The Correctional Officer

D1235692

The Correctional Officer

A Practical Guide

Second Edition

Gary F. Cornelius

CAROLINA ACADEMIC PRESS

Durham, North Carolina

Library of Congress Cataloging-in-Publication Data
Cornelius, Gary F.
  The correctional officer : a practical guide / Gary F. Cornelius. -- 2nd ed.
      p. cm.
  Includes index.
  ISBN 978-1-59460-310-5 (alk. paper)
  1. Corrections--United States--Handbooks, manuals, etc. 2. Correctional
personnel--United States. 3. Correctional institutions--United States. I. Title.

  HV9471.C6675 2010
  365'.973--dc22

                                        2009037918

Cover photo: Hampton Roads (VA) Regional Jail

CAROLINA ACADEMIC PRESS
700 Kent Street
Durham, North Carolina 27701
Telephone (919) 489-7486
Fax (919) 493-5668
www.cap-press.com

Printed in the United States of America

Dedication

The corrections field is a demanding one, and sometimes a thankless one. I have been fortunate to pass on my observations and experiences to the current and new generation of correctional officers. I dedicate it to them, as I am going out to pasture and you all are coming in.

I could not have done this without the support and guidance of several people. I dedicate this work to my children Gary Jr., Amber and the loving spirit of their late mother and my wife, Nancy.

I also dedicate it to a loving person, Deborah. Also, my friend and colleague Tim Manley provided support when the going got rough. Finally, little Isaiah and his dad Pernell will hopefully pick this book up in later years and treasure it.

I love you all and thanks.

Contents

Acknowledgments

The following people were helpful in the preparation for this book, supplying photos and allowing me to take photos. The author wishes to thank:

Barbara Tate-Stephens

Clarke-Frederick-Winchester Regional Adult Detention Center (currently known as Northwestern Regional Adult Detention Center): Superintendent Fred Hildebrand, Lt. Patty Barr and staff

Alexandria, Virginia Office of the Sheriff

Manatee County (FLA) Sheriff's Office: Charles T. Wells, Sheriff, and special thanks to Lt. Jim Conway

Maryland Department of Corrections: Lt. Martin Ice

Albany County (NY) Correctional Facility: Ed Szostak, Superintendent (retired), photos by Al Roland, Senior Identification Officer

Fairfax County (VA) Office of the Sheriff: Sheriff Stan Barry, Sgt. Charles Taggart and Andrea Ceisler

Rhode Island Department of Corrections: Director A.T. Wall and Tracey Zeckhausen

Hampton Roads (VA) Regional Jail: Major Chris Smith

Colonial Williamsburg (VA): Office of Public Affairs: Penna Rogers

The following organizations were gracious enough to permit a listing of their organizations and including material from their publications:

The American Correctional Association: Gabriella Daley Klatt and Alice Heiserman

The American Jail Association: Gwyn Smith-Ingley, Executive Director

International Association of Correctional Training Personnel: Linda Dunbar, President

The Corrections Connection: Laura Noonan and Jeff Ware

Doug Cooley: Executive Director: Southwest Virginia Criminal Justice Training Academy, Bristol, VA

About the Author

Lt. Gary F. Cornelius retired in 2005 from the Fairfax County (VA) Office of the Sheriff, after serving over 27 years in the Fairfax County Adult Detention Center. His career included assignments in confinement, work release, programs and classification.

He has been an adjunct faculty member of the Administration of Justice Department at George Mason University from 1986–2009, where he taught four corrections courses. He also teaches corrections in-service sessions in Virginia, and has performed training and consulting for the American Correctional Association, the American Jail Association, and the National Institute of Justice. *The Correctional Officer: A Practical Guide Second Edition* is Gary's ninth book in corrections. His most recent books are *The American Jail: Cornerstone of Modern Corrections*, 2008, from Pearson and *The Art of the Con: Avoiding Offender Manipulation Second Edition* 2009, both available from the American Correctional Association. In 2008 he co-founded ETC, LLC: Education and Training in Corrections with Timothy P. Manley, MSW, LCSW. Gary resides in Williamsburg, Virginia.

Introduction

Correctional officer.... When most people hear the words, they think of a "guard"—a uniformed person patrolling Spartan looking cell blocks, keeping an eye on sinister looking inmates. In reality highly trained, professional and motivated men and women patrol the cellblocks, hallways, recreation yards, towers and walls of our nation's jails, prisons and lockups.

The job of a correctional officer in the 21st century is a demanding one. The days of a correctional officer being a "watchdog" are long gone. Gone also is the notion that correctional officers are merely "custodians" of wrongdoers. The philosophy of merely warehousing and keeping an eye on inmates has given way to such revolutionary concepts such as direct supervision, improved electronic monitoring, improved medical care, and alternatives to traditional forms of incarceration.

Another demand on the correctional officer of today is the keeping up with information about offenders. More knowledge is available now thanks to the Internet and improved communications about inmates. More information is now known and being updated about offenders' medical issues, mental health, gang affiliations and civil rights, to name a few. There have been new developments in institutional security and procedures; for example the development of emergency procedures, correctional emergency response teams and new methods of security. Correctional officers face dangers—for some working in correctional facilities and being around offenders have resulted in injuries and death.

Public opinion and criminal justice policies throughout the 1980s and 1990s resulted in mandatory sentencing, "three strikes and you're out" and the abolition of parole in many states. These changes, combined with more research on inmate violence, security threat groups, recent legislative acts and court decisions all have impacted the job of the correctional officer. Today's correctional officers need as much knowledge and skills training as possible in order to be the best and safest at their jobs.

This book while concise, is a relevant "hands on" informational tool for correctional officers. Its purpose is to be a training resource for correctional officers in correctional facilities such as lockups, prisons, jails and community corrections facilities. This book is specifically designed for entry level and in-service training with the following goals:

- To serve as a written training guide for corrections agency instructors and field training personnel.
- To provide an understanding into the history, philosophy and evolution of past and present correctional systems.
- To serve as a guide for correctional officer job skills training.
- To provide an understanding of the sociological, educational and behavioral characteristics of inmates.
- To give the correctional officer an understanding of the positive traits and characteristics needed to maintain a successful career in corrections.
- To give understanding as to the future of corrections and the skills needed by the correctional officer to meet future challenges.

This version has been updated and will be hopefully more reader friendly. In the first chapter, the previous edition focused on the three correctional ideologies. In this revised version, there is a discussion of the functions of corrections and how they fit in and overlap into each ideology. The text is updated throughout to reflect current statistics and operational practices, as well as current information on offenders. The final chapter, The Rights of Inmates, has been modified to provide a good, common sense look at liability, the basic civil rights of inmates and has a strong emphasis on how correctional officers can avoid inmate litigation.

This book can be used in an undergraduate class in corrections, especially where the instructor wishes to interject a realistic view of operations and staff in different types of correctional facilities. By doing so, college students considering a career in corrections will be provided a good look at the field. No matter in what way the book is used, it is a valuable resource for the "unsung heroes" of the corrections field—the correctional officers.

Gary F. Cornelius
1st Lt. Deputy Sheriff (Retired)
February 2010

The Correctional Officer

Chapter 1

Corrections: Definition, Offenders, Goals and Functions

What Is Corrections?

Most people in the public sector, when they hear the term *corrections*, think of a large walled prison or county jail with bars, guards, and keys. In reality, the term *corrections* generically describes a set of agencies, both public and private, that attempt to control the behavior of persons either accused of or convicted of a criminal offense—a violation of the law. The underlying foundation of corrections is *social control:* the set of methods that are designed to encourage or force people to obey the norms of society (Quinn, 1999, p. 1).

More simply, corrections can also be defined as including all government agencies (such as police, judiciary, treatment programs, probation and parole, federal, state and local departments of corrections, sheriff's offices etc.), facilities (such as prisons, jails, lockups, community corrections centers, juvenile detention facilities), programs, procedures, personnel, and techniques involving the investigation, intake, custody, confinement, supervision, or treatment of adult offenders [or inmates], delinquent juveniles, or status offenders; whether they be accused (alleged) or adjudicated or convicted (Allen, Latessa, Ponder and Simonsen, 2007, p. 465).

In examining this definition more closely, corrections involves simply dealing with criminals and other types of offenders after their arrest by law enforcement and while being adjudicated by the judicial system. Dealing with these offenders—called inmates or detainees after incarceration—means keeping them confined in order to protect the correctional staff, the public by the prevention of escape, and the offenders themselves from being harmed by others.

The term *correctional staff* means all of the workers in a correctional facility: the correctional officers who are responsible for security and confinement, the medical officers who tend to inmate health problems, the counselors who classify inmates into housing areas, the programs staff who operate and supervise rehabilitation programs, and the service workers who perform maintenance and food service functions. These staff roles will be discussed in detail later.

Who Are the Offenders?

One of corrections' main goals, which involve the staff described above, is to answer these two questions (Allen, et al., 2007, p. 1):

- Who are the offenders?
- What should we [the correctional system] do with them?

The first question can be answered by identifying several categories of offenders. While it is easy for corrections officers to "lump" offenders together into a general category of inmates, the types of lawbreaking offenders are (American Correctional Association, 1998, pp. 63, 79):

> *Offender:* a person convicted or adjudicated of a criminal offense, i.e. a violation of criminal law.
> *Juvenile offender:* any individual who is subjected to the juvenile court jurisdiction for the purposes of adjudication and treatment based on his or her age (under age 18) and the limitation of offenses as defined by state law.

During the past several years, law enforcement and corrections began dealing more with mentally ill persons coming into conflict with authorities, persons entering the United States illegally, and sexual offenders being confined after they have served their sentence. These individuals fall into the category of *civil commitment,* which can be defined as (American Correctional Association, 1998, p. 17):

> *The action of a judicial officer, court or administrative body ordering a person to be confined in an institution or facility for custody, treatment, protection or deportation, including those administered by a mental health service.*

Civil commitments can include the indefinite commitment to a mental institution of habitual sex offenders, sexual predators, and pedophiles after completion of a prison sentence. These are offenders who have been convicted of sex offenses and are also deemed a danger to the community by a panel of psychiatrists and other treatment experts. The United States Supreme Court up-

Exterior view: Hampton Roads Regional Jail, Portsmouth, VA. Many correctional facilities have a modern look. Photo by author.

held these types of commitments in 1997, and at least 15 states have sexual predator statutes. These commitments are reassessed annually to determine when the offender can be released into the community (Alarid and Reichel, 2008, p. 108). Civil commitments can also include the placement of mentally ill persons into residential mental health treatment if legal criteria is met — generally that they are an inherent danger to themselves or others.

Another group is illegal aliens, apprehended due to entering the United States in violation of immigration laws. Illegal aliens are held in the custody of the Department of Homeland Security, Immigration and Custom Enforcement or ICE. According to estimates, ICE arrests about 1.5 million aliens each year, the majority along the United States southwest border. Most of these arrestees are detained and deported, but many are detained for longer periods of time due to criminal activity, subject to prosecution in state and federal courts. This group of offenders — both categories — has put a tremendous strain on our nation's corrections system, forcing ICE to enter into contracts with private correctional facilities, the Federal Bureau of Prisons, state correctional institutions and local jails (Alarid and Reichel, 2008, p. 129).

Juveniles are also treated in a special manner by the corrections system. Some minors may be judged by the court to be dependent (without family or support) or neglected (in a harmful family or home situation). The only category of juvenile offender involving criminal acts is the *delinquent*. The juvenile delinquent offender category has three components: minors who have committed acts which would be considered crimes if they were adults; status offenders who have violated juvenile regulations such as a curfew, not attending school, etc.; and incorrigible or unruly juveniles who their parents, guardians or the juvenile court have deemed unmanageable. Status offenders and incorrigibles are also referred to as minors in need of supervision (MINS), children in need of supervision (CHINS) and persons in need of supervision (PINS). Juvenile institutions, sometimes called *juvenile detention centers*, are facilities designed to provide specialized programming such as counseling and education to prepare the juvenile for an eventual return to the community (Allen, et al., 2007, pp. 332–333).

In certain circumstances youthful offenders are certified by juvenile court to be tried as an adult or sentenced in adult court as an adult. In such cases juvenile criminal offenders can be held in adult local jails and/or sentenced to adult correctional facilities.

The Goals and Functions of Corrections

To understand what corrections is about at any level—whether it be federal, state or local, one must understand what corrections is supposed to do (functions) and its goals. By doing so, one can also understand the types of correctional facilities, the types of inmates and offenders confined in them and the job categories of correctional workers.

The main goal of corrections is to punish the criminal offender. The overseeing and management of this punishment are performed by the correctional systems mentioned previously. Historically, there have been disagreements among criminologists, social workers, sociologists, law enforcement and the courts as to just how offenders are to be punished (Champion, 2005, p. 14). The correctional system is diverse. Its goals and functions reflect the philosophies of those professionals in the criminal justice system and have impacted corrections operations and the development of correctional facilities and staffing.

The main functions of corrections surpass these disagreements. Whether one believes in strict punishment for criminals or rehabilitation, professionals generally are in consensus as to its main question as to its functions: what the correctional system is trying to do with the offender. The main functions of corrections are: retribution, deterrence/prevention, incapacitation/isolation, rehabilitation, reintegration and control (Champion, 2005, p. 14). Each function has its own types of correctional facility, staffing, and management of inmates.

The functions and current state of corrections are based on three philosophies or ideologies. The definition of the term ideology is defined in Webster's Dictionary as "a systematic body of concepts, especially about human life or concepts." A *correctional ideology* is defined by researchers Allen, Latessa, Ponder and Simonsen as a "body of ideas and practices that pertain to the processing of offenders as determined by the law." By understanding these three philosophies or ideologies correctional officers will better understand the various purposes of different correctional institutions and programs. The three ideologies are punishment, treatment and prevention. Frequently they overlap into one another; for example, treatment programs support the prevention of crime. Punishment by long sentences also is designed to prevent crime (Allen, et al., 2007, pp. 44–46).

Retribution

Another description of *retribution* can be the term revenge—which is most likely the oldest goal of corrections—society giving the lawbreaker his or her "just deserts." It is also based on punishment. Capital and corporal punishment (discussed in chapter 4) owe their roots to authorities taking out revenge on the criminal; sentencing practices in federal and state courts have resulted in a "retributions" philosophy. Examples include restitution by the offender to victims, numerous hours of community service, heavy fines, and forfeiture of property (Champion, 2005, p. 14). Flogging, mutilation, harsh physical labor and execution by various methods were illustrations of this function. In the United States, we have seen several methods of capital punishment that sought to extract the ultimate retribution on the offender: firing squad, hanging, electrocution, gas, and lethal injection.

When Michael Fay, an American, was due to be punished for vandalism by caning (lashes on the buttocks), a $2,220.00 fine and four months imprisonment in Singapore, a *Newsweek* poll found that 38% of Americans *approved* the caning, 52% did not (Elliott, 1994).

Views on whether severe punishment deters crime are split. For example, a 1997 *Time Magazine* poll found that 45% of Americans believe capital punishment deters crime; 52% did not (Pooley, 1997).

In summary, retribution delivers like punishment to those offenders who commit particular crimes. Punishment is deserved and offenders must be made to "pay their debts" and it adheres to the biblical philosophy "an eye for an eye and a tooth for a tooth" (Clear and Cole, 2000, p. 56).

Deterrence

Deterrence of crime is an important function of corrections, and in a perfect world criminal wrongdoers would realize that "crime doesn't pay." The truth is that many offenders are not deterred by legal sanctions and punishment. The meaning of *deterrence* or prevention is to "send a message" to others that if they commit crimes, they too will suffer the fate of wrongdoers who are incarcerated or under some type of correctional supervision. In doing so, people are deterred from committing future crimes. Programs such as "Scared Straight" where convicts in prison and jails would bluntly talk to young people including high school students about the negative consequences of living a life of crime illustrate the deterrence function. Treatment programs in correctional facilities such as substance abuse education, vocational programs and those designed to change patterns of criminal thinking have deterrence and prevention as main goals.

Deterrence can have a strict, "no nonsense" side, based on the punishment ideology. According to researchers, these are exemplified by two types of deterrence: general and specific. *General deterrence* is the concept of punishing criminals overall and showing the general public that crime does not pay and the consequences are harsh. The citizen must believe that if he or she commits a crime, arrest, prosecution and incarceration or other type of corrections sanction will result (Clear and Cole, 2000, p. 57). This is especially true for specific crimes; in recent years changes in laws for driving under the influence (DUI) for example, have become harsher.

Special deterrence or specific or individual deterrence believes that those already convicted of crimes are made to say through severe sentences that "The results and consequences of my crimes are too painful; it was not worth it; it was not worth the risk. I do not want to be punished like this again." Examples of special deterrence could be offenders convicted of driving while intoxicated or committing sexual offenses against children. Penalties for both of these offenses became stricter in the past several decades.

General deterrence is difficult to measure, because we will never know how many general population citizens have potentially been deterred. Deterrence does not factor in when examining offenders who commit crimes due to mental illness and other psychological factors (Clear and Cole, 2000, pp. 56–57).

The way a correctional institution is operated could be a result of deterrence philosophy. A jail or prison operating on a "no frills" basis where inmates are not given access to many amenities and programs may wish the environment to be so uncomfortable that inmates hopefully think twice about coming back.

Incapacitation/Isolation

Corrections strives to keep the people safe in its environment. The inmates, public and staff—both civilian and sworn are all at risk if inmates confined in a facility escape or commit crimes, including physical and sexual assault. The function of *incapacitation* through strict and controlled punishment prevents criminal offenders from committing future crimes by making it physically impossible for them to do so—they are isolated. Supporters of incapacitation often justify it by saying that it is the surest means to safeguard the public, other inmates and staff from the most dangerous criminals. Proponents of incapacitation believe that this "warehousing" approach will discourage crime due to the years of incarceration, solitary confinement and the maturation of the inmate (Quinn, 1999, p. 11).

Criminals who continue to engage in repeated criminal behavior despite repeated arrests, convictions and sentences are known as *habitual offenders* (Quinn, 1999, p. 11). By enacting such statutes as *three strikes laws*, it is hoped that society is isolated from offenders who never appear to refrain from a life of crime. Three strikes laws, when first enacted in 1994 in California stipulated that any three felony convictions could lead to a life sentence. Ruled as too broad by the California Supreme Court in 1996, a new law was proposed that allowed some discretion in sentencing by judges and repeat offenders were guaranteed punishment (Quinn, 1999, pp. 11–12).

Despite the consensus that all states have enacted three strikes and you are out laws, many courts do not consistently enforce them. Also, many prosecutors do not uniformly enforce them, but use them legally as persuasive tools to extract confessions, plea bargains and guilty pleas (Champion, Hartley and Rabe, 2008, p. 417).

Three strikes laws, as they are commonly called, are types of *mandatory sentences*, or sentences mandated through legislative acts at both the state and federal level for specific crimes. Mandatory sentencing removes discretion from the sentencing judge; the punishment is fixed by law. Mandatory sentences stipulate a minimum time to be served by an offender convicted of a specific crime, usually for crimes of violence, crimes committed with a firearm, habitual offenders and drug law violations (Clear and Cole, 2000, p. 65).

Many have disagreed with the goal of rehabilitating offenders through light sentences, programs, and probation. This has resulted in legislatures passing mandatory sentences, in which the term of punishment is a fixed term, minus good time earned by the inmate. For example, the sentence for the crime of burglary is ten (10) years. *Good time* is time off a sentence earned by an inmate through participation in rehabilitative, vocational and educational programs and activities. It is granted at the discretion of the correctional facility administrator after the inmate has demonstrated that he or she has *worked* at positive participation in such programs. For example, some good time policies state that if an offender is participating in an educational program (such as GED) or a substance abuse program, and shows clear progress (such as completing assignments), he or she may receive one to five days good time to be deducted from the sentence for every thirty days of participation in the program.

The other type of determinate sentence is the ***presumptive sentence*** where a minimum and maximum term is fixed, such as one to five years, six months to one year, etc. (Clear and Cole, 2000, pp. 64–65). This is also known as ***indeterminate sentencing***.

A clear example of using sentencing to support the incapacitation function is the enactment of ***truth in sentencing laws***. These types of laws mandate that offenders serve a substantial time in prison, approximately 85 percent, before being released on some type of supervision or parole. As of 1999, forty states had adopted a version of truth in sentencing laws. This tool came about because the public, including those serving on juries learned that the time that the convicted offender would actually serve differed significantly from the actual sentence (Clear and Cole, 2000, p. 68). For example, if an offender was sentenced to 10 years for burglary, good time, credit for good behavior and a parole date given at the discretion of the parole board could result in a release sooner than the 10 years—significantly sooner. Political leaders, supported by public opinion, felt that this did not send a clear enough message to criminals. The result was the enactment of truth in sentencing laws.

The result was the steady elimination and revision of parole and supervised release laws to reflect a "get tough" policy towards criminals. Maine was the first to abolish parole in 1976, and as a result, many states and the federal government markedly changed or abolished their parole systems. In 1984, Congress enacted the Comprehensive Crime Control Act, eliminating parole beginning in 1992 and substituting post release supervision for federal prisoners beginning in 1993. By 2000, twenty states had abolished their parole systems and/or barred certain categories of violent offenders from being paroled by the discretionary decisions of parole boards. States that abolished discretionary parole by 2000 included the following: Arizona, California, Delaware, Florida, Illinois, Indiana, Kansas, Maine, Minnesota, Mississippi, North Carolina, Ohio, Oregon, Virginia, Washington, and Wisconsin. In addition, discretionary parole for certain types of violent offenders was abolished in Alaska, Louisiana, New York and Tennessee. The elimination of parole is being considered by the legislatures in several states (Champion, 2005, p. 469).

The impact was noticeable. For example, in 1994, Virginia eliminated parole and lengthened sentences. Offenders convicted of murder, robbery and burglary under this would serve 125% to 500% more prison time (Cauchon, 1994, p. 9A). Inmates under the old parole laws in their states are not affected, and the previous policies still apply to them. However, the granting of parole in these circumstances will be under closer scrutiny, as the mood of the nation has "toughened up" on letting offenders be released early.

Rehabilitation

It is always hoped that criminals will be rehabilitated and not engage in any more criminal behavior, both in and out of a correctional facility, or while on some type of community supervision such as on parole or probation. According to the American Correctional Association, *rehabilitation* is defined as "an approach to offender management which attempts to change the offender's criminal behavior through appropriate treatment" (American Correctional Association, 1998, p. 99).

Staffs who work in rehabilitation supervise and operate programs designed to make the inmate a more law abiding citizen when he or she is released. Correctional programs vary in size, curriculum and purpose. Examples of rehabilitation efforts in corrections are:

- General Education Development (GED) programs in jails and prisons
- Adult Basic Education (ABE)
- Substance abuse education
- English as a Second Language (ESL)
- Vocational programs: landscaping, barbering, hairstyling, auto repair, furniture repair, reupholstering, refurbishing office furniture
- Programs addressing the changing patterns in criminal thinking
- Life skills
- Alcoholics Anonymous
- Narcotics Anonymous
- Training dogs for the visually impaired
- Janitorial/custodial education
- Volunteer and mentoring programs
- Religious programs
- Individual and group therapy on mental health issues and substance abuse

Rehabilitation has several approaches or doctrines, all based on the treatment of offenders. *Treatment* is the correctional rehabilitative approach that begins with qualified staff diagnosing the needs of offenders, designing a program or programs to address these needs and the application of the program (Allen, et al., 2007, p. 51).

Correctional officers work in facilities that operate rehabilitative treatment programs. The aforementioned list of programs all are designed to address needs of offenders whether they be educational, vocational, substance abuse or criminal thinking. Rehabilitation and treatment is based on several doctrines, or schools of thought. Each of these doctrines has been tried in American corrections and some have been modified to adhere to modern corrections. These doctrines are (Allen, et al., 2007, pp. 52–53):

- *Quaker Doctrine:* The Quakers in the newly independent United States of America began in 1790 to support the view that if a criminal was to free himself or herself from wrongdoing, he or she would have to repent sins and get in touch with God. Through religious instruction, prayer and studying the Bible, crime would decrease.
- *Educational Doctrine:* A result of the reformatory movement in the late 19th century, this doctrine believes if inmates are given opportunities for education in several areas, such as learning a trade, an occupation, reading/writing skills, and discipline, internal controls would result and lead to non criminal behavior.
- *Medical Model:* Developed through the United States Bureau of Prisons in the late 1920s and early 1930s, it was believed that the answers to crime were inside the individual; crime was to be treated after the problem was diagnosed much as in the way a physician diagnoses a disease. A treatment program attempts to "cure" the problem, and the inmate is released into the community on supervised release (parole) and authorities would continue therapy and casework. Correctional programs would make the "ill" well. This model has been the target of much criticism in corrections, and has been replaced by programming targeting individual criminal behavior rather than dealing with a defect or disease.

The Quaker Doctrine has been modified to operate in such organizations as the Good News Jail and Prison Ministry that supplies chaplains and coordinates with local churches to work with inmates in jails and prisons. Its programs, such as individual mentoring and religious classes work in conjunction with other programs. Religious and spiritual progress is part of the rehabilitative foundation.

To be law abiding, it is necessary to have an education and a job or marketable skill. In many correctional facilities, inmates are getting an education and job training. Through community corrections programs such as work release, they can be legally released to work in the community as they near the end of their sentences. Treatment programs using the medical model approach work in conjunction with other programs; inmates cannot simply blame their problems on a "disease." However, there are significant rates of mentally ill or disordered inmates that need psychological diagnoses by qualified mental health personnel and subsequent treatment plans implemented. The same is true for substance abuse, when as viewed as a disease of addiction, a treatment plan is developed by qualified staff. Increasingly, developments are being made in corrections where treatment staff works across the board with staff from other disciplines.

In the Alexandria, Virginia, Adult Detention Center, the Sober Living Unit (SLU) is an intensive program that uses the Twelve Step cure to substance abuse developed by Alcoholics Anonymous. The SLU program started in 1990 with the support of Sheriff James H. Dunning. At that time, research revealed that 95% of SLU inmates had been previously incarcerated and 80% had never had *any* prior treatment (Mclain, 1990). Many jails and prisons conduct programs to identify and treat inmate problems, particularly in substance abuse and mental health. Programming in correctional facilities have improved greatly, with facilities using computers and state of the art programming curriculum and well trained staff to assist offenders.

Reintegration

A major concern of the public—one of the key groups served by corrections officers—is the release of offenders back into the community. Questions arise such as "are they rehabilitated?" or "are we safe?" The public expects corrections to do something with wrongdoers while they are in correctional custody. Depending on one's philosophy and opinions, that "something" could be the traditional (but one dimensional) approach of just locking them up and making them do hard labor.

Reintegration is the treatment model concept that states that offenders need to be released into the community as productive citizens, using community resources to teach them tools to handle problems (American Correctional Association, 1998, p. 99). The community is examined as a causative factor of the inmates' problems (such as easy availability of drugs, no jobs, peer influences such as gang activity, etc.) *and* as an environment where the resources contained within can assist offenders with the handling of problems that caused them to commit crimes. For example, it is recognized that illegal drug use in the community combined with unemployment can cause criminal behavior. However, substance abuse programs such as a neighborhood Narcotics Anonymous (NA) meeting is a place where an offender who is newly released and off drugs can go when he or she feels the urge to do drugs. Concerning employment, an offender in a reintegration program such as work release can be hired with the help of corrections staff, learn a job skill, and make money.

Reintegration is based on the concept of restorative justice. *Restorative justice* views crime as an injury done by the offender to people—the victims— and the community. It concerns itself with meeting the victim's needs, their impact as stated at the penalty or sentencing phase at court, repairing the harm inflicted in a meaningful way, and holding offenders to strict standards of accountability and responsibility. It is the opposite of *retributive justice,* which views the offender being punished by guilt, pain and suffering such as in the methods of harsh penalties and sentences (Zehr, 2002, pp. 22–24, 58).

The best way to understand reintegration based on restorative justice is to contrast it with retributive justice. Retributive justice, sometimes called traditional criminal justice, believes the following (Zehr, 2002, p. 21):

- The criminal act is a violation of the law and the state.
- Violations of criminal law create guilt of the offender.
- The blame (guilt) and the pain (punishment) of the criminal will be determined by the state.
- The central focus is on giving the offender what they deserve.

Restorative justice believes (Zehr, 2002, p. 21):

- The criminal act is a violation of people and relationships in the community.
- Violations of criminal law create obligations by the offender.
- Justice involves the victims, the offenders, and the community all working together to make things right and repair the harm that has been done.
- The central focus is on both the repairing of harm by considering the needs of the victims and the offender repairing the harm done to the victims.

While some view reintegration as part of the treatment approach, it is a unique function of corrections due to the fact that the offenders can be incarcerated and attend programs designed to prepare for release. Some reintegration programs are work release, electronic monitoring and halfway houses (see Chapter 5).

Most inmates who are incarcerated will be released at some point. According to the United States Department of Justice, Bureau of Justice Statistics (Hughes and Wilson, *Reentry Trends in the United States,* p. 1):

- At least 95 percent of all inmates in state corrections systems will be released from incarceration at some point; almost 80 percent will be released to supervision on parole.

- Approximately 592,000 inmates in state correctional facilities were released into the general population after serving time.
- In 1999, almost 33 percent of released inmates from state correctional facilities were drug offenders, 25 percent were violent offenders, and 31 percent were property offenders.

The reintegration approach combined with treatment programs addresses these needs. Correctional officers working in this area need to be flexible as to offender needs and problems, and be able, through specialized training to work with offenders, programs staff and employers of offenders in the community. If the reintegration process goes well, the offender can resume his or her role in society, with the stigma of being an ex offender minimized. For example, if offenders are participating in electronic monitoring or work release programs, they can keep that to themselves, thus facilitating regaining the role of a normal citizen.

Control

The final function of corrections is control. In corrections, security and safety are the key aspects of a well run correctional system. The public expects that offenders or inmates will be under staff *control:* safely confined, which means that certain acts are prevented: escapes, criminal acts inside the facility, conspiracy to commit criminal acts outside the community, rule violations, assaults on staff and other inmates, gang activity, and contraband smuggling.

Being in control also means enforcing the security policies and procedures of the agency and more specifically the correctional institution. Controlling what inmates may possess and use is part of control, as is conducting searches and headcounts. Control means that inmates are escorted within the facility, to outside work assignments, and to court. They are also securely transported to other law enforcement agencies, other correctional facilities for court, and to places such as hospitals and doctors' offices as is necessary.

While the inmates are expected to control their behavior and follow the rules, correctional officers are also held to a standard of control. In correctional facilities there must be some uniform operation, adhered to and followed by all staff. Directives and orders are communicated to all staff, sworn and civilian, and followed. Offenders are expected to follow the rules and regulations of the facility. They may be called "inmate regulations," "Code of Inmate Offenses," etc., and have punishments for disobedience ranging from disciplinary segregation (see Chapters 8 and 13) to loss of privileges and/or loss of good time. Control can also be wielded over problem inmates through the use of administrative hearings, such as formal classification hearings to place an inmate on administrative segregation (see Chapters 8 and 13).

Correctional organizations are managed according to a combination of the bureaucracy of government agencies and the military. Three basic principles guide the controlling of correctional agencies through staffing. A *chain of command* allows the communication of policies, procedures and orders from the hierarchy of the agency—the administrators, managers, and supervisors down to the line staff responsible for dealing with offenders on a daily basis and/or the carrying out of operations of the facility. Each staff member, including correctional officers has a supervisor which clarifies his or her duties and responsibilities. This is known as the *unity of command*. Finally, each manager or supervisor, from corporal on up, has a *span of control*—a section, division, squad, etc. consisting of a specific number of employees that report to him or her. By keeping this communication and staffing plan intact, the facility follows a "paramilitary" organizational chart, where the correctional officers are recognized as the first line of authority (Quinn, 1999, p. 322). Control in correctional facilities cannot be maintained if inmates do not recognize officers' authority and engage in obedience to their orders.

Summary

Corrections is the discipline that involves all of the public and private agencies and staff that deal with the treatment and confinement of inmates, based on the theory of social control—encouraging people to obey the norms and rules of society. Offenders can be either adult or juvenile criminal offenders, and in recent times, commitment has become either criminal—placement in corrections facility, or civil, such as in the case of apprehending illegal aliens, the further commitment of sex offenders and the commitment of the mentally ill.

The discipline of corrections consists of three philosophies—punishment, treatment, and prevention, each supported by the main functions of corrections—retribution, deterrence, incapacitation/isolation, rehabilitation, reintegration and control. These functions overlap from one philosophy into the other depending on what each function is trying to do.

"Three strikes and you're out," mandatory sentences and truth in sentencing laws are trends supporting the incapacitation function of corrections.

Rehabilitation is based on the Quaker Doctrine, the Educational Doctrine and Medical Model. Their one goal is to help inmates stay out of prison and prevent future criminal behavior. Many treatment programs are innovative, such as the Sober Living Unit, and vary—from educational and vocational programs to religious programs.

Reintegration concerns the release of offenders from incarceration back into the community. Statistics support the view that most offenders who are incarcerated will be released back into the community at some point, and will need help dealing with their problems. Reintegration is based on the concept of restorative justice in which offenders must repair the harm done to victims and meet obligations by working with the victim and the community. This is the opposite of the more traditional retributive view of justice, where the offender receives pain in the form of harsh sentences.

Control is the last function of corrections that is discussed in this chapter. The public expects correctional staff to keep offenders confined in such a way that escapes, criminal assaults, smuggling contraband, and other similar acts are prevented as much as possible. Also, staff must control offenders through the enforcement of rules and policies of the correctional agencies. Staffing and communications must be in a clear way, using the paramilitary model, a chain of command, and an organizational chart that recognizes correctional officers as the first line of authority.

Review Questions

1. What are the functions of corrections and the ideologies that each supports?
2. Define the three strikes laws, mandatory sentencing, and truth in sentencing.
3. Explain the three doctrines of rehabilitation.
4. Explain the differences between restorative justice and retributive justice.
5. What is meant by control when discussing corrections?
6. What is reintegration?

Terms/Concepts

civil commitment

control

correctional ideology

correctional staff

corrections

delinquent

deterrence

Educational Doctrine

general deterrence

good time

habitual offenders

incapacitation

indeterminate sentencing

juvenile detention centers

juvenile offender

mandatory sentences

Medical Model

offender

presumptive sentence

Quaker Doctrine

rehabilitation

reintegration

retribution

social control

special deterrence

three strikes laws

treatment

truth in sentencing laws

References

Alarid, Leanne F. and Philip L. Reichel. (2008). *Corrections: A Contemporary Introduction.* Boston: Pearson Allyn and Bacon.

Allen, Harry, Ph.D., Latessa, Edward J., Ph.D., Ponder, Bruce S., and Simonsen, Clifford, Ph.D. (2007). *Corrections in America: An Introduction, Eleventh Edition.* Upper Saddle River: Pearson Prentice Hall.

American Correctional Association. (1998). Dictionary *of Criminal Justice Terms.* Lanham, Maryland.

Cauchon, Dennis. (September 30, 1994). Virginia Jumps on Get-Tough Train with No-Parole Plan, *USA Today,* p. 9A.

Champion, Dean J. (2005). *Corrections in the United States: A Contemporary Perspective: Fourth Edition.* Upper Saddle River: Pearson Prentice Hall.

Champion, Dean John, Hartley, Richard D., and Gary A. Rabe. (2008). *Criminal Courts: Structure, Process and Issues, Edition 2.* Upper Saddle River: Pearson Prentice Hall.

Clear, Todd R. and George F. Cole. (2000). *American Corrections: Fifth Edition,* Belmont: West/Wadsworth.

Elliott, Michael. (1994, April 18). Crime & Punishment: The Caning Debate: Should America Be More Like Singapore? *Newsweek, Vol. CXX, No. 16,* 18–23.

Hughes, Timothy and Doris James Wilson. (Revised August 30, 2003). *Reentry Trends in the United States.* U.S. Department of Justice, Bureau of Justice Statistics. Retrieved from: www.ojp.usdoj.gov/bjs/.

Mclain, Buzz. (1990, August 31). Program Sobers Prisoners' Lives. *Fairfax Journal*, p. A3.

Pooley, Eric. (1997, June 16). Death or Life? *Time, Vol. 149, No. 24*, 31–36.

Quinn, James F. (1999). *Corrections: A Concise Introduction.* Prospect Heights: Waveland.

Zehr, Howard. (2002). *The Little Book of Restorative Justice.* Intercourse: Good Books.

Chapter 2

Types of Correctional Facilities

Most people in the public sector when they hear the word "corrections" think of the local jail, the state prison or what the media—television and motion pictures—portray. While this view is simplistic, the truth is that correctional facilities come in different varieties.

The most common facilities for adult corrections are in order of usage. The usage of each type of correctional facility depends on several things: its function in the correctional system, its particular mission and the type of offenders that are confined within. These facilities are as follows, considering the order of events in corrections:

- lockup
- jail
- prison

There are other, more specialized types of correctional facilities. They include:

- community corrections centers
- juvenile detention centers
- boot camps
- geriatric correctional facilities
- mental health correctional facilities
- Indian Nation correctional facilities
- Immigration and Custom Enforcement (ICE) detention centers
- US Military Correctional Facilities

Types of Correctional Facilities

Lockup

A lockup is a temporary holding facility and is primarily found at the local level. The local lockup is often the offender's first step in being incarcerated. Lockups are generally operated by the local police or sheriff's office and are located in police headquarters, station houses, or a designated area of the jail building.

A *lockup* is defined as a temporary holding facility, usually operated by a police department that holds offenders pending bail or transport to the local jail for processing, inebriates (those offenders arrested for public drunkenness) until they are ready or sober enough to be released, and juvenile offenders pending release to parental custody or placement in a juvenile detention center at the order of the juvenile court (American Correctional Association, 1998, p. 68).

Due to the various locations of lockups, it is difficult to pinpoint exactly how many lockups there actually are in the United States. For example, a police station may have one or two holding cells in an area adjacent to the main police department booking desk. Lockups can also be located in court buildings, but are not designed for long term care and do not offer the wide range of services that local jails do. Lockups are short term and usually hold offenders for a short time—no more than 48 hours (Seiter, 2005, p. 65–66).

The function of lockups is a critical first step on the path of incarceration. Arrestees are held for no more than forty-eight hours, excluding weekends and holidays. Arrestees are held until they are taken before a magistrate, a judge, or are released through personal recognizance, bail or bonding. Inebriated arrestees remain in custody until they sober up or "dry out." Juveniles detained by the police are held until their parents can be contacted or placement in a juvenile detention center or shelter can be arranged. In other words, the lockup is a critical part of the system (Cornelius, 1996, p. 2).

Generally, lockups are operated by the police or sheriff's departments— the agencies whose members arrest the offenders. Lockups are similar to jails in several respects—they confine people, the staff is responsible for the health and safety of the prisoner, and many problems that jail officers have to deal with also are displayed in lockups. These problems may include aggressive behavior, effects of substance abuse, suicidal behavior, or mental illness. It is imperative that lockup officers, like jail officers, be trained in these areas. Escapes, suicides, and assaults can happen at a lockup just as in a jail or prison. Wherever people are held against their will, incidents such as these can occur.

Lockup officers must also be trained in the fundamentals of corrections security. Prisoners brought into a lockup must be carefully searched, observed and restrained if necessary. Releases from a lockup must be legal and proper. Lockup prisoners must not be allowed to escape. Although lockups are temporary holding facilities, prisoners' property must be properly confiscated, inventoried, documented, and stored.

Catastrophic incidents do happen in lockups. One of the most serious incidents is suicide. For example, in 1985, a 38-year-old man arrested for driving while intoxicated hung himself at a Maryland State Police barracks lockup (*Washington Post*, 1985). The offender hung himself one hour after being placed in the lockup by pulling an electrical cord from the ceiling of the holding cell, wrapping it around his neck, and jumping off a bunk bed to the floor.

A problem with lockups that has been recognized is that many are staffed by police officers and not custodial personnel who are trained in the recognition and handling of offender problems. In the event of an offender being physically or sexually assaulted, committing suicide, or suffering a life threatening medical problem, lockup staff must be trained to properly respond to these situations. If they are lacking in such training, the agency and the officers are open and liable to lawsuits. Some police departments have incurred liability in such litigation because they did not have sufficient staff to operate a lockup. Progress is being made in this area. The Commission on Accreditation for Law Enforcement Agencies (CALEA) has guidelines for lockups for police departments seeking CALEA accreditation. Organizations such as the American Jail Association are assisting law enforcement agencies with improving lockup operations. Some researchers define the time span of holding offenders from a few hours up to 72 hours, which means that no matter how long offenders are held, the holding agency is responsible for their welfare and safety (Kerle, 2003, p. 99).

Jail

Jail: The next major type of correctional facility is the jail. Prisoners who do not get released from the lockup are transported to the local jail of the jurisdiction in which they were arrested. For many offenders, incarceration in the local jail (if not confined in a lockup immediately after arrest) means experiencing what it means to be locked up for the first time.

A *jail* is defined as *a correctional facility administered by a local law enforcement agency, such as a sheriff's office or local corrections department; confines adult offenders and juveniles under certain circumstances who are awaiting trial or sentenced to one year (12 months) or less* (Cornelius, 2008, p. 473).

In the past 20 years, in a cost saving measure and to pool staffing, finances and other resources many jurisdictions throughout the United States have constructed *regional jails*. Regional jails are defined as *jails that are operated by*

Dayroom: work release center: Fairfax County (VA) Pre-Release Center. Notice the vending machines and other amenities. Photo by author.

several jurisdictions jointly by mutual agreement with each jurisdiction contributing funds for operations and staffing (Cornelius, 2008, p. 476). This has met with success in several states, including Virginia.

Jails are known by a variety of names—adult detention center, detention center, correctional facility, county prison, workhouse, or house of corrections. Six states—Delaware, Alaska, Hawaii, Rhode Island, Vermont, and Connecticut administer combined jail/prison systems (Cornelius, 2008, p. 2).

The local jail has several functions, which have adapted from the early history of jails where they were only holding local lawbreakers for trial to dealing with the today's offenders and their problems. These functions are (Cornelius, 2008, pp. 1–2):

- Detain and confine criminal offenders who are awaiting trial for both major and minor crimes, including those who cannot be released through bail, bond or on their own recognizance.
- Confine criminal offenders who are sentenced to short sentences (generally one year/12 months or less) for non violent felonies or misdemeanors.
- Confine convicted offenders who are sentenced to prison terms; jails will confine those offenders awaiting transport to state or federal correctional facilities.

- .Confine mentally ill offenders who are awaiting transfer per order of the courts to state mental health facilities.
- Confine substance abusers who are court ordered to transfer to an alcohol/drug treatment facility.
- Confine juveniles ordered to jail by the juvenile court or due to the jurisdiction having no appropriate facilities to confine juveniles.
- Confine parole violators who are awaiting revocation hearings before the parole board.
- Confine probation violators who are awaiting probation revocation hearings before the sentencing court.
- Confine federal prisoners awaiting pickup by the United States Marshals Service for further action by the federal judiciary or ICE (Immigration and Customs Enforcement).
- Confine criminal offenders being held due to outstanding warrants from other jurisdictions. These charges, called *detainers*, are on file from other jurisdictions, holding the offender pending transfer to that jurisdiction (Cornelius, 2008, p. 471).

In some cases, overcrowding and security breaches from inmates who are management problems have resulted in jails transferring inmates to other facilities for holding. By doing so, the inmate has been *farmed out* (see Chapter 6). This is an informal jail term meaning that an inmate has been transferred from one jail to another for overcrowding or security reasons (Cornelius, 2008, p. 471).

Characteristics of Local Jails

Jails are more restrictive than prisons. Where prisons confine inmates for long periods of time and allow inmates more freedom of movement in the facility, jails confine inmates for a shorter time and as a rule, place more restrictions on inmate movement. Whereas inmates being committed to a prison type correctional facility will spend the majority of their sentence in that facility; jail populations are more fluid and transient.

State and federal prisons will have programs in place that address inmates' problems in a long term manner. Also, they will have the space, funding and physical plant capability to have more industrial and vocational programs.

The development of correctional facilities including the local jail will be discussed in Chapter 5. The following is a summary of the status of jails in the United States, based on the benchmark publication, *Who's Who in Jail Management*,

Fifth Edition, published by the American Jail Association in 2007 (American Jail Association, 2007, p. 2):

- The 3,096 counties in the United States are served by 3,163 jail facilities.
- The rated capacity of U.S. jails stands at 810,966.

The *rated capacity* is defined as the number of inmates or beds assigned to a correctional facility by an official body such as a jail board, a local corrections department, a sheriff's office, or a state or federal department of corrections. The *operational capacity* is the level or population at which the correctional facility can operate safely and is usually decided by the agency head or person supervising the facility operations (American Correctional Association, 1998, pp. 81, 97). The rated capacity is usually determined based on the architectural design and construction of the facility.

For example, a county contracts to build a 500 bed jail. The architectural design is for 350 male inmates and 150 female inmates. This is approved by the county jail board and the sheriff. This is the rated capacity. The jail becomes operational, and in two years is holding over 600 inmates. The sheriff decides to double bunk several male and female housing areas, increasing the bed space to 700. The jail supervisors report that they can safely handle the increase of bed spaces. The operational capacity—considering operations and safety— is now 700.

Overcrowding

It is clear that many jails are overcrowded and have exceeded their rated capacities. In many, their operational capacities have been pushed to the limit, and budgets are strained due to food costs, health costs, cost of inmate uniforms, personnel costs, salaries and the costs of overtime. The count of inmates in our nation's jails is always fluctuating due to the nature of jail operations. Offenders are constantly being released due to time served on their sentences, transfers, court releases or meeting bond or bail.

At mid year 2006, according to the Bureau of Justice Statistics, the total rated capacity of U.S. local jails was 810, 863 beds. Local jails at that time were operating at 94 percent of rated capacity; and when considering the peak or highest numbers of jail inmates incarcerated on a given day during the year, jails were operating at 100 percent capacity (Sabol, Minton and Harrison, *Prison and Jail Inmates at Mid Year 2006,* 2007, p. 7). In many jails, overcrowding forces jail administrators to be creative in making both bed space and adequate staffing available.

Population in jails as well as other correctional facilities is measured by the *average daily population,* or *ADP.* The ADP is measured by the adding the sum of the number of inmates confined in a correctional facility for one year and dividing it by the total number of days in that year. In examining the number of inmates in jails held at a "snapshot" glance at a specific time, the number held are significantly above the total ADP for U.S. jails (Sabol et al., 2007, p. 5).

Year	ADP	Number of inmates held on June 30
2000	618,319	621,149
2005	733,742	747,529
2006	755,896	766,010

Types

Due to the nature of our political system, there are individual local government agencies such as sheriff's offices, county correctional departments, etc., who have influenced the types of jails that have developed in their respective jurisdictions. Some jails are the old-fashioned linear design, some indirect supervision, and some are moving towards the direct supervision style of inmate management (see Chapter 8).

Research on jails has been conducted by the American Correctional Association (ACA). Jails are placed into several categories, depending on size. They are, with the number in the United States published in 2002 by ACA survey (American Correctional Association, 2002, pp. 10, 12):

- *Mega Jails:* jails having 1000+ bed capacity: 195
- *Large jails:* jails having 250–999 bed capacity: 571
- *Medium jails:* jails having 50–249 bed capacity: 1,303
- *Small jails:* jails having 1–49 bed capacity: 1,549
- Total: 3,618

The total from AJA differs from the ACA total (3,163 to 3,618, respectively) as described previously in this chapter. Why? Many jurisdictions are closing old jails, renovating existing jails, building new ones, or combining resources to place offenders in their jurisdictions into regional jails. Placement in regional jails can result in old jails being closed.

According to noted corrections author and college professor (Texas A&M International University) Dean John Champion, some professionals are in disagreement as to the definition of a jail, some authorities count short term, locally funded facilities as jails, while others count state run jails in reports. Facilities that may be excluded from the definition of jails may include work release facilities and work farms. Lockups may be also counted as jails. These factors, combined with closing jails, new construction, renovations and combining housing into regional jails results in different figures of the total number of jails (Champion in Cornelius, 2008, p. 9).

Problems with Jail Operations

Jail operations and management philosophies are not uniform; neither is the amount of funding, staffing or equipment that is provided to local jails. One county or city may have enough funding to adequately hire, train and equip staff; in another locality this may not be the case. According to Champion, the problems in jails may be attributed to three factors. First, many jails are old, the majority being constructed before 1970 and many of those were built five decades before that. Second, the local control of jails and the political factor of sheriffs being elected result in erratic, changing policies, procedures and management philosophies that staff and inmates have to adapt to. Third, many jurisdictions consider jail funding a low priority, resulting in limited operations and a lower quality of services and personnel as compared with state and federal corrections departments (Champion in Cornelius, 2008, p. 9).

Prisons

The third type of facility that comes to mind upon hearing the word "corrections" is the *prison*. A *prison* is defined as a correctional facility that houses convicted offenders under long sentences, usually over one year. Prisons are administered by state governments, the federal government or a private corrections company (American Correctional Association, 1998, p. 91). The term "prison" is often interchangeably used with the term "penitentiary" or may be called a "reformatory."

Prisons hold adult inmates or juveniles adjudicated (sentenced) as adult criminals serving long terms for serious crimes. Characteristics of prisons are high custody levels, solitary confinement for high risk dangerous inmates, and single cell occupancy whenever possible. However, where a jail may restrict inmate movement and have more confining architecture, such as cellblocks, prisons allow inmates more freedom of movement—in dormitories, program areas, exercise yards, etc., plus allowing a more flexible daily routine.

Entrance to facility: Rhode Island Department of Corrections.

Photo by Stephanie Ewans.

Number, Types and Characteristics

A benchmark study to examine the numbers and types of prison facilities in the United States is the *Census of State and Federal Correctional Facilities, 2005* published in October of 2008 by the United States Department of Justice. Statistics change annually as new facilities are opened, old ones are closed, or facilities are renovated for different use in their respective correctional systems. This is an official and accurate picture of the number of adult correctional facilities as the following types of correctional facilities were excluded from the census: jails or other types of local or regional facilities, private correctional facilities not primarily holding State or Federal inmates, military correctional facilities, Immigration and Naturalization Service facilities, Bureau of Indian Affairs facilities, the U.S. Marshals Service, or correctional hospital wards not operated by correctional authorities (Stephan, *Census of State and Federal Correctional Facilities 2005*, 2008, 1).

The number of adult facilities is increasing, most markedly in the number of private facilities, which increased from 264 to 415 of all correctional institutions, representing a 16 percent to 23 percent increase. The overall occupancy rate of adult facilities has increased significantly. In 2000, adult correctional facilities were operating at 2 percent above capacity; in 2005 the rate was 11 percent over capacity (Stephan, 2008, pp. 1, 2). In other words, adult prison facilities overall are overcrowded.

The following table is a concise, "snapshot" look at the number and types of adult correctional facilities including prisons, and their inmate population figures (Stephan, 2005, Appendix Tables 1, 2, 10):

Federal	Type	Population
Confinement facilities	102	145,780
Community based	0	
State		
Confinement facilities	1,190	1,230,195
Community based	529	54,233
Private		
Confinement facilities	107	85,604
Community based	308	22,847

Concerning security levels and facilities, slightly more than one third of inmates in state and federal correctional facilities are confined in maximum security type institutions. Medium security facilities housed two-fifths of inmates; a fifth was housed in minimum security facilities. Overall, in 2005 there were a reported 372 maximum security facilities, medium security facilities totaled 480 and 969 facilities were designated minimum security (Stephan, 2008, pp. 2, 4).

Specialized Correctional Facilities

There are types of correctional facilities that are specialized in the mission of their operating division, home agency, and also in the types of inmates that they confine. Staffs that operate these facilities are specialists and require training in specific areas that focus on handling certain types of offenders and the problems that they have. These special corrections facilities are as follows:

Community Corrections Facilities

Community corrections facilities are corrections facilities, generally minimum security, that house low risk offenders who are participants in rehabilitative programs using community resources. These programs deal with offenders in the community or allow carefully screened and selected offenders to enter the community to work, attend school, or participate in programs that address the problems that brought them into conflict with the law.

These programs include, but are not limited to the following: probation and parole, electronic monitoring, work release, study release, community service, community labor, and fine options (American Correctional Association, 1998, p. 20). These facilities are also called work release centers or pre-release centers.

Juvenile Detention Centers

Juvenile detention centers are facilities responsible for the custody and/or care and treatment of juveniles determined by juvenile court authorities to be in need of care, services or to have allegedly committed criminal acts and offenses (delinquent). The court can also determine that the juvenile detained may be dependent or a status offender (American Correctional Association, 1998, p. 63). Some detention centers detain only juveniles in need of services or protection until their cases are disposed of by juvenile courts and may be called shelters.

The centers holding serious juvenile offenders are very similar to jails and other secure confinement facilities, where a restricted environment is necessary. This environment is for the protection of the juvenile, the staff and the public. Juvenile detention centers and state facilities holding serious juvenile offenders provide a wide range of services and programs, whose goals are to support the juvenile's physical, emotional, and social development. At a minimum, these facilities provide education classes, recreation, counseling, nutrition, medical and health care services, visitation, and constant supervision. Juvenile detention centers also have staffs perform clinical assessments and report their findings to the court (American Correctional Association, 1998, p. 62). In many ways, juvenile detention centers are similar to adult correctional facilities: security hardware, rules and regulations, security patrols, and staff trained in handling juveniles and defensive tactics.

Boot Camps

A popular term in corrections is the "boot camp." A *boot camp* is defined as a special type of correctional facility, conducting short term reintegration programs for selected offenders that employ the method of military discipline. A boot camp has strict programming and physical conditioning to prepare offenders (usually youthful offenders) for a return to the community having the ability to resist criminal behavior (Cornelius, 2008, p. 434).

Boot camps were popular with the public in the 1990s and politically were very attractive. Staffs at boot camp are strict, formal and custody staffs are very similar to military drill instructors.

Statistically, boot camps are not that prevalent in American corrections. According to the *Census of State and Federal Correctional Facilities, 2000*, there were 84 boot camps in 2000: 3 Federal, 78 state, and 3 private. Of these, 11 were community based—9 state and 2 private. The majority of boot camps was minimum or low security (41); followed by medium security (30) and maximum security (13). Some local jail corrections facilities operate boot camps, but statistically, most fall into state corrections departments (Stephan and Karberg, *Census of State and Federal Correctional Facilities, 2000,* 2003, pp. 5, 6). The boot camp environment is strict, clean and orderly. Offenders follow a routine and are treated in the same way as military recruits.

Geriatric Correctional Facilities

The clock of aging does not stop when one enters incarceration. Studies are indicating that there is an aging trend among inmates. Offenders who are given long sentences of incarceration at a young age, such as life without parole, will "grow old and die" in prison. Also, there are offenders that get arrested at an older age. Whatever the reason, aging and elderly inmates pose several health and security concerns. They suffer physical and mental ailments associated with aging and may fall victim to younger, immature and predatory inmates. *Geriatric correctional facilities* are separate correctional facilities or units that are specifically designed to supervise and provide services for inmates aged 55 and older. These elderly or older inmates do not have contact with younger inmates, and are assisted with physical and medical needs. Programming that is provided target the older inmate, and there is an emphasis on family contact. These facilities are found in Alabama, Connecticut, Florida, Georgia, Maryland, Minnesota, Ohio, Pennsylvania, Tennessee, Texas, Virginia, and Washington (Alarid and Reichel, 2008, p. 344).

Several examples of geriatric correctional facilities are the Hamilton (Alabama) Prison for the Aged and Infirm and the Deerfield Correctional Center in Virginia. The Hamilton facility is a small (200 bed unit) which houses elderly inmates that are too infirm to be housed in a traditional correctional facility or are waiting to die. The reasons for placement there include physical disabilities, medical problems, mental incompetence and prone to harassment or assault from younger inmates. The Deerfield facility resulted in a transformation from the Deerfield Correctional Facility into an assisted living facility for disabled and elderly inmates, helping to manage the three percent of Virginia state prison inmates that are 55 years of age and older. One sixth of that number requires assistance with daily activities such as meal preparation and bathing. The Laurel Highlands Correctional Institution in Pennsylvania has sections or wings designed for geriatric inmates—with wheelchairs and oxygen generators. Housing elderly inmates in this fashion allows for better use of corrections personnel—such as freeing staff to work in areas that require more staff presence and supervision (Alarid and Reichel, 2008, pp. 344–345).

Mental Health Correctional Facilities

According to the *Census of State and Federal Correctional Facilities, 2000,* a total of 1,038 state, Federal and private correctional facilities provided psychological and psychiatric counseling for inmates. The highest number was among state facilities (849), followed by private facilities (112) and Federal facilities (77). Of these programs, 906 were confinement and 132 were community based (Stephan and Karberg, 2003, p. 11).

There are not generally a large number of correctional facilities devoted solely to the supervision and treatment of mentally ill inmates. According to the Bureau of Justice Statistics, 143 state correctional facilities specialize in the confinement of mentally ill offenders among other corrections functions. Twelve state facilities report psychiatric confinement as their primary task (Beck and Marushak, *Mental Health Treatment in State Prisons, 2000,* p. 1)

Frequently there is a segregation unit designated to house inmates with mental problems—"a facility within a facility." For example, the mental health staff may consult with classification and house an inmate in this unit until such time that he or she is deemed manageable and can live with other inmates.

An example of this is the result of the 2007 court case *Disability Advocates, Inc. v. N.Y.S. Office of Mental Health* 02 CIV. 4002 (GEL) (S.D. N.Y., 2007). In this case, advocates supporting the improvement in treatment for mentally ill inmates gained in a settlement with the New York Department of Correctional Services. The settlement resulted in the establishment of a 100 bed Residential Mental Health Unit. It will provide four hours per day of out of cell programs for inmates suffering from serious mental health problems; these inmates would otherwise be in a special housing unit. Other improvements include the addition of 215 Transitional Intermediate Care Program beds for mentally ill inmates in general population and 90 beds in an Intermediate Care Program for mentally ill inmates who cannot tolerate being housed in the general population (Cohen, 2007, pp. 33–34).

Indian Nation Correctional Facilities

There are correctional facilities on American Indian reservations and tribal lands, often referred to as "Indian Country." There are approximately 562 federally recognized Native American tribes; 341 tribes are recognized in the lower continental 48 states. Over 92 percent or 341 tribes took part in the *Census of Tribal Agencies in Indian Country, 2002.* Over half (59%) had some type of judicial system (Perry, *Census of Tribal Agencies in Indian Country, 2002,* p. iii).

Correctional facilities and corrections are present in the Indian Country judicial system. Approximately 23 percent or 71 of the tribes responding to the survey provided their own detention functions and facilities, while two thirds relied on a local or county corrections agency to provide a jail or detention facility for offenders. Out of the 314 tribes, only 24 had their own residential juvenile detention facility for the detention of juveniles committing offenses on Indian tribal land. Most of the tribes surveyed (approximately 68 percent or 119) placed juvenile offenders in neighboring county or non tribal juvenile residential facilities (Perry, 2002, p. iii).

In 2004, the federal government released a very uncomplimentary report on 74 jails and detention centers on Indian reservations in the United States. Investigators inspected 27 jails and concluded that staff lacked training and found problems with the physical plant and maintenance. Major problems cited included suicides, attempted suicides, escapes, and several inmate deaths due medical conditions such as seizures, alcohol poisoning and appendicitis. There are success stories, however, such as the Southern Ute Indian Tribal Center in Colorado, which provides a well trained, diverse (Native American, Anglo and Hispanic) staff, counseling and programming including programs in Native American culture, substance abuse and educational needs of tribal offenders (Cornelius, 2008, pp. 43–44). It is clear that improvements are needed in Indian Country correctional facilities.

Immigration and Custom Enforcement (ICE) Detention Centers

A new development in corrections has been the illegal immigration problem. Illegal immigrants—those individuals who are in the United States as a result of illegal entry are detained by the United States Immigration and Customs Enforcement service, or ICE. Local jails and corrections facilities can contract with ICE to hold illegal aliens until arrangements are made for them to appear in court, be deported or be transferred to an *immigration detention facility.* This facility houses offenders who have violated immigration laws and are awaiting deportation, court action or other dispositions of their cases.

This detention can be through a contract with a local public or private correctional facility and ICE or at an ICE facility. In local jails having contracted with ICE, the trend is to have that facility meet standards in the ICE Detention Operating Manual. As of July, 2008, ICE detention of illegal aliens was in operation at 22 ICE and contracted facilities in the United States. This does not include illegal aliens being temporarily detained at local jails pending transport to an ICE facility or a contracted ICE facility (*U.S. Immigration and Customs Enforcement, Public Information, accessed July 27, 2008*).

In 2008, ICE announced an initiative to identify and remove criminal aliens for U.S. jails and prisons. The agency estimates that about 300,000 to 450,000 convicted criminal aliens are eligible to be removed and deported annually from federal, state and local correctional facilities. It is expensive—costing an estimated $2 to $3 billion dollars per year. The aim of this initiative is to free space in correctional facilities and deport convicted illegal aliens and not release them back into the community (*U.S. Immigration and Customs Enforcement, News Releases, March 28, 2008*).

U.S. Military Corrections Facilities

Individuals who break the law while in the United States military are incarcerated in military corrections facilities. *Military corrections facilities* are correctional facilities that incarcerate offenders who commit crimes while active members of the United States Armed Forces. They may also be known as "the stockade" or "the brig."

According to recent statistics, the Army, Air Force, Marine Corps and the Navy held 1,135 prisoners in 2006, a decrease from 2,322 in 2005 (*Sourcebook of Criminal Justice Statistics Online Table 6.64.2006*).

Some of the offenders held by the military have been turned over to the military for trial, sentencing and have been sentenced to terms of incarceration after committing criminal offenses in civilian jurisdictions. Other offenders have been charged and/or convicted of violating the Uniform Code of Military Conduct. These offenses include desertion, disrespect for a superior officer, or being AWOL (absent without official leave). Military corrections differ from civilian corrections as the primary objective is to restore the offender to active duty, on a case by case basis (Stinchcomb, 2005, p. 169). Offenders who are on active duty in the U.S. military may be confined in local jails and lockups until arrangements are made by military authorities for transfer to military confinement.

Costs of U.S. Corrections

Corrections is an expensive discipline. Not only does it take funding to build new facilities and renovate old ones, it takes funding to hire and train

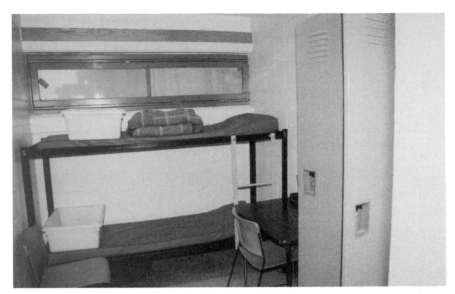

Some community corrections facilities "double bunk" inmates, similar to jails and prisons. Community corrections facility room, built for one, housing two. Fairfax County (VA) Pre-Release Center. Photo by author.

staff, provide services to the inmate population, and maintain the operations in a facility.

The expenditures of a correctional facility are dependent on several factors, such as location, the number of inmates it confines (overcrowding can have an impact), the number of personnel needed to staff and operate it, its security hardware and measures and how extensive its programs (Stinchcomb, 2005, p. 169). The age of the facility can be a factor—renovation and repairs can be expensive.

According to the U.S. Bureau of Justice Statistics, total expenditures for corrections between 1982 and 2003 increased a staggering 423 percent. During the same time period, the federal government increased its spending on corrections 925 percent, followed by state corrections expenditures increasing 550.9 percent and local corrections expenditures increasing by 519.6 percent. Overall, from 1982–2003, the number of employees in corrections—including correctional officers and probation and parole staff more than doubled in size, from 300,000 to 748,000 (Hughes, *Bureau of Justice Statistics, Justice Expenditure and Employment in the United States, 2003*, pp. 2, 3, 7).

A frequently asked question in corrections from the public—the taxpayers—is "how expensive is it to house inmates"?

When correctional administrators compute the costs of running a facility, they examine the daily costs of incarcerating inmates. This is based on the cost of security staff, medical care, clothing, feeding, etc. According to the Bureau of Justice Statistics, the average operating costs per State inmate in 2001 were $62.05 per day or $22,650 per year. This was very close to the Federal cost per inmate: $62.01 per day or $22,632 per year (Stephan, *State Prison Expenditures, 2001*, p. 1).

Population of U.S. Correctional Facilities

Corrections population statistics are very carefully examined and researched in the United States. Correctional policy, procedures, operating decisions and standards are based in part on the population of the facility. Population statistics of correctional facilities change constantly due to inmates being processed in or released.

A benchmark report on the incarceration rate in the United States was The PEW Center on the States *One in 100: Behind Bars in America 2008*. The highlights of the report stated (The PEW Center on the States: *One in 100: Behind Bars in America 2008*, pp. 5, 29):

- The U.S. incarcerates more people than any other country in the world.
- In the two decades from 1987 to 2007, the prison population in the U.S. has nearly tripled.
- The actual U.S. incarceration rate is 1 per 99.1 adults.
- The breakdown of prison counts as of January 1, 2008 were:
  - Total prison population: 1,596,127
  - Total Federal prison population: 198, 989
  - Total State prison population: 1,397,138
- The local jail incarceration rate was 723,131

Security Levels

Maximum, medium, and minimum security or custody levels define the type of facility. They also considered the levels of supervision by the facility custody staff. Many prisons and jails are tasked to provide security through assigning levels of custody to the inmate population. In every type of correctional facility, some inmates cause trouble for the staff due to negative behavior—escape attempts, thefts, trafficking in contraband, causing disturbances, assaults on staff and other inmates, etc. Other inmates adapt to being incarcerated and obey the rules. Some inmates need higher levels of staff supervision and secure custody based on their charges such as murder, sex offenses or felonious assault. For these reasons, custody is designated into three types of security levels. In many institutions, particularly jails, all three types are incorporated into the same facility. The basic definitions are (Cornelius, 2008, p. 474):

Maximum security: Maximum security is designed to exercise maximum control and constant supervision over the inmate population. Through use of officer escorts, prisoners in restraints when out of their cells, security cameras, numbers of locked doors, solitary confinement, frequent head counts, searches, incidents such as escapes, violent acts and disturbances are minimized. Inmates in maximum security are the most serious in terms of crimes, have behavioral problems, are hard core, dangerous and very institutionalized. Participation in rehabilitation programs is not a priority. If a correctional facility is designated as maximum security, inmates are carefully watched if in general population or are segregated (housed alone) as risks to security.

Medium security: At this level, the prevention of escapes, violence and disturbances are still priorities. However, the security measures are less strict. Fewer cameras and the allowance of inmates to move more freely and unrestrained typify some trust in the inmates. Inmates may live two to a cell or in a dormitory. In medium security, the inmates have demonstrated that they can behave, and their criminal histories and behavior do not indicate a problem. They are usually non violent, and are eligible to work in the facility or participate in programs.

Minimum security: Inmates are allowed greater degrees of movement and responsibilities such as attending programs or in cases of community corrections facilities, attending programs or working in the community. Inmates are generally not a security risk and may be short term (close to release date).

A simple axiom is this—the higher the security—cameras, officers, razor wire on outside perimeters, checks, counts and searches, for example—the higher the level of custody.

Summary

There are many types of correctional facilities. Prisons, jails and lockups are the most familiar. There are specialized correctional facilities: community correctional centers, juvenile detention centers, boot camps, geriatric correctional facilities, mental health correctional facilities, Indian Nation correctional facilities, ICE detention centers, and U.S. military correctional facilities.

Correctional facilities are expensive. Besides just housing a prisoner, other factors such as construction, operation and staffing influence the total costs. The daily cost to incarcerate federal inmates and state inmates is about the same.

Population statistics are constantly changing. What is noteworthy is that the U.S incarcerates more people than any country in the world; 1 out of every 99 adults is in the correctional system.

The three supervision levels are maximum, medium and minimum. In descending degree, they restrict surveillance and movement of the prisoner. These levels define the type and function of the facility.

Review Questions

1. Explain the differences between a jail, prison and lockup.
2. What are the ten main functions of a jail?
3. What are the four types of jails?
4. Explain maximum, medium and minimum security.
5. What are factors in the costs of incarceration?
6. Identify and discuss three types of specialized correctional facilities.

Terms/Concepts

average daily population (ADP)   maximum security
boot camp   medium jails
community corrections facilities   medium security
detainers   mega jails
farmed out   military corrections facilities
geriatric correctional facilities   minimum security
immigration detention facility   operational capacity
jail   prison
juvenile detention centers   rated capacity
large jails   regional jails
lockup   small jails

References

Alarid, Leanne F. and Philip R. Reichel. (2008). *Corrections: A Contemporary Introduction*. Boston: Pearson Allyn and Bacon.

American Correctional Association. (1998). *Dictionary of Criminal Justice Terms*. Lanham, Maryland.

American Correctional Association. (2002). *2002–2004 National Jail and Adult Detention Directory*. Lanham: American Correctional Association.

American Jail Association. (2007). *Who's Who in Jail Management, Fifth Edition*. Hagerstown: American Jail Association.

Beck, Allen J., Ph.D. and Laura M. Marushak. (July, 2001). *Mental Health Treatment in State Prisons, 2000*. U.S. Department of Justice: Bureau of Justice Statistics. Washington, DC: U.S. Government Printing Office, [available on line at www.ojp.usdoj.gov/bjs/].

Bureau of Justice Statistics. *Sourcebook of Criminal Justice Statistics Online Table 6.64.2006*.

Champion, Dean. (2008). Point of View: Jails and Jail History. In: Cornelius, Gary F. (2008). *The American Jail: Cornerstone of Modern Corrections*. Upper Saddle River: Pearson Prentice Hall.

Cohen, Fred. (2007). New York Settles on Behalf of Inmates With Mental Illness: Disability Advocates, Inc. v. N.Y.S. Office of Mental Health, 02 CIV.4002 (GEL) (S.D. N.Y., 2007). *Correctional Mental Health Report, Vol. 9, No. 3*, 33–34, 40.

Cornelius, Gary F. (2008). *The American Jail: Cornerstone of Modern Corrections*. Upper Saddle River: Pearson Prentice Hall.

Cornelius, Gary. (1996). *Jails in America: An Overview of Issues, 2nd Edition*. Lanham: American Correctional Association.

Drunk Driving Suspect Hangs Self in Waldorf State Police Barracks. *Washington Post*, 6/2/85.

Hughes, Kristen A. (April, 2006, revised 05/10/06). *Justice Expenditure and Employment in the United States, 2003*. U.S. Department of Justice: Bureau of Justice Statistics. Washington, DC: U.S. Government Printing Office, [available on line at www.ojp.usdoj.gov/bjs/].

Kerle, Kenneth E., Ph.D. (2003). *Exploring Jail Operations*. Hagerstown: American Jail Association.

Perry, Steven W. Bureau of Justice Statistics. (December, 2005). *Census of Tribal Justice Agencies in Indian Country, 2002*. U.S. Department of Justice: Bureau of Justice Statistics. Washington, DC: U.S. Government Printing Office, [available on line at www.ojp.usdoj.gov/bjs/].

Sabol, William J., Ph.D., Todd Minton and Paige M. Harrison. (June, 2007, revised 06/27/07). *Prison and Jail Inmates at Midyear 2006*. U.S. Department of Justice: Bureau of Justice Statistics. Washington, DC: U.S. Government Printing Office, [available on line at www.ojp.usdoj.gov/bjs/].

Seiter, Richard P., Ph.D. (2005). *Corrections: An Introduction*. Upper Saddle River: Pearson Prentice Hall.

Stephan, James J. (October, 2008). *Census of State and Federal Correctional Facilities, 2005*. U.S. Department of Justice: Bureau of Justice Statistics. Washington, DC: U.S. Government Printing Office, [available on line at www.ojp.usdoj.gov/bjs/].

Stephan, James J. (June, 2004) Bureau of Justice Statistics. (2004). *State Prison Expenditures, 2001*. U.S. Department of Justice: Bureau of Justice Statistics. Washington, DC: U.S. Government Printing Office, [available on line at www.ojp.usdoj.gov/bjs/].

Stephan, James J. and Jennifer Karberg. (August, 2003, revised 10/15/03). *Census of State and Federal Corrections Facilities, 2000*. U.S. Department of Justice: Bureau of Justice Statistics. Washington, DC: U.S. Government Printing Office, [available on line at www.ojp.usdoj.gov/bjs/].

Stinchcomb, Jeanne, Ph.D. (2005). *Corrections: Past, Present and Future*. Lanham: American Correctional Association.

U.S. Immigration and Customs Enforcement, *Public Information, accessed July 27, 2008.*

U.S. Immigration and Customs Enforcement, *News Releases, March 28, 2008.*

Warren, Jennifer. PEW Center on the States: *One in 100: Behind Bars in America 2008*. www.pewtrusts.org.

Chapter 3

Correctional Officers: Personnel Issues and Training

The public image of a prison or jail usually focuses on the correctional officer. Sometimes they are called guards, jailors, turnkeys, etc. Due to movies and television, these men and women are sometimes portrayed as undereducated, out of shape (overweight), sadistic, and brutal. That is not the case. Our nation's jails, prisons and community corrections centers are staffed with trained, skilled and conscientious men and women who must perform a difficult mission—keeping people safely and securely locked up against their will.

This chapter will discuss six areas concerning correctional officers:

number, race gender
salaries
hiring, retention and employment outlook
duties of correctional officers
training
traits of a good correctional officer

Number, Race and Gender

According to the Bureau of Justice Statistics, full time corrections employees are running second to full time police employees. According to 2003 statistics, full time police protection makes up 44.7 percent of total justice system (state and local) employment, corrections comprises 35 percent and judicial and legal workers total 20.4 percent (Hughes, *Justice Expenditure and Employment in the United States, 2003*, p. 8).

The mainstay of any correctional facility is the correctional officer or *CO*. The United States Department of Labor reported in 2006 that overall, correctional officers held about 500,000 positions. Approximately 3 out of every 5 correctional officer positions were in state corrections facilities, including pris-

Correctional Officers take pride of their agencies: Rhode Island Department of Corrections Honor Guard. Courtesy of the Rhode Island Department of Corrections.

ons, prison camps, and corrections facilities for youthful offenders. The Federal correctional system had approximately 18,000 CO positions in 2006; about 16,000 COs worked in private correctional facilities. The majority of the remaining CO positions were in local jails at the city, county or regional level. Most COs at the local level are employed in correctional facilities located in rural areas with small inmate populations. Correctional officers also work in facilities supervising individuals being held by the U.S Immigration and Customs Enforcement (ICE), ending court action or deportment (U.S. Department of Labor, *33-3012 Correctional Officers and Jailors*).

By correctional system facilities, the number of correctional officers and CO to inmate ratio breaks down as follows in 2000 (*Sourcebook of Criminal Justice Statistics 2003 online, table 1.104*):

Federal: custody/security staff:	12,376
State: correctional systems custody/security staff:	243,352
Private: correctional systems custody/security staff:	14,589
Ratio of inmates to COs (overall):	4.8

The gender of correctional employees is predominantly male. According to the *Sourcebook of Criminal Justice Statistics online,* males made up 288,306 of the correctional work force, while females composed a total of 141,727 employees. In examining the jail CO work force, jail correctional officers are mostly male. The national estimate is that 108,700 jail correctional officers are males, while 42,500 are females (*Sourcebook of Criminal Justice Statistics 2003 online, tables 1.104, 1.100*).

It is important that the correctional officer work force be diverse. Correctional officers supervise male and female offenders, as well as offenders from different ethnic groups. Cultural diversity training is mandated in many jurisdictions per corrections standards. The correctional officer ethnic makeup should mirror that of the offender population. Hispanic offenders who cannot speak English will communicate with Hispanic COs who speak Spanish. Black inmates may find it more comfortable to speak more openly with black correctional officers. The breakdown of correctional staff ethnicity in 2000 was (*Sourcebook of Criminal Justice Statistics 2003 online, table 1.104*):

Uniform Inspection. Maryland Department of Corrections.

- White, non Hispanic: 272,436
- Black, non Hispanic: 83,697
- Hispanic: 31,697
- Other: Native American, Alaska Natives,
  Asians, Pacific Islanders: 7,890

The total staff of a facility includes correctional officers. In reality, many employees' having multiple jobs make up the staffs of correctional facilities.

Support staff: clerical, administrative workers

Maintenance workers: electrical workers, repair personnel

Food service workers: cooks, dieticians

Medical staff: physicians, dentists, nurses, correctional health care workers (usually called medics)

Treatment staff: substance abuse counselors, teachers, mental health workers, classification staff, teachers, vocational instructors and auxiliary staff including volunteers

Religious staff: chaplains and assistants

Mental health staff: psychiatrists, psychologists, counselors.

Salaries

The pay scale is improving in the corrections field, but the amount of pay depends on the tax base of the jurisdiction responsible for the agency and the amount of funding available from sources such as the federal or state government. The median annual salary of a correctional officer including jail correctional officers was $35,760 as of May, 2006. In 2007, the Federal Bureau of Prisons starting salary for COs was $28,862 (U.S. Department of Labor, *33-3012 Correctional Officers and Jailors*).

There are supplemental factors to the correctional officer pay scale. Due to overcrowding and staff shortages, paid overtime opportunities and the ability to accrue compensatory time exist in many departments. Benefits in agencies include retirement after 25 years of service at any age or after 20 years at age 50, and civil service coverage and protections, including merit systems and benefits. Also, in many agencies COs are given an allowance to purchase uniforms and/or equipment (U.S. Department of Labor, *33-3012 Correctional Officers and Jailors*). Paid annual leave, life insurance and the opportunity to choose a medical plan are a few examples of how benefits have improved for correctional officers.

Hiring, Retention and Employment Outlook

To effectively perform these duties, correctional officers are hired through a screening process taking into consideration their education and physical fitness. More correctional agencies are looking for candidates on line, at job fairs, from government agencies, at other law enforcement agencies, at colleges and from honorably discharged military personnel. A new process in correctional hiring is the *integrity interview*, where applicants are asked questions about financial difficulties, drug and/or alcohol abuse, or any situation that could put the CO into a compromising position with inmates. If the screening is successful, the applicant is offered a conditional position, contingent on passing a physical examination, passing a drug test, and completing mandatory basic training. In recent years, more correctional agencies are requiring applicants to take a test to determine recent drug use, as well as staff performing detailed background investigations (Seiter, pp. 317–319). It is correctional officers, through their interaction with inmates, who set the stage for whatever the correctional environment becomes. If they are screened, interviewed and trained correctly, the environment will be a positive one.

According to the U.S. Department of Labor, all corrections facilities have basic job requirements, namely (U.S. Department of Labor, *33-3012 Correctional Officers and Jailors):*

- To be at least 18 to 21 years of age
- To be a U.S. citizen or permanent resident
- High School diploma or graduation equivalency degree
- Have no felony convictions
- Pass background examination
- Demonstration of job experience and stability (not necessarily related to corrections) for at least 2 years
- Prior military or law enforcement experience (optional); college credits can be substituted for this (the Federal Bureau of prisons requires all CO applicants to have a bachelor's degree, 3 years of full time experience in a field counseling, assistance or supervision to individuals, or a combination of the two)
- To be in good health, meeting standards in physical fitness, vision, and hearing
- Have good judgment and the ability to act quickly
- Pass a drug screening
- Pass standardized written exam
- Have a positive response and impression at an interview

Retention

There must be incentives for the CO to remain at the agency and make his or her tenure there into a meaningful career. Promotional opportunities, cost of living raises, merit salary raises and good retirement benefits can assist in this, as well as opportunities to learn other skills such as firearms instructor, academy instructor, tactical response team officer, computer technician, classification counselor, etc. In many agencies, specialized training and college classes can enhance promotional prospects. It is important that the agency grows and when a facility expands, more supervisory positions such as corporal, sergeant, and lieutenant open up for advancement (U.S. Department of Labor, *33-3012 Correctional Officers and Jailors*).

Employment of correctional officers is estimated to grow at a rate of 16 percent between 2006 and 2016, which is faster than the average of all other occupations. This is due to many states abolishing or limiting parole, mandatory sentencing, longer sentences of incarceration, and rising populations (U.S. Department of Labor, *33-3012 Correctional Officers and Jailors*).

Duties of Correctional Officers

Correctional officers are the foundation of a correctional facility. Champion (2005) defined a correctional officer as a guard in a prison whose function is to supervise or manage inmates (Champion, 2005, p. 683). While the image of the correctional officer (or CO) is one of the traditional prison guard, the term is more complex. A more specific definition of a *correctional officer (CO)* is:

> *A trained law enforcement officer in a correctional facility whose function is to supervise and manage inmates, enforce the laws of the jurisdiction, enforce the rules of the facility, maintain the inmates in a safe and secure environment, and prevent escapes.*

Though correctional agencies, both adult and juvenile, have various general orders and procedures that govern officers and provide guidance, the basic goal of a CO and those in specialized correctional facilities is to *securely* and *safely* confine inmates/offenders in their care.

Secure and safe confinement simply means that the public is protected from escapes, staff and visitors are protected from aggressive acts by inmates, and the inmates/offenders are protected from each other (murders, assaults, thefts, etc.), and themselves (self-mutilation and suicide). If order is maintained, lives and property are not harmed and the public is protected.

Correctional officer checking a segregation unit. Clarke-Frederick-Winchester (VA) Regional Adult Detention Center.

According to the Honorable Helen Corrothers, former president of the American Correctional Association and former Commissioner of the United States Sentencing Commission, the goal of public safety can be achieved by COs through the achievement by two objectives (Corrothers, 1992, p. 4):

1. Preventing escapes and humanely incarcerating offenders until they are legally released; and
2. Provide an appropriate safe environment (for inmates *and* staff) which may influence inmates to learn and adopt positive values. Hopefully, the second objective will create a will or desire in the inmate to stay crime free once released.

To achieve these two objectives, the duties of a CO take both a formal and an informal track (Partial source: U.S. Department of Labor, *33-3012 Correctional Officers and Jailors*).

Formal Duties of a CO

1. Perform regular checks and headcounts on inmates in living, programs, and work areas. These checks are performed at intervals (every thirty minutes, every fifteen minutes, etc.). Some checks, such as in

Two correctional officers conducting a "shakedown," or cell search. One looks for contraband, and the other documents the search and records its findings. Clarke-Frederick-Winchester (VA) Regional Adult Detention Center.

inmate segregation or in jail booking/receiving are performed more frequently. These checks are logged or documented.

2.   Perform searches on inmates' persons, living areas, and work areas; the purpose of these searches are to look for several things such as contraband, signs of illegal or self-destructive activity (needle tracks due to drug use, tattooing themselves, cutting wrists, etc.) or any sign of breaking the rules or the law. *Contraband* is defined simply as any item (illegal drugs, weapons, etc.) that is not authorized by the facility administration. Contraband can also be any authorized item in excess such as extra blankets, hoarded food, etc.

3.   Process inmates into the facility: all correctional facilities have intake centers. Inmates must be properly committed — legal paperwork must be in order, the inmates must be searched, placed in confinement, have his/her property inventoried, and medically checked.

4.   Observe inmate behavior and activities. CO's must observe inmates for rule violations, work performance, unusual behavior, hygiene, signs of depression, etc. The CO must observe inmates constantly in living units, segregation units, work assignments, in recreation, programs,

etc. Problems must be documented and reported. This is the formal role of *patrol officer* (Cornelius, *Stressed Out, 1994,* p. 28).

5. Supervise inmates on work assignments. Carefully selected and screened inmates who perform work for the facility, called "*trusties*," must be supervised by officers. These officers must also provide direction and issue instructions.

6. Enforce rules and laws, investigate violations. All correctional facilities have rules that must be followed. A CO as *investigator* (Cornelius, *Stressed Out,* 1994, p. 28) must enforce these rules and settle disputes, showing no favoritism. Violators must be reported. Also, inmates must obey the laws of the jurisdiction and may be criminally prosecuted. For example, if an inmate stabs another inmate, he/she can be charged with felonious assault and face criminal prosecution. A CO must be able to fairly and objectively investigate events with an eye for detail and prepare a case for prosecution.

7. Inspect the facility security system and environment. COs inspect daily the cells, cellblocks, dormitories, program areas, recreation facilities, offices, locked windows, bars, gates, grilles, cameras, and fire safety equipment for signs of tampering. Intercoms, radios, handcuffs, and other staff equipment must be checked for flaws and malfunctions. All areas are inspected for fire safety and/or unsanitary violations. Incoming mail and packages are inspected for contraband.

8. Escort or transport inmates and admit authorized visitors. COs escort inmates to and from housing areas, court, programs, recreation, visiting, sick call, classification or other institutions. COs also escort authorized visitors inside the facility.

9. Participate in disciplinary hearings/administrative hearings. Not only will the CO be asked to participate in disciplinary and administrative hearings, he or she may be asked to chair them, taking on the formal role of *judge* (Cornelius, *Stressed Out, 1994,* p. 28).

All of the above functions require documentation. Checks, rule violations, escorts, and inspections usually require some kind of written report. To be in corrections, one must know how to communicate clearly in writing. Formal duties such as observation, looking into rule violations, investigating crimes in the institution, and being part of hearings result in formal CO roles such as patrol officer, investigator, and judge.

Documentation of observations, events, and interactions with inmates is a critical part of the correctional officer's job. Clarke-Frederick-Winchester (VA) Regional Adult Detention Center.

Informal Duties of a CO

Officers perform many functions informally in the facility; not all duties and jobs are formal. The informal roles that officers perform include (Cornelius, *Stressed Out, 1994*, p. 28):

Psychologist: recognizing symptoms of mental illness and referring inmates to appropriate mental health staff.

Legal advisor: when asked, providing answers to inmates' legal questions — sentence, court dates, bond, etc., or representing an inmate in a disciplinary hearing.

Parent: being a strong, positive role model for immature inmates, teaching inmates better hygiene. For example, correcting an inmate who exhibits a body odor problem, telling an inmate to clean his cell, etc.

Information agent: when asked, giving answers to inmates about facility policies, programs, rules, etc. Some officers conduct orientations for newly arriving inmates.

Counselor: giving advice to inmates on how to properly conduct themselves, how to handle a personal problem, etc.

Diplomat: intervening in and defusing inmate disputes, before verbal disagreements escalate into full scale physical altercations.

It has been said that working in a correctional institution can prepare one to deal with a variety of people. Corrections officers can learn first hand how to handle resistant people while maintaining a calm demeanor. This is especially true of COs who work with specialized populations such as the mentally disordered.

Training

All correctional officers must have training. Working with offenders and dealing with inmates require special observational, communicative and interpersonal skills.

Training for correctional officers comes in three basic types: (Cornelius, 2008, p. 469, 472, 473):

1. *Basic training:* training conducted in a training academy that is measured in a set number of hours, that newly hired correctional officers must successfully complete within their first year of employment, subjects covered include the agency mission, rules and regulations, and the skills that must be developed for job performance. Officers are tested and must meet performance standards. Standards and guidelines of training are set down by state and federal agencies responsible for correctional facility standards and correctional officer training.
2. *In-service training:* training designed to maintain certification and job skills; the CO is required to attend a specific number of hours of training in subjects applicable to his or her job during a particular time period. For example, the correctional officer may be required to complete 40 hours every year, or every two years, depending on mandates by the state or organization that grants accreditation.
3. *On the job training (OJT):* training that is conducted on the job for a specific number of hours per agency policy, and usually after the new correctional officer graduates from basic training, but before he or she is permitted to work independently on a post or job assignment. This training is conducted by a *FTO*, or *field training officer*. The FTO is a veteran staff member who serves as the training supervisor of the new CO, requiring him or her to perform job tasks, such as searches, headcounts, writing reports, etc. The FTO will rate and grade the

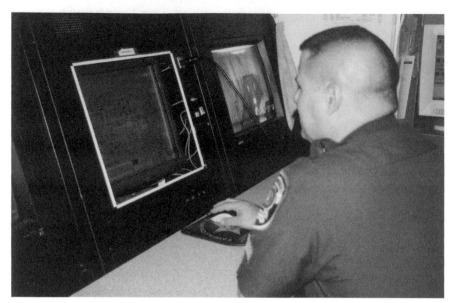

Correctional officers must be constantly vigilant, whether inside a control center or in an inmate housing unit. Fairfax County Adult Detention Center. Photo by author.

trainee officer and can recommend retention or dismissal. The first year of employment is called the ***probationary year***, where new officers must demonstrate that they can complete basic training and OJT. If they do not satisfactorily meet job expectations, including passing basic training, they can be dismissed.

Some correctional agencies are accredited by professional organizations such as the American Correctional Association or by the boards of corrections in their states, or by the federal government in cases of federal correctional facilities. These organizations mandate the number of training hours that COs must have in order for the facility to maintain accreditation.

For example, a new correctional officer in the Federal Bureau of Prisons must complete 200 hours of formal training during the first year of employment and within 60 days; 120 hours of specialized training at the U.S. Bureau of Prisons residential training center in Georgia (U.S. Department of Labor, *33-3012 Correctional Officers and Jailors*). Due to new developments in corrections, the number of mandatory hours may change.

The American Correctional Association standards mandate the number of training hours for correctional officers in different types of correctional facilities. The training is backed up by curriculum, training records, and agency policies and procedures. For example (American Correctional Association, *2008* pp. 42, 70, 71):

- ACA Standards 4-4084 and 4-4084-1 state that all new correctional offi-cers in adult correctional institutions receive 120 hours of training dur-ing their first year of employment, and at least 40 hours of training annually.
- ACA Standards 4-ALDF-7B-10 and 4-7B-10-01 state that all correc-tional officers working in adult local detention facilities receive 120 hours of training during their first year and at least 40 hours of annual training.

The sources of training vary. Most agencies rely on a training academy to provide training. A training academy may be a branch of the agency or, as a cost saving move, be composed of staff from the several agencies it serves (re-gional academy). Other methods of providing training are roll call training where training is presented at shift change, or one- or two-day seminars held at the facility sponsored usually by the academy. Staff members who meet cer-tain criteria can become certified instructors in their jurisdictions. Training can also be in the form of seminars conducted by such correctional organiza-tions as the American Correctional Association (ACA), the American Jail As-sociation (AJA), and the National Sheriff's Association (NSA).

Specialized training is training in a specific task or job skill, often requir-ing certification or a showing of proficiency. For example, if correctional of-ficers are to be trained in a specific piece of equipment, such as a semi automatic

Corrections Officers at Roll Call. Maryland Department of Corrections.

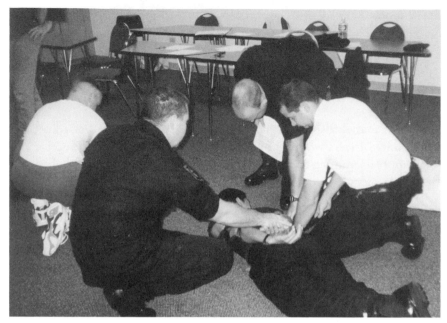

Restraints training, Manatee County Corrections Facility. Manatee County (FLA).

handgun, shotgun, rifle or expandable baton, they will be tested or have to qualify with that equipment before being permitted to carry it and subsequently use it. Another area of specialized training is emergency response. If a CO is selected to be on a facility emergency response team, he or she will be trained on such equipment as pepper spray, plexiglas shields, inmate extraction techniques, restraining inmates and riot control. If new computers are being installed in a jail's booking and receiving area, the correctional officers working there must undergo specific training with the new software and demonstrate that they can perform their job tasks.

Training Topics

There is no limit to the subjects offered in training, and like the number of hours, these subjects can be increased. For example, as a result of the passage of the Prison Rape Elimination Act, or PREA (see Chapter 13), ACA added the subject of sexual abuse/assault intervention to the 40 hours of annual training for correctional officers in adult correctional institutions, local adult detention facilities and juvenile detention facilities (American Correctional Association, 2008 pp. 42, 70, 7, 197).

The following is representative of areas of effective correctional training:

Security procedures: counts, searches, key and tool control
Supervising inmates
Use of lethal/non-lethal force
Defensive tactics
Inmate discipline
Inmates' civil rights
Report writing/documenting events
Fire procedures/safety
Escape prevention
Firearms training
Communicating with inmates
First aid/cardiopulmonary resuscitation (CPR)
Blood-borne/air-borne pathogens
Criminal code
Agency policies and procedures
Code of Conduct/ethics
Staff communications/use of computers/information systems
Emergency operation of motor vehicles
Suicide prevention
Crisis intervention
Handling special inmates (mentally ill, etc.)
Cultural diversity
Gangs and security threat groups
Prevention of riots and disturbances
Stress management and wellness
Physical fitness and agility
Juveniles in custody
Safe transport of inmates
Prevention/investigation of sexual assault

Many states have standards of training which in detail describe subject areas to be taught, the required number of hours, and performance based objectives that the officer must pass. Academies may combine formal classroom-type training with on-the-job training, putting the trainee with veteran staff in the facility and grading them on job performance. These standards also govern the selection of training of instructors. Certified instructors must have formalized training in teaching techniques and lesson plan development.

An example of a comprehensive, up to date correctional officer training program can be found at the Denver, CO Sheriff's Office. The following is a list of subjects covered in basic training and the hours mandated (Cornelius, 2008, pp. 308–309):

Subject	Number of Hours
Academic Training Topics	
Communication, conflict management, human relations	20
Contraband detection and control	14
Department rules, policies and professional standards	16
Emergency procedures	24
General operations and security (additional covered elsewhere)	48
Restraints	8
Prisoner handling	24
Classification, etc.	6
Law and legal issues	30
Unusual and suicidal prisoner behavior	18
Use of force (practical and other information covered elsewhere)	8
Miscellaneous	20
Skills Training	
Firearms/related weapons (shoot, don't shoot, use of force)	95
Defensive and practical driving	19
Incident evidence/scene preservation/report writing*	22
CPR, first aid, life safety skills	30
Physical fitness, defense and control tactics	62
Inmate supervision	16
* also covered in testifying	
Total training hours	480

Specialized topics, such as inmate con games, high risk prisoners, stress management, and defensive tactics are offered at most training academies. Training in the juvenile corrections system is very similar to adult corrections training—security issues and dealing with offenders are addressed.

Training for correctional officers who deal with youthful offenders including juveniles is improving. Researchers are recommending that correctional staff in juvenile facilities be afforded training in these areas (Silverman, 2001, pp. 187–188):

- conflict resolution: important to positive role modeling and showing youthful offenders and juveniles how conflicts should be handled
- role modeling: youthful offenders and juveniles should be exposed to staff who are stable, fair and mature
- self defense: use of force and gaining control

- adolescent behavior patterns: gaining knowledge in adolescent stages of development and stages of behavior and maturation
- security: adherence to same principles as in adult facilities
- supervision: in units, and during activities and leisure time

New Trends

One new trend in correctional officer training is technology. The field is changing. New equipment ranging from firearms to radios is making the job of the CO easier. One example is booking or processing offenders into a facility. In Norfolk, Virginia the local jail system will *read inmates' eyes* in order to keep them confined to their areas inside the facilities. Scanners will record the "fingerprint" of each inmate's and staff member's eyes and memorize the information. This technology will determine exactly who a person is in the facility, as inmates have been known to attempt escape by wearing civilian clothes (*The Corrections Professional*, February 2008, p. 2). To make this system work, staff will have to be trained on the scanners and their proficiency demonstrated.

A new trend in corrections training is *scenario based training*. This training puts trainees in certain situations through the involvement of role players or by electronic means (Cornelius, 2008, p. 477). For example, through the use of computer animation, a trainee may be presented with a situation in which he or she has to make a decision to shoot or not to shoot a firearm. In a class on interpersonal relations and communication, other COs in the class may play inmates who try to intimidate or argue with the trainee. The goal of such training is to bring the real world of corrections and law enforcement into the classroom to ascertain how the trainee should handle the situation. In Illinois, juvenile services supervisors dress up staff members to look like juveniles and run them randomly through the yard to test staff reaction (*Corrections Professional*, 6/6/97).

Cross training staff and giving them insight as to what others do inside the facility is also a new trend. At the Washington Department of Community Corrections, an in-house training program was developed to provide quality training within the agency. By the use of focus groups from different job sections, it assessed training needs and developed implementation through a training advisory committee. This utilization of staff resources has saved money and provided staff with a way of having input concerning training needs (*Corrections Professional*, 11/7/97).

As new subjects are developed for corrections training, so are new methods to deliver them. Such non traditional methods are roll call training, where subjects are discussed at correctional officer roll calls, on line training, where classes are taught from a web site to the CO on line at a computer, and correspondence course training, such as offered by the American Correctional Association.

Often events on the outside can make new training necessary. For example, concern over the number and activities of illegal aliens has been reported in the United States. Sheriff's deputies—including those working in local jails—are being trained in procedures for screening inmates' immigration status, including the prevention of suspected illegal aliens from being released on bail if they lack legal papers to be in the United States. The training is the result of a partnership between local agencies and the federal government and lasts 6 weeks; as of July 2008, the Department of Immigration and Customs Enforcement has trained 700 officers in 47 law enforcement agencies in the United States (*The Corrections Professional*, July, 2008, p. 2).

Traits of a Good Correctional Officer (CO)

While training methods have improved for workers who deal with adult and juvenile offenders, training alone does not make an effective correctional officer. As many staff members know, the job of correctional officer is like no other occupation.

Training for correctional officers has greatly improved, such as in this state of the art roll call training room. Fairfax County (VA) Adult Detention Center. Photo by author.

Correctional officer on rounds. Clarke-Frederick-Winchester (VA) Regional Adult Detention Center.

Not everyone or just anybody can become a correctional officer. It takes a special type of person to work with offenders. Staff development and training must bring out the best traits.

Much has been written and researched about what traits a correctional officer should have. The following is based on research from Karen Campbell, women's program manager at the Federal Correctional Institution in El Reno, California; Linda Zupan, researcher; and Susan McCampbell, former jail director, Broward Co., Florida:

- have a desire to help people
- have an ability to work without fear or anxiety
- have a knowledge of human behavior
- be able to maintain good health and an organized lifestyle
- have an ability to manage a safe and humane environment
- be able to handle inmate discipline and maintain order
- have a desire to respond promptly to inmates' requests
- have an ability and desire to build and maintain personal creditability with inmates, as well as developing an ongoing rapport with them
- be able to perform duties among inmates in a clear, well organized, attention-getting manner

- be able to resolve inmate conflicts and problems fairly and promptly
- have effective relations with the facility administration and staff
(Cornelius, 1994, McCampbell, 1990).

Correctional officers are required to manage the inmate population through face-to-face, interpersonal interaction with inmates. The ways that this is accomplished assists to maintain an orderly and safe environment. COs must have "job related competencies" in two areas: security and procedural skills, and human relation skills as listed below:

Security and Procedural Skills

knowledge of rules, regulations and procedures concerning custody
ability to:
- be a team player
- locate and identify contraband
- prevent escapes, riots and disturbances
- prevent violent physical and sexual predatory behavior
- when necessary, use appropriate degrees of physical force
- accurately use weapons and to know under what circumstances deadly force can be applied
- defend self if attacked
- intervene in an assault, fight, confrontation, or argument between inmates
- rescue inmates and staff from fire or smoke hazards
- correctly use emergency equipment
- protect the safety and lives of injured or sick inmates or staff through the correct application of emergency first aid and life-saving techniques
- to maintain control over inmates without creating hostility or compromising security
- to understand and describe inmates' rights and not violate them
- to communicate clearly verbally and write clear, concise and informative log entries, memoranda and reports
- be physically proficient in order to protect inmates and staff rights to health, safety and welfare

Human Relations Skills

ability to:
- remain non-prejudiced, non-judgmental, and humane, treat inmates as people, be consistently fair and honest

- establish and maintain positive relationships with inmates, to be genuinely concerned as to the welfare of inmates and staff
- listen, watch, and care about what happens to inmates
- clearly, politely and understandably orally communicate to inmates
- when confronted with an inmate problem, handle it calmly, being non-judgmental or abusive, offer counseling and practical advice
- recognize physical and behavioral changes in inmates as signs of potential problems and offer assistance, if applicable
- refer an inmate for help if he/she has a serious personal problem
- be non-defensive and open to any honest dialogue
- effectively manage people
- defuse or de-escalate a crisis situation effectively and safely
- through interviewing, determining what the inmate believes to be the causes of a crises
- mediate and informally resolve conflicts and interpersonal disputes between inmates where practical
- handle the rigors, pressures and stresses associated with correctional work
(Gilbert and Riddell, 1983, p. 31–36)

Training Resources

The following organizations can be very useful to corrections training personnel and supervisors. They are:

American Correctional Association
206 North Washington Street, Suite 200
Alexandria, Virginia 22314
Phone: 1-800-ACA-JOIN / 703-224-0000
www.aca.org

American Jail Association
1135 Professional Court
Hagerstown, MD 21740-5853
Phone: 301-790-3930
www.aja.org

International Association of Correctional Training Personnel
PO Box 473254
Aurora, CO 80047
Phone: 877-884-2287
www.iactp.org

The Corrections Connection
159 Burgin Parkway
Quincy, Massachusetts 02169
Phone 617-471-4445
www.corrections.com

The Commonwealth of Virginia is a good example of how corrections training have improved. Not only are there regional jails being developed and professional organizations that support them being formed such as the Virginia
Association of Regional Jails, training academies offer a variety of training. An
example of this is the Southwest Virginia Criminal Justice Training Academy
in Bristol, Virginia. Typical of many progressive academies, it offers online
training, classroom in-service training, links to regional training, links to local
colleges offering criminal justice training as well as basic law enforcement and
jail officer training (www.svcjta.com).

*Correctional officers use specially trained dogs to search for drugs inside correctional fa-
cilities. K9 Unit, Rhode Island Department of Corrections. Courtesy of the Rhode Island
Department of Corrections.*

Summary

Correctional officers are trained law enforcement officers and also are the mainstay of any correctional facility. Recent trends have shown that COs are primarily male in gender, and the correctional officer workforce is diverse. There have been improvements in the pay scale and benefits of correctional officers, but they depend on the agency and jurisdiction. Hiring, screening and retention techniques have improved, as well as corrections officer training. Training encompasses a variety of subjects and special functions and needs resulted in the development of specialized training. COs receive training through pre-service and in-service schools and seminars offered by training academies, in-house, on line and through professional organizations. Training is improving significantly as demonstrated by the use of on the job training and field training officers. Good COs must exhibit abilities in the security and human relations areas. The main goals of correctional officers' work are to prevent escapes and maintain a safe environment. These goals are accomplished by formal and informal duties. The job and promotional outlook for corrections officers looks promising.

Review Questions

1. What is the definition of a correctional officer?
2. What groups comprise the staff of a correctional facility?
3. Describe the formal and informal duties of a correctional officer.
4. What are the three basic types of training for correctional officers?
5. What have researchers indicated are traits of a good correctional officer?
6. What is being done to hire and retain good correctional officers?
7. Discuss five security and procedural skills and five human relations skills.

Terms/Concepts

basic training   on the job training (OJT)
contraband   probationary year
correctional officer (CO)   scenario based training
field training officer (FTO)   specialized training
in-service training   trusties
integrity interview

References

American Correctional Association. (2008). *2008 Correctional Standards Supplement*. Alexandria: American Correctional Association.

Champion, Dean J. (2005). *Corrections in the United States: A Contemporary Perspective Fourth Edition*. Upper Saddle River: Pearson Prentice Hall.

Cornelius, Gary F. (2008). *The American Jail: Cornerstone of Modern Corrections*. Upper Saddle River: Pearson Prentice Hall.

Cornelius, Gary. (1994) *Stressed Out! Strategies for Living and Working in Corrections*, Lanham: American Correctional Association.

Cornelius, Gary. (1994). Twenty Minute Trainer: Direct Supervision: Who's Right for It? *Journal of Correctional Training, No. 22*. International Association of Correctional Training Personnel.

Corrothers, Honorable Helen G. (1992). Career vs. Job: Why Become a Correctional Officer? In M. Nunan (Ed.) *The Effective Correctional Officer* (pp. 1–10). Lanham: American Correctional Association.

Gilbert, Michael J. and Jack Riddell. (1983). Skills for Achieving Security, Control, and Public Protection. In Julie N. Tucker (Ed.) *Correctional Officers: Power, Pressure, and Responsibility*. College Park: American Correctional Association.

Hughes, Kristen A. (April, 2006, revised 05/01/06). *Justice Expenditure and Employment in the United States, 2003*. Bureau of Justice Statistics. Washington, DC: U.S. Government Printing Office [available on line at www.ojp.usdoj.gov/bjs/].

LRP Publications. (2008). Deputies Train for Immigration Checks. *The Corrections Professional*, July, 2008, Volume 14, Issue 2.

LRP Publications. (1997). In-House Training Yields Cost Savings, Increase Staff Buy In. *The Corrections Professional*. 11/7/97, Vol. 3, Issue 5.

LRP Publications. (2008). Virginia jails to use eye scanners. *The Corrections Professional*. February, 2008.

LRP Publications. (June 6, 1997). National Survey Shows Juvenile Leaders Should Improve Training. *The Corrections Professional* Vol. 2, Issue 18.

McCampbell, Susan. (1990, November–December). Direct Supervision: Looking for the Right People. *American Jails, Vol. IV, No. 4,* pp. 68–69.

Seiter, Richard P. (2002). *Correctional Administration: Integrating Theory and Practice.* Upper Saddle River: Prentice Hall.

Silverman, Ira J. (2001). *Corrections: A Comprehensive View Second Edition.* Belmont: Wadsworth Thomason.

Sourcebook of Criminal Justice Statistics online, tables 1.104, 1.100.

Southwest Virginia Criminal Justice Training Academy, www.svcjta.com.

U.S. Department of Labor, *33-3012 Correctional Officers and Jailors, 33-3012.* Last modified date, October 16, 2001.

Chapter 4

Early Development: Punishment and Early Prisons

The corrections facilities and practices of today did not develop overnight. The discipline of corrections is a product of hundreds of years of beliefs and opinions on what society should do with society's wrongdoers.

This chapter will explore how the concept of criminal punishment developed. This chapter, in conjunction with Chapter 5, will give the reader a clear insight into the development of corrections.

Early Behavior

Throughout the history of man, societies, whether they be in tribes, nomadic groups, city-states (such as in ancient Greece), countries, etc., have held that certain acts (or groups of acts) have been looked upon as wrong. Acts such as these were discouraged or proscribed. Examples of *proscribed behavior* or wrong behavior include murder, rape, thievery, kidnapping, destruction of another's property, etc. Societies also encouraged certain acts which were deemed acceptable—marriage, bearing and rearing children, growing food, hunting, protecting the family, helping others, etc. These acts were called *prescribed behavior* (Allen, Latessa, Ponder and Simonsen, 2007, p. 4).

As societies developed, people learned that behavior, both prescribed and proscribed, could be controlled by social rules called *folkways* (Allen, et al., 2007, p. 4). Folkways can also be described as customs or more simply, habitual, acceptable ways of doing things. Growing food and sharing with others, taking care of elders and not stealing from the group could be considered early folkways.

We have folkways in everyday life such as working for a day's pay, paying for what one wants or needs—purchasing, etc. Folkways are mildly encouraged (i.e., applause or smiling) or discouraged (i.e., a look of dismay or shock). If the behavior either prescribed or proscribed was stronger, the encouragements

69

(financial security, status) or discouragements (physical beatings, banishment) were more pointed and strong. These stricter rules were called *mores*. Violations of mores could result in punishments such as verbal abuse, beatings, temporary ostracism from the group, or being banished from the group. Obedience to mores were encouraged by social rewards such as dowries, securing one's finances and money, social status or engaging in fertility rights and ceremonies. However, as society evolved and the well being and protection of the group became more important, mores and their sanctions (or punishment) were written down and became known as *laws*, or rules for all to follow (Allen, et al., 2007, pp. 4–5).

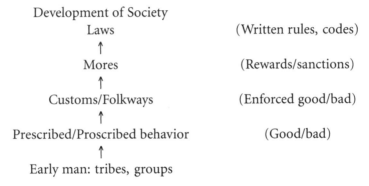

Development of Society

Laws	(Written rules, codes)
↑	
Mores	(Rewards/sanctions)
↑	
Customs/Folkways	(Enforced good/bad)
↑	
Prescribed/Proscribed behavior	(Good/bad)
↑	
Early man: tribes, groups	

Retaliation

Early groups accepted and encouraged the *earliest* forms of punishment on a wrongdoer — personal retaliation. If a person committed a wrongful act against a person, he could simply seek personal revenge. This theme of vengeance on the wrongdoer continues as a theme in corrections today — long, harsh sentences, no parole, three strikes and you are out, etc. The practice of seeking retaliation or revenge evolved into the *blood feud* — the victims' people, families or tribes seeking revenge on the offenders' people, families or tribes (Allen, et al., 2007, p. 5). These feuds or vendettas could continue for long periods of time — spilling much blood and causing suffering, much of it probably needless.

Men were "duty bound" by religious beliefs and expectations to avenge deaths of kinsmen by killing the offender's nearest male relative, who in all likelihood was not involved in the crime (Kocoureh and Wigmore, 1915, Allen, et al., 2007, p. 5). Some people, sick of bloodshed and suffering, began to accept property — land, castles, goods, etc., or money in place of vengeance. Vengeance was still practiced, but as rulers needed to exert control, this practice of restitution became more widespread. If a wrongdoer stayed away by his choice, he became an *outlaw*; this term evolved into labeling offenders who eluded the law.

Pillories and stocks were used to inflict shame, public humiliation and corporal punishment on lawbreakers. Colonial Williamsburg, VA. Photos by author.

Early Legal Codes

As civilization developed, so did the practice of writing. Early taboos, customs and mores were written into codes. The earliest code that has been discovered is of Ur-Nammu, founder of the Third Dynasty of Ur in Mesopotamia in 2050 B.C. There are references to written codes existing before that date by other rulers. The King of Lagash, Urgakina made reference in a reform document to a legal code that gives the entire population the right to the justification for each conviction of wrongdoing and its punishment (Lyons, 2003, p. 15).

The Code of Ur-Nammus contained a system of justice that was administered on behalf of the king by head priest and governors of individual towns. Temples were courtrooms due to their size. Some of the practices parallel modern law, such as lawsuits by private parties, the taking of sworn oaths by witnesses, documentary written evidence and a system of appeals (Lyons, 2003, pp. 15–16).

In the Code of Hammerabi (from King Hammerabi of Babylon) and the Sumerian Code, the concept of "*lex talionis*" (an eye for an eye and a tooth for a tooth) was evident. Codes in these times were vengeful and very harsh. Both the Hammurabic and Sumerian Codes called for death, mutilation, whipping, or wrongdoers being made to perform forced labor. Slavery was also used as a punishment. The Romans used *penal servitude* as a way of using criminals sentenced to long terms as manpower to row galleys, building public works or working in mines. Slaves had their heads shaved identify them as criminals (*mark of the slave*). This was still practiced in the twentieth century, where the heads of women who collaborated with the Nazi authorities were shaved after the liberation of France during World War II. Also, the concept of *civil death* took root, where the wrongdoer had many aspects of his life stripped away: his property was confiscated in the name of the state, his wife was declared a widow and could remarry, and had all status as a citizen and liberties taken away until death (Allen, et al., 2007, p. 6).

The "Scales of Justice" depicted in Roman art comes from the Emperor Justinian's efforts to enforce a code in sixth century A.D. where the punishment fit or balanced the crime, depicted in Roman art as the scales of justice. Like today, these laws, called the "Code of Justinian," had many administrative procedures which hampered its execution. When the Roman Empire fell, this code did not survive, but it left building blocks on which today's Western legal codes were built. In nearby Greece, the "Code of Draco" was harsh and included previous practices such as the blood feud, vengeance, and outlawry. The significance of the Greek Code is that any citizen could prosecute a wrongdoer in the name of the wronged citizen (Allen, et al., 2007, p. 6).

In ancient Greece and Rome, the question arose as to where to confine law-breakers, political dissidents and social misfits. A novel approach at the time in Rome was to confine them underneath the sewers of Rome in the squalid and inhumane *Mamertime Prison* and also in rock quarries and cages (Champion, 2005, p. 6).

Soon religion began to have an impact on the development of corrections. In the thirteenth century, the powerful Spanish Inquisition, described as a religious tribunal, punished those who disagreed with and did not conform to the church. Early examples of victims of this type of punishment for disagreeing with powerful religious bodies were Joan of Arc and the Apostle Paul (Champion, 2005, p. 6).

During the Middle Ages, the church enjoyed great influence and reforming criminals was deemed a religious process. An offender had to pay a debt to society and *another* debt to God. Accused people were subjected to "trials by ordeal" in which painful tests were administered. If an offender was innocent, it was believed that he or she would emerge unscathed and unharmed; the guilty would suffer excruciating pain and finally die. The authorities did not care about rehabilitating an offender except through a painful punishment in the hope that God would be pacified. However, one lasting concept of the Middle Ages and its religious influence has been the term *"free will." Free will* is a concept whose basic premises are that a person chooses good or bad actions and as a result of these choices, he/she must be held accountable for the consequences of them. The church during the Middle Ages used this concept to reinforce harsh punishment. Its position was that harsh treatment would not be necessary if the wrongdoer had not chosen these actions (Allen and Simonsen, 2001, p. 10).

The concept of free will echoes throughout our modern correctional facilities, but in a secular tone. Although many inmates have serious problems, such as substance abuse, etc., they have chosen illegal acts and must pay the consequences through doing time. Correctional officers say frequently of prisoners—no one made them come here; they chose to do the crime.

Free Will v. Criminal Responsibility

Today's public thinks that many criminals will "get off" by using the criminally insane defense. While this defense is mentioned frequently in the media, it is only brought up in 1% of felony cases and is successful in only one quarter of that amount. The courts have ruled that for an offender to qualify for the insanity defense, they must show suffering from a "serious mental disease or defect" which impairs their behavioral controls or somehow hinders the understanding of what they did. The majority of criminals know what they did and understands the proceedings affecting them. "Criminal responsibility" takes the Middle Ages term "free will" to a modern plane—their mental state did not interfere with their understanding of what they did. It did not impair controls of their behavior. Simply, they acted on free will—the modern translation being: they *rationally* chose to commit an illegal act and should suffer punishment for their actions (Lally, 1997, p. C2).

Early Methods of Punishment

Corporal Punishment

Early punishments of wrongdoers had two distinct characteristics: variety and brutality. Until the 1700s, the main rule of punishment was *corporal punishment* or as defined as "infliction of pain on the body by any device or method" (Champion, 2005, p. 8). Methods of corporal punishment were numerous; brutality and pain were the rules of the day.

Methods of Corporal Punishment: Early methods of corporal punishment were quite imaginative (Champion, 2001, pp. 9, 645):

> *Flogging:* whipping on back or buttocks; accepted practice in schools, prisons and on naval vessels.
> *Dismemberment:* pickpockets and thieves suffered the cruel amputation of their hands.
> *Mutilation:* Liars and those punished as committing perjury would have their tongues removed.
> *Stocks and Pillories:* offenders were seated with their feet protruding through holes or were forced to stand with their heads and arms protruding through holes. The devices were meant to be uncomfortable and the citizenry could jeer, taunt and humiliate them.
> *Ducking stool:* a device consisting of a chair at the end of a long lever; the offender seated in the chair is dunked in a pond or river to the point of almost drowning.

Other methods included: adulterers having an "A" branded on their faces; tongues cut out of "liars;" mutilation (cutting off of hands, dismemberments), and branding. Authorities were inventive in devising ways of inflicting pain to force wrongdoers to "think." In America, corporal punishments were practiced well into the 20th century. Flogging was practiced in Delaware's prisons. As recently as 1937, Georgia inmates were placed in stocks that painfully secured both their feet and hands. In Middle Eastern countries, mutilation is still a practice (Leinwand, ed., 1972, pp. 13, 33).

Capital Punishment

When the authorities decided to punish an offender by taking his or her life, the concept of *capital punishment* originated. Similar to corporal punishment, various methods were devised to ensure the wrongdoer suffered a very painful death. A simple rule was the more harsh and brutal, the better. Consider this account by an explorer in Florida in the 1500s of an Indian tribal execution of a village sentinel. Because of his carelessness, the village had been burned. He noted that other offenses warranted the same punishments (Leinwand, ed., 1972, p. 16).

> *The chief sits alone, his principal men placed on a long semi-circular bench nearby. The executioner orders the sentinel to kneel down before the chief ... He sets his left foot on the offender's back and with a sharp-edged club made of ebony or some other hard wood, he strikes him a blow on the head hard enough to split open the skull.*

Early Methods of Capital Punishment

Early methods of execution were brutal, inhumane by today's standards, and were designed to elicit the utmost suffering from the wrongdoer. Among those methods, often carried out in public so that citizens could see the death throes and suffering of the criminal were (Lyons, 2003, pp. 157–170):

> *Burning:* Offender is tied to a wooden stake in a public area; kindling is piled around the stake and set afire; other methods included being thrown into burning pits of cauldrons of boiling oil or molten lead.
> *Hanging:* Offender's neck is broken by dropping with a noose tied around the neck.
> *Beheading:* taking off the offender's head by sword, ax, or guillotine.
> *Crucifixion:* nailing or tying the offender to a crossbeam and leaving him to die a lingering death.
> *Poison:* offenders were forced to drink hemlock or other poison.

Some methods were simple, such as *starvation,* where the offender is simply placed in a locked box with the head showing to starve to death (Leinwand, ed., 1972, p. 16).

In Colonial America, the death penalty had an interesting development. Colonial authorities used the death penalty for crimes against morality such as adultery and sodomy. In the Massachusetts Bay Colony in 1644, a married woman and her lover were executed for the crime of adultery. However, executions for adultery ceased in the mid 1600s due to the reluctance of juries to convict (Friedman, 1993, p. 41).

Early colonial jail with cells opening into a small courtyard. Inside the cells, a method to keep order was to simply chain the inmate to a wall. Colonial Williamsburg, VA. Photos by author.

Overall the colonies sparingly used the death penalty, in contrast with English law. Before 1660 in the Massachusetts Bay Colony, only fifteen executions took place. In Pennsylvania, until the American Revolution, only 94 out of 170 condemned prisoners were actually executed; the remainder were reprieved or pardoned. On the whole, Pennsylvania executions averaged only one execution per year. Pardons were also a factor; Virginia and New York used them extensively (Friedman, 1993, pp. 41–42).

Concerning capital offenses, murder was the most common capital offense. However, rape and statutory rape were also punishable by death. Rape, including statutory rape was made a capital offense after an incident where three servants had sex with their employer's nine-year-old daughter. Also, in Virginia, a 1748 law imposed the death penalty on repeat offenders or recidivists. Livestock in those times was important property. For a first offense of hog theft, for example, the wrongdoer received a fine and twenty-five lashes; the second offense had a penalty of two hours in a pillory nailed by the ears; a third offense resulted in death (Friedman, 1993, p. 42).

Mitigating factors were considered in early Colonial America. The "two witness rule" in the Massachusetts Bay Colony said that no offender was to be executed without the testimony of two or three witnesses. But if the prisoner confessed, the rule did not apply. Another rule that was used by criminals to stay alive was "*benefit of clergy.*" Benefit of clergy was basically a "dodge." In the Middle Ages, priests accused of a crime could have their trials in Church courts. Ordinary citizens generally could not read, priests could, and by reading from the Bible, they proved that they were clergymen. Around 1600, benefit of clergy protected any wrongdoer who could read at all from the death penalty; they then received a lesser penalty such as branding. This was practiced in the English colonies (Friedman, 1993, p. 43).

Of course, the practice of capital punishment has been refined; the "two witness rule" and "benefit of clergy" are no longer practiced. While a detailed discussion of capital punishment today would be too impractical for this work, the reader should note that court proceedings and the appeals process for capital offenses are strict, detailed, and subject to several levels of judicial scrutiny. Methods of capital punishment, such as lethal injection and confinement on death row are considered more humane.

Corporal punishment was generally conducted in public view. The pillory, stocks, burning at the stake, etc., were public. It was hoped that not only the wrongdoer would suffer shame, but the punishment would serve as a warning and deter future wrongdoing. The debate as to whether capital punishment is a deterrent has continued for decades without a definitive conclusion. Some think that executions should be made public while others think that the spectacle of a public execution would commercialize and cheapen a process, though depressing—which should maintain some dignity. The fact that in some jurisdictions victims' families are permitted to view an execution is a compromise.

Early Prisons and Methods of Confinement

In the early stages of civilized society, methods of punishment were numerous and brutal, as has been stated. Not much thought was given to humanely housing wrongdoers until trial and caring for their needs. This has changed as evidenced by today's modern facilities.

Prior to our modern facilities, prisons were meant to be painful for the offender. Wardens of early prisons or any places of confinement simply did not care about decent treatment for prisoners. Early places of confinement were horrible in methods of supervision, squalor and in the lack of decency. Early prisons were "self consciously punitive and controlling; their internal regimes were intentionally inhumane ... [they] were haphazardly arranged, inflicting pain without purpose ... meeting out pain for pain's sake" (Johnson, 2002, p. 19).

Early Prisons

Probably the first prison was the aforementioned *Mamertime Prison* built under the sewers of Rome in 64 B.C. This prison was nothing more than dungeons and its purpose apparently was to cause offenders great suffering due to "neglect, the darkness and the stench" (Peck, 1992; Johnson, 2002, p. 19). It did not matter where wrongdoers were confined; the public did not concern itself with rehabilitation and humane treatment—quite a contrast with prisons today.

As time went on, fortresses, castles, and any secure buildings were all pressed into the service of housing prisoners. Feudalism of the Middle Ages ended and more people moved to urban areas. In London in 1557, *Bridewell*, a workhouse named after London's Bridewell Palace was built to deal with wrongdoers by using them as cheap labor. Prisoners were physically abused and required to labor at manufacturing products, milling and baking. Conditions were miserable, but the practice of confining criminals and making them work took hold. "Bridewells" were soon required to be in every county by the English Parliament (Roberts, 1997, p. 6).

Another institution that authorities used to house outcasts were debtors' prisons—"prisons" which housed the poor until their monetary debts were paid by family or friends. Some were housed until they died. These institutions, primarily in England and Scotland, were not true correctional institutions; they just warehoused debtors without concern for rehabilitation or correction (Champion, 2005, p. 6).

Gaols

The term "jail" originated from the old English word *gaol* which is pronounced the same. In 1166 A.D., Henry II, King of England, established gaols as part of the Constitution of Clarendon. Gaols were locally operated by English "shire-reeves" (now sheriffs) and were meant to be holding facilities to confine or detain persons accused of breaking the law, such as misfits, paupers, vagrants, drunkards, thieves, murderers, debtors, robbers (called highwaymen), orphaned children, prostitutes, trespassers and religious dissidents. They were held until courts convened and guilt or innocence was established (Champion, 2005, p. 202).

Throughout the 16th, 17th, and 18th centuries, an estimated 200 common jails were in operation in England, under the responsibility of the local sheriff and the justices of the peace. The justices of peace used county funds to repair and rebuild jails. The sheriffs were the keepers and legal owners of the jails. As with early places of imprisonment, jails took many forms—parts of castles, rooms in old towers or gatehouses, or two or three dungeons under a public building. The sheriff appointed the keeper, who was not paid a salary. The *fee system* developed where fees were charged for every item (such as a bed, mattress) and process (being housed in squalid quarters or a private room). Also under the fee system, jail keepers could sell goods to the inmates and use them for forced labor. The jail business was corrupt and profitable. Prisoners had to support themselves through family, friends or begging. Extortion was practiced, resulting in pain and death for inmates who could not pay the required fees (Kemble, 1996, pp. 14–19).

Underground Prisons

Early societies, such as Rome, used underground confinement as a convenient way to house criminals and keep them securely confined out of the public's view in squalid conditions. Prisoners were also housed in sulfur pits and quarries.

In Colonial America, this belief resulted in what some researchers say is the United States' first state prison, Newgate Prison, in an underground copper mine converted into a prison in Simsbury, Connecticut. Established in 1773, it became a permanent prison in 1790.

Inmates were shackled at the ankles and worked long hours. Offenses such as burglary and counterfeiting drew sentences of up to ten years; a second offense resulted in life imprisonment. Inmates were crowded into chambers; 32 men would be crammed into a cage only 21 feet long, 10 feet wide and under seven feet high. A year after the prison opened, the inmates rioted. Another underground prison, located in a quarry, opened in Maine. Chained inmates cut stone by day and were confined in unheated, dark, underground chambers at night (Champion, 2005, p. 277, Roberts, 1997, p. 26).

Conditions in jails were filthy, leading to outbreaks of "*jail fever*," a form of typhus. An example of these conditions was London's Newgate Gaol, where the cells were poorly ventilated, gloomy and dark. Inmates suffered from an appalling stench and inadequate water supplies. The gaol was paved in stone; the prisoners had no beds and endured miseries by having to lie on the stones. Fees were even charged to inmates to warm themselves by a fire! (Moynahan and Burke, 1991, pp. 76–77).

Another type of early punishment that had a decidedly different aspect than just throwing inmates into squalid quarters was banishment into the wild or exile. The practice had English roots; errant children in Coventry, England, were sentenced to having all communications cut off with everyone—a practice knows as being placed "in Coventry." Criminal offenders heard sentences banishing them to unknown misfortunes such as storms, shipwrecks, famine or death by the hands of savages or wild beasts. With the onset of mechanization in the Industrial Revolution, slavery became less profitable. Countries began to export prisoners through transportation, sending them away (Stinchcomb and Fox, 1999, p. 93).

Transportation

A form of banishment, transporting inmates to remote areas or colonies, was widely used after the onset of the Industrial Revolution. Russia sent convicts to Siberia; Africa received prisoners from Spain and Portugal; France sent prisoners to South America.

England sent prisoners to the North American colonies beginning in 1630 and in 1717, Parliament officially ruled America was Britain's penal colony. By the start of the American Revolution in 1776, an estimated 100,000 prisoners had been transported to America. Transported prisoners were a free, thrifty, economical source of labor. Private contractors and businesses took advantage and allowed convicts to work as "indentured servants" where convicts satisfied their sentences by working for wealthy colonists for specific time periods. The American Revolution effectively closed the colonies to prisoners; England turned to Australia for use as a penal colony until 1879. Eventually the usage of prisons ended banishment and transportation (Stinchcomb and Fox, 1999, p. 93–94).

In England from 1776 to 1858, the overload of convicts forced English authorities to house prisoners in old, abandoned transport ships anchored in harbors and rivers. These *hulks* housed young and old, hardened criminals and misdemeanants and men and women all together without regard to segregation, safety or hygiene. Because of practices such as flogging, use of inmate labor and squalid, filthy conditions, hulks were horrible places. Hulks were generally in use until 1858. However, they were used in the 19th century in California. The idea of housing inmates in ships was considered as recently as 1976 when Washington State considered using decommissioned U.S. Navy warships. Old ferries and barges were used in New York as recently as the 1980s (Allen, Simonsen and Latessa, 2004, p. 17).

Improvement of Confinement

In the discussion of the history of corrections, two early cellular prisons bear mention—the *Maison de Force* at Ghent, Belgium, and the *Hospice of San Michel* in Rome, Italy. The Maison de Force (House of Enforcement) fed prisoners well. Prisoners were also supplied with adequate clothing and lodged in a humane manner, separately at night. The institution was operated by administrator and disciplinarian, Jean Jacques Vilain, who had some revolutionary practices. He instituted a classification procedure—separating women and children from hardened prisoners and minor offenders from felons. Vilain's discipline was based on the Biblical rule that if a man [prisoner] will not work, he will not eat (Champion, 2005, p. 276; Allen, et al., 2004, p. 276).

The Hospice of San Michel was located in Rome and was built by Pope Clement XI. He placed the following inscription over the door which is still there to this day:

> It is insufficient to restrain the wicked by punishment unless you render them virtuous by corrective discipline.

Its target group was juveniles under age twenty. Inmates were exposed to hard work and lessons in Scripture. Strict silence was the rule; violators were flogged. Separate cells were used for sleeping and a large central hall was for work. This practice would influence discipline in later institutions (Allen, et al., 2004, p. 18).

The panopticon or prison cupola central observation point designed by Jeremy Bentham is still evident today in prison architecture. Courtesy of the Rhode Island Department of Corrections.

Three Key Philosophers

Not all observers and practitioners of corrections during the 1600s and 1700s were callous, brutal and harsh. Montesquieu (1689–1755) and Voltaire (1694–1778) called for penal reforms such as punishment fitting the crimes, more humane conditions for the imprisoned and judicial reform. In England, Jeremy Bentham (1748–1832) called for a unique form of punishment where criminals would see clearly the losses and pains of punishment due to punishment being swift, certain and painful. Bentham also developed the architectural concept of the "*panopticon.*" The panopticon was a circular design for prisons that allowed guards to observe and monitor many prisoner housing areas from a central location (Champion, 2005, p. 9). This concept is in wide use today in many jails and prisons. The correctional officer is stationed inside a booth or tower and can observe the inmate living or activity areas around him.

Three philosophers of the field of corrections bear mentioning because their influence continues to this day. They are: Cesare Bonesana, Marchese de Beccaria or Cesare Beccaria; John Howard, High Sheriff, Bedfordshire, England; and William Penn, Quaker, Governor of Pennsylvania.

Cesare Beccaria (1738–94): An Italian jurist and economist, Beccaria opposed the death penalty, torture and harsh treatment of inmates. His philosophy was that the "true measure" of crime is the "harm [that is] done to society." He authored and published the book *Essay on Crime and Punishment* in 1764. Becarria's philosophies had a great influence on the jurisprudence and legal philosophies of many countries, including the United States. His philosophies are summarized below and became known as the "classical school of criminology."

1. Laws only can determine the punishment of crimes, punishments stay within the law and cannot be increased by any one magistrate. Laws are to serve the needs of society, which is united and are only made by the legislator. The basis for all social actions must be the concept of the greatest good for the greatest number of people.
2. Punishments for crimes are to be determined by the injury done to society. The punishment of a nobleman (rich) should not differ from punishment to the "plebian" (the poor).
3. Punishments should be swift and certain; the certainty and swiftness of it rather than severity better meets the goal of prevention.
4. Prevention of crime is more important than punishment and the mode of punishment should leave an impression on the citizens. Prevention is two fold: the criminal is prevented from doing further harm to society and others are also prevented from committing like offenses. The impressions on society concerning punishments should be strong and lasting. Legal codes must define prohibited behaviors and their punishments so that citizens will support the law.
5. All accused persons should be allowed to present evidence in their behalf and be treated humanely before trial.
6. Criminal procedures should not include secret accusations and torture. Trials should be speedy.
7. Imprisonment of offenders should be more widely used, but the mode should be improved. This can be done by providing better living quarters and by separating and classifying prisoners by sex, age and degree of criminality (the offense/their criminal histories).
    (Beccaria in Killinger and Cromwell, 1973, pp. 1–5; Clear and Cole, 2000, pp. 30–31)

In jails and prisons today, his idea of separating offenders by sex, age and degree of criminality is practiced through classification procedures. Also, inmates in our nations' prisons and jails are not as a rule treated inhumanely.

John Howard (1726–1790): Next to Beccaria, the contributions of John Howard (1726–1790) to the discipline of corrections are noteworthy and his influence is still felt in today's jails and prisons. Howard was Sheriff of Bedfordshire, England, and traveled outside of England to examine other prison systems. Impressed with the humane treatment of prisoners in the Maison de Force, he published *The State of Prisons* in 1777. This classical essay led to reforms in European and American correctional institutions. In 1779, the British government passed the Penitentiary Act (Clear and Cole, 2000, pp. 31–32, Killinger and Cromwell, 1973, pp. 5–11).

This significant law dictated the creation of new correctional institutions, where prisoners would work *productively* at hard labor. Prisoners were to be adequately fed, clothed and housed singly in sanitary isolated cells. There were to be no fees for the prisoners' incarceration. Other reforms included regular inspections. Howard believed that hard and productive labor would result in prisoners realizing how serious their crimes were and the consequences of lawbreaking.

From Howard's ideas of reform and penance came the term *penitentiary*, a word derived from Latin meaning a place that a man is sent to do penance for sins against society. He believed that if penal authorities made prisoners think, they would see the errors and mistakes of their ways (Leinwand, ed., 1972, p. 24).

The State of Prisons, 1777

The publication of this essay by John Howard helped to change the course of corrections. Howard's views on the management of inmates were unique.

Location and Construction of Prisons: areas that are "airy," near a clean river or brook in order to avoid "the stench of sewers." Men-felons wards should be raised on arcades; small rooms and cabins should allow prisoners to sleep alone and reflect in solitude and silence. Baths should be "commodious" with an adequate water supply. Ovens can be used for cleaning clothes. Day rooms should have a kitchen and fireplace.

Classification of Inmates: Women felons are housed separately from the men, the same separations apply for old, hardened offenders from young criminals.

Hygiene: Howard detailed how wards should be cleaned (scraped and then swept and washed), prisoners entering the gaol should be bathed and have his/her clothes washed. Prison uniforms should be worn for hygiene and to detect escapees. Bedding should be changed weekly.

Food: Food should include "good household bread," having good meals would encourage prisoners to behave.

Rules: No fighting, quarreling, abusive language, or gaming (gambling). Injured inmates could complain to the keeper who "must hear both parties face to face" and make a decision. The aggressor is then punished by "closer confinement." More serious offenses are examined by a magistrate or inspector. Rules should be "made known ... and intelligibly drawn up."

Staff and Management: No fees are charged and no profit gained from the prisoners. Gaolors (jailors) are to be paid a suitable salary proportioned to "trust and trouble." They are to be "honest, active, and humane ... sober" ... having no contact with the sale of liquors. Inspectors must be appointed for every prison. They are to hear all complaints and correct serious wrongs. Inspectors should visit once per week without [prior] notice.

Security: Alarm bells, double doors, surrounding high wall, clothes of two colors, jailor's window looking into the yard.

The influence of this document is still felt today in penal housing, disciplinary procedures and hiring practices.

[Adapted from *Penology: Evolution of Corrections in America*, George Killinger and Paul Cromwell, editors; Howard, *State of Prisons—1777*, West, 1973, pp. 5–11.]

The *State of the Prisons* influenced the establishment and operations of the gaol at Wymondham, in Norfolk, England. The gaol, built in 1785, had cells for separating different types of prisoners and men and women. The founder of the gaol, Sir Thomas Beever (1786–1814), had prisoners sleeping and working in separate cells. Beever believed that this was more effective than corporal punishment, such as whipping. This idea worked: prisoners earned double their maintenance by working at hard labor six days per week. Judges reported fewer offenders being committed to the gaol, so it was believed that it was a deterrent. Ironically, the founder of the gaol's principles, John Howard, died of jail fever (typhus) in 1790. Representative of the poor health conditions of English jails, this disease killed many prisoners (American Correctional Association, pp. 14–16, 1983).

William Penn (1644–1718): Arriving in Colonial America in 1682, this Quaker governor of Pennsylvania instituted reforms. Penn established a penal code which did two things: (1) retained capital punishment only in cases of homicide; and (2) punished wrongdoers by hard labor instead of bloody corporal punishment. There were also other significant provisions. All prisoners were eligible to be released on bail. Prisoners who were wrongfully incarcerated could recover double damages and prisons could not charge fees for food and lodging. Injured parties could claim double restitution from the land and goods of felons and all counties were to erect "houses of detention" to replace such brutal methods as the pillory, stocks, etc. (American Correctional Association, 1983, p. 24).

This code or the Great Law of 1682 took a humane approach to corrections. However, flogging was still used as punishments for the crimes of adultery, arson and rape. The Great Law and the policies that followed created a need that continues to today—the need to find housing for felons who are sentenced to a length of incarceration. Beginning in Pennsylvania in 1725, county jails began to emerge with sheriffs maintaining administrative and operational control (Kemble, 1996, pp. 14–19). However, one day after Penn died in 1718, his code and reforms were repealed and replaced by the Sanguinary Laws, which remained in effect until the American Revolution. Punishment began to be harsher and to a large degree, capital punishment was re-established. Whereas Penn's Code punished only homicide by capital punishment; the new laws took a harsher view, making the following crimes punishable by death: treason, murder, burglary, rape, sodomy, buggery, malicious maiming, manslaughter by stabbing, witchcraft by conjuration, and arson (American Correctional Association, 1983, p. 25).

Walnut Street Jail

The Walnut Street Jail in Pennsylvania was built in 1773 and closed in 1835. The reforms of William Penn had long since grown obsolete. By 1730, legislation had passed reinstating inmate fees. Extortion and corruption among inmates had grown. There was no classification of inmates with regard to age, gender, race, crimes or the physical and mental state of the inmate (Kemble, 1996, pp. 14–19).

In 1790, reform-minded Quakers, trying to change the treatment of convicted criminals, requested that the Pennsylvania legislature declare a wing of the Walnut Street Jail a penitentiary house for *all* convicted felons. Exceptions were those prisoners condemned to death (American Correctional Association, 1983, p. 25). This era spawned the birth of the prison reform movement and, in practicality, the first corrections volunteer organization. The efforts to change prisoner treatment were primarily due to the group formed in 1787— the Philadelphia Society for the Alleviation of the Miseries of Public Prisons.

Members visited the prisons once per week bringing food, clothing, religious tutoring, and teaching basic reading and writing skills. They also made inquiries about inmates' conditions and reported abuses. The Society wanted to know if society's morals were influenced by punishment and confinement. The Society still exists today as the Pennsylvania Prison Society (American Correctional Association, 1983, p. 25, Champion, 2001, p. 83).

The Walnut Street Jail was revolutionary. The reformers' efforts had resulted in humane treatment for prisoners and genuine concerns for their welfare. In practice, the Walnut Street Jail treated inmates well by doing the following:

- More serious offenders were separated from others in sixteen large solitary cells; other inmates were separated by degree of offense and by sex.
- Inmates were assigned productive work according to gender and the offense conviction. Women made clothing, mended clothes and did laundry. Inmates who were skilled could work as carpenters, shoemakers or craftsmen. Unskilled prisoners also worked by beating hemp or jute for caulking in ships. Prisoners who worked, except women, received a daily wage, which was applied to defray the cost of their incarceration.
- Religious groups provided religious instruction for offenders. (Champion, 2001, p. 83)

Medium, maximum and minimum security institutions can trace their roots to the Walnut Street Jail. The jail also was the forerunner of the usage of solitary confinement. During the next several decades, many institutions and management practices were modeled on the Walnut Street Jail (Champion, 2001, p. 84).

Summary

Early methods of punishing wrongdoers developed from early views of vengeance and inflicting pain. From early civilizations through the establishment of the Walnut Street Jail, criminal offenders suffered the pains of capital punishment, corporal punishment, and housing in unsafe and unsanitary structures. Enlightened philosophers such as Bentham, Beccaria, Howard, and Penn set the course for change. While many institutions were not conducive to positive treatment of prisoners, institutions such as the Maisons de Force, Hospice of San Michel, and the Walnut Street Jail started penal reform. Beccaria's views, John Howard's *The State of the Prisons* and the Walnut Street Jail all have had a profound effect on American corrections.

Review Questions

1. What were the revolutionary views of Beccaria and how do they relate to corrections today?
2. How did churches influence the punishment of wrongdoers?
3. Describe methods of capital and corporal punishment.
4. What were the views of John Howard concerning jails, prisons and the treatment of inmates?
5. Why was the Walnut Street Jail revolutionary?

Terms/Concepts

benefit of clergy	*laws*
blood feud	*lex talionis*
Bridewell	*Mamertime Prison*
capital punishment	*mark of the slave*
civil death	*mores*
corporal punishment	*outlaw*
fee system	*panopticon*
folkways	*penal servitude*
free will	*penitentiary*
hulks	*prescribed behavior*
jail fever	*proscribed behavior*

References

Allen, Harry, Edward J. Latessa, Ph.D., Bruce S. Ponder and Clifford Simonsen Ph.D. (2007). *Corrections in America: An Introduction, Eleventh Edition,* Upper Saddle River: Pearson Prentice Hall. *See also:* Albert Kocoruek and John Wigmore. (1915). Evolution of Law, Volume 2, *Punitive and Ancient Legal Institutions,* Boston: Little Brown and Jeffrie Murphy (2000). Two Cheers for Vindictiveness. *Punishment and Society 2:2,* 134–143.

Allen, Harry and Clifford Simonsen. (2001). *Corrections in America: An Introduction, Ninth Ed.* Upper Saddle River: Prentice Hall.

American Correctional Association. (1983). *The American Prison from the Beginning: A Pictorial History,* Laurel: Maryland.

Beccaria, Cesare. (1973). On Crimes and Punishments, 1764. In Killinger, George G. and Paul Cromwell, (Eds.). *Penology: The Evolution of Corrections in America* (pp. 1–5). St. Paul: West.

Champion, Dean J. (2005). *Corrections in the United States: A Contemporary Perspective, Fourth Edition.* Upper Saddle River: Pearson Prentice Hall.

Champion, Dean. (2001). *Corrections in the United States: A Contemporary Perspective, Third Edition.* Upper Saddle River: Pearson Prentice Hall.

Clear, Todd and George F. Cole. (2000). *American Corrections: Fifth Edition.* Belmont: West Wadsworth.

Friedman, Lawrence. (1993). *Crime and Punishment in American History,* N.Y. Basic Books.

Howard, John. (1973). State of the Prisons 1777. In Killinger, George G. and Paul Cromwell, (Eds.). *Penology: The Evolution of Corrections in America* (pp. 5–11). St. Paul: West.

Johnson, Robert. (2002). *Hard Time: Understanding and Reforming the Prisons, Third Edition.* Belmont: Wadsworth. *See also:* Peck, H.T. (Ed.). (1922). *Harper's Dictionary of Classical Literature and Antiquity.* New York: American Book.

Kemble, Tod. (May–June, 1996). Jails in America. *Texas Journal of Corrections,* pp. 14–19.

Lally, Stephen. (1977, November 23). Drawing a Clear Line Between Criminals and the Criminally Insane. *The Washington Post,* p. C2.

Leinwand, Gerald, (Ed.). (1972). *Prisons.* N.Y. Pocket Books.

Lyons, Lewis. (2003). *The History of Punishment.* London: Amber Books.

Moynahan, J.M., and Burke, Troy. (May–June, 1991). London's Famous Newgate Gaol (1188–1902) [part of "Some Old English Institutions]. *American Jails,* 76–77.

Roberts, John. (1997). *Reform and Retribution: An Illustrated History of the American Prison.* Lanham: American Correctional Association.

Stinchcomb, Jeanne B., Ph.D. and Vernon B. Fox, Ph.D. (1999). *Introduction to Corrections, Fifth Edition.* Upper Saddle River: Prentice Hall.

Chapter 5

The Development of the Modern Correctional Facility

The development of the modern correctional facility in the United States has its roots in three penal systems—the Pennsylvania System, the Auburn System, and the Reformatory System. By understanding the philosophies and daily operations of the institutions in these systems, one can see the reasoning behind today's penal facilities.

The Pennsylvania System

The Pennsylvania System was a result of the disciplinary system of the Walnut Street Jail. This school of thought was primarily developed by the penal reformer, Dr. Benjamin Rush (1745–1813), a famous physician, politician, and signer of the Declaration of Independence. Dr. Rush believed that dangerous, assaultive prisoners should be housed singly from the rest of the inmate population. He advocated gardens for food and exercise. Prisons should sell goods that were manufactured in the prisons in order to help financially support the prisons. Dr. Rush believed that prisoners must reform and be prevented from committing crimes. Dangerous criminals must be removed from society. Dr. Rush's ideas were incorporated into the *Pennsylvania System* of discipline at the Walnut Street Jail—an inmate was to be in solitary confinement with no work. The objective was to get offenders to repent and reflect on their crimes throughout their stay. However, such isolation and inactivity was detrimental to the inmate's well being so minimal labor such as handicrafts and piecework was allowed. Inmates also received moral and religious education (American Correctional Association, 1983, pp. 30–31).

Two institutions were constructed. The Western State Penitentiary in Pittsburgh was built in 1826. It had an octagonal shape, based on the cellular isolation wing of the Walnut Street Jail. Inmates were kept in isolation without work. The cells were replaced with larger, outside cells in 1833. Inmates were allowed to work in their cells in 1829. The Eastern State Penitentiary was influenced by the Western State Penitentiary and was built in 1829. It became the model for the Pennsylvania or "separate" system. It had seven cellblocks radiating from a hub like center. This central structure had a rotunda equipped with an alarm bell and observation tower. The entire prison was surrounded by a wall (American Correctional Association, 1983, pp. 38–39).

For an inmate, life inside a Pennsylvania system prison was not easy. The routine has been described as "one of solitary confinement and manual labor, a simple monastic existence in which the prisoners were kept separate from one another as well as from the outside world." Its aim was a fundamental conversion of character, focusing on simple things of nature and as result — thoughts of God (Johnson, 2002, pp. 36–37).

Inmates lived in solitude — eating, sleeping, and working alone. Exercise was alone in private yards and they saw and spoke to only visitors carefully selected by staff. The only reading material allowed was the Bible. Officials would not let inmates see or speak to each other for fear of contamination. For example, upon arrival at the prison, the officials would place a shroud over the head of the inmate so that he could not be seen by other inmates. The goal of total solitude was to arrest or deter the progress of corruption, thus receiving no additional contamination. Inmates could receive labor as a welcome diversion after a time and learn regularity and self discipline. If an inmate showed good behavior, he could receive books and visitors more frequently. Security was maintained due to close confinement and no communication with the other inmates was allowed (Rothman, 1971, pp. 82–86).

This system was expensive. Solitary confinement mandated the construction of large cells. Crafts and piecework could not generate much income to the prison, although prison staff was minimal due to the isolation of the inmates. It was more financially feasible to use prisoners in penal factories due to the short supply of workers in nineteenth-century America (Johnson, 2002, p. 38).

The Auburn System

While some prison authorities embraced the Pennsylvania System as the answer to the question of how to reform the criminal, others believed in another system first developed at a prison in Auburn, New York.

Built in 1816, the Auburn prison was modeled after other prisons using solitary confinement. An experiment to test the separate system was tried from 1821 to 1823. A test group of inmates was confined to their cells without participating in labor. The majority became ill and insane; also the majority of the test inmates were pardoned. Authorities then began a policy of inmates sleeping in their cells at night, but worked and ate meals together during the day. This system became known as the "congregate system" or the *Auburn System* (American Correctional Association, 1983, pp. 48–49).

The Auburn system developed a system of cell construction that continues to this day: the *interior cellblock*. This economical building of prison cells simply was constructing cells back to back in tiers, which were stacked on top of one another. The tiers were constructed in a large, hollow building. The cell doors opened out on a gallery or "catwalk" which was eight to ten feet from the exterior wall of the building. Thus, many prisoners could be "stacked up" (American Correctional Association, 1983, p. 49).

Inmates in Auburn type prisons slept singly and congregated for eating and working. Like the Pennsylvania system, there was no communication with other prisoners. Silence was the rule in order to have a monastic type environment by night and a military type of routine by day (see below feature on Discipline). Inmates labored all day and the only sounds they heard were guards' orders, machines and tools. They were in a "prison within a prison." Movement was in unison, with inmates in lockstep and eating was sitting at attention with backs straight (Johnson, 2002, p. 38).

Discipline: Silence and Regimentation

Both the Pennsylvania and Auburn prison systems believed in order to prevent contamination and cross-infection from prisoners and to encourage improved behavior, silence and penitence must be enforced. Authorities in the Pennsylvania system believed that silence and penitence resulted in more control of prisoners, a prisoner's individual needs could be addressed, and he would not be "contaminated" from other prisoners. An inmate could be released with his background known only by a few penal administrators.

In the Auburn system, inmates ate with backs straight at attention in silence. Corporal punishment for rule breaking was common. Maine prisons used the ball and chains; Connecticut prisons used the cold shower. Whipping was also used. Regimentation in daily routines became the mainstay. Bells signaled when the prisoners could leave their cells. Tasks such as emptying chamber pots were done in line formation. Marching to and from meals and work was done in *lockstep* (close order, single file, each prisoner looking over the shoulder of the man in front, facing towards the right, feet stepping in unison).

It was believed that existing in silence, thinking about their crimes, and severe discipline and regimentation would teach proper behavior and good habits (Rothman, 1971, pp. 102–106; Johnson, 2002, p. 38).

Eventually a debate took place as to which system was better. While Pennsylvania system advocates argued control and anti-contamination, Auburn supporters showed that it was cheaper to construct interior cellblocks, vocational training was offered in congregate shops, and as a result, more money was earned for the states. The Auburn system won. From 1825–1870, twenty-three Auburn type prisons were built in the United States (American Correctional Association, 1983, p. 51).

The Reformatory Movement

As Auburn type prisons flourished in the 1860s, a new prison reform movement began to develop. From 1870 to 1900, the reformatory movement arose and left a definite mark on corrections. The *Reformatory System* advocated education, vocational or trade training, grades and marks, the indeterminate sentence, and parole. Two things influenced the reformatory type of inmate management: the *Mark System* under Captain Alexander MacConochie and the *Irish System* under Sir Walter Crofton, an Irishman. Both systems believed that inmates through proper behavior and participation in rehabilitative activities could earn their release from prison *early* (American Correctional Association, 1983, p. 66).

Manatee County County (FLA) Corrections Facility.

MacConochie was an Englishman who took charge of the penal colony of Norfolk Island in the South Pacific Ocean in 1840. He believed that an offender can be reformed if given an incentive for good behavior. He experimented with indeterminate sentencing. While a *determinate sentence* fixes a flat maximum term (i.e., ten years) that the inmate must serve minus any time off for good behavior; indeterminate sentencing fixes a range of time (i.e., five to ten years). Prisoners in MacConochie's charge could be released sooner by earning marks for proper behavior and hard work. Inmates earned marks, received privileges, and earned an early release. MacConochie believed that the *Mark System*—earning marks by behaving and working hard for early release—better prepared inmates for a return to society (Stojkovic and Lovell, 1997, p. 456).

Crofton developed the *Irish System* during the 1850s in which the indeterminate sentence was used as an incentive for inmates to move through stages toward release. This system provided a model for parole supporters in the United States. The first stage consisted of the inmate housed for nine months of solitary confinement; the first three months consisting of reduced rations and no labor. After three months, it was reasoned that even the laziest inmate would want *something* to do. He would be afforded full rations, instructed in useful skills and be exposed to "religious influences," church, prayer, etc. In the second stage, the inmate was assigned to a special prison working with other inmates and earning marks to qualify for transfer to the third stage. In the third stage, the inmate was assigned to an "open institution." In this stage, the inmate could earn a conditional release on a *ticket of leave.* Convicts released under tickets of leave were supervised by the Inspector of Released Prisoners who secured employment for released convicts, required them to report regularly to him, inspected their homes, and verified their employment. The inspector was the forerunner of today's parole officer. These ideas and the "ticket of leave" concept evolved into what we now know as *parole:* the conditional release of an offender into the community before the expiration of sentence based on good behavior and rehabilitative activities, such as work and attending programs (Stojkovic and Lovell, 1997, pp. 456–457).

One key event that occurred during this period of American penology was the 1870 National Prison Congress held in Cincinnati by corrections professionals. In this unprecedented conference, twenty-two resolutions were adopted in a "Declaration of Principles." Included in these principles were promotions of reformation of inmates, classification based on the Mark and Irish Systems, rewards for good conduct, endorsements of religious programs, educational programs, vocational training, and improvements in penal management and architecture. These principles are still advocated today by the organization born at that Congress — the American Correctional Association (American Correctional Association, 1983, pp. 71, 73).

The Reformatory Movement and the use of indeterminate sentencing started with the 1870 National Prison Congress and in 1876 with the opening of the *Elmira (New York) Reformatory* under the leadership of Zebulon Brockway. Targeting young offenders from 16 to 30 years of age, this prison placed inmates into one of three classes or grades. If they behaved, they could move to the first grade and parole eligibility. Moving to the third grade was a demotion. As a result, sentences to this prison were indeterminate. Movement from grade two to grade one was based on earned "marks" and education and trade training was available. The type of prison in this era, the reformatory, had several distinct features: indeterminate sentences with fixed maximum terms, use of parole when inmates' records warranted early release, and the placement of all inmates into a particular class based on conduct and achievement. However, by 1910, the Reformatory movement was on the decline due to not luring adequate staff to maintain high quality rehabilitation programs and staff feeling that the old style discipline was easier to administer than the grade system (American Correctional Association, 1983, pp. 76–85).

Women's Prisons

Women offenders were not excluded from the developments in corrections. Typically, female inmates were confined to the "leftover" spaces in the male prisons — the attics, basements and corners. Female inmates were subjugated to degrading treatment, abuse and the supervision of male staff, which was commonplace. London's Newgate prison had similar conditions and was criticized by the British penal reformer Elizabeth Fry (1780–1845) who called for women's prisons to be improved, administered by women, and offer rehabilitative, educational, and vocational programs (Roberts, 1997, p. 106).

As a result, Fry's views were taken up by United States penal administrators; in 1825, a separate building for female juvenile offenders opened in New York, and improvements were made in the 1840s for females housed in the women's section of Sing Sing. Private and religious organizations also aided in efforts to improve conditions for female offenders. Some progress was made, but it was not until the 20th century that substantial changes and programs were instituted. One reason was because there were fewer female than male offenders and the number of women's institutions were small. More latitude and flexibility occurred concerning programs for female offenders. The need to have women supervise offenders and run the facilities was recognized (Roberts, 1997, pp. 108–112).

The Industrial Type Prisons

A common myth or mistaken image of the 20th century prison is that only large state and Federal prisons used inmates as a type of "factory worker." In reality, prisons have been used by government and private industries for the production of goods.

Post Civil War South

After the Civil War (1861–1865), the South was in economic ruin. Slavery was gone so a new source of labor had to be found—the convict. In the South, some states leased out their entire convict populations to contractors. Another method was for prison administrators to take in contract work from businesses. Either way, convict labor was cheap and cost effective. Many Southern convicts were black plantation workers and were exploited due to the fact that the post war South afforded them little opportunity, guidance or services. Leasing continued into the 1920s and was eventually replaced by prison farms. The post Civil War South was a dark chapter in American penology; the South ignored the Auburn and Reformatory Systems and developed its own unique prison style (Allen, Latessa, Ponder and Simonsen, 2007, pp. 34–35). Conditions were brutal. If a business leased convicts, they were transported in *prison wagons* to the work site. These "mobile cages" could hold up to thirty convicts and provided sleeping quarters. If a prison "contracted" out work, the convicts worked inside the prison (American Correctional Association, 1983, p. 90).

The goal of turning profits and producing goods for the state gave rise to the prison or penal farm and the prison camp. Both provided work for convicts in agriculture, road building, and prison construction. The tracts of land cultivated for prison farm use were vast; in 1921, Mississippi had 28,750 acres and Texas cultivated 73,461 acres. Prison farms began to decline by 1973; privately produced food was cheaper than convict grown and parolees from the farms couldn't find agricultural jobs. Some states, such as Louisiana, still use the camp system (American Correctional Association, 1983, pp. 91, 104, 105).

In the early 20th century prisons were used as factories. The expansion of railroads and the development of the automobile resulted in convicts building and maintaining roads—working for long hours under conditions that were likely less favorable than in private industry. The zenith of prison industries occurred in 1923 where $74 million of convict-made material was produced. From 1929 through the Great Depression to 1940, Congress and the states passed laws that severely restricted the manufacture of prison goods which were competing on the market with private goods. Many of these laws are still in effect today. Today, there is inmate labor, but it is restricted to goods that are sold in restrictive markets within the state, goods for usage in other state agencies and institutions, and public works projects such as construction and maintenance of roads, parks, public facilities, etc. (Stinchcomb and Fox, 1999, pp. 108–109).

The Big House

Beginning in the early 20th century and lasting primarily through the 1950s, a type of prison known as the *Big House* developed. These prisons were walled institutions containing a mixture of both old and new large cellblock buildings. These buildings contained stacks of three or more tiers of one or two inmate cells. The average institutional population was about 2,500 inmates; some cellblocks alone held 1,000 inmates (Irvin, 1980, p. 3).

The "Big House" prison was maximum security where custody was strictly enforced. Very little was offered in terms of rehabilitative programming. Punishments were brutal; routines were monotonous. According to Johnson, three things made life in the "Big House" bearable—tobacco, abolition of corporal punishment, and some internal freedoms. Convicts could smoke, they were not beaten or tortured, and they could move around inside the prison. But cells were

Inmate Housing Unit, Manatee County (FLA) Corrections Facility.

drab, food was part of a monotonous menu, and the work and leisure routines were devoid of any goals or initiative. Prisoners were told to keep silent and guards could use force to maintain control (Johnson, 2002, p. 41).

The era of the "Big House" resulted in the construction of well known prisons such as San Quentin (California), Sing Sing (Ossining, New York), Jefferson City (Missouri), Canon City (Colorado) and Stateville (Illinois) (Irvin, 1980, p. 5). It also ushered in the "isolation" type prison such as Alcatraz in San Francisco and more recent models of Pelican Bay (California) and Marion (Illinois).

Isolation Type Prisons

Alcatraz, Pelican Bay and Marion are representative of super maximum security, isolation type prisons.

Officially known as the United States Federal Penitentiary, Alcatraz Island, *The Rock* was known to house famous criminals such as Al "Scarface" Capone and George "Machine Gun" Kelly. Formerly a fort and a military prison, Alcatraz was a Federal prison from 1934 to 1963. The majority of the inmates imprisoned at Alcatraz were problems in other Federal prisons—troublemakers, escape risks, etc. Security was tight not only by guards, but by its location, an island surrounded by the cold water and swift current of San Francisco Bay. There were fourteen attempted escapes, the last being in 1962. Due to increasing maintenance costs, Alcatraz was closed in 1963 and is now a tourist attraction. Contrary to the image portrayed in movies, Alcatraz was clean, the food was good, and the inmates were not mistreated. Also, the operational capacity was 336, the average population was 260 and the maximum population was 302 (*Discover Alcatraz: A Tour of the Rock* by the Golden Gate National Parks Association, 1996).

Pelican Bay State Prison is located in a remote area of Northern California. Its Security Housing Unit (SHU) holds approximately 1,200 of the worst inmates in the California penal system. The prison is set in a 270 acre clearing and built of reinforced concrete in an "X" shape. SHU prisoners are monitored, escorted and cared for under very tight security. All recreation, exercise and leisure activities and programs are strictly controlled (Hentoff, 1993, pp. 21–27).

The United States Penitentiary at Marion, Illinois replaced Alcatraz. Marion inmates are considered the most dangerous security risks in the Federal system. The average sentence is 39.5 years. In 1990, 98% of the inmates had violent histories and 51% were convicted murderers. Inmates are restricted to their cells for twenty-two hours per day and restraints are applied when the inmate is moved inside the prison. Searches are very frequent and extremely thorough. Marion is located 100 miles southeast of St. Louis near a wildlife refuge (Dickey, 1990, pp. 66–69).

The most well known recent development concerning super max prisons is the opening of the federal Administrative Maximum Facility or ADX in Florence, Colorado in 1994. Its mission is to house the worst of the worst federal prison system inmates. Some cells have been described as "Hannibal Lechter" cells (in reference to the film *The Silence of the Lambs*). Solitary confinement is the routine, 40 percent of inmates stay in their cells 22 hours per day; 33 percent (the most dangerous) stay in their cells 23 hours per day. Exercise is an hour per day—alone. Cell dimensions are 8 ft., 8 inches by 12 feet, 3 inches; furnished with no view windows, a concrete desk, stool and bed and a shower equipped with a timer to prevent flooding. The television is black and white with a 12 inch screen. High profile inmates such as Ted Kacyzynski (the "Unabomber"), New York Latin Kings gang leader Luis Felipe, and Ramzi Yousef (1993 World Trade Center bombing mastermind) are there. Felipe is convicted of six murders, and is allowed no other visitors except his attorney. ADX has withstood criticism from human rights groups; the management style represents a new trend in prison security. As a result, 30 state prison systems now have similar "super max" prisons (Annin, 1998, p. 35).

Development of the Modern Jail

Jails in the United States from the 1800s to today have had a colorful and diverse history. Since jails were under the authority of local sheriffs, jails in the United States have existed in different sizes and modes of operation. Much of this is due also to the funding base of the jurisdictions and the differing philosophies of those responsible for administering the jail: the sheriff, the chief jail officer, or the jail board.

Rabble Management

Early American jails practiced what is called *rabble management* or housing people such as drunkards, vagrants, public nuisances, and the mentally ill. These people were not a criminal threat, but it was convenient to just lock them up. We still see that today in a reduced degree in some jails. From the po-

Inmate Dining Area, Manatee County (FLA) Corrections Facility.

lice, through the courts and ending in the correctional facilities, some people that the public through its laws finds offensive and dangerous are controlled and sometimes removed from society. The "rabble" can be defined as law-breakers, outcasts (such as the homeless or mentally ill) who commit crimes, or people that offend the public (Stojkovic and Lowell, 1997, p. 67). If they break the law, the correctional facilities have custody over them. As a result the correctional officer has to deal with them. Many jurisdictions deal with inebriates by releasing them after a short time or transporting them to a detoxification center.

A "Hodgepodge" of Facilities

During the 19th and early 20th centuries, there was no recognizable system or area of corrections that could be identified as jails. The jail system, if one could call it that—was a potpourri of buildings and places that confined society's wrongdoers. Jails were holding facilities used for housing problematic people, such as the criminal offender, the sick, the neglected, the drunk, the drug addict and the mentally ill. There were not any other ways to deal with the problem (Stojkovic and Lowell, 1997, p. 68). Jails took the form of sheriffs' homes in some jurisdictions. In others, workhouses, barns, and other buildings confined wrongdoers and were sometimes called jails. Little interest was paid to jails because they were operated locally and little communication existed between sheriffs' agencies. State governments did not concern themselves with where inmates were housed, how they were treated and if their situation needed improvement (Champion, 2005, p. 204).

The keeping of jail statistics started in 1880 under the United States Census Bureau. The Bureau obtained statistics every ten years concerning race, ethnicity, gender and age. In 1923, this information was incorporated into jail statistics. Joseph Fishman, a Federal prison inspector, reported "horrible" conditions in the 1,500 jails he visited (Cornelius, 1996, p. 4).

By the mid 1960s, studies reported that some jails built prior to George Washington's inauguration in 1789 still were in use. Also, 25 percent of jails were built more than 50 years previously. Most jails reportedly were not administered properly, were overcrowded and poorly staffed. Services such as medical care and recreation were substandard and funds were lacking (Kemble, 1996, pp. 15–16).

Starting in the mid 1960s, the Federal courts began to take an interest in jail and prison conditions based on lawsuits filed by inmates. Conditions began to improve in many U.S. jails. As a result of the Federal Bureau of Prisons policy of maintaining a "normalized living environment" for inmates, the concept of direct supervision was born. This "normalized" environment conveys to the inmate the expectations of positive behavior, or how to act appropriately. Secondly, this approach would result in less expensive operating costs in terms of equipment and construction. In other words, direct supervision uses larger spaces to house inmates, and if they behave, there is less wear and tear on the facility. The first local direct supervision correctional facility—the Contra Costa County Detention Center—opened in 1981 (Kemble, 1996, p. 16).

As recently as 1980, jails in the United States were a mixture of modern and substandard facilities. A Mississippi jail housed four inmates in a cell with an open toilet in the middle of the room. Inmates were confined to the cellblock except to see a family member at visiting. The local court was very critical of the condition of the jail; the sheriff admitted that his jail was poor and asked what he could do when the jail was built in 1845 and last renovated in 1901. In Philadelphia, the jail psychiatrist estimated that he needed an additional 80 beds per day to handle the growing numbers of mentally ill inmates. An Alabama judge ordered officials in one facility to stop scraping dead animals off highways and cooking them for the inmates' dinner. In contrast, a Colorado jail housed inmates in individual rooms and inmates were afforded the opportunities for programs (Press, Kirsch, Smith, Reese and Gelman 1980, pp. 75, 77).

In the 1980s, primarily due to inmate lawsuits and court rulings (see Chapter 13), jail management and design underwent a significant overhaul with conditions beginning to improve. Jails now fall into one of the following types of inmate management—linear/intermittent, podular/remote surveillance, and podular/direct supervision (see Chapter 8). Jails are overcrowded, but there are many examples of well run, modern jails that have state of the art equipment, good medical care, staff training and inmate management. Examples of modern jails include Alexandria Detention Center in Virginia, Butler County Prison in Pennsylvania, the Fairfax County (VA) Adult Detention Center and the Clark County, Nevada Detention Center in Las Vegas.

Even though overcrowding remains a problem, jails' operations and quality of life for the inmates will continue to improve into the next century.

Development of Community Corrections Facilities

While the roots of community corrections can be traced back to MacConochie's Mark system and Crofton's Irish system, today's corrections' systems— federal, state and local—operate a variety of *community based corrections programs* and facilities. These facilities can be part of the main correctional facility (such as a dormitory or wing) or can be in a separate facility which is part of a local, state or federal correctional agency.

Community Based Corrections Defined

Community based corrections is defined as "non-institutional," having programs for criminal offenders. Three main elements that give authorities options for dealing with offenders in the community are part of this definition. They are (McCarthy, McCarthy, Jr., and Leone, 2001, p. 1):

- Efforts, programs and staff designed to divert accused offenders from further involvement in the criminal justice system or jail incarceration. Included here are diversion, fines, community service, pre trial electronic monitoring, house arrest, day reporting and pre trial release programs.
- Enforcing sentences and programs that impose restrictions on convicted offenders while they live and work in the community. Offenders can be sentenced to *probation* or being released into the community by the court and being required to obey conditions (maintaining employment, participating in substance abuse treatment, going to school, etc.) enforced by a probation officer. Parole is the release of an offender prior to the expiration of his or her sentence. This early release is due to good behavior and participation in prison rehabilitation programs. The conditions that the offender must adhere to are similar to the conditions of

probation; the enforcing person is a parole officer. Parole is granted by the parole board of the state or federal system. Parole has been abolished in many states; it has been replaced by a similar method — supervised release. Another method is electronic incarceration, where offenders are allowed to live at home, work and attend programs in the community under the supervision of an electronic surveillance device.

- Efforts by correctional facilities, the courts and programs to smoothly prepare and facilitate the reintegration of the offender from correctional supervision back into the community with the goal of being a law abiding system.

Partial incarceration programs such as work release, weekend confinement, home incarceration and service programs require the inmate to be inside the facility if not engaged in work. For example, inmates selected for or court ordered into a work release program may go unsupervised into the community to work, subject to random checks by staff. Weekend confinement programs require that inmates sentenced to weekends in jail perform work which produces cost saving labor to the jurisdiction.

The goal of community-based programs is reintegration (see Chapter 1). In 1967, the President's Commission on Law Enforcement and Administration of Justice defined reintegration as "… building or rebuilding ties between offender and community, integrating or reintegrating the offender into community life, restoring family ties, obtaining employment and education, securing in the larger sense a place for the offender in the routine functioning of society" (McCarthy, et al., 2001, p. 4). Community-based corrections makes use of community programs, volunteers, and resources including Alcoholics Anonymous (AA), Narcotics Anonymous (NA), education centers, vocational training programs, community substance abuse and mental health centers, and churches.

Probably the most well known of the community-based programs or community corrections is work release. Modern work release dates back to 1913 in Wisconsin, where by statute, misdemeanants could work their jobs while serving short sentences in jail. By 1957, North Carolina enacted a similar law, followed shortly by Michigan and Maryland. In 1965, the Federal Prisoner Rehabilitation Act took effect allowing Federal prisoners to take part in work release, furloughs, and community treatment centers. This act has served as a model in many states for today's work release and community corrections programs (Allen, et al., 2007, p. 438).

From the 1960s community corrections programs and facilities have been put into operation for two purposes — to attempt to treat inmates' problems using people and resources in the community and to give federal, state and local correctional systems a cost saving alternative to traditional incarceration. Community corrections inmates working at gainful employment and paying room and board are generating revenue more than the inmate existing in a cell draining tax dollars.

Types of Programs

Community corrections programs such as diversion programs and day reporting centers are usually handled by probation officers or staff from a court treatment program. There are, however, several types of facilities/programs that are usually staffed by correctional officers. This staffing requires careful selection and specialized training. Working in community corrections supervising offenders on work release or on electronic detention differs from patrolling cellblocks. Offenders are in the community working, and COs must use tact and civility, plus be aware of the many temptations awaiting the offender in the community such as drugs, alcohol, and seeing unauthorized people. The main community corrections programs are:

- *Work/study release:* Through court order or screening and approval by the sentencing judge, inmates are permitted to reside in a community corrections center, pre-release center, or halfway house, and work and/or attend school in the community. Inmates can wear civilian clothes, must have their urine and breath tested for substance abuse, and are subject to on-site checks by staff. Inmates can be court ordered or be placed in the program through a screening process in the agency in accordance with statutory guidelines. These facilities have rules and regulations and a disciplinary system. If the inmate breaks the rules of the program and/or a criminal statute, he or she is subject to revocation from the program and re incarceration. Inmates must find a job that is subject to staff approval at the prevailing community minimum wage. Inmates may be permitted to attend community treatment programs and earn visits to families (furloughs).
- *Home detention/electronic monitoring:* Court ordered or screened inmates with approval by the sentencing judge may reside in their homes and go into the community to work, attend treatment programs, attend school and take care of emergencies with prior staff approval. While confined at home, inmate is tracked electronically by staff through an electronic transmitter that is worn on wrist or ankle. These transmitters usually operate over a telephone line to a central computer and verify that the offender is at home. If the offender leaves without staff author-

ization the signal is broken and he or she is treated as an escapee. Schedules and times in the community are subject to staff approval. Inmates may apply, be screened, or court ordered. Inmate is subject to home/job checks similar to work release including urine and breath tests for drug and alcohol use, respectively. Offenders must pay a program fee to defray the costs and meet regularly with staff.

- *Weekend confinement:* to ease overcrowding, offenders at the local level are sentenced to serve their sentences on weekends, from Friday to Monday. They can be used to work around the local jail or in the community under staff direction.

Several types of local programs require correctional officer security. Public works projects using inmates with short sentences performing work in public areas (parks, schools, recreation areas, public roads, etc.) use correctional officers to escort and direct inmates. Correctional officers may supervise offenders completing community service hours or working off fines if the court decides that they do not have the ability to pay.

Community-based facilities are defined by the Bureau of Justice Statistics as correctional facilities that permit 50 percent or more of offenders to leave the facility and enter the community to work or study unescorted by staff. Included are halfway houses, residential treatment centers, restitution centers and pre release centers (Stephan, *Census of State and Federal Correctional Facilities, 2005,* p. 8).

These facilities are increasing in number. The number of state and federal community based facilities increased from 460 in 2000 to 529 in 2005. More than one quarter (28 percent) of state and federal correctional facilities had a work release program in operation, with approximately 25,000 inmates enrolled. It should be noted that only 7 percent or 135 facilities offered study release (Stephan, 2005, pp. 6, 8, Appendix Table 2).

Concerning jails, jail officials reported in 2006 that 60,222 inmates were supervised outside of jail facilities; this represents 7.3 percent of the total jail population. Of these inmates, the most were in community service programs (14,667), weekend confinement programs (11,421), electronic monitoring (10,999) and work programs (8,319) such as work release, work gangs, and other work programs (Sabol, Minton and Harrison, *Prison and Jail Inmates at Midyear 2006,* pp. 7, 21). All of these programs serve to combat overcrowding.

As correctional facilities become more and more overcrowded, community corrections programs may provide "breathing room" by keeping less hard core offenders in alternative programs and putting the more serious offenders behind bars.

Boot Camps

Another type of correctional facility that has received much press in the past decade is the boot camp (see Chapter 2). This facility is based to a degree on the strict basic training regimen used in our armed forces. Boot camps as we see them today originated in 1983, when in an effort to relieve prison over-crowding, the state correctional systems of Oklahoma and Georgia opened the first military style boot camps. Female offenders make up only 9 percent of the boot camp inmate population. Boot camps can be most simply defined as follows (Schmalleger and Smykla, 2009, p. 188):

> A short term institutional type of confinement, modeled after military training, that includes strict discipline and regulations, and is designed to promote self discipline, respect for authority, responsibility, and a sense of achievement and accomplishment.

Boot camps incorporate programs and aftercare planning. According to the National Institute of Justice boot camps are distinguished from other correc-tions programs by the presence of the following (Schmalleger and Smykla, 2009, p. 188):

- Military drill, ceremony, chain of command and authority
- Hard labor and physical training incorporated into a rigorous daily schedule
- Separation of boot camp inmates from the rest of the general prison population
- The concept is an alternative to long term, traditional confinement in jails and prisons.

Boot Camp: Manatee County, Florida

One example of a modern "boot camp" for multiple offenders ages 14 to 18 is the Manatee County (Florida) Sheriff's Office Boot Camp. In providing long-term residential treatment, inmates are exposed to role modeling, physical training, practical problem solving and training in educational and social skills.

Six hours per day is spent in school and recruits (offenders) are ordered into the program for a minimum of six months. An average day starts at 5:00 a.m. and ends at 9:00 p.m. The nineteen basic rules are strict. Recruits are also appraised of their rights—visitation, health care, phone use, etc. To successfully complete the program, re-

cruits must meet goals set by the program and develop the skills necessary to return to the community and family.
[Source: Manatee Co.: Sheriff's Office *Boot Camp Recruit Handbook*, Juvenile Justice Division pamphlet]

Boot camp goals are to reduce the recidivism rate of young offenders, reduce overcrowding, and save on operating costs. While the concept is very attractive, research has shown that these goals were not being reached. First, offender volunteers for boot camps were not materializing because boot camps target non violent offenders and drug law violators who are open to changing their criminal lifestyle. Many jurisdictions were either releasing such offenders early or finding them placement in community corrections programs such as work release. The pool of eligible offenders was significantly reduced. Secondly, rigorous physical activity produced very fit offenders, but due to no model to follow, issues such as recidivism, reduced operating costs, and reduced corrections populations were not effectively addressed. Third, there was no real consensus on programs and aftercare, which are critical in fighting recidivism. Some camps had them, some did not. With such varying degrees of programming, any benefits from boot camp participation were short lived (Schmalleger and Smykla, 2009, pp. 188–189).

Privatization of Corrections

One of the most interesting developments in corrections in the past several decades has been the use of private companies and organizations to deliver goods and services in adult and juvenile correctional facilities as well as operate facilities. Not only are several companies such as the Corrections Corporation of America operating facilities, other firms such as Aramark are providing commissary and kitchen services. In many facilities, health care providers ("medics") were county, state or federal employees. Now, private correctional health care firms provide the same services to the inmates.

Privatizing operations and services to offenders is not new. Victims and their families performed many functions that are now performed by correctional and law enforcement authorities. In 1648, the Society of St. Vincent De Paul built the first permanent home for "wandering children," whom we now call juvenile delinquents or children in need of services. The noted penal reformer, John Howard used his own resources to travel throughout Europe, visiting jails and eventually drafting reforms that we see today. The American penitentiary and the Walnut Street jail were influenced by the reform efforts of a private group affiliated with the Quakers. The father of probation—John Augustus—provided bail, supervised and assisted offenders assigned to him by the courts. The Chicago Women's Clubs exerted pressure and as a result, the juvenile court systems that we know today were started (Stinchcomb, 2005, p. 563).

Assistance to Corrections

Private agencies can assist corrections in many ways. In some facilities, the correctional officers work for the company that is running the facility. In facilities where the COs are sworn and are employed by a federal, state or local corrections department, private companies can help in several areas, such as (Stinchcomb, 2005, pp. 564–565):

- Treatment services: providing substance abuse and mental health therapy and counseling
- Community based corrections: drug testing and providing surveillance equipment
- Technical assistance: computers, renovating facilities and architecture
- Health services: providing medical services, dental services and running infirmaries
- Food services: operating a facility kitchen
- Commissary: operating an inmate "canteen"
- Security: supervising a security staff: corrections officers, transportation officers, etc.

Privatization: Pros and Cons

Private corrections companies cite advantages such as reduced costs due to being competitive, flexibility and creativity in addressing the needs of operations and the staff, and performing well due to the contractor (government) having other choices or competition. There is a debate, with critics saying that private companies that cut costs to save money can compromise quality assurance. Critics also say that private firms can "pick and choose" what types of offenders they want to deal with, leaving government correctional agencies with the least desirable inmates. Finally concerning liability, government cannot transfer liability to a private contractor simply because they have a contract in place. In 1997, the United States Supreme Court ruled that the state (government body that hires the private contractor) cannot transfer its sovereign immunity to a contractor in a response to litigation filed under 42 United States Code Section 1983 or the Civil Rights Act (Stinchcomb, 2005, pp.

569–570). The debate is ongoing about the use of private facilities, and as governments grapple with tight budgets and getting the most results for their money, private operations may look very attractive. In agencies that have employed private medical care, commissary, and technical support, the private agencies have blended well into the operations. The key is to bring their staffs on board with good hiring practices and training in security and properly dealing with inmates.

Recent Trends

Dr. Jeanne Stinchcomb of Florida Atlantic University has calculated a breakdown of private facilities in terms of the level of security. Based on the *Census of State and Federal Correctional Institutions 2000,* most privately operated prisons are minimum security (74 percent), followed by medium security (24.5 percent) and maximum security (1.5 percent) (Stinchcomb, 2005, p. 571).

In the years between 2000 and 2005, the number and capacity of private adult prisons increased markedly. In that time frame, the number of private adult correctional facilities increased from 264 to 415 representing an increase from 16 percent to 23 percent respectively of all state and federal correctional institutions. The inmate population in private facilities grew from 91,184 in 2000 to 105,451 in 2005, representing 7 percent of the U.S. average daily prisoner population. Approximately two thirds of private correctional facilities had contract agreements with state authorities; one third were under contract to the Federal Bureau of Prisons (Stephan, 2005, p. 1).

Corrections Standards

Corrections officers may find themselves working for agencies that have to comply with standards. Generally correctional facilities—prisons, jails, community corrections facilities or juvenile facilities—must be in compliance with standards from the government agency responsible for the operation of the correctional facility. These standards may be from the federal government in cases of Bureau of Prison facilities, the state boards of corrections that oversee conditions in state and local facilities, or from professional organizations such as the American Correctional Association (ACA) and the National Commission on Correctional Health Care (NCCHC). Since the 1970s, correctional standards have consistently emerged due to court decisions and case law resulting from inmate litigation.

Many designs of correctional architecture developed in the 1800s are still in use today. Interior cellblock, Rhode Island Department of Corrections. Courtesy of the Rhode Island Department of Corrections.

History of Correctional Standards

Corrections standards had its roots in the Declaration of Principles adopted at the first National Prison Congress held in Cincinnati, Ohio in 1870. Penal reformers and advocates for prison reform worked to make changes in the ways that inmates were supervised, housed and treated, as well as changes for staff training and development of programs. From that Congress evolved the American Prison Association which eventually became the American Correctional Association (ACA). Compliance with standards is critical to the operation of a correctional facility, because the safety of the staff, the safety of the inmates, and the safety of the public weigh in the balance (Roberts, 1997, pp. 62, 77, 219).

For the first 150 years of corrections history in the United States, correctional institutions and managers lacked any cohesion, central management, correctional standards and operational consistency. To improve the profession, correctional agencies examined the standards from organizations such as the American Bar Association and the American Medical Association. In an effort to be seen as a profession, correctional agencies created standards for self regulation, ethical behavior for staff, and guidelines for operations and training (Seiter, 2008, pp. 530–531). States and the federal governments began to write standards for the correctional facilities, and required compliance from the correctional facilities. Compliance is determined by an audit of the agency policies and procedures. Documents such as incident reports, inmate observation logs, post logs, programs lists and medical records all can show an audit team that the correctional facility is following the policies and procedures that are based on the standards being checked.

Concerning the meeting of standards through accreditation, ACA has been the leader. The Commission on Accreditation for Corrections was formed in the 1970s to coordinate and administer national accreditation programs for all components of juvenile and adult correctional agencies. Corrections professionals were recruited to write standards for different operations such as security, training, food service, programs, medical, etc. Corrections administrators must decide if accreditation from ACA and NCCHC is feasible and best serves the mission of their agencies. According to ACA, the purpose of the standards and accreditation process is to improve the institution's management, defend against inmate lawsuits by demonstrating "good faith" and proper documentation, improve conditions of confinement, increase staff accountability, create better credibility to the public, foster a safer and humane environment for staff and inmates, and establish measurable criteria for the upgrading of programs, personnel, medical care, services, and the physical plant on a continuing basis (Seiter, 2008, p. 531).

Correctional officers must realize that meeting standards protects them and their agencies from litigation, criticisms and violating the public trust. This is an ongoing process. Audits from state and federal government corrections agencies are generally annual; ACA audits are every three years. Documentation supports the compliance with the standards, and must be regularly collected and filed, ready to show the auditor or audit team. To prepare, correctional staff is asked to supply documentation. The agency may perform a pre audit or self audit in preparation.

Key Terms Defined

Standards are constantly being revised, combined or deleted to keep up with the developments in corrections, such as developments in health care, inmate rights, training, etc. or court decisions. Standards can be mandatory, where the agency must meet them to be in compliance, or non mandatory. Recently standards have changed from a simplistic statement to performance based and expected practices. To understand the often detailed aspect of performance based standards and accreditation, COs should know these definitions and how they apply to each other. The best illustration of this is from *Performance Based Standards for Adult Local Detention Facilities, 4th Edition* from ACA, published in 2004. These terms are, with illustrating examples, are (*Performance Based Standards for Adult Local Detention Facilities, 4th Edition*, 2004, pp. xxx, xxxi, 17, 18):

> *Goal statement:* a general statement on what is desired within a facility functional area. For example, a goal statement is: **Protect the community, staff, contractors, volunteers and inmates from harm.**
>
> *Standard:* a statement that defines clearly a required or essential condition that staff must achieve and maintain.
>
> *Performance standard:* describes the "state of being," but not the measures that staff takes to achieve it. This is stated: **The community, staff, contractors, volunteers, and inmates are protected from harm. Events that pose risk of harm are prevented. The number and severity of events are minimized.**
>
> *Outcome measures:* Events, occurrences, conditions, behaviors and attitudes that demonstrate the extent to which the performance standard has been achieved. This data is compiled and consists of such items in a time period such as incident reports, number of physical injuries, number of emotional traumas, number of unauthorized inmate absences, and number instances of unauthorized access to the facility, etc.
>
> *Expected practices:* actions and activities when properly implemented according to protocols will produce the desired outcome. Concerning security, these practices are controlled (control center staffed 24 hours per day, staffing of essential posts, inmate counts, etc.).
>
> *Protocols:* written instructions that provide guidance for staff, such as policies and procedures, post orders, training curriculum, etc. Policies and procedures are the "guiding light" for staff.
>
> *Process indicators:* Evidence and documentation that shows that the expected practices are being implemented. They are monitored, evaluated and revised as necessary by agency supervisors as standards are revised or rescinded.

Changing Face of Accreditation

State minimum standards may not be as detailed as ACA, but the facility must meet them to receive funding. They may be more general and not written the same. Whether they are called standards or performance standards, changes are on going. At the time of publication, the ACA adult local performance based standards totaled 384 (62 mandatory and 322 non mandatory expected practices). ACA accreditation, which is every three years, requires that the facility meet 100 percent and 90 percent of mandatory expected and non mandatory expected practices, respectively (*Performance Based Standards for Adult Local Detention Facilities, 4th Edition*, 2004, pp. xix, xxxviii).

Accreditation has taken hold in corrections. The first accreditation of correctional agencies occurred in 1978. By January 1, 2002, 501 state and federal prisons, or 72.9 percent of the prisons in operation at that time were accredited by ACA. This figure represented accredited prisons in 28 state or federal agencies. But—if a facility is not accredited by ACA or NCCHC, that in no way means that it cannot operate constitutionally and use good management practices. The agency head, sheriff, or corrections administrator may feel that ACA accreditation is too costly and time consuming. ACA accreditation is not mandatory or regulatory such as in state and federal standards. These facilities may operate just as well, adopting ACA principles, but are content with state or federal accreditation (Seiter, 2008, p. 533).

Summary

Today's prisons, jails and community corrections facilities were born out of well meaning conflicts among learned men as to how inmates should be housed and treated. Out of the Pennsylvania and Auburn systems' debate came new ways to house inmates (silent solitary confinement cells vs. the interior cellblock). The reformist ideas of MacConochie, Crofton and Brockway resulted in rehabilitative programs for inmates. Though the original programs were short lived, their philosophies resulted in community corrections programs such as today's work release and parole. Not all developments in U.S. corrections were positive as the brutal conditions in southern prisons attest. Inmates were exploited and used as cheap labor. However, women's corrections did improve as the need for women offenders to be both understood and properly supervised began to be realized.

Industrial prisons developed as did the "Big House," large prisons that warehoused inmates. Isolation type prisons such as Alcatraz developed and are still in use. Jails started as a mixture of facilities and philosophies and have modernized. Alternatives to traditional incarceration such as community corrections facilities, boot camps, and privately run prisons started to save funds and reduce overcrowding. Community corrections operate work release, electronic monitoring and weekender programs. Private corrections companies operate facilities and provide services. Boot camps provide a structured program for young offenders, but not without debate as to effectiveness.

With the advancement of corrections has come the development of correctional standards based on court decisions and developments in such areas as training and health care. COs should be familiar with what standards are and how they benefit the facility.

Review Questions

1. Explain the philosophies of the Pennsylvania, Auburn and Reformatory Systems.
2. How was prison discipline maintained by silence and discipline?
3. Describe the Mark and Irish Systems and their influence on the Reformatory Movement.
4. Describe the development of the Industrial type prison.
5. Describe several community corrections programs.
6. What are boot camps?
7. Describe how privatization has changed corrections.
8. What is the importance of correctional standards and accreditation?

Terms/Concepts

determinate sentence   *prison wagons*
home detention/electronic monitoring   *probation*
interior cellblock   *rabble management*
Irish System   *ticket of leave*
lockstep   *weekend confinement*
Mark System   *work/study release*
parole

References

Allen, Harry, Edward J. Latessa, Ph.D., Bruce S. Ponder and Clifford Simonsen Ph.D. (2007). *Corrections in America: An Introduction, Eleventh Edition,* Upper Saddle River: Pearson Prentice Hall.

American Correctional Association. (1983). *The American Prison from the Beginning,* Laurel: American Correctional Association.

American Correctional Association. (2004). *Performance Based Standards for Adult Local Detention Facilities Fourth Edition.* Lanham: American Correctional Association.

Annin, Peter J. (1998, July 13). Inside the New Alcatraz. *Newsweek,* 35.

Champion, Dean J. (2005). *Corrections in the United States: A Contemporary Perspective, Fourth Edition.* Upper Saddle River: Pearson Prentice Hall.

Cornelius, Gary. (1996). *Jails in America: An Overview of Issues, 2nd Ed.* Laurel: American Correctional Association.

Dickey, Christopher. (1990, January 15). A New Home for Noriega? *Newsweek,* 66–69.

Golden State National Parks Association. (1996). *Discover Alcatraz: A Tour of the Rock.*

Hentoff, Nat. (1993, September). Buried Alive in Pelican Bay, *Prison Life, Vol. 1, No. 9,* 21–27.

Irwin, John. (1980). *Prisons in Turmoil.* Boston: Little, Brown.

Johnson, Robert. (2002). *Hard Time: Understanding and Reforming the Prisons, Third Edition.* Belmont: Wadsworth.

Kemble, Tod. (1996, May–June). Jails in America. *Texas Journal of Corrections,* 14–19.

Manatee County, Florida Sheriff's Office. (1998). Boot Camp Recruit Manual/Juvenile Justice Division.

McCarthy, Belinda Rodgers, McCarthy, Jr. Bernard J., and Matthew C. Leone. (2001). *Community Based Corrections,* Fourth Edition. Pacific Grove: Brooks-Cole.

Press, Aric, Jonathan Kirsch, Vern Smith, Michael Reese and Eric Gelman. (1980, August 18). The Scandalous U.S. Jails. *Newsweek,* 75–77a.

Roberts, John. (1997). *Reform and Retribution: An Illustrated History of the American Prison.* Lanham: American Correctional Association.

Rothman, David. (1971). *The Discovery of the Asylum: Social Order and Disorder in the New Republic.* Glenview: Scott Foresman.

Sabol, William J., Ph.D., Todd Minton and Paige M. Harrison. (June, 2007, revised 06/27/07). *Prison and Jail Inmates at Midyear 2006.* U.S. Department of Justice: Bureau of Justice Statistics. Washington, DC: U.S. Government Printing Office, [available on line at www.ojp.usdoj.gov/bjs/].

Schmalleger, Frank, Ph.D., and John Ortiz Smykla, Ph.D. (2009). *Corrections in the 21st Century Fourth Edition.* New York: McGraw Hill.

Seiter, Richard P., Ph.D. (2008). *Corrections: An Introduction: Second Edition.* Upper Saddle River: Pearson Prentice Hall.

Stephan, James J. (October, 2008). *Census of State and Federal Correctional Facilities, 2005.* U.S. Department of Justice: Bureau of Justice Statistics. Washington, DC: U.S. Government Printing Office, [available on line at www.ojp.usdoj.gov/bjs/].

Stinchcomb, Jeanne, Ph.D. (2005). *Corrections: Past, Present and Future.* Lanham: American Correctional Association.

Stinchcomb, Jeanne B., Ph.D. and Vernon B. Fox, Ph.D. (1999). *Introduction to Corrections, Fifth Edition.* Upper Saddle River: Prentice Hall.

Stojkovic, Stan and Rick Lovell. (1997). *Corrections: An Introduction, 2nd Ed.* Cincinnati: Anderson.

Chapter 6

An Examination of Today's Inmate

The conventional term for persons housed in correctional facilities is inmate. More specifically, persons incarcerated but not yet convicted of a crime are called "*pre-trial detainees*;" those adjudicated and sentenced to terms of incarceration are "*convicts*." For the everyday correctional worker, all prisoners in the facility are collectively called "inmates." In some minimum security facilities such as community corrections centers, inmates may be called offenders, residents, participants or clients.

Inmates come in various ages, races, physical sizes and social backgrounds. No two inmates are alike. While the average correctional officer may find it easy to "lump" all the inmates in one basket and try to treat them all the same, the reality is that inmates have different personalities and tolerances for incarceration. Correctional officers must realize this and adjust their styles and methods of dealing with inmates accordingly.

Correctional officers are not paid to be psychologists to try to get into the minds of inmates in their care. To deal with today's inmates a correctional officer should understand their backgrounds. The nature of work in today's correctional facilities is the same as it has always been—adversarial, or "us v. them." Correctional officers *must* know their adversary.

In this chapter, we will look at the relationship of officers to inmates from a knowledge point of view: knowing inmates' problems, backgrounds and limitations socially; and the "survivalist" part of inmates: how they adapt to and survive incarceration.

Sociological Characteristics of Today's Inmate

While the numbers of prisoners incarcerated in the United States has been previously discussed, this section will deal with the following areas:

- Age
- Gender
- Race and ethnicity
- Educational level
- Vocational level
- Substance abuse
- Medical problems
- Criminal history and type of offense

This is meant to give the reader a concise "snapshot" of who is locked up currently in the United States. The reader hopefully will draw his or her bottom line conclusions about the inmate population. Probably the best source of correctional statistics is the United States Department of Justice Bureau of Justice Statistics (BJS), which publishes statistics annually or at regular intervals.

Age

In 2007, the breakdown of age groups among inmates incarcerated in U.S. prisons (federal and state) and jails are as follows. Almost 34 percent (33.8%) were aged 20 to 29, meaning one in three were relatively young. Regarding females, almost 36 percent (35.9%) were aged 30 to 39 (Sabol and Couture, *Prison Inmates at Mid Year 2007*, p. 7):

	Males	Females
Ages 18–19	86,600	5,500
Ages 20–24	353,300	31,000
Ages 25–29	354,100	32,000
Ages 30–34	328,600	35,500
Ages 35–39	303,100	39,000
Ages 40–44	273,600	32,700
Ages 45–49	184,200	18,200
Ages 50–54	96,800	8,000
Ages 55–59	50,500	3,300
Ages 60–64	21,700	1,200
Ages 65+	17,700	800
Total	2,090,800	208,300

(reported by BJS)

No discussion of statistics on the age of inmates would be complete without the mention of juvenile offenders. The number of offenders reported incarcerated in state prisons under age 18 has averaged 2,300 between 2005 and

2007. The number reported by state correctional authorities are (Sabol and Couture, *Prison Inmates at Mid Year 2007*, p. 9):

Year (June 30 to June 30)	Number
2005	2,208
2006	2,364
2007	2,280
Average	2,284

According to the last published official profile of jail inmates published by BJS in 2004, jail inmates were older in 2002 as compared to the last profile in 1996. In 2002, approximately 38 percent were age 35 or older, increasing from 32 percent in 1996. The number of offenders age 17 and younger decreased from 1996 to 2002: 2.3 percent to 1.8 percent, respectively (James, *Profile of Jail Inmates, 2002*, p. 2).

Gender

Historically, the majority of inmates incarcerated in the United States have been male. At the local level, jails have more cell space for male inmates than females. It was not uncommon for a local jail, especially an old one, to transfer female inmates to local jails that had cell space. This practice of transferring inmates to other facilities for management reasons including the reduction of overcrowding is called *farming out* or *farmed out* (see Chapter 2). With the improvement of corrections management, more cell space is available for females, but overcrowding can continue to be a problem, no matter what the gender. As of mid year 2007, the gender breakdown for state and federal prison inmates was (Sabol and Couture, *Prison Inmates at Mid Year 2007*, p. 1):

Male	92.8%
Female	7.2%

In the last in depth look at the local jail population, statistics indicated that the number of female jail inmates was increasing, in a comparison of 1996 and 2002 jail inmate profiles reported by BJS (James, *Profile of Jail Inmates, 2002*, p. 2):

Gender	1996	2002
Male	89.8%	88.4%
Female	10.2%	11.6%

With the increase of the female inmate population in jails comes the need for awareness of the problems and concerns of female inmates. This means that training and management must address such issues as female inmates with medical problems unique to their gender, such as pregnancy, and the mental strain of being incarcerated when one is the mother of dependent children being cared for by relatives, friends and social services. This is especially important in training male staff for cross gender supervision.

Race

Any person of any race can be incarcerated, as corrections knows no color barrier. In terms of BJS statistics, the following was reported in 2008 concerning the mid year report of federal, state and local jail inmates in 2007. It should be noted that the highest percentage is black males (35.4%), followed by a 32.9 percent rate for white males and a 17.8 percent rate for Hispanic males (Sabol and Couture, *Prison Inmates at Mid Year 2007*, p. 7):

Total incarcerated male	2,090,800
Total incarcerated female	208,300
White male inmates	755,500
Black male inmates	814,700
Hispanic male inmates	410,900
White female inmates	96,600
Black female inmates	67,600
Hispanic female inmates	32,100

One concern among the corrections field is the high rate of Hispanic inmates, which is reaching a total of almost a half million inmates. Language barriers between these inmates and non-Spanish speaking staff are only one problem. Officers learning how to deal with the behaviors of incarcerated Latinos is being discussed and dealt with more by conducting cultural diversity training (see Chapter 7).

Race and ethnic statistics are more closely examined in the 2002 jail population profile by BJS. In 2002, whites were 36.0 percent of the jail population, blacks were 40.1 percent, Hispanics were 18.5 percent. Among the smaller groups, American Indian/Alaska Native composed 1.3 percent, Asian/Pacific Islander totaled 1.1 percent and multi racial stood at 3.0 percent. Jail officers should be aware that 6 in 10 jail inmates were racial or ethnic minorities (James, *Profile of Jail Inmates, 2002*, p. 2).

Education Levels

Many correctional officers feel that if inmates cared about their education, they would not be incarcerated. Lack of education is only a piece of the puzzle as to why individuals choose a life of crime. Studies have confirmed what correctional officers already know—inmates are not well educated.

In January 2003, the Bureau of Justice statistics published the special report *Education and Correctional Populations*. This report was based on data collected from several BJS Studies, the Current Population Survey sponsored by the Bureau of Labor Statistics, and the National Adult Literacy Survey. Among the findings were (Harlow, *Education and Correctional Populations*, p. 1):

Level Attained	State Prison Inmates	Federal Prison Inmates	Jail Inmates
Some high school or less	39.7%	26.5%	46.5%
GED	28.5%	22.7%	14.1%
High School diploma	20.5%	27.0%	25.9%
Postsecondary	11.4%	23.9%	13.5%

Other notable findings were that an estimated 1 in 6 jail inmates dropped out of school because they were convicted of a criminal offense, sent to a correctional facility or became otherwise involved in criminal activity. The most important reasons for dropping out of school were having behavioral or academic problems, losing interest or having family or personal problems. Concerning recidivism, less educated inmates are more likely to repeat criminal behavior than are more educated inmates (Harlow, *Education and Correctional Populations*, pp. 3, 10).

A general rule in society is that education is a must in achieving success in life, but according to Dr. Stanton Samenow, a clinical psychologist and author of *Inside the Criminal Mind*, the delinquent youths and future criminals do not appreciate school and the value of education. They use school to exploit others, engage in criminal activities and stake out territory (Samenow, 1984, pp. 67–71).

There has been progress in this area. Educational programs are offered in many prisons, jails, community corrections centers and juvenile facilities. Minnesota took a progressive view. About 35% of the inmates were functionally illiterate and were made to participate in a reading course before joining other classes. In 1994, a reported 90% of those illiterate inmates had enrolled (Smolowe, 1994, pp. 54–59).

Educational programs for inmates have flourished, partly thanks to the passage of the federal Second Chance Act, signed by President George W. Bush in 2008, providing $165 million dollars annually for correctional education programs. Consider these examples from several jurisdictions (Barnett, 2008):

- In South Carolina, the Palmetto Program affords inmates the opportunities to achieve their GED diplomas. At one institution, 186 out of 217 enrolled earned their GEDs in the 2007–2008 school year.
- In Tennessee, female inmates at the State Prison for Women earn college credits from Lipscomb University.
- Pennsylvania inmates incarcerated in the state Department of Corrections have Individual Plans of Instruction developed to meet educational needs. They are also required to take a victims awareness class to teach them the consequences of their criminal acts.
- In 2008, the Arkansas state prison school system had a record 872 inmates earning their high school equivalency diplomas.

Vocational History

A more realistic way to look at inmates and vocational history is to examine jail inmates. Prison inmates are incarcerated in the local jail first as their cases wind their way through the criminal justice system. In 2002, 71 percent of jail inmates reported that they were working in the month before their arrest. Out of that number, 57.4 percent reported full time employment. Over half (63.2 percent) reported that their source of income were wages/salaries. About 41 percent reported an income of $1,000 or more per month. However, it should be noted that almost 16 percent (15.8) of jail inmates reported that their source of income was from family and friends; almost 12 percent (11.8) received their income from illegal sources (James, *Profile of Jail Inmates, 2002*, p. 9).

Substance Abuse

It is clear to correctional officers that many inmates in their custody both in prisons and jails have abused drugs and alcohol. Jail COs see the effects of substance abuse as offenders are booked into jails right off the street. Prison COs combat drug smuggling and inmates' manufacture of homemade "booze."

Concerning alcohol abuse, an estimated 50 percent of convicted male jail inmates reported in 2002 that they had used alcohol or drugs at the time of their criminal offense; the rate for convicted females was 46.3 percent. The rate of alcohol use by all jail inmates at the time of offense declined from 1996 to 2002 (41 percent to 33 percent respectively). However, approximately 77 percent of convicted jail inmates could be placed in the category of alcohol or drug involved; this has remained at the same rate since 1996, posing a challenge for correctional rehabilitation personnel (James, *Profile of Jail Inmates, 2002*, p. 8).

The following is a concise table on regular drug usage (percentages) from inmates in federal and state prisons (2004) and in 2002 in local jails (Mumola and Karberg, *Drug Use and Dependence, State and Federal Prisoners, 2004*, p. 2) and (James, *Profile of Jail Inmates, 2002*, p. 8):

Type of Drug	State Inmates	Federal Inmates	Jail Inmates
Any drug	69.2	64.3	68.7
Marijuana/hashish	59.0	53.0	58.5
Cocaine/crack	30.0	27.5	30.9
Heroin/opiates	13.1	9.2	12.0
Depressants	9.9	8.6	10.7
Stimulants*	17.9	14.8	17.1
Hallucinogens	13.3	11.9	13.4
Inhalants	4.5	3.0	4.2

* The stimulant methamphetamine was reported to be used regularly by 14.9 percent of state prison inmates and 12.8 percent of Federal prison inmates.

As in prisons, drug offenses are responsible for a significant number of jail arrests. As veteran jail and prison officers realize, as well as treatment personnel, many offenses "spin off" from substance abuse, but are not labeled drug offenses by the ordinary public. For example, grand larceny, selling stolen goods or robbery may all have a goal of obtaining drug money. Reactions to drugs or the influence of alcohol may result in assaults.

Combating substance abuse has been the focus of many corrections programs for many years. In jails and prisons, groups such as Alcoholics Anonymous (AA) and Narcotics Anonymous (NA) try to show inmates the consequences of such abuse. Many facilities contract with substance abuse staff in local jurisdictions to provide individual counseling, group counseling, and therapy. It is important that COs support inmate participation in these programs.

Medical Problems

It is not surprising that many inmates do not take care of their hygiene and health. COs have to deal with their many health problems that inmates suffer and ensure that they get the medical care that they need. Most inmates surveyed had received some type of medical service since admission and during incarceration; approximately 9 out of 10 were asked about their medical history. About 70 percent of state and 76 percent of federal inmates reported seeing a correctional medical staff person about a current medical problem. Inmates in state and Federal prisons were surveyed in 2004 and the main findings were (Marushak, *Medical Problems of Prisoners,* on line report):

- An estimated 44 percent of state prison inmates and 39 percent of federal inmates reported having a current medical problem when surveyed, other than a cold or virus.
- The two most common medical problems reported by state and federal inmates were arthritis and hypertension.
- State and federal female inmates (57 and 52 percent, respectively) were more likely to report a current medical problem.
- The reported rates of hearing and vision impairments increased with age; the percentages of state and federal inmates reporting surgery since admission, dental problems and medical problems increased with age.
- The most commonly reported impairment by state and federal inmates was learning (23 and 13 percent, respectively).
- Concerning pregnancy, 4 percent of state female inmates and 3 percent of federal female inmates stated that they were pregnant when admitted.
- Inmates reporting ever having tuberculosis (TB) or having TB totaled 9.4 percent of state inmates and 7.1 percent of federal inmates.
- The percentages of state and federal inmates reporting HIV were 1.6 and 1.0 respectively. Less than 1 percent of state and federal inmates reported having a sexually transmitted disease.

Criminal Offenses

BJS keeps detailed statistics on the criminal offenses of both juvenile and adult offenders. The following table is a general "snapshot" of all state prison inmates in 2002 (*Sourcebook of Criminal Justice Statistics 2003, online* Table 6.0001.2002):

Category	Total: Inmates (%)	Males (%)	Females (%)
Violent Offenses	50.5	51.7	33.0
Property Offenses	20.4	19.9	28.7
Drug Offenses	21.4	20.7	31.5
Public Order Offenses*	7.1	7.1	6.1
Other/unspecified**	0.6	0.6	0.8
Total:	**100**		

  * Includes weapons offenses, drunk driving, court offenses, commercialized decency, vice and morals offenses, court offenses, and other offenses against public order.
  ** Includes unspecified felonies and juvenile offenses.

In regards to Federal inmates the three highest rates for offenses in 2003 were drug offenses (54.8 percent), weapons, explosives and arson offenses (11.5%) and immigration offenses (10.6%) (*Sourcebook of Criminal Justice Statistics 2003, online* Table 6.56).

Juvenile Crime

Juveniles who are charged and/or certified as adults can be incarcerated in adult prisons and jails. Juvenile offenses can be just as serious as adult offenses. According to the U.S. Department of Justice, in 2004, juveniles were involved in 12 percent of violent criminal offenses cleared. This involved 5 percent of murders, 12 percent of forcible rapes, 12 percent of aggravated assaults and 14 percent of robberies (Snyder, *Juvenile Arrests 2004*, p. 1).

Female juveniles accounted for 24 percent of juveniles arrested for aggravated assault in 2004. From 1980 to 2004, the rate of juvenile arrests for simple assault increased 290 percent for females and 106 percent for males. However, juvenile offenders are predominantly male; 30 percent of juvenile arrests in 2004 involved a female. Surprisingly, young offenders *under age 15* accounted for an estimated one third of all violent and property crime offenses (Snyder, *Juvenile Arrests 2004*, pp. 1, 3, 8).

Correctional officers cannot be swayed by age. A juvenile offender may be brought into the jail and look chronologically young, but also may have a serious juvenile crime record. COs must be on their guard, no matter if the offender is an adult or juvenile.

Recidivism

Recidivism simply defined is offenders being rearrested for new crimes or inmates being released and reincarcerated for committing new crimes. It is the "scourge" of the field of corrections. While the most idealistic of corrections professionals believe that inmates can be rehabilitated, the fact that some always will be rearrested cannot be ignored. While it is important to know what an inmate is charged with as it tells a lot about the inmate, it is impossible for COs in a prison or a jail to know an inmates' charges at a glance.

The Bureau of Justice Statistics has tracked the repeat crime rate of 272,111 inmates who were released in 15 states in 1994. Studies found that many (67.5%) were rearrested for a serious misdemeanor or felony within three years. Out of these, almost 47 percent (46.9%) were reconvicted and an estimated half (25.4%) were sentenced to prison again for a new crime (BJS *Criminal Offenders Statistics*). It is not surprising for COs to see the same offenders coming in over and over.

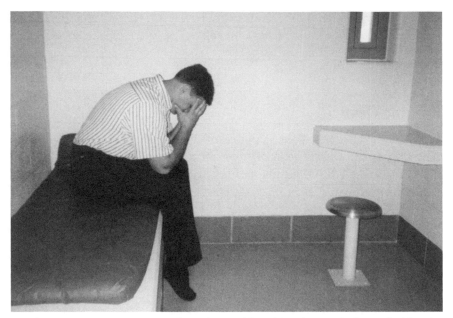

For the inmate, incarceration can bring his world crashing down. Clarke-Frederick-Winchester (VA) Regional Adult Detention Center.

Inmates as Survivors: The Pain of Incarceration

There are two ways to look at inmates: in a detached, statistical way or as human beings who live an atypical lifestyle and learn to adapt to the harsh rigors of prison life. They learn to survive.

To work every day with inmates, correctional officers must learn about how they think, how they adapt and how they do their time. By doing so, they can *empathize* with the inmate and can understand what they go through. The benefits are better communication and a lessening of tensions between staff and inmates.

Prisonization

When working with inmates, no matter what type of facility, correctional officers must realize that offenders are not "born" inmates, they *become* inmates through a process called prisonization.

First coined by Donald Clemmer in 1940, the term *prisonization* means "... the process by which the inmate learns, through socialization, the rules and regulations of the penal institution, as well as the informal values, rules and customs of the penitentiary culture." In other words, the inmate learns how to be an inmate: how to sleep, eat, dress and talk differently in order to survive (Allen, Latessa, Ponder and Simonsen, 2007, p. 177).

Observers of the process note that not only does the inmate learn behaviors, they learn things about the staff from other inmates around them—what officers are "easy" to lie to, manipulate or influence; and what officers are "hard," sticking to policy, procedures and are not easily manipulated. Also, inmates will learn quickly which inmates are predators, thieves, liars and untrustworthy. They learn from inmates they befriend and who are similar to themselves; they see inmates trying to survive.

Prisonization besides the learning of everyday habits is influenced by three things: the needs of inmates, the development of niches and the "inmate code."

A Lesson in Prisonization

Not all lessons an inmate learns through prisonization are negative and destructive. Ralf Dean Omar, an ex-convict, advises inmates to avoid these eight pitfalls:

1. *Gangs:* An inmate may be considered a gang member if he associates with a gang; gangs engage in illegal activities. Inmates should not accept favors from a gang and should decline tactfully any offers to join a gang.
2. *Drugs:* Using drugs impedes an inmate's judgment and ability to defend oneself.
3. *Sex:* Inmates entering the homosexual prison culture may be victims of rape, violence and sexually transmitted diseases.
4. *Debts and gambling:* Inmates should not lend things or gamble. If they cannot collect, it may be considered a sign of weakness.
5. *Stealing:* Inmates should guard their own property and not steal from fellow inmates.
6. *Snitching:* Inmates should stay away from illegal activity and not believe staff promises. Inmates observing such activities may be labeled a snitch by the guilty inmates.
7. *Trickbags:* When opportunistic inmates let an inmate borrow something and say its broken or not the same upon its return, they have the naive inmates in a "trickbag"—indebted to them. Omar says that "if a [prison] deal looks too good to be true, it probably is."
8. *Riots:* Inmates should avoid becoming a spokesperson or being in areas where hostages are held. Avoid speaking to the media. Do not cross prisoner picket lines.
    (Omar, 1995, pp. 66–67)

The Needs of Inmates

Inmates have needs, needs beyond the simple everyday necessities of a bed, food and clothing. To safely manage inmates, officers must realize these needs and try to have them met in a positive way without jeopardizing security.

These needs can be viewed as "seven ecological dimensions" that serve to express the preferences and needs of inmates. Research by Hans Toch in 1977 described these dimensions or needs as:

1. *Activity*: to be occupied, do something to pass the time, be entertained and distracted. In jails and prisons, programs, recreation, television and radio serve this purpose as well as trustee (inmates performing work for the prison) jobs.

2. *Privacy*: to be alone, to try to survive in peace and quiet, away from noise, crowded living conditions, and immature, bothersome inmates. Inmates generally crave privacy and will ask at times to be transferred to single housing, away from the pressures of crowding. In certain cases, such as an inmate "on the edge" mentally, this may be possible so as to avoid future problems. Generally, in an overcrowded facility, inmates living alone are not luxuries that can be granted. Classification staffs generally have the burden of finding such housing; inmates must be told if that is not possible.

3. *Safety*: inmates are concerned about their physical well being and that their belongings are left alone.

4. *Emotional feedback*: all of us want to be loved, liked and looked upon as a worthy person deserving of others' appreciation. Inmates do not want to be considered just inmates, they want to be loved, appreciated and cared for. There is loneliness in prison and inmates will find emotional support in friendship and relationships with other inmates.

5. *Support*: some inmates *do* take advantage of programs, counseling, volunteer assistance and other tools that can aid rehabilitation. Those inmates wish to have such support available to them.

6. *Structure*: inmates prefer predictability when it comes to rules, regulations and routines. Rules must be clear-cut, according to Toch. Enforcement of them must be consistent and fair. A common complaint from inmates is that one team or shift (squad, etc.) works differently from another.

7. *Freedom*: all inmates want freedom in the usual sense of the word. Toch states that inmates want minimal restrictions, minimal supervision and to be able to govern their own conduct. For example, many inmates covet trusty jobs to escape the restrictiveness and staff sur-

veillance of the housing units. Being a trusty gives them more freedom of movement. Inmates who have been transferred to jails from
prison for court hearings, for example, find the county jail housing more
confining and do not like the increase in staff presence.
(Johnson, 2002, pp. 168–171)

Niches

Everyone has his or her own niche and inmates are no exception. The average citizen has a job, home and family—important things that can bring
happiness and assist in survival. Inmates in prison look for the same supports.
In 1977, J. Seymour (in Toch, 1977) defined niches as they fit in the prison
setting. A *niche* is:

> A functional subsetting containing objects, space, resources, people and
> relationships between people (Johnson, 2002, p. 172).

Inmates, by forming their niches, will try to have the seven needs Toch described met. They will form friendships, make arrangements with each other
to look out for danger, engage in recreational activities or procure a work assignment in order to be active. In essence, they will try to cope with incarceration as best they can using the people and resources around them.

The corrections officer must realize that niches not only give an inmate relief from stress, they can also serve to keep the institutional climate calm.
Niches must then be viewed as a realistic aspect of prison life.

However, niches can be both good and bad. While positive objects that
Seymour mentions in his definition could be commissary items, family pictures, etc., they could also mean smuggled drugs or weapons. Space could
be a private cell gained through lying to staff or manipulation. Resources
could be a contraband smuggling operation trafficking in drugs. People and
their relationships could mean power through membership in a gang or extremist group. While activity means positive distraction and entertainment,
it could also mean using staff, lying and manipulating staff—entertainment
for the inmates.

The Inmate Code

Much has been written about the *inmate code* or the social rules
in prisons and jails that inmates live by. This code permits inmates
to live by *their* own rules, not so much the institution's. Violations of
this code could result in physical assault, murder or ostracism, at the
minimum. Violators can be labeled weaklings or snitches. One of the

best descriptions of this code is from the Kansas Department of Corrections training manual:

1. *Be loyal:* Keep silent about what other inmates do, including criminal acts. Lie if you must. Never take a problem to the institution staff. Be loyal to your fellow inmates no matter what the cost.

2. *Be cool:* Be calm and in control, no matter what the pressure you receive from staff. Do your time—don't make waves.

3. *Be straight* (with fellow inmates): Don't take advantage of another inmate—don't steal, don't lie, don't break your word. Inmates should share goods and do favors. It is permissible to tell staff "half truths" to get your way or avoid a problem.

4. *Be tough:* Don't be weak, don't whine, don't say that you are guilty. Inmates must "take it." The code says that inmates should not start fights; inmates should not run from a fight that another inmate starts.

5. *Be sharp:* Correctional officers must not be trusted, suspect them. Concerning a conflict between an officer and an inmate, the officer is always wrong.

Recently, some penal reformers and convicts have been speaking out against the code saying that through silence, it protects inmates who are brutal and should face the consequences of their actions. One convict said that he will accept responsibility for his actions and never would burden another. Bo Lozoff, director of the Prison-Ashram project, relates the true story of a convict who witnessed a vicious gang rape of a young inmate. The convict, a year later, said that the incident still bothered him, but has said nothing because of the "code." Lozoff says that his "biggest problem with the old convict code is that even at its best, it has been basically selfish. Its rule of silence allows all manner of brutality to take place."

Clearly, any revision of the code is in the hands of the inmates. Could a revision of the code be a twinge of conscience? (Bayse, 1993, pp. 35–36, Lozoff, 1995, p. 32, Renaud, 1995, pp. 31–32)

The Pains of Imprisonment

Being locked up away from families, loved ones and children is painful. No matter what prior record an inmate has or how many years of experience in prisons, prison life is uncomfortable and many inmates think about life on the outside and what they are missing. Many try to compensate by developing their niches.

Correctional officers must realize that for all the inmate "bravado" and cockiness, being incarcerated, especially at a younger age, can be devastating to the inmate. Robert Johnson wrote:

> *Imprisonment is a disheartening and threatening experience for most men. The man in prison finds his career disrupted, his relationships suspended, his aspirations and dreams gone sour* (Johnson, 2002, p. 82).

Some inmates will deal with this pain by acting tough, exhibiting a tough veneer or mask. When wearing this mask, inmates will act like nothing bothers them—not other inmates, not the staff and their rules or, in general, being locked up. According to Johnson, based on 1954 research by McCorkle and Korn, inmates feel a need to "reject their rejectors" and live as though the pains of incarceration are of little or no consequence. To illustrate how weak society is having to "cage" its "manly" outlaws, inmates may flaunt big muscles and tough behavior (McCorkle and Korn, 1954, in Johnson, 2002, p. 163). To the average law abiding citizen, contact with authorities (from being given a warning to receiving a traffic citation or being arrested) is a traumatic, fearful experience. To many inmates, being written up in prison on a disciplinary charge is nothing; for some it is a way to verbally defy authority by appearing before a hearing acting like "it's no big deal."

However, when looking inward, many inmates realize their situation. Two quotes from two 18-year-old inmates both convicted of murder illustrate (Buckley, 1997, pp. 6D–7D):

> *It dawns on me every day, I'm going to be in here for life.*
> *Jail ain't a place to be. It's the emotional pain of being without your family.*

In order to cope in this negative world, many prisoners will follow a "prison career." These careers had their origins in the Big House type prisons, but are evident today in our nation's correctional facilities. They are (Irwin, 1980, p. 14–21):

Doing time: The inmate's concern is doing his/her own time, getting out with minimum pain in the shortest time.
Jailing: Learning the inmate culture, similar to carving out a niche, getting very familiar with inmate life, looking on other inmates like family.
Gleaning: Taking advantage of any available resource, programs, counseling, etc., to better themselves and prepare for life after prison.

Improvisation: Gathering whatever items or materials that are available and substituting them for "luxuries" on the outside, i.e., making home-made alcohol, making weapons, etc.

Fantasy: Fantasies, daydreaming, etc., is conducted in private to shut out the drabness and despair of imprisonment.

Stupefaction: Due to the deprivation of outside contact, especially with long-term inmates, inmates learn to "blunt their feelings," fantasize and turn inward. Incarceration numbs them.

Being incarcerated affects different types of inmates in different ways. The inmate prone to suicidal behavior may try to take his own life, the female prisoner with small children may cry a lot, the substance abuser may try to smuggle drugs. This will be discussed more in Chapter 7.

Summary

When discussing the question of who inmates are, the answer must be approached from two directions: social characteristics and a humanistic view.

Socially, inmates generally are young; many lack education, and are mostly male. Violent offenses comprise the most number of state inmates, drug offenses the most in the federal system. High numbers of inmates have had previous problems with the law. Juvenile violent crime is a concern. Inmates exhibit high rates of alcohol and drug abuse.

From a humanistic view, inmates are people who learn the culture of the prison through prisonization. Inmates have needs, as we all do, and these needs are met through niches. Incarceration is painful, resulting in the prisoner finding coping mechanisms, including exhibiting a tough shell.

The much discussed inmate code apparently gives inmates informal guidelines to live by. However, recent research has indicated that the blind loyalty to this code may be waning.

Review Questions

1. What is a niche?
2. Describe the seven inmate needs as researched by Toch.
3. What pitfalls of prison life should inmates avoid?
4. Define prisonization.
5. Describe the inmate "code" and explain how it may not be beneficial to inmates.

6.   What trends concerning the inmate population can one understand from inmate statistical data?

Terms/Concepts

convicts	*jailing*
doing time	*niche*
fantasy	*pre-trial detainees*
gleaning	*prisonization*
improvisation	*recidivism*
inmate code	*stupefaction*

References

Allen, Harry, Edward J. Latessa, Ph.D., Bruce S. Ponder and Clifford Simonsen Ph.D. (2007). *Corrections in America: An Introduction, Eleventh Edition,* Upper Saddle River: Pearson Prentice Hall.

Barnett, Ron. Incarcerated Getting Educated. *USA Today.* Available on line: usatoday.com (Accessed 09/25/08).

Bayse, Daniel. (1993). *Helping Hands: A Handbook for Volunteers in Prisons and Jails,* Laurel: American Correctional Association.

Buckley, J. Taylor. (1997, April 19). Growing Up and Growing Old in Prison. *USA Today,* pp. 6D–7D.

Clemmer, Donald. (1940). *The Prison Community.* New York: Rinehart.

Criminal Offenders Statistics. U.S. Department of Justice: Bureau of Justice Statistics, [available on line at: http://www.ojp.usdoj.gov/bjs/crimoff.htm] (Accessed 08/18/07).

Harlow, Carolyn Wolf. (January 2003). *Education and Correctional Populations.* U.S. Department of Justice: Bureau of Justice Statistics. Washington, DC: U.S. Government Printing Office, [available on line at www.ojp.usdoj.gov/bjs/].

Irwin, John. (1980). *Prisons in Turmoil.* Boston: Little Brown.

James, Doris J. (July 2004 revised 10/12/04). *Profile of Jail Inmates, 2002.* U.S. Department of Justice: Bureau of Justice Statistics. Washington, DC: U.S. Government Printing Office, [available on line at www.ojp.usdoj.gov/bjs/].

Johnson, Robert. (2002). *Hard Time: Understanding and Reforming the Prisons,* Third Edition. Belmont: Wadsworth.

Lozoff, Bo. (1995, July–August). Revising the Inmate Code—One Step Further. *Prison Life,* p. 32.

Marushak, Laura M. *Medical Problems of Prisoners, on line report,* U.S. Department of Justice: Bureau of Justice Statistics.http://www.ojp.usdoj.gov/bjs/pub/html/mpp/mpp.htm (Accessed 09/21/08).

McCorkle, J.W., Jr., and R. Korn. (1995, May). Resocialization Within Walls. *The Annals of Political and Social Science, 293,* 88–98.

Mumola, Christopher J. and Jennifer Karberg. (October 2006). *Drug Use and Dependence, State and Federal Prisoners, 2004.* U.S. Department of Justice: Bureau of Justice Statistics. Washington, DC: U.S. Government Printing Office, [available on line at www.ojp.usdoj.gov/bjs/].

Omar, Ralf J. (1995, May–June). Eight Pitfalls to Avoid in Prison. *Prison Life,* pp. 66–67.

Renaud, Jorge. (1995, July–August). Challenging the Convict Code. *Prison Life,* pp. 30–33.

Sabol, William J., Ph.D. and Heather Couture. (June, 2008). *Prison Inmates at Mid Year 2007.* U.S. Department of Justice: Bureau of Justice Statistics. Washington, DC: U.S. Government Printing Office, [available on line at www.ojp.usdoj.gov/bjs/].

Samenow, Stanton. (1984). *Inside the Criminal Mind.* New York: Times Books.

Smolowe, Jill. (1994, February 7). And Throw Away the Key. *Time. Vol. 143, No. 6,* pp. 54–59.

Snyder, Howard N. (December 2006). *Juvenile Arrests 2004.* Office of Juvenile Justice and Delinquency Prevention, [available on line at www.ojp.usdoj.gov/ojjdp].

Sourcebook of Criminal Justice Statistics 2003. Bureau of Justice Statistics: online Table 6.0001.2002.

Sourcebook of Criminal Justice Statistics 2003. Bureau of Justice Statistics: online Table 6.56.

Toch, Hans. (1977). *Living in Prison: The Ecology of Survival.* New York: Free Press.

Chapter 7

Special Populations and Methods of Handling

In keeping with the theme of this text in presenting a useful information guide to the correctional officer, this chapter will focus on nine special types of inmates. Statistical data on all but the mentally ill has been discussed in Chapter 6. To correctional officers, it is known that the mentally ill in jails and prisons can present serious problems concerning management and safety.

There are many avenues of advice on how COs should handle the "special" or unusual types of offenders. This chapter will give the CO practical advice concerning managing the following types of "special" offenders:

- Substance abusers
- Suicidal inmates
- Security threat groups
- Mentally disordered
- Female offenders
- Juveniles
- Elderly
- Medical issues
- Culturally diverse inmates

Substance Abusers

Realistically, drug abuse by male and female offenders continues to be a decisive factor when discussing inmates. The "war on drugs" has accounted for many offender commitments. Statistical data and tests reported by BJS and published by correctional researchers in the 1990s of inmates at adult male prisons and correctional facilities indicate an ongoing usage of drugs behind the walls. These tests revealed that at least 1% tested positive for cocaine and heroin, 2% for methamphetamines, and approximately 6% for marijuana

(Allen, Latessa, Ponder and Simonsen, 2007, p. 314). Correctional officers in both jails *and* prisons have to be aware of the "pull" that illegal substances have on inmates. While jail staffs see the effects of substance abuse when inmates under the influence of alcohol and drugs are booked in from the street, prison correctional officers must be aware that inmates can use drugs and alcohol that are smuggled in.

Signs of Abuse

Correctional officers must be able to recognize the signs and symptoms of alcohol and drug abuse, but should do so cautiously. Diabetic emergencies, serious illness/injuries, and mental and emotional conditions can also exhibit similar symptoms. These symptoms are (Va. Dept. of Mental Health and Mental Retardation, 1986, pp. III-3, III-4):

> abscesses/scars on arms and legs
> cannot walk/stand
> confusion/disorientation
> delirium/hallucinations
> inmate feels very hot or very cold

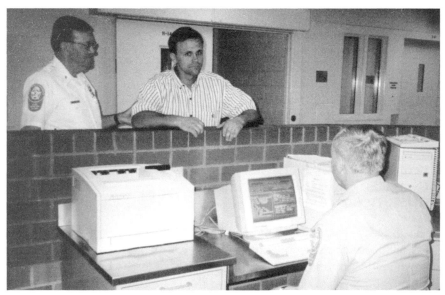

Booking area at a local jail. Correctional staffs never really know if a newly admitted inmate will or won't be a problem; observation is critical. Clarke-Frederick-Winchester (VA) Regional Adult Detention Center.

lethargic behavior
nausea—cramps, vomiting, diarrhea
needle marks (tracks) on arms and legs
odor of alcohol
pupils dilated/pinpoint
rapid and/or shallow breathing
restlessness/agitation/aggressiveness
slurred speech

The withdrawal from alcohol and drugs can pose serious health and management problems for the inmate. Inmates undergoing drug withdrawal (especially from heroin) may complain that they are "sick" and want medical help. Most jails observe inmates under withdrawal going *cold turkey*—withdrawal without maintenance doses of the drug. Correctional officers must take note of these alcohol and drug *withdrawal* symptoms (Va. Dept. of Mental Health and Mental Retardation, 1986, p. III-4):

agitation
delirium
difficulty breathing
fear/anxiety
hallucinations
insomnia
nausea/vomiting
pupils pinpointed
sweats
talkativeness
tremors (shakes)
violent excitement

Any inmate undergoing withdrawals or showing signs of alcohol and drug abuse must be *closely observed*; all interactions with staff, meals, medical checks and behaviors must be documented. The inmate must be reported *immediately* to the medical staff and mental health staff, if applicable.

For substance abusers in our nation's correctional facilities, programs are available if the inmate wants help, such as Alcoholics Anonymous (AA), Narcotics Anonymous (NA) and in *therapeutic communities*. These are correctional units where inmates live as a group, follow unit and program rules and guidelines and undergo treatment and therapy.

SLU: Sobering Prisoner's Lives

In 1988, the Alexandria, Virginia, Adult Detention Center initiated the Sober Living Unit (SLU)—a housing unit ninety-day program using AA's twelve-step approach. Daily routines are rigidly structured; inmates must go by the rules. It is a non-stop, intensive program that helps inmates that want to live a "drug free life."
(From "Program Sobers Prisoners' Lives," Buzz McClain, Fairfax *Journal*, 8/31/90)

Prisons offer treatment for longer periods of time due to inmates' sentences. Some jail systems are offering revolutionary treatment programs in order to change offenders into sober, clean, and persons from the onset of incarceration in the local jail. The goal is to release this type of offender back into the community.

Suicidal Inmates

One special group of inmates that all correctional officers and staff should be aware of is the inmate prone to suicide. Inmates may become suicidal due to the trauma of being arrested, loss of stable resources in their lives (such as job, family, etc.), shame, fear, depression, or withdrawal from drugs or alcohol. Whatever the reason, the suicidal inmate, if successful at self-destruction, can cause the institution embarrassment, scrutiny and liability. Correctional staff has the responsibility to protect inmates not only from other inmates, but from themselves.

Training in suicide prevention must be ongoing. Correctional officers, with heavy workloads, demands from inmates, and stress may become indifferent. This indifference is not conducive to helping a suicidal inmate, who is looking for help.

Four Types of Suicidal Inmates

Researchers have identified four types of suicidal inmates:

1. *Morality shock:* becomes suicidal shortly after admission; has to come to terms with criminal behavior and the losses and consequences that it has caused.
2. *Chronic despair:* in post-sentencing incarceration, has become depressed and hopeless about the future, feeling disconnected and distant from family, friends and attorneys.

3. *Manipulative anti-social inmate:* who, by non-lethal acts, attempts to gain a softer assignment (hospital/infirmary), sympathy, or *escape* (during transport to the hospital).
4. *Self-punishment:* inmate wishes to humiliate him/herself and make life painful and miserable.
(Lester and Danto, 1993, pp. 34–36)

Methods

Methods include hanging (which appears to be the most used method) ingesting hoarded medications, jumping headfirst from heights (such as tiers) or slashing themselves. Correctional officers must be aware that critical times for inmates include before/after court, after visiting, first few hours after admission and before release. Staff, when confronted with a suicidal inmate, should move the inmate to a high observation area, observe *very* frequently, such as every 5–10 or 15 minutes, and get the inmate to talk while staff acts as supportive listeners. Correctional officers should document their observations and call in qualified mental health staff to intervene, as well as notify their supervisors. These observations must be passed on in writing to staff relieving officers on post. Some inmates, if considered extremely suicidal, may have to be placed in a constant line of sight observation by staff, such as a holding area directly across from a booking desk, for example.

One method of dealing with the suicidal inmate is to isolate them and place him or her on *restricted issue (RI)*, or the taking from the inmate all items including clothing with which the inmate can make a noose, cutting instruments, any sharp objects including pencils, etc. Correctional officers, with the notification and approval of their supervisors can place an inmate on RI status and should immediately notify the mental health staff. In a properly run facility, only qualified mental health staff can take an inmate off restricted issue.

The following is a general list of suicidal behavior symptoms (Va. Office of Mental Health and Mental Retardation, 1986, pp. IV-9–IV-11, Cornelius, 1996, p. 40, Duncan, 2008, p. 105):

• creating poems or pictures with suicidal intent
• crying
• depression
• feelings of excessive self-blame
• giving away personal belongings such as commissary items
• lack of interest
• lacking the will to eat or sleep

- making comments such as "I want to die," "I want to kill myself," "I don't care any more," or "I don't want to live any more" or any type of suicidal threat
- previous or very recent suicide attempt
- tenseness
- varying moods
- withdrawal from activities
- worthlessness/guilt
- writing journals or notes with suicidal intent

In the past twenty years, much information has been made available about suicidal inmates. Every facility should have entry level and in-service training. In this training, COs should be made aware that no matter what the inmate's charge, behavior, mental status, disciplinary record, etc. they are *people* that are to be protected by the COs from self harm.

Correctional officers must be good listeners, showing compassion and encouraging inmates to talk about their problems. Also, the families and friends of inmates may contact the facility and ask if the inmate is all right, or inform the staff of the inmate's suicidal history, recent talk of suicide or give other

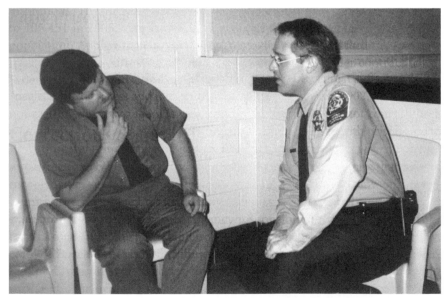

Correctional officers must be good listeners; assisting inmates who have problems promotes a positive climate in the facility. Clarke-Frederick-Winchester (VA) Regional Adult Detention Center.

critical information. Staff must give such communication credence, listen and take the proper action. COs are the first line of responsibility.

Inmates as a rule do not have coping skills that can handle life's challenges, including the stress and trauma of incarceration. Statistically, inmates have higher rates of suicide than those in the general population. This is especially true if they are suffering from the effects of alcohol abuse, drug abuse, substance abuse withdrawal, or have committed a crime that has a high shame factor such as a sexual offense, including crimes against children. Suicidal ideation can occur in an anxious spur of the moment, and they may not take the time to think the situation through rationally (Duncan, 2008, p. 104). Death may appear to be the only option for them.

Besides such interventions as described, other actions that can be taken by COs in dealing with a suicidal inmate include, with consultation with the mental health staff, (Duncan, 2008, p. 105):

- Keeping the inmate occupied through positive activities and interactions with staff—including mental health staff, religious staff, treatment staff and volunteers.
- Increasing headcounts and observations.
- Placing the inmate in a living area or cell that is very close to staff.
- Providing them with a cellmate.

The issue of inmate suicide has been one of the most discussed and litigated areas in corrections. It also requires on going training and review. Inmate suicides cannot be totally prevented. When a suicide or attempted suicide does occur, the incident should be examined and discussed with the staff to determine what happened, what went wrong and what can be done to improve staff actions and procedures. Every inmate—no matter if they are being booked into a jail, or is housed in the jail or prison general population—is a suicide risk.

Security Threat Groups

Recently, the prevalence of groups such as gangs in jails and prisons has posed a serious security problem for correctional staff. In a parallel development, the existence of extremist and terrorist groups also poses a security nightmare for correctional officers. In a post 9/11 world, correctional officers must be on guard for inmates advocating terrorist points of view. By doing so, in their (inmates') view they may be striking back at the law enforcement authorities that are keeping them confined. No matter what the organization, any group that advocates racist views, violence, and terrorist acts must be dealt with by the correctional officer.

Groups such as gangs, racial supremacist groups, extremist and terrorist groups are called *security threat groups*, or *STGs*. These groups, in the most basic sense are groups, because of their organization, views, ability to recruit new members and carry out actions and illicit activities in support of their views, disrupt the security and orderly operation of the correctional facility (Cornelius, 2008, p. 109). For example, in a correctional facility STG members can spread hate speech, engage in the smuggling of contraband (including weapons) into the facility and assault inmates or correctional officers that they consider enemies or wish to intimidate.

Gangs

Most gangs originate from street gangs and are based on racial attitudes and ethnic origins. Members adhere to a strict code of lifelong membership, behavior and silence. Gangs group together for power and protection, and have a hierarchy and leaders. Research by the American Correctional Association and the corrections departments in Ohio and Florida have revealed much information about gangs. Gang objectives of power and control are met through actions such as contract murder, homosexual prostitution, drug trafficking, gambling and contraband smuggling. Conflicts and struggles with rival gangs are settled through violence. This violence disrupts facility operations, takes its toll on staff by creating fears for safety, and results also in many inmate requests for administrative segregation (Allen, et al., 2007, p. 200). In a correctional facility, the inmates belonging to a gang want to do time on *their* terms, and do not allow security procedures and the authority of staff get in their way. Gangs are definitely a security threat group.

Gangs Defined

For all the information and media attention given to gangs in movies, books, etc., the exact definition of a gang is commonly thought to be a group of "toughs" disrupting society through violence. The state of California defines in clear terms both the criminal street gang and the gang member. These below paraphrased definitions can be helpful to the correctional officer who has to be on the lookout for gang activity (Ross, 1995):

- *Criminal street gang:* An organization, association or group of three or more persons, whether formal or informal which has a continuity of purpose, seeks a group identity and its members engage [or have engaged] in criminal activities either individually or collectively.

- A *gang member* is an individual who participates in a criminal street gang and has knowledge of members engaging in criminal gang activities. A gang member also is one who willfully promotes, furthers and/or assists members' criminal behavior and promotes and furthers such activities.

For correctional officers to deal with gangs, their origins must be examined. Up until the early 1980s, "gangbanging" meant gang members "hung out" with neighborhood toughs or homeboys. Gang violence and fights occurred with fists, guns, knives or baseball bats. With the crackdown on crime, street gangs had their power bases relocated from the street to prison. Conversely, some gangs that have started in prison have relocated to the street. Prisons have become the new recruiting and training group for our nation's gangbangers (Cozzone, 1995, p. 44).

Current Research on Gangs

How many STGs, or more specifically prison gangs are there? Beginning in 1950, the United States Bureau of Prisons has studied the problem, trying to identify the more problematic and prevalent prison gangs. A partial list includes (Cornelius, 2008, p. 110–111):

- Aryan Brotherhood
- Mexican Mafia
- La Nuestra Familia
- Texas Syndicate
- Black Guerilla Family
- Black Gangster Disciples
- Jamaican Posse
- Hell's Angels
- MS-13 (Mara Salvatrucha 13)
- Almighty Latin Kings
- Bloods
- Crips

In 2002, the *CQ (Congressional Quarterly) Researcher* released data on the growing criminal gang problem in the United States which spills over from the street to our correctional facilities (Cornelius, 2008, p. 111):

- The estimated number of gangs in the United States stands at 21,500; in 2002 increased gang activity was reported in over 40 percent of police jurisdictions, up from 27 percent in 2001. These gangs have an approximate membership of 731,000.

- According to the National Alliance of Gang Investigators, the gang threat has changed from an urban scourge to a nationwide threat; gang members have crossed the socioeconomic, ethnic and racial boundaries.
- Crimes committed by gang members are serious, including assault, illegal drug trafficking, extortion, fraudulent identification documents (used by terrorists and illegal aliens), property crime, homicide, and home invasions.
- Offenders belonging to gangs attempt to thwart law enforcement investigations by threats, assaults, rapes and killing potential witnesses.
- High rates of immigration from Latin America and Asia have resulted in the proliferation of gangs such as MS-13 (originating from El Salvador) and the Almighty Latin Kings Nation.

There has been research on prison gangs at the adult correctional institution level in both prisons and jails. In 2002, the National Major Gang Task Force conducted a survey of all adult prison systems in the United States, Canada, Guam, Puerto Rico, and the U.S. Virgin Islands. The response rate to the survey was 80 percent, and results indicated over 1,600 security threat groups being identified with an estimated membership—inmates belonging to these groups—of 114,000 (Schmallger and Smyrka, 2009, p. 503).

Concerning jails, in 2004 researchers from two universities (California State University at Chino, University of Missouri at St. Louis) and the National Youth Gang Center examined the perceptions of jail administrators of problems and disruptions that STGs cause in their facilities. They also examined the prevalence of these groups, methods of classifying membership in a gang, and tools and approaches used by staff that could reduce the disruption and violence caused by these STGs. Jail administrators said that designation of gang membership by another law enforcement agency, such as local police, etc., was a commonly used tool, as well as identifying tattoos, gang colors and clothing, hand signs and the offender declaring that he or she was a gang member. The jail administrators estimated that membership in STGs was at 13.2 percent. When researchers figured in the June 2005 national jail population, an estimated 98,673 STG members were being held in jail on any given day (Schmallger and Smyrka, 2009, p. 508).

Recently, police departments and other law enforcement agencies have started sharing gang information with correctional staff. In some correctional agencies, *gang intelligence units* have been formed. These specialized units investigate suspected gang members who are incarcerated, investigate crimes committed by gang members in the facility, assist in disciplining gang members, provide staff training, and work with local and federal anti gang law enforcement agencies. Other measures include tracking known gang members in the prison or jail inmate population and using criminal statutes and in-house disciplinary charges to the fullest extent possible.

Racial Supremacist Groups

Another type of STG group is the racial supremacist group or, more commonly the racist, bigoted groups that have members in our corrections facilities. Groups that are racial supremacist are well known, such as the American Nazi Party or the Ku Klux Klan. Inmates adhering to these groups and views or belonging to them may not want to be housed with minorities, or may engage in abrasive behavior and harassment towards inmates and staff of a different race, ethnic group or religion.

Often, racial supremacist STGs hide under the guise of being religious. One example is the Nation of Gods and Earth, otherwise known as the "Five Per-centers," whose members, although recognized in some facilities as being in a prison gang, claim to be in a religious group. Another group is the Christian Identity, whose members believe that Jews are the descendants of Satan, Jews are "imposters," that the British are the true Israelites, non white people are "mud" people and are on the same level of animals. They also predict a cata-clysmic Biblical race war in which all non white people are destroyed (Cor-nelius, 2008, pp. 110–111). This is in opposition to inmates who are members and believers of more tolerant, non biased mainstream, positive religions where hate is not spewed.

Terrorist Groups

It is clear that the United States is under a terror alert, especially after the attacks in 1993 and 2001 on the World Trade Center. Also, in the past two decades terrorists have attacked abroad, targeting Americans, United States embassies and military personnel. Terrorism takes direct action against established authorities. Correctional officers must be aware of the possibility of these views held by inmates. Also, correctional institutions are representative of government authority and are subject to terrorist attack, like any other government and public building. In this age of terror, jails and prisons have improved their perimeter security.

Correctional officers should realize that inmates are ripe for recruitment for terrorist criminals. According to terrorist researcher Chip Ellis of the National Memorial Institute for the Prevention of Terrorism, inmates often strive for some type of self identity and are disenfranchised; these aspects can be capitalized on by terrorist groups or inmates who believe in terrorism. Correctional officers must be alert for terrorism and extreme anti authority oral and/or written views from inmates, especially in notes, letters and literature (Schmallger and Smyrka, 2009, pp. 382–383).

According to the FBI, terrorist groups such as al-Qaeda are continuing to recruit inmates in our nation's correctional facilities. The 9,600 Muslim inmates in the federal correctional system are looked upon by Islamic terrorists as possible converts. In 2004, according to a report from the Office of Inspector General of the U.S. Department of Justice, the primary threat of radicalization and recruitment of terrorist groups comes from inmates and not chaplains, volunteers, or contractors (Schmallger and Smyrka, 2009, p. 383).

Identification of STGs

There has been much research on how correctional staff can identify gang members in STGs. They are similar in content.

There are three factors in labeling a group as a STG, according to Deputy Sheriff Loran Hatcher, Intelligence Coordinator for the Arlington County (VA) Sheriff's Office. They are (Cornelius, 2008, p. 110):

- Having a common name or common identifying signs (hand signs), colors, language or symbols. These are exhibited openly with other STG members and with a sense of pride.
- Having members or associates who either as individuals or members of a collective group engaging in or having been engaged in a pattern of gang activity, illegal activity, etc. and/or violating department rules.
- Having the potential to act in concert resulting in a threat or potential threat to staff, visitors, or to disrupt the secure and orderly operation of the correctional facility.

Research by George Wilcox in 1992 resulted in a six-point classification system to identify if a group is extreme. These points are:

1. They are absolutely certain that they have the truth; their way is the *only* way.
2. Some evil, conspiratorial group controls to a greater or lesser degree the United States.
3. The group hates their opponents openly. They make no secret of their animosity.
4. Group members have little or no faith in the democratic process. Compromise is scorned.

5. The group believes that its enemies are to be denied basic civil liberties; they do not deserve them.
6. Groups will irresponsibly accuse opponents and engage in "character assignation." Opponents will be charged with having wicked motives and agendas.
   (Mason III and Becker, 1994, p. 62)

Correctional officers must circulate among the inmate population, getting to know the inmates. Many do not subscribe to racist dogma, and having good interpersonal relations with COs can help to combat supremacist groups' activities.

Correctional officers must be trained to identify inmates as possible STG members. The research by Levinson and Ross is a good foundation for an effective checklist on STG identification:

1. *Self-admission by inmate*: Inmates may boast about gang affiliation, either among inmates in living areas or during an intake or classification interview.
2. *STG markings or tattoos*: Inmates who possess marks or tattoos such as gang emblems, colors, etc., are easily identifiable.
3. *Possession of STG paraphernalia*: Paraphernalia could be certain clothing and jewelry. For example, Laron Douglas (aka "Scoobie G") describes his "Gangster Disciple Nation" uniform: black sweatshirt over a long blue T-shirt, black tweed belt turned to the right, saggy black Levis, black ProModel cap turned right. The jewelry worn is a Turkish gold rope and a ring in the shape of a six-pointed star on the right index finger (Douglas, 1995, p. 45).
4. *Information from Law Enforcement*: Law enforcement sources do not mean only the police; there are many agencies that participate in gang intelligence. Information could be gathered from local police, neighboring agencies, probation and parole, the U.S. Marshal's service, the Federal Bureau of Investigation (FBI), the Bureau of Alcohol, Tobacco and Firearms (ATF) and the U.S. Bureau of Prisons.
5. *Information from Internal Investigations*: Some results of any investigation conducted regarding gang activities should be released to all sections who deal with inmates on a daily basis.
6. *Information from Confidential Informants*: Not all inmates want to be caught up in gang activities. Informant information must be initially taken seriously and confirmed.
7. *Inmate Mail/Outside Contacts*: While correctional officers cannot usually read private mail or listen to personal visits except by court order,

they can observe the visitors, especially if they are sporting gang colors or emblems. The outside of envelopes may have gang symbols drawn on them.

8. *Individual or Group Pictures*: Some inmate gang members are proud of their STG affiliations and/or the affiliation of friends. Their cells may contain photos of them or those close to them in gang pictures. These photos can be in plain view and can be easily seen by the officer. (Levinson, 1995)

In addition to this list, these groups assume that they have the absolute right to revolt or reform the "corruption" of the social system and members who are inspired or hailed are elevated to martyrdom or sainthood (Mason III and Becker, 1994, p. 62).

Tattoos and markings are excellent clues that an inmate is a member of an STG. Crude tattoos in black or dark blue ink often are done in prison, due to the lack of commercial dyes which are used on the outside. Tattoos are symbolic of gang affiliation and beliefs. Swastikas are symbolic of the Aryan Brotherhood; shamrocks or clovers represent the white race; skulls, demons and serpents state that the wearer is alienated from society's social values. The number of murders committed for the "cause" is indicated by the number of dots between the thumb and forefinger (Mason III and Becker, 1994, p. 62). A well-informed security network can get such information about STGs to the line staff.

To the correctional staff, STGs cannot be thought as basic white and black groups. There are Asian gangs consisting of Chinese, Korean and Vietnamese subgroups who form separate gangs. Asian gangs tend to keep to themselves and appear quiet and respectful. The number of Asian gangs in the U.S. jails is predicted to increase. Hispanic gangs are considered the most structured with leaders who tightly control operations and discipline (Ross, 1995).

A General Guide to Security Threat Groups (STGs)

Mexican Mafia: Formed in 1958, it is thought to be the most powerful gang in the California penal system. Membership is for life, restricted to Mexican Americans. Criminal activities include gambling, drugs, homosexual relations and crimes in the community such as murders ordered from prison.

Black Guerilla Family: Follows a revolutionary philosophy, its goal being to control the destiny of the black inmate through education about racism and advocating pride and dignity. It is highly organized and correctional authorities are its number one enemy. This group is responsible for serious murders and assaults on California correctional staff.

Christian Identity: Racist theology based on religion, which provides justification for all white supremacist groups. Christian Identity churches in jails and prisons serve to recruit members. Christian Identity members believe that non-whites are "mud people" and are on the same spiritual level as animals; Jews are Satan's descendants and are imposters; British people are true Israelites; and a race war which will destroy all non-whites is predicted in the Bible.

Black Gangs: Crips and Bloods: Very little formal structure and strong leadership. Members may act for themselves instead of the gangs. Correctional staff members enforcing prison rules are considered a personal affront. Members file many complaints and will not hesitate to use violence against inmates or staff.

[Adapted from: Ross, 1995 and Mason III and Becker, 1994, pp. 61–65 and Stinchcomb and Fox, 1999, p. 381]

In the mid 1980s, a new type of STG emerged—roving gangs of Vietnamese criminals who specialize in home invasion, car theft and robbery. What is different about this type of group is that they are loosely organized with 3–10 members, ages 16–25, have no group name and have no permanent leaders. Apprehension is difficult due to members using multiple identification and adults claiming to be juveniles (Carton, 1986, pp. C1, C5).

What can correctional staff do about STG activities? One positive trend in corrections has been the increase of informative studies and articles on STG activities (see References). This material contains some useful steps to curb STG activity. Correctional officers, both line staff and supervisors should:

- Have operating procedures and training for the recognition, secure housing, classification, and management of STGs.
- Implement gang intelligence units, or have a liaison with local, state and Federal law enforcement concerning STGs.
- Use tools at staff's disposal such as: Institutional Classification Committee (ICC) administrative hearings to segregate STG members and leaders, increase custody levels, restrict privileges, remove from programs and establish conditions of confinement such as CO escorts, restraints, etc.; enforce criminal laws, and use the facility disciplinary code to its full extent to segregate STG members on disciplinary segregation (see Chapter 8).
- In housing STG members, keep them apart as much as possible and determine who are not enemies from whom are.
- Be alert concerning recruiting by STG members, especially young, angry impulsive inmates.

- Aggressively and frequently pursue such existing security measures such as strip searches, cell shakedowns, incoming property searches, visitation monitoring, monitoring of STG inmates' commissary/financial accounts (big deposits may indicate a "payoff" for criminal activity inside the institution) etc. Prohibit visits to known STG members; restrict visitors if necessary (Ross, 1995).
- Monitor incoming and outgoing mail and telephone calls. Court orders may be needed. Inmate financial accounts should be monitored (Ross, 1995).
- Credits for good time and work time credits should be cancelled as a result of STG activity (Ross, 1995).
- *All* indicators of STG activity, such as tattoos and hate literature, should be photographed and documented. *All* behavior and activity should be documented by memorandum, incident report or log entry in the inmate's file (Mason III and Becker, 1994, p. 65).
- *All* material found in inmates' property, such as tattoo patterns, ink, material marked with tattoos, boots/heavy footwear (can be used for weapons), should be placed in the inmate's property, sent out at the inmate's expense, or if the inmate signs a waiver, destroyed (Mason III and Becker, 1994, p. 65).

The development of an STG intelligence network should consist of several components:

- A very detailed classification procedure that asks the inmate detailed questions about tattoos, markings, gang activities, etc. Also, the staff should ask the inmate such questions as (Mason III and Becker, 1994, p. 65):
  - Are you a racist?
  - Will/can you freely associate with members of other races and religious groups on an equal basis, including being housed with them?
  - Do you think that you have been a victim of political, racial or religious persecution? (Mason III and Becker, 1994, p. 65)
- A mechanism for trained STG intelligence personnel to analyze all STG information, recommend proactive strategies, and to regularly brief the institutional staff. Also, continuous training should be provided.

Progress is being made. For example, the New York City Department of Corrections initiated a gang tracking program that shares computerized data with other law enforcement agencies. Correctional officers collect intelligence on gangs and maintain a digitized photo data base. Gang members who commit crimes are aggressively prosecuted and the crimes are examined for intelligence gathering. The message to the inmate population is that gang violence *will not* be tolerated (Nadel, 1997, pp. 16–19).

Mentally Disordered Inmates

It is no secret that our jails and prisons house inmates that are mentally ill. Jails are often viewed by veteran COs as the biggest mental hospital in the community. Prison COs know that many inmates in their custody are mentally disordered or may deteriorate mentally due to incarceration.

The Scope of the Problem

Correctional officers should have a basic understanding of the scope of this problem. Mentally ill people are arrested, jailed, convicted and incarcerated. In a prison, the staff may have a warning that an inmate transferred to the prison is mentally disordered, if there is information communicated from the local jail from where he or she is being transferred. In a jail, COs get the offender, occasionally out of control, right from the scene of the arrest and off the street. The mental illness that the person is suffering from is more acute, but still as serious as a prison inmate with a mental disorder. Offenders may be off their medications, suffering from hallucination, delusions, paranoia, or have a disorder exacerbated from substance abuse. In a jail booking area, it is not uncommon to see and hear mentally ill offenders banging on cell doors, eating feces, screaming, refusing to obey staff instructions, talking to themselves, not talking, refusing to cooperate with medical staff, and refusing to eat and/or bathe.

The Bureau of Justice Statistics (BJS) has looked at the problem, and the statistics are interesting. In mid 2005, BJS stated that (James and Glaze, 2006 *Mental Health Problems of Prison and Jail Inmates*, pp. 1, 2, 10):

- Over half of all prison and jail inmates in the U.S. had a mental health problem
- Percentage wise, 56 percent of state prison inmates, 45 percent of Federal prison inmates and 64 percent of jail inmates reported having any mental health problem.
- Recent mental health histories were reported in 24 percent of state prison inmates, 14 percent of federal prison inmates and 21 percent of local jail inmates.
- Percentages of inmates reporting symptoms of mental health problems were 49 percent for state prison inmates, 40 percent of Federal prison inmates and 60 percent of local jail inmates.

- Psychotic disorders were examined by looking at the prevalence of delusions and hallucinations. According to the BJS researchers using a modified interview with the fourth edition of the Diagnostic and Statistical Manual of Mental Disorders, (DSM-IV), psychotic disorders are characterized by any signs of hallucinogens or delusions. An estimated 24 percent of jail inmates, 15 percent of state prison inmates and 10 percent of Federal inmates reported at least one symptom of psychotic disorder. *Delusions* are characterized as beliefs that other people are controlling their brain, their thoughts, can read their minds or are spying on them. *Hallucinations* are characterized as the offender sees things and/or hears voices that other people state that they do not hear or see.
- While the survey inquired as to what mental disorder symptoms inmates were experiencing since admission or in the past 12 months, persistent anger or irritability were reported by 37.8 percent of state prison inmates, 30.5 percent of federal inmates and 49.4 percent of jail inmates.
- Mentally disordered inmates have a significant rate of rule violations: 57.7 percent of state prison inmates, 40 percent of Federal prison inmates and 19 percent of local jail inmates.

Signs of Inmate Mental Disorders

According to the Virginia Department of Mental Health and Mental Retardation, mental disorders may be categorized as disturbances in behavior, thinking (cognitive) or emotion (affect). Schizophrenia and paranoia are cognitive disorders while mania and depression are affective (Virginia Department of Mental Health and Mental Retardation, 1986, p. II-5).

Symptoms may range in severity, depending on the seriousness of the disorder. The best rule to follow is that the inmate is not acting normally. Trust your gut—the inmate is not acting as a normal person would in the situation.

The following are general symptoms that may indicate mental illness, distinguished by degree and the inappropriateness of behavior for the surroundings and situation (Virginia Department of Mental Health and Mental Retardation, 1986, p. II-6):

anger
anxiety
confusion
delusions (for example they think they are God)
depression/suicidal thoughts and ideations

fear
hallucinations: hears voices, sees visions
manic behavior: non-stop energy
states that others are plotting against him or her
thinks others are plotting against him/her
unusual/unreal physical symptoms
withdrawal

Abuse of alcohol and drugs can contribute to odd behavior. The correctional officer, if possible, should try to ascertain if there is any history or signs of substance abuse and notify qualified staff. An inmate under the influence may state that "I can fly," "the light fixture talks to me," etc. They may be under the influence of a drug, alcohol, or both. Offenders suffering from mental illness in combination with substance abuse are *dually diagnosed*.

Some serious and life threatening medical conditions can produce symptoms similar to mental illness. All symptoms of possible mental illness must be reported to qualified medical staff for follow up and referral to the mental health staff. These medical conditions include (Virginia Department of Mental Health and Mental Retardation, 1986, p. II-6):

- Diabetes
- Severe infections
- Head injuries
- Medication side effects
- Usage of alcohol and other drugs
- High Blood Pressure
- Epilepsy
- Hardening of the arteries

Some inmates may suffer from "*prison psychosis*" or a form of mental disorder where the inmate cannot cope with prison life any longer. This could be due to prison routine, assault, fear of rape/assault, depression, falling apart of social life (family, marriage, etc.) and the deterioration of their lives on the outside such as losing their jobs, losing their homes, etc. Not all inmates who suffer from mental illness are new arrivals—the overwhelming problem of being incarcerated can contribute to a breakdown of mental health. COs must be aware of this and realize that being incarcerated can drive some inmates "over the edge" mentally. This type of episodic mental illness must not be treated in a "band aid" fashion, such as "get him to the shrink and they will give him a pill," but in a way that the mental health staff can help the inmate adjust long term (Allen, et al., 2007, p. 358).

A Thumbnail Guide to Mental Disorders

The science of psychology covers a wide range of material. Often, the correctional officer must be able to ascertain that something "isn't quite right" with an inmate. Ongoing training by qualified mental health staff is crucial to a well run facility.

The following will serve as a general guide which can be expanded upon by in-depth training:

Substance Abuse Disorders: Caused by alcohol and drug abuse which affects behavior and functioning. Depression can be induced by alcohol, heroin and its derivatives (narcotics), inhalants, barbiturates, etc. Stimulants (cocaine, amphetamines) can result in mania, while hallucinogens (LSD, PCP, marijuana) can alter one's sense of reality. As the person sobers up, the symptoms disappear.

Mood Disorders: Non-substance abuse and person's moods appear abnormal—depression (sadness, despondent), bipolar disorder (manic depression) and mania (rapid speech, agitation, no need for sleep). These disorders are treatable with drugs.

Anxiety Disorders: Involve being overly anxious and exhibiting repetitive behavior—general anxiety disorder (fear or worrying about non-specific problems), obsessive compulsive disorder (doing things a certain way such as washing hands repeatedly, etc.), post-traumatic stress disorder (PTSD), anxiety resulting from a past event like an assault, etc. and phobias such as fear of certain things (i.e., insects) or situations. These disorders are treatable with medication and counseling.

Thought Disorders: Offenders' thought processes are severely affected such as in schizophrenia; delusional disorders and paranoia are frequently aggravated by stress resulting from, for example, being incarcerated in a jail. Hallucinations may occur, such as someone or something seen and heard only by the inmate commanding suicide. Treatment includes anti-psychotic medications.

Sexual Disorders: Mental illness characterized by abnormal sexual behavior such as exhibitionism, voyeurism, frotteurism and sadism. Information concerning these disorders needs to be kept confidential to ensure the safety of the inmate.

Personality Disorders: Five that are of concern to the correctional officer are: anti-social (deceitful, lack of remorse, lack of respect for others), borderline personality disorder (lacks self-identity, may act suicidal, empty feelings), histrionic personality (draws attention to self through physical appearance, seductiveness, etc.), narcissistic per-

sonality disorders (overblown sense of self, being special) and para-
noid personality disorders (believe they are being used, distrust people, hold grudges, feel like they are being attacked).
[Adapted from: "Identifying and Referring Inmates with Mental Disorders. A Guide for Correctional Staff," by Gary L. Lupton, *American Jails*, May–June, 1996, pp. 49–52]

Handling of the Mentally Disordered Inmates

Documentation is of primary importance in the handling of mentally ill
inmates. Staff should document in writing through reports, logs, memos, etc.,
all observations of behavior and symptoms of mentally ill inmates; the more
information is known and shared, the more effective the management of the
inmate will be. Any inmate exhibiting signs of mental illness or showing behavior that is "not quite right" should immediately be referred to the mental
health staff in the facility and watched very closely. However, some jails do not
have full-time mental health personnel. In such cases, arrangements must be
made with local community mental health centers or nearby hospitals to have
a qualified mental health therapist come in to assess inmates. Under no circumstances should correctional officers diagnose inmates; they should only
report what they observe. CO observations and well written reports are the
crucial first lines of dealing with mentally disordered inmates.

Inmates who are believed to be behaving irrationally due to a mental disorder should be housed near an officer's or medical post and checked at least
every fifteen minutes or sooner if thought to be necessary. Closed circuit television and audio systems should not be a substitute for "eyeballing" the inmate
personally and frequently.

Inmates who are suspected to be mentally ill should be treated with caution. Though the inmate may be on medication and/or in treatment, his/her
behavior may be unpredictable. Caution is a must. Expect the unexpected.
Also, to keep the inmate on a calm level, correctional officers should speak to
inmates calmly, listen to what they have to say and not be sarcastic and condescending. COs should realize that the mentally ill process communications
and the interactions with others much differently than the normal person. Patience is a key factor.

The Developmentally Disabled Offender

A recent development in the subject of mentally disordered inmates is the study of the *developmentally disabled offender* or "mentally retarded." These inmates are characterized by low intellectual

ability (IQ) and show an inability in social or life skills. Estimates of the rate of developmentally disabled inmates in the general inmate population run from 3 to 10 percent.

Developmentally disabled offenders may distrust the system or become angry when asked to read or sign something. They do not understand what is happening to them. For example, in South Carolina, out of forty-five such inmates who were evaluated, seven did not know what the word "guilty" meant.

Guidelines for correctional officers include observing appearances such as clothing and hygiene for unusual characteristics. Also, the inmate may have problems with motor skills such as using a pen. Communications should be calm and clear and precautions should be taken against the inmate from becoming a victim for predators. Referrals concerning such inmates should be made to the mental health staff, courts and attorneys.

[Adapted from: "Working with the Developmentally Disabled in Jail, by Wendy R. Jones, *American Jails*, Nov–Dec, 1995, pp. 16–20]

The author had an experience with a developmentally disabled offender, a young male in his 30s. He was arrested for assaulting a counselor in a group home and was brought to the jail. The classification staff with mental health personnel housed the young man in a cell next to the receiving medical station, in a well traveled section of the jail. He was frequently checked on by staff until the charges were disposed of and was released to his family. At a local meeting of the county Mental Health Committee, the author explained to the board that though it was unfortunate that this man was placed in jail, pro active and humane management kept him safe until release.

Female Offenders

More attention has been devoted in recent years to the problems of the female inmate. The basic statistical data for female offenders has been discussed in Chapter 6. Correctional officers realize that some female inmates can be as streetwise, conniving and anti authority as male inmates.

Profile of Female Offenders

Recent studies have resulted in a national profile of the typical female offender. In May, 2005, the National Institute of Corrections (NIC) published a report on women offenders. A national profile indicates that female offenders (Bloom, Owen and Covington, 2005, p. 3):

- are disproportionately women of color.
- are in their early to mid thirties.
- are most likely to be convicted of a drug related offense.
- have fragmented family histories; other family members may also be involved in the criminal justice system.
- have survived as adults and/or children sexual and/or emotional abuse.
- have significant substance abuse problems.
- have multiple substance abuse and mental health problems.
- are unmarried mothers of minor children.
- are individuals with a high school diploma or GED; however many have limited vocational training and sporadic work histories.

While females have been traditionally viewed as the "fairer sex," veteran correctional officers know that there are female inmates who are as hard core and streetwise as males. However, female inmates should be encouraged to enroll in vocational and educational programs while incarcerated. Since many are mothers, such rehabilitation programs can assist in maintaining a crime-free life for them and their children. Correctional officers must remember that family ties are important and not being able to see their children or participate in their upbringing can lead to despair and depression.

Programs for Females

Conditions of confinement and programs for female inmates are improving. Class action lawsuits filed in courts on the behalf of female inmates can have an effect. At the Huron Valley Correctional Institution in Ypsilanti, Michigan, female inmates could receive minimal job training as housekeepers, cooks and craft workers—the traditional "female" jobs. Male inmates in the Michigan system could choose from *twenty* job training courses such as auto repair, air conditioning service and repair, commercial baking and drafting. A 1979 class action suit improved jobs training for females. In 1981, another class action suit improved conditions for females at the Women's Prison in Rehee Valley, Kentucky. Until the suit, new inmates could not set their hair or display photos of their children in their cells. By 1987, the availability of programs for women was not at the same level for male inmates, but conditions had improved (Rubin, 1987, pp. 36–42).

Programming for female offenders has improved in the areas of parenting, substance abuse and education. One of the main tools in female inmates' rehabilitation have been programs that allow them to have contact with their children, especially newborn children, either born in custody or right before incarceration. Often the burden of raising a female inmate's children falls on her relatives, such as aunts, uncles, grandparents, etc. Programs that promote the bond between mother and children should be used as an incentive to stay crime free once released.

Examples of programs allowing female inmates to maintain positive contact with their children and learn parenting skills are the Children's Visitation Program at the women's prison in Plymouth, Michigan. This program recognizes that the children of inmates are angry, confused and need help. Family Foundations is a California prison program where non violent female offenders can live with their minor children in a community based drug treatment program. In New York the Bedford Hills Correctional Facility opened the nation's first prison nursery over 100 years ago; today its parenting program continues to show good results with only a 10 percent repeat offender rate, much lower than the 52 percent recidivism of inmates overall (Drummond, 2000, p. 108).

Managing Females

Correctional officers should be aware that females have different medical and behavioral issues than males. They must be supervised and treated differently in some ways. Pregnancy and medical issues such as menstruation can make incarceration extremely uncomfortable.

The problem of being the incarcerated mother of minor children can cause much stress and anxiety; the lines of contact to the family responsible for caring for the children should be encouraged to be kept open. While male inmates may become angrier in an incompatible situation and may act out physically such as fighting, females tend to be more vocal in their complaints to staff. However, this in no way suggests that females cannot be violent or combative with each other or the staff. COs must be also on their guard.

The inmate population in our nation's correctional facilities is predominantly male and female housing can be limited. However, problem female inmates are subject to administrative and disciplinary segregation if necessary as well as being charged with criminal offenses. Sometimes the traditional "fair sex" cannot be given any favoritism when locked up.

Finally there is the issue of privacy. Staff sexual misconduct is a problem and in most states, carnal knowledge of a female inmate is against the law. COs should be careful in giving female inmates their privacy—such as while dressing, in the shower or using the toilet. Having other staff present when making rounds, conducting themselves professionally and announcing "man on the floor" are several tools that can prevent accusations of misconduct.

Juvenile Offenders

To the correctional officers in our nation's jails and prisons, some juvenile offenders are as hard core and streetwise as some adult offenders. The plan of attack on juvenile crime has been in the past several years to certify more juvenile offenders as adults so they can be tried and punished in adult courts. The debate continues as to whether this approach is the right answer.

In 1986, juvenile justice experts recommended strategies to deal with the juvenile offender. Upon release, juvenile offenders should be given effective caseworker attention in community-based programs with positive peer group activities and responsible citizens acting as role models. Chronic offenders should receive long-term incarceration if other strategies fail. Courts, schools and juveniles' families must work with the offender together. If the juvenile's family situation is negative and contributes to a lack of supervision and crime, the youth should be placed in foster care. Finally, courts must sentence consistently and fairly. The juvenile should not be able to "skate by" on an offense and manipulate the system by false promises of rehabilitation (Santoi, 1986, p. 16–17).

If a juvenile is transferred by the court to an adult jail from a juvenile facility for security or behavioral reasons, the jail staff should find out as much as possible about the offender's criminal history, institutional record and any behavioral problems.

Management of Juveniles

Handling juveniles in adult facilities is not easy. "Juvies" may be impulsive and immature. Some are drug abusers and gang members. Problems associated with these offender characteristics must be dealt with the same as with adult offenders. Hard core juveniles also engage in disciplinary violations and get into confrontations with staff. Young offenders need daily recreation and leisure activities; their energy levels are higher than adult offenders. Correctional officers must take time and exhibit patience in dealing with juveniles due to immaturity and emotionally not being able to handle the stresses of incarceration. While a juvenile may be cocky when first incarcerated, a realization may set in that once the facility doors close, he or she has hit the "big time" and the situation is now much more serious.

Juveniles confined to adult jails are generally handled and housed separately from adult inmates by sight and sound. Inmates need social contact and juveniles are no exception. Staff should check juveniles at least every fifteen minutes and should watch for signs of suicidal behavior, despair and depression. Suicides of juveniles in adult jails occur at an alarming rate. According to the late expert on inmate suicides, Joseph Rowan, who wrote and researched extensively on the subject, juvenile offenders commit suicide at a rate nearly eight times higher than those confined in separate juvenile facilities (Cornelius, 2008, pp. 278–279).

Dealing with juvenile offenders takes skills above and beyond the normal attributes of the correctional officer. Keeping in mind that juveniles emotionally and chronologically are younger than the average adult inmates, COs should exercise patience and concern. Also, juveniles may have adjustment problems and extra time may be needed when conversing with juveniles. Some juvenile offenders are immature and engage in harassment and horseplay. A strong measure of control including enforcement of the facility disciplinary rules may be necessary. COs should realize that many juvenile offenders have serious criminal histories, are streetwise and may rebel against correctional authorities, including engaging in physical resistance and assault. It is necessary at times to exert physical control and force on juveniles.

Finally, COs must keep in mind that juveniles because of their age may be victimized and harassed by adult inmates. Jails have a "no contact with adults" rule or separation from adults by sight and sound. However, if a juvenile is incarcerated as an adult after adjudication, their youth, size and possible lack of experience being incarcerated should not allow them to be a victim inside the facility.

Elderly Inmates

Due to the current trends of abolishing parole and handing down tougher sentences, the fact that inmates will be growing old in prison is becoming a concern among corrections professionals. These trends will result in young inmates getting convicted and doing time into middle age and beyond for serious crimes. The correctional officer reading this book should examine the number of inmates older than age 50 incarcerated in the United States (see Chapter 6). Some of these inmates commit crimes at an older age, while others start their criminal careers earlier in life, get convicted, and will grow old and either die in prison or be released at a much older age. For purposes of training and reading this book, they will be referred to as "older inmates"—age 50 and older.

Older Inmates: Housing and Medical Concerns

There are definitive concerns about the management of older inmates. Older inmates may be vulnerable to attack by younger, predatory inmates. Older inmates cannot be housed with inmates who are younger, less mature and noisier. One veteran correctional officer said that in the jail he was frequently approached by older inmates—men and women—asking to be relocated to a cellblocks housing older, more mature and quieter inmates.

Older inmates may be experiencing problems in two areas. One is depression, as families become estranged because older elatives are locked up at a time in their lives where normal seniors are retired and enjoying life. Secondly, if an older person is incarcerated, their spouses and relatives may pass away or cut off communications with them; this is a sad situation that can lead to depression.

Corrections systems have to look for different methods and approaches for dealing with inmates who are aging in our nation's correctional facilities. As the baby boomer generation becomes older behind bars, correctional staff and COs will have to deal with them and the problems they that they encounter. Statistics from the U.S. Justice Department reported in 2003 indicate that the number of criminal offenders age 55 and older has increased 85 percent since 1995, and all signs point to a continued increase. Several states, including Virginia and Maryland, have operated under a *medical parole* system, which means an inmate can be released for medical reasons after serving a portion of his or her sentence. In Virginia, this system in operation since 2001, stipulates that a geriatric offender can be paroled at age 65 with 5 years of incarceration or at age 60 with a minimum of 10 years of incarceration. In Maryland, offenders can request a release for circumstances related to health care (Gaseau, 2004).

Incarcerating older offenders is costly. Once imprisoned, they are no longer eligible for Medicare or Medicaid, the medical assistance programs were costs are paid by the federal government. The correctional agencies pick up the burden of medical costs. From fiscal year 2005 to 2006, prison health care costs, particularly the costs for older inmates, were largely responsible for a 10 percent increase in spending in state prisons. Some researchers estimate that it costs more to house older inmates than the $18,000 to $31,000 annual costs of housing an inmate. Medical problems of elderly and aging inmates mirror the same ailments as those in the outside population: Alzheimer's, dementia, memory loss, senility, cardio-vascular disease, stomach problems, kidney disease, bladder problems, arthritis, diabetes, cancer, bad backs and joints, vision problems, loss of hearing, etc. Some older inmates walk with walkers and canes or use wheelchairs. The list of medications required for these inmates can be long and expensive (Associated Press, 2007).

Management Guidelines for Older Inmates

Correctional officers are responsible legally and morally, through sworn oath, to provide for the safest housing possible for the inmates in their custody. As a result, older inmates require good management practices, such as (Gaseau, 2004):

- Being aware that due to medical and mental health issues, older inmates may not move or react as fast as younger inmates. Patience from staff is a factor.
- Being aware that older inmates may need assistance with bathing, walking, dressing, eating, toilet functions, etc.
- Having clear communication with the facility medical staff in referring to them older inmates who are having difficulties.
- Referring older inmates suspected of having mental health problems such as depression, Alzheimer's, etc. to the mental health staff.
- Realizing that older inmates may be concerned with family matters, such as spouses that are ill, facing loss of income, etc. or are about to be released. Such situations and inmates should be reported to the facility social worker if available, or to the local social service agencies or organizations that assist inmates who are being released.
- Prevent victimization of older inmates by other, predatory and violent inmates, from such acts as stealing food, stealing commissary, harassment, assault, teasing, etc.

Medical Issues

The state of an inmate's health is important to all who work and live in the institution. Inmates have a right to basic medical care. More importantly, some illnesses and ailments can spread throughout an overcrowded facility to both other inmates and staff. Veteran COs can tell stories of the spread of colds, flu, etc. throughout inmate living areas.

Some inmates receive good medical care only when they come into a jail or prison. Alcoholics and drug addicts may be malnourished or suffer from various medical problems resulting from their lifestyle. Some inmates have bad teeth, skin problems, colds, skin or dental abscesses, etc., because they do not take care of themselves. As one veteran correctional officer states:

> *I have seen inmates come into jail with rashes, sores, bleeding gums, rotten teeth, infected ears, severe colds and flu, venereal diseases, lice, etc. It*

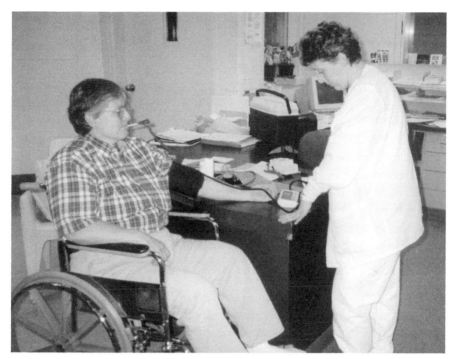

Most jails and prisons have qualified medical staff in order to treat a variety of medical problems and physical conditions. Clarke-Frederick-Winchester (VA) Regional Adult Detention Center.

appears that the only time some inmates see a medical practitioner is when they are locked up.

While a very detailed examination of inmates' medical afflictions would take up a book in itself, this section will consist of a general overview of management techniques when dealing with serious inmate health problems, such as AIDS, tuberculosis, hepatitis or any serious medical condition.

AIDS (Acquired Immune Deficiency Syndrome): AIDS is a disease resulting from the Human Immunodeficiency Virus (HIV). AIDS is a blood-borne disease and it defeats the human body's ability to fight off infections and diseases. Some people become infected with the HIV virus and show no signs of illness for years while others become sick and die in a short period of time. Individuals infected with HIV have a 50% greater chance of developing "full blown AIDS" over a period of 10–20 years. AIDS infections vary from pneumonia, cancers and central nervous system disorders (Hyzer, 1989, p. 2).

Tuberculosis (TB): Mycobacterium Tuberculosis is spread through the air and an infected inmate can easily spread the disease to others in a crowded living area. The immediate isolation of an inmate with TB can interrupt its spread to others. Inmates who are infected with the HIV virus, are substance abusers or come from a low socioeconomic class where they did not take care of themselves health wise are prime candidates for contracting TB. All inmates should be screened for active TB or latent TB exposure through a skin test. Positive results should be checked with a chest x ray within 72 hours after the skin test is interpreted. All correctional staff having close contact with inmates should be regularly checked for TB exposure. Besides a medication regimen, the best precaution is medical isolation of the infected inmate and the checking as much as possible of all inmates that he or she has lived around, interacted with, etc. (Bales, ed., 1997, p. 96–98).

Hepatitis: Viral hepatitis is caused by five viruses: hepatitis A, B, C, D and E. The hepatitis B (HBV) and C (HCV) strains are transmitted by needle stick exposures to blood and/or sexual contact. Hepatitis D (HDV) is also transmitted in this manner, but only to persons infected with HBV. The A and E strains are spread by fecal/oral route and a chronic infection does not occur. HBV infection damages the liver which becomes the site of infection and reproduction of the virus. Correctional workers have recognized the dangers of HBV infection for years and more information about HCV has become available. Correctional officers today can be vaccinated against Hepatitis B (Bales, ed., 1997, pp. 93–94).

The three diseases discussed here—HIV/AIDS, TB and Hepatitis B and C represent dangerous diseases in correctional facilities and correctional workers must always keep in mind how they are transmitted and take preventative measures.

HIV can be spread by blood to blood contact by infected needles or by infected blood coming into contact with an open cut or wound. It can also be spread by sexual fluids to blood contact, primarily through anal sexual intercourse or, as is now being documented, vaginal intercourse. While the HIV can be found in other bodily fluids, it is almost always found to be present in blood and sexual fluids (Bales, ed., 1997, p. 95). The HIV organism does not live long outside the body. The primary transmission method is intimate transfer of certain bodily fluids, particularly from inside an infected person to the bloodstream of another (Hyzer, 1989, p. 3). Homosexual/bi-sexual men, persons who engage in casual, unsafe sex and intravenous drug users all run the risk of getting HIV.

TB is spread through breathing the air that contains the bacteria put there by an infected person. Hepatitis B and C are primarily spread by needle stick exposures to infected blood and sexual contact. However, HBV has been found in lower concentrations in semen, saliva, vaginal fluid and sweat (Bales, ed., 1997, pp. 93–94). A good rule to remember is TB by air, and HIV, HBV and HCV by exposure primarily to blood or sharps (needles) containing infected blood.

All inmates entering a correctional facility must be asked about their medical history at a minimum. If an inmate is sick or is showing the symptoms of a serious disease, he or she should be examined by a qualified medical staff person as soon as possible. Inmates should be tested for TB and if there are symptoms present or they request it, HIV/AIDS. In a jail, the turnover rate of inmates is high; many are released before a medical exam can be conducted. In a prison, decisions about treatment and housing can be made with the information gained in a complete medical exam.

Medical Operations

Medical operations in any correctional facility have several basic, critical components. The first is screening, where all inmates that enter the facility are seen by a trained and qualified medical staff person, sometimes informally called a "medic." A medical interview is conducted. If the inmate refuses to cooperate—and some in a sense of bravado do not—he or she will be housed in a receiving area until they do cooperate. The facility medical staff cannot risk exposure of diseases and contagious medical conditions to other staff and inmates. State correctional standards, along with standards from the American Correctional Association and the National Commission on Correctional Health Care mandate screening procedures. The CO may notice a medical problem or condition when the inmate is booked in—and must notify the medical staff immediately. Also, suspected mental disorders or unusual behavior must be reported to the medical staff for follow up screening and referral to mental health. COs should be familiar with referring procedures.

Every inmate is different medically. While jails screen offenders "right off the street," prisons have the advantage to have newly arrived inmates' medical histories and files from the last facility where they were incarcerated. A partial list of medical problems that must be addressed with a medical screening include (Duncan, 2008, p. 49):

- On prescription medications or having a medical condition and is without medication
- Under the influence of drugs or alcohol
- Withdrawals from drugs or alcohol
- Head injuries
- Cuts, abrasions or injuries from the scene of the arrest (should be treated at a hospital before taking custody)
- Suspected mental disorder
- Diabetes

- Physically handicapped
- Communicable disease
- Sexually transmitted disease
- Respiratory ailment (asthma, etc).
- Hygiene issues: lice, scabies, etc.
- Suicidal ideation
- Heart problems

Secondly, all facilities' medical staff operates some version of *"sick call"* a scheduled procedure where inmates who complain of medical problems can see the nurse or facility physician. Some jails charge the inmate a fee for this service with payment coming from the inmates' financial account. Placing the inmate in a dispensary or in an outside hospital under guard may be necessary if the medical condition warrants it and authorization is given by the facility physician. Security and transport must be strict as some inmates have escaped or attempted escape from hospitals. Correctional officers *must* be at a heightened level of security. Hospitals and doctors' offices contain many items lying around that the inmate can pick up and bring back into the institution.

Medication can be dispensed by calling the inmate to the medical station or by the medical staff making rounds or "medication [med] runs" to the inmate housing areas. Medication can be placed into envelopes with the inmate's name and dispensed or can come ready to dispense in a "blister pack" assigned to each inmate. The medication is "popped" out and given to the inmate. Over the counter (OTC) medications such as headache remedies, antacids, etc., are sold through the inmate commissary in many facilities.

Giving an inmate a pill and proceeding on is not thorough security for a medical staff person. Inmates have been known to fake taking their medications, and then hoarding them for sale to other inmates or taking them in a large quantity later in order to commit suicide. Medical staff must exercise patience and caution, observing the inmate taking the pill/liquid, and then observing an open mouth to make sure the substance was ingested properly.

The CO and Inmate Medical Problems

The medical staff cannot be in every inmate housing area all the time; the most present staff person is the correctional officer. COs should act proactively, namely:

- Be trained in first aid (responder) and cardio-pulmonary resuscitation (CPR) per agency policy. This requires training conducted by qualified staff, written and practical tests for proficiency and regular refresher classes including recertification. Training includes the usage of automatic defibrillators, CPR masks, eyewash apparatus, etc.

- Inform inmates as to facility procedures on notifying staff when they have a medical emergency or illness.
- Know the procedures for informing medical staff and mental health staff of a medical/mental/dental condition concerning an inmate, especially in emergencies.
- Know the facility policy and procedures for sick call and medication distribution, especially taking actions in searching inmates and living areas for hoarded medications.
- Report in writing as necessary all observations and information pertaining to an inmate's medical and mental health situation.
- Ensure that inmates receive their medications or are seen by medical staff if required for their well being.
- Be familiar with and do not deviate from security procedures when transporting inmates to outside medical services or to a hospital. Inmates might wish to have visitors in the hospital, but prudent procedures dictate NO.
- Ensure that inmates are seen by medical staff after a physical altercation, use of force incident or any kind of assault, including sexual assault.

Culturally Diverse Inmates

Correctional facilities have no control concerning what foreign born or ethnic inmates become incarcerated. At the local jail level, for example, a Latino inmate who speaks little or no English could be booked in for drunk driving, followed an hour later by a Vietnamese person charged with assault. Rather than concern oneself with the current illegal immigration problem, the debate over border security and the fact that many in the U.S. are from other countries and do not speak English, correctional officers should accept reality and realize that some inmates come from foreign or culturally diverse groups, they may be in the U.S. illegally, they do get arrested, some may not speak English, and their incarceration must be safe and secure just as for inmates who are American and speak English.

The "Smooth" Shift

For correctional officers to effectively deal with inmates of different cultures and ethnic groups, they must make an effort to understand them. This can only be accomplished through cultural diversity training. Law enforcement officers, including corrections personnel, need to understand the cultural aspects of inmates' communication and behavior. If they do not, frustrations will mount as staffs ignore the fact that inmates come in all cultures (Weaver, 1992, p. 1). All correctional officers want to work a "smooth" shift—one where inmates will not feel hesitant in communicating with officers, there is back and forth communications between inmates and COs, and culturally diverse inmates will view COs in a positive way and as persons who care about their safety and welfare.

For example, inmates of other cultures may find adjusting to being incarcerated difficult. There could be a language barrier or the impatience of correctional officers in dealing with a foreign inmate or with one who does not speak English. Inmates may not understand the language or words—but they will understand its inflection and tone. An inmate from another foreign or culturally diverse group who is treated in a stereotypical, bigoted and condescending way by some COs may not communicate information about being assaulted, other inmates being victimized or assaulted, problems in the cellblock, harassment or personal problems. He or she may view COs as negative people that do not really care about inmates.

What must be developed is a mind set of COs putting themselves in other people's [foreign/ethnic inmate] "cultural shoes." This concept is called *cultural empathy*. A key point to remember is that America is not "all the same;" we are a diverse society (Weaver, 1992, p. 4).

Here is an example of misreading an inmate's behavior due to a lack of cultural empathy from a jail officer:

> *I remember a time where we booked in a Vietnamese inmate, about 30–35 years old. He did not speak English. We noticed that he kept turning away food. He was charged with a felony and we all thought he was on a hunger strike. After a few days, the classification staff managed to get a Vietnamese interpreter as we had no Vietnamese speaking officers on the department at the time. Through the interpreter, we discovered that the inmate had only been in the United States a very short time and could not digest American food. He requested rice; the jail cook made up a batch. The inmate ate and started to interact more with the staff.*

Correctional officers tend to "lump" foreign inmates together by using common terms—Hispanics, Asians, etc. However, most Asians prefer *not* to be called Orientals, but by their nationality, such as Korean-American, Japanese-American, etc. Instead of "Hispanic," some Spanish speaking inmates prefer "Chicano" (Mexican-American), Latino (Central American), or El Salvadoran, Costa Rican, etc. American Indians do not like the term "Native American" because it is an invention of the United States government. They prefer

"American Indian" or being called by their trial ancestry such as Sioux, Chero-kee, etc. The terms African-American and black American are used often; younger people prefer African-American (Weaver, 1992, p. 6).

It is impossible in this book to cover all aspects of all the different cultures and ethnic backgrounds of inmates. It is impossible to know all of the cultural practices of a diverse population. Training must be afforded to all correctional staff who encounters inmates from different ethnic backgrounds. Staff must not develop an attitude of *ethnocentrism* or a belief that one's own culture is "in-herently superior." Inmates should not be viewed as an inferior class of people (Fernandez, 1992). In general, training should focus on these points:

1. People from different cultures can react in different ways to interac-tions with staff. For example, an Arab inmate may be reluctant to talk to an American correctional officer sitting cross-legged with a shoe near the inmate's face or having his feet up on the desk. Americans usually do not casually touch each other, but in Italian or Spanish cul-tures, it is acceptable (Weaver, 1993).

2. In some cultures, families may cut off relations with the inmate. In Asian families, individualism and rights of individuals are secondary to the collective good. To bring attention to oneself, especially criminal ac-tions, is shameful to the family or group. The family bears the shame of the wrongdoer, and this is a terrible burden. The offender feels this shame also, feeling personal weakness (Grubb and Crews in Toth, Crews, and Burton, 2008, p. 76). One jail officer recalled a young Vietnamese inmate on suicide watch. He was getting out in 90 days, which would have been good news to a non Asian inmate. However, he has never told his family that he was in jail; his sister had lied for him to the family concerning his whereabouts, and had even gone as far as receiving his letters and re mailing them to his parents using a false address. He could not face release and confronting his family with the truth as they were very traditional.

3. Ethnicity or common culture traditions or a sense of identity becomes important to the inmate. They become loyal to other inmates in a similar culture. For example, Hispanic inmates are loyal to their eth-nic subgroup (Mexican, etc.) for brotherhood and protection (Fer-nandez, 1992).

4. Training should stress that there is no place in corrections for ethno-centrism or prejudice. Being bigoted is not a good practice for cor-rectional officers in overcrowded institutions where staff and inmates must engage in positive interactions and communications.

5. Cultural diversity training cannot be "glossed over" in roll calls. Seminars of at least two to four hours are recommended. Community leaders from ethnic groups in the community could provide training to correctional staff.
6. Staff who use racist and bigoted slurs, harass or ignore inmates from culturally diverse groups should be counseled, reprimanded and disciplined if necessary.

Some correctional officers are of the opinion that foreigners and people from different cultures should learn English and the ways of our (American) culture. One veteran in-service instructor informs his classes that it is counter productive to be overly angry or concerned with that. He tells them that COs have to deal with whomever is incarcerated; no matter if they are foreign or culturally diverse. He has also heard COs speaking in a condescending fashion to inmates from other cultural or ethnic groups and says that even if the language is not understood by the inmate, the inflection and tone of the remarks are. This behavior is not good, he continues, in a facility where good interpersonal relations between inmates and staff can greatly promote a positive, less tense atmosphere. Finally, he asks the class a question: if they were under arrest in a foreign country, they would want the person holding them to know a little about Americans—and respect them.

Use of Interpreters

When encountering a foreign inmate that speaks little or no English, it is advantageous to have the services of an interpreter. In some agencies, a memorandum is distributed to all staff listing the staff personnel that are be fluent in a particular language, the contact phone numbers of organizations in the community that could provide interpreters either by phone or in person or any persons fluent in another language that may work in the courts.

Correctional officers using interpreters should use their services not only for routine procedures like booking, classification interviews, etc., but for more unusual events such as medical emergencies, sick call, suicide intervention and any situation that calls for further investigation, especially concerning the inmate's welfare and safety.

Effective guidelines for using interpreters include the following (Carrera, 2003):

- Do not be rushed; pace it. Allow the conversation to take place in a private area if possible.
- The interpreter cannot omit or add anything to what the inmate is saying. The interpretation should be word for word, even foul language, as that may be relevant.

- Keep the interpreter on track and focused.
- Interpreters should not give any personal advice as that may interfere with the duties of the CO. Advice should only be given at the direction of the correctional staff.
- Interpreters should not give personal opinions, but there may be times when COs may ask interpreters what they think. The interpreters generally know the culture, especially if they are of the same ethnic background or are from or have spent time in the country of origin.
- Written translations may be necessary for staff review, watching for intent and tone.

Summary

Correctional staff must deal daily with many different types of inmates, each with their own unique characteristics and problems. Substance abusers, suicidal inmates, security threat groups, mentally disordered, females, elderly, juveniles, foreign, and inmates with medical problems must all be understood and managed, keeping in mind the welfare of the inmate and the safety of the CO. Each of these groups exhibit symptoms and signs; the CO is the first line in managing them and taking the first steps in handling whatever adjustment issues there are as well as notifying the proper staff for follow up.

Substance abusers can be "high" on alcohol, drugs or both and the CO must notify medical staff so as the effects and the withdrawals that inmates suffer can be managed. Suicidal inmates cannot be ignored; COs must take precautions against self harm by the inmate and report what they see to the medical and mental health staff. Positive interpersonal intervention can work to prevent suicides. Mental disorders can be wide ranging and the inmates must be seen by qualified staff, carefully observed and observations documented. COs must play it safe, as inmate behavior is unpredictable.

Security threat groups include gangs, racial supremacist groups and terror organizations. Besides certain behaviors and signs, the actions of these groups pose definitive threats to security. COs have tools varying from gang intelligence units to enforcing the criminal and disciplinary codes in the facility.

Female inmates pose problems due to substance abuse and being mothers of dependent children. The management of female inmates has improved as more is being revealed about them and how they adjust to incarceration. Older inmates are increasing in number as our society becomes more conservative in sentencing offenders to longer sentences. Their problems must be handled, namely medical and mental health issues as well as victimization by younger inmates.

Juveniles require special handling, especially concerning suicide. Some are as bad as adult inmates, even though their chronological age is young. Foreign inmates should not be lumped together in a group. COs should not practice bigotry and ethnocentrism. Having good and respectful relations with culturally diverse inmates promotes a safer atmosphere in the facility.

Medically, AIDs, HIV, hepatitis and TB all pose a threat to the correctional officer, but training has improved greatly. COs are responsible for ensuring that inmate medical needs are addressed and being proactive is a good management tool.

Review Questions

1. What are several signs of alcohol and drug abuse?
2. What are drug and alcohol withdrawal signs?
3. What are the four types of suicidal inmates?
4. Name several identifying criteria to determine the identification of an STG.
5. Identify four symptoms of suspected mental illness.
6. Discuss the problems that females face when incarcerated.
7. What are some concerns about older and elderly inmates?
8. What are some tools that COs can use to manage juvenile offenders?
9. What are some inmate medical problems that can be addressed with a medical screening?
10. Discuss guidelines for the use of interpreters.

Terms/Concepts

cold turkey	gang member
criminal street gang	hallucinations
cultural empathy	medical parole
delusions	prison psychosis
developmentally disabled offender	restricted issue (RI)
dually diagnosed	security threat groups (STGs)
ethnocentrism	sick call
gang intelligence units	therapeutic communities

References

Allen, Harry, Edward J. Latessa, Ph.D., Bruce S. Ponder and Clifford Simonsen Ph.D. (2007). *Corrections in America: An Introduction, Eleventh Edition.* Upper Saddle River: Pearson Prentice Hall. For more gang information, *see also:* American Correctional Association (1993). *Gangs in Correctional Facilities.* Laurel: American Correctional Association; Reginald Wilkinson, M. Meyer and T. Urwin (1996). *Ohio Prison Gangs: A Counterfeit Community.* Columbus: Ohio Department of Rehabilitation and Correction and *Major Prison Gangs.* Security Threat Group Intelligence Unit, Florida Department of Corrections, www.dc.state.fl.us.

Associated Press. (2007, September 29). Aging Inmates Clogging Nation's Prisons. AOL News [Online] Available: www.aol.news.com/.

Bales, Don, (Ed.). (1997). *Corrections Officer Resource Guide 3rd Ed.* Lanham: American Correctional Association.

Bloom, Barbara, Owen, Barbara and Stephanie Covington. (2005, May). *Gender Responsive Strategies for Women Offenders.* Washington, DC: National Institute of Corrections.

Carrera, Angie. Cultural Diversity Seminar. Fairfax County Government, VA. 10/24/03.

Carton, Barbara. (1986, September 25). Roving Vietnamese Bands Seen as New Crime Pattern. *Washington Post,* pp. C1, C5.

Cornelius, Gary F. (2008). *The American Jail: Cornerstone of Modern Corrections.* Upper Saddle River: Pearson Prentice Hall.

Cornelius, Gary F. (1996). *Jails in America: An Overview of Issues 2nd Ed.* Lanham: American Correctional Association.

Cozzone, Chris. (1995, March). Gangbangers Speak Out, Part I. *Prison Life,* pp. 44–55.

Douglas, Laron. (1995, March). In the Mind of a True Disciple. *Prison Life,* pp. 46–48.

Drummond, Tammerlin. (2000, November 6). Mothers in Prison. *Time,* pp. 106–108.

Duncan, Peria. (2008). *Correctional Officer Resource Guide: Fourth Edition.* Alexandria: American Correctional Association.

Fernandez, Victor. (1992, Winter). Cultural Diversity Training in the Correctional System. *Journal of Correctional Training,* pp. 11–12.

Gaseau, Michelle. Caring for the Aging Inmate: Solutions for Corrections. Corrections.com [Online]. Available: http://www.corrections.com/ (Accessed December 6, 2004).

Grubb, Skip and Gordon A. Crews. (2008). Asian Americans in the Criminal Justice System. In Reid Toth, Gordon A. Crews and Catherine E. Burton (Eds.), *In the Margins: Special Populations and American Justice* (pp. 72–82). Upper Saddle River: Pearson Prentice Hall.

Hyzer, Walter, Capt. (1989). Infectious Diseases in the Jail. *Jail Operations Bulletin, American Jail Association, Vol. 1, No. 9.*

James, Doris J. and Lauren E. Glaze. (September 2006, revised 12/14/06). Bureau of Justice Statistics. (2006, September). *Mental Health Problems of Prison and Jail Inmates.* Washington, DC: U.S. Government Printing Office.

Jones, Wendy. (1995, November–December). Working with the Developmentally Disabled in Jail. *American Jails*, Nov–Dec 1995, pp. 16–20.

Lester, David, Ph.D. and Brice L. Danto, Ph.D. (1993). *Suicide Behind Bars: Prediction and Prevention.* Philadelphia: Charles Press.

Levinson, Robert B., Ph.D. (January 23, 1995). Security Threat Groups. Presented in "Controlling the Influence of Gangs in our Jails," *Large Jail Network Meeting,* National Institute of Corrections, Longmont, Colorado.

Lupton, Gary. (1996, May–June). Identifying and Referring Inmates with Mental Disorders. *American Jails,* pp. 49–52.

Mason III, John J. and Paul Becker. (1994, September–October). Know Your Bigots: Identifying and Supervising White Supremacists in a Correctional Setting. *American Jails,* pp. 61–65. *See also:* George, John and Laird Wilcox (1992). *Nazis, Communists, Klansmen and Others on the Fringe Political Extremism in America.* Buffalo: Prometheus Books.

Mclain, Buzz. (1990, August 31). Program Sobers Prisoners' Lives. *Fairfax Journal.*

Nadel, Barbara A., AIA. (1997, Winter). Slashing Gang Violence, Not Victims. *The Keeper's Voice, Vol. 18, No. 4,* pp. 16–19.

Ross, Roger D., Sgt., L.A. Sheriff's Office. (January 23, 1995). Controlling the Influence of Gangs in Our Jails. *Large Jail Network Meeting,* National Institute of Corrections, Longmont, Colorado.

Rubin, Nancy. (1987, August). Women Behind Bars. *McCalls,* pp. 36–42.

Santoi, Al. (1986, April 20). How Should We Handle Young Offenders? *Parade,* pp. 16–17.

Schmalleger, Frank, Ph.D., and John Ortiz Smykla, Ph.D. (2009). *Corrections in the 21st Century Fourth Edition.* New York: McGraw Hill.

Stinchcomb, Jeanne B., Ph.D. and Vernon B. Fox, Ph.D. (1999). *Introduction to Corrections, Fifth Edition.* Upper Saddle River: Prentice Hall.

Virginia Department of Mental Health and Mental Retardation. (1986, June). *Trainer's Manual: The Mentally Ill, Mentally Retarded and Substance Dependent,* Project Consultant: Joseph Rowan; Project Director: Frank Patterson.

Weaver, Gary, Ph.D. "Cultural Diversity," seminar, Fairfax Co. Office of the
    Sheriff, 4/2/93.
Weaver, Gary, Ph.D. (1992, September). Law Enforcement in a Culturally Di-
    verse Society. *FBI Law Enforcement Bulletin,* pp. 1–7.

Chapter 8

Physical Plant and Classification

The word "security" is heavily used in the field of corrections. From the time that COs begin training in the academy and throughout their careers until retirement, every duty and action that COs perform have the goal of security. Correctional staffs familiarize themselves with facility policies and procedures concerning security. One rule of thumb is:

Security will not work if procedures are not followed.

This chapter will examine what is meant by the "physical plant" of a correctional institution as it pertains to safe and secure operations, especially relating to the classification unit, which is a key part of the facility staff. Also, since a correctional institution is mostly comprises inmate housing areas, the reasons for housing inmates in different population areas will be examined. Another way to think of security is to think of security as safety—safety of the institutional staff, the inmate population and the public by preventing escapes. Classification and security work hand in hand.

Layout of Facilities

While prisons, jails and community corrections facilities are different in functions and goals, many are unique in design to themselves. For example, a maximum security prison can differ in design from another prison one hundred miles away or two jails in neighboring counties can have different designs. However, all correctional facilities have these areas in their physical plant:

Entry/Exit Points

These points are located throughout the facility: the entry points are for staff entry, receiving inmates, receiving personal visitors (families, etc., of in-

Entrance door to the Maryland House of Correction.

mates), receiving professional visitors (attorneys, probation officers, etc.) and receiving services (deliveries, trash removal, maintenance entries, etc.).

Procedures must be in place for receiving visitors, no matter who they are. Personal and professional visitors must check in with the staff, show identification and be logged into an official record. Some institutions search visitors' bags, briefcases, etc., for contraband (illegal items, drugs, etc.). Improvements have been made in this area, as most facilities require some type of photo identification to be shown by the visitor.

The main entry point for inmates is the *receiving area,* or "*booking,*" the area where incoming prisoners must be legally committed, searched, submit their property to a search and be photographed. Depending on the type of correctional facility, certain data must be recorded, such as:

- Legal commitment order, court order, arrest warrant or transfer order
- Inmate's full name
- Aliases (other names the inmate uses, often called *AKAs*—also known as)
- Address, phone number
- Emergency contact (friend or family member)
- Attorney
- Physical description: height, weight, hair and eye color

- Scars, marks, tattoos
- Charges: court date, bond, court dates or sentence
- Photograph
- Fingerprints
- Information from transferring facility if applicable

The commitment paperwork *must* be in order. Generally, the receiving area is separate from personal visiting and the public entrance. Newly arrived inmates can receive professional visits from their attorneys, police officers, probation and parole officers and social workers.

Prisons have a long term function, where they accept inmates who are sentenced. Community corrections facilities may be at the federal or state level, where they are accepting inmates who are sentenced to the department of corrections and a record of their incarceration has been established. Jails incarcerate newly arrested or sentenced offenders. Local community corrections centers in a jail system may either book in offenders directly or take them in a transfer from the jail. No matter how it is done, a good booking procedure is the foundation for the institutional record.

In prisons and community corrections centers, entry points for inmates into the facility may vary. For example, inmates returning from the community on work release or from work details are already part of the population, so the entry points for them may or may not be through booking.

Perimeter

While jails and community corrections facilities generally are in close proximity to public streets, prisons are usually located in open, relatively remote areas for security purposes. Some facilities are, however, located in urban areas. The goal of perimeter security is that the facility border is sealed and secure: that is the *perimeter*—the secure boundary of the correctional facility. Inmates do not get out; nothing or no one gets in. Devices such as closed circuit television, CO towers, alarms, motion sensors, chain link and mesh fences, walls and rolled razor wire maintain a physical security barrier. Visual observation from strategically placed towers, guard posts and mobile patrols (walking and vehicle) maintain a presence of the correctional officer. "Blind spots" can be overcome by closed circuit television cameras or mirrors. The perimeter and surrounding areas should be well lit and must be clear; overgrown vegetation provides hiding places for weapons, drugs, messages and other forms of contraband that someone could leave for an inmate. While not all inmates may have access to the fence or perimeter border, an inmate in a work crew may have an opportunity to smuggle contraband in (Henderson, et al., 1997, pp. 59–63). Perhaps the most memorable security perimeter of the past century has been San Francisco Bay, which surrounded Alcatraz Federal Penitentiary.

Internal Operations Areas

Administration areas: Administration areas consist of a main records section, staff offices, mail rooms, property rooms, equipment storage areas, etc. Good security practices do not allow any inmates or inmate workers in these areas unless they are escorted by staff. Also, administrative offices are located throughout the facility. Counseling offices, medical exam rooms and other rooms in which staff can see inmates may be located in different buildings or on different floors. Locker rooms and weapons/emergency equipment storage areas are administrative areas and are located away from inmate housing areas.

Control centers: Control centers are the hub of any good institutional security system. Control centers are areas where all electronic surveillance communications are coordinated and routed to the staff. Modern correctional facilities have closed circuit television systems, intercoms, fire/smoke alarms, door alarms, etc., for maintaining security. Phone lines to police and fire departments are located in these centers and provide instant access to outside help in case of emergencies. Staff in these centers must be constantly alert for security violations and in constant contact with staff members, especially those posted in inmate housing areas.

Visiting areas: Visiting in correctional facilities is located near entry points. Visiting is divided into two types: personal and professional. ***Personal visiting***

Old style linear supervision; cellblocks are off a main corridor. Fairfax County (VA) Adult Detention Center. Photo by author.

Entrance, Clarke-Frederick-Winchester Regional Adult Detention Center.

is defined as friends and family members of inmates coming to visit per facility policies and procedures (such as per an approved visitors' list); *professional visiting* are visits from attorneys, social workers, police officers, psychologists, probation and parole officers, clergy, etc. Generally, each type of visiting has its own area. In jails, personal visiting areas are usually no contact, but professional visiting areas have no physical barriers between visitor and the inmate and allow contact (of a professional nature) between inmate and visitor. All visitors and their possessions, such as a purse or briefcase, are subject to search. Metal detectors are being used more frequently. Good security policies dictate that packages, purses, etc., of personal visits must be left in another area. While visitors are usually not required to go through a body search such as a pat down, a visit may be denied if the correctional staff suspects that the visitor possesses contraband. The staff may call, at the direction of a supervisor, the local law enforcement agency to investigate. Visitors can volunteer for a search, but this is rare. The visiting area requires good staff observation and surveillance. All visiting areas should be thoroughly searched after visiting; contraband can be left behind by a visitor for pickup later by an inmate work detail (Henderson, et al., 1997, pp. 173–177).

Some correctional facilities allow *contact visits*, where the personal visitor and inmate are allowed to visit without any type of physical barrier. In jails, this is not the standard practice. Some inmates, such as those working in the jail as inmate workers, or trusties, *may* earn such a visit as a privilege. In some prison systems inmates may have personal visits in visiting rooms or outside in "picnic" type areas. Records should be maintained of all visits to inmates by professionals, personal family members and friends of inmates.

Correctional officers should be very familiar with the visiting policies and procedures of the facility. Each correctional institution has its own rules and regulations concerning visiting. Visitors and inmates are not permitted to act inappropriately, including boisterous conduct, being loud and disorderly, or acting in any way that is suggestive and sexual in nature, including "flashing" of bare skin in a suggestive manner, exposing sex organs, exposing breasts, exposing sexual genitalia, fondling, etc.

Visitors that do not adhere to the facility visiting rules must be asked to leave and possibly be banned from the facility. Occasionally the visitor and the inmate are both to blame. A veteran jail supervisor was informed by a jail mail room officer that while inspecting a female inmate's mail, he had found photographs of her (taken by a visitor) posing in sexual "horseplay" (exposing a breast) in the jail non contact visiting area. He advised the officer to charge her with sexual misconduct, a violation of the jail rules, and find out the names of the visitors involved (if possible) so that they can be barred from visiting her. Discipline must be enforced. If inmates misbehave, charge them under the rules; if visitors misbehave, they should be charged criminally (such as in cases of disorderly conduct, public drunkenness, etc.) and/or banned from visiting inmates. Visiting rules, facility policy on contraband, and any legal statutes under which a visitor could be arrested should be posted where the public and visitors can see them. The inmate population should be aware of these policies and should communicate them to their families and friends who want to visit them. Unfortunately, there incidents where visitors have misbehaved, appeared at the facility drunk or "stoned," attempted to pass in contraband (such as hidden in property to be given to the inmate) or have refused to obey staff instructions.

Service areas: These areas are operated by staffs that provide services and support to the inmate population such as medical, laundry, janitorial, food service and maintenance. These areas are located away from inmate housing, but medical staff may have exam rooms located throughout the facility. Inmate workers or trusties may work in these areas under staff supervision.

Concerning services, facilities receive shipments of supplies, food, etc., as well as maintenance worker visits. Trash is removed by refuse services. It is crucial to security that *all* such visitors be identified and escorted by staff, especially if trusties are assigned to the area.

Programs and recreation areas: Programs areas (classrooms, religious service areas and chapels, law/leisure libraries, gyms, exercise rooms) are located away from inmate housing areas. Only inmates authorized by staff, generally classification can participate. Programs staff offices may be located here. In the direct supervision style living areas, each housing unit may have an adjacent exercise area and study rooms for use by inmates in programs and programs staff.

Inmate Housing

In a correctional facility, inmate housing is generally divided into these areas: receiving/booking, intake, general population, administrative segregation and disciplinary segregation. All of these housing areas are linked to one key section of the facility: the classification section.

Classification

Classification is more than just separating inmates into different housing areas. Classification is an ongoing process and an inmate management tool, based on staff analysis and diagnosis of inmate information, resulting in informed inmate housing and custody level decisions. This information allows staff to predict and control inmate's behavior (Cornelius, 2008, p. 470). To meet this goal, the classification process has three important objectives (Bales, ed., 1997, p. 118):

- to assess the inmate's background (social, economic, criminal, etc.) and behavior. The inmate is assigned to the appropriate custody level/housing in the facility or to the appropriate institution in a large correctional system, such as a state or federal system. The proper assignment aids the staff in supervising the inmate; for example hard core inmates are placed in maximum security; extreme high risk inmates are segregated.
- to develop a program or treatment plan for the inmate based on a prior assessment and staff input. This involves the placement of inmates into work programs, community corrections programs, educational programs, substance abuse programs or mental health programs.
- to periodically review and calculate the inmates' progress. Program and housing/custody levels could be modified, based on information received from several sections of the facility staff, such as mental health, medical and from correctional officers via incident reports.

Classification staffs perform additional duties, such as holding disciplinary hearings, holding administrative segregation hearings, assigning/removing inmates from inmate worker (trusty) status, conducting inmate orientations and communicating inmates' institutional adjustments to concerned personnel such as a probation/parole officer. They also reassign inmates coming off disciplinary segregation to the facility general population or refer them to an ICC hearing for assignment to administrative segregation. Besides the custody control centers of the facility, classification is one of the main "nerve centers."

Classification Process

Classification teams or unit teams begin the process by analyzing the information obtained by the inmate in the initial interview—criminal, social and medical histories. Other information that is looked at includes psychiatric/psychological examinations and assessments by programs staffs in terms of education, substance abuse and religious needs or requests. In *receiving/intake*, the inmate is interviewed by the classification staff. This **initial interview** is an in depth interview conducted by the classification staff where crucial information is first gathered about the inmate. The inmate is asked about his/her:

> criminal history and prior incarcerations
> mental health history
> education
> social history: addresses, etc.
> emergency contact
> job history
> sexual preference
> current offense
> substance abuse history
> suicidal ideation
> religious preference
> special needs: diet, etc.
> medical needs/problems/history

Other information that can be useful to the classification or unit team is information obtained from the **pre sentence investigation (PSI)** report. This is a comprehensive report about an inmate written either by a probation officer or a social worker and is submitted to the sentencing judge in felony cases. It contains detailed information about the inmate ranging from family history, education, etc. to the inmate's version of the crime. It also contains the recommendation of the person writing the report as to whether the inmate should or should not be incarcerated.

All of the information obtained by the classification team is consolidated into the *classification file*, or the file generated by the classification section that serves as the central repository for information obtained from and about an inmate, including the classification interview, criminal and institutional histories, correspondence from and about the inmate, mental health reports and evaluations and notably incident reports filed by correctional officers about the inmate. These reports can be the basis for disciplinary charges, criminal charges, and the segregation of the inmate (Cornelius, 2008, p. 470). Correctional officers must realize that their input is crucial to the accuracy of the classification file. The information is turned over to the ICC or unit teams that will decide where and under what custody level the inmate will be housed.

Classification, in addition to assigning inmates to custody levels and suitable housing, also has much input in the correctional process. Court staff, probation/parole officers and other agency staff can inquire as to an inmate's background, conduct, etc. All facility staff should be made aware of the fact that the classification interview and assignment creates a file that has valuable information about the inmate. All staff should be encouraged to submit documented incidents about inmates to the classification staff, such as behavior observations, all infractions and "information only" reports or memos. Disciplinary actions are filed usually in the classification file.

The inmate is housed in an intake area if they are cooperative and exhibit no problems. If an inmate refuses to be interviewed; is mentally disordered; is on special custody, such as a high risk inmate, witness, escape risk, etc., he/she may remain in receiving until they cooperate or the matter is discussed by the classification staff. Generally, in intake, no visiting is allowed, except for attorneys, bondsmen, police, etc., and the inmate is observed for a period of time and receives an orientation.

The orientation process is crucial. A good orientation conducted by an experienced staff member should address the following:

- facility schedule: TV, lights out, cleanup, etc.
- facility disciplinary system including rules and penalties
- contacting the staff with any concerns for safety, well being and medical/mental health needs
- medical and sick call procedures
- inmate services: laundry, canteen, monies, etc.
- visiting: personal and professional
- property authorized by the facility, including what property can be brought by visitors
- mail procedures

- telephone procedures
- library services including access to law library
- recreation
- programs
- use of the *inmate request form:* a form used by inmates to communicate in writing to the staff; inmate indicates the appropriate facility staff where request is to be sent and writes a message
- grievance procedure
- familiarization with any written guidebooks, handbooks, etc. issued to the inmate

Classification Decision Making

Classification decisions can be handled by either the *Institutional Classification Committee (ICC)* or a unit team The ICC is a committee consisting of various sections of facility staff that have to consider and make decisions based on the behavior, criminal background, custody level and housing location of the inmate. They bring to the table concerns that they have for the safety of the staff and other inmates. The committee membership is primarily the custody, mental health, medical and classification staffs. In most facilities, the chairperson is the head of classification that chairs the meeting and ensures that all pertinent information is discussed; programs personnel, social workers, counselors, chaplains and supervisors that deal with inmate treatment and housing may also be contributing members of the ICC (Bales, ed., 1997, pp. 114–115).

Unit Management

Some facilities use the *unit management* approach where each housing unit has a management team, similar to the ICC. This team decides initial housing assignments, programs issues, and classification decisions. The team can also recommend parole for inmates. This team comprises the unit manager, case manager, unit education staff, unit psychologist and unit correctional officer(s) (Bales, ed., 1997, p. 115).

Units in a correctional facility can be a dormitory, cellblock or wing. The unit management system has several basic requirements, which makes it different from the more traditional ICC approach, even though its decision making functions are very similar (Duncan, 2008, p. 147):

- Units should hold a relatively small number of inmates—fewer than 150, even though in overcrowded institutions this could range up to 500.

- Inmates in the unit are housed there for long periods of time, or for the major portion of their confinement. This allows the counseling and treatment staff to have the time to work with them.
- Inmates in the unit work closely with multidisciplinary staff; positive working relationships are developed.
- Staff members assigned to the unit have input into the programming, living conditions, and the enforcement of facility regulations, rules and policies.
- Inmate assignments to the unit are based on the criteria of the inmate's need for control, security, and the programs that are offered to the inmate.

Housing Assignments

As previously stated, inmate housing assignments are based on classification decisions. However, if the correctional facility incurs an emergency such as an escape attempt, an inmate committing a crime or a serious breach of discipline, or any type of security problem, the shift supervisor can order an inmate or inmates to be placed in the most secure housing available. This is also true for the facility medical staff. If an inmate is suffering from a serious medical condition or injury that requires medical isolation or housing, the medical staff can have the inmate transferred to medical housing or a hospital. In all cases of medical transfer, the facility supervisors and classification must be notified.

Types of Inmate Housing

In most correctional facilities, there are four types of housing for inmates after receiving/intake, dependent on their custody levels which are determined from information obtained by the classification staff and discussed by a unit management team or the ICC. They are:

- General population: includes inmate worker housing/community corrections housing
- Administrative segregation
- Disciplinary segregation

General Population

If the ICC/unit team reviews the inmate's file and decides that *general population* housing is appropriate, the inmate is assigned to a cellblock or unit with other inmates. In this type of housing inmates live together and are afforded all privileges, such as commissary or canteen, television, programs and recreation. Inmates in general population are considered to have the social skills necessary and the behavior to live with other inmates. The committee decides on the custody level: maximum, medium, minimum. Some facilities do a subjective "gut feeling" approach while more sophisticated use an objective, numerical scale approach.

Depending on the facility and agency policy, general population can be any housing that is not segregation. This may include work release and inmate worker housing. In some facilities, especially older ones, work release and inmate labor inmates are housed in living units inside the main facility. Inmate workers or trusties may be housed also in designated areas. Certain criteria must be met such as minimum or medium custody, non violent charge, no sex offense, good institutional record, medical approval, and not having a long sentence.

Administrative Segregation

Classification staff through an ICC or unit team, can also assign an inmate to *administrative segregation,* or *A/S* defined as where the inmate is housed separately from inmates in general population for other than disciplinary reasons.

Interior of a cell, Clarke-Frederick-Winchester Regional Adult Detention Center.

These reasons may include mental state, incompatibility, at their own request or for any reason for increased attention, surveillance or supervision. As much as is possible, the inmate receives the same privileges as inmates in general population (Cornelius, 1996, p. 67). In some A/S units there is no television, recreation may be alone, and programs may be restricted depending on the reason for A/S. Overall, A/S inmates get library services, chaplain's services, recreation, commissary and personal visiting. A/S housing is not considered punishment.

A comprehensive list of reasons to put inmates on administrative segregation can be found in *Inmate Handbook*, published by the Alexandria, Virginia Detention Center. It is distributed to every inmate. The reasons are (Alexandria Office of the Sheriff, 2004, *Inmate Handbook*, p. 4):

- Incidents that occurred during prior incarcerations.
- You are a safety risk to the staff or other inmates.
- You are a security risk.
- There are concerns about how well you can handle being in jail.
- You have an extensive criminal history.
- We do not have enough information about you.

There are unusual "special cases." In a jail, the ICC may deal with inmates who are so mentally ill that they will not understand staff instructions, may refuse their medications, and be totally unmanageable and unpredictable. The ICC should discuss thoroughly and in great detail the case with the mental health staff, deciding on the best course of action that will benefit the inmate and keep the staff and other inmates safe. However, some inmates will most likely remain on A/S status due to their mental state. Another case could be in a jail, where a newly arrived inmate in a show of "bravado" may refuse to be changed into jail clothes, refuse any cooperation with the staff, and refuse to be subjected to a medical exam. The ICC must look at this problem, conduct an administrative hearing and make it clear to the inmate that the privileges that he or she could enjoy in general population will not be afforded, namely television, recreation, programs or personal visiting. These inmates must have access to their attorneys, who also may try to convince them as to the futility of their actions.

Medical Housing

Being housed in a correctional facility *dispensary* for medical reasons is a form of administrative segregation. The dispensary is a form of "mini hospital" in the facility where inmates needing medical attention are housed under the supervision of the medical staff. Correctional officers are also assigned to these areas. Inmates on medical A/S may be hospitalized at some point. In some cases, it may be necessary to house mentally disordered inmates in the dispensary based on medical issues. Some correctional staff may argue that such housing is less secure, but inmates must be treated for medical problems, especially serious life threatening ones even if they pose a security and safety threat to other inmates or staff. Inmates housed in a dispensary are only released when cleared for general population or other appropriate housing by the medical staff.

Protective Custody

Protective custody is another type of A/S. Inmates who fit into a special risk category may be assigned to protective custody or P/C. Protective custody is the housing of an inmate on administrative segregation in order to protect him or her from being harmed by other inmates. Reasons for an inmate being on P/C may include possible harm from gang enemies, being a current or former law enforcement officer, being an informant (which must remain confidential), being a material witness in a crime inside or outside the institution, or for any reason that has been investigated and the inmate's safety is determined to be in jeopardy.

For example, one jail classification director [the author] recalls an inmate who requested P/C:

> He was a member of a local street gang. He just had become a new father and for the sake of his girlfriend (the baby's mother) and his new child, he asked gang leaders in the jail for "permission" to be released from the gang. He was refused—word spread throughout the jail—and we had to honor his request for P/C. He wasn't a bad sort—but we saw his reasons.

He also recalled:

> My institution received a call from the local Federal Bureau of Investigation (FBI) office. An inmate in a nearby prison had witnessed a homicide of another inmate and was willing to testify. The FBI asked if we could take him and hold him in P/C "incognito." We held him under wraps for two months; the jail staff was instructed not to divulge to anyone calling in that we were holding him.

Another reason is protection from sexual assault. If an inmate has been the victim of an attempted or completed sexual assault, he or she may be placed on P/C to prevent further attacks, harassment or ridicule.

A frequent but no less important reason to employ administrative segregation is *incompatibility*. Incompatibility occurs when an inmate demonstrates

Dayroom in a podular living unit. Fairfax County (VA) Adult Detention Center. Photo by author.

Double bunked cell in podular unit. One inmate gets the bunk, the other gets the floor. Fairfax County (VA) Adult Detention Center. Photo by author.

by actions, behavior or request, that he or she cannot live with other inmates in the general population. This can also be brought to the staff's attention by other inmates. In incompatibility cases, the classification staff has a choice— to segregate the inmate on administrative segregation by authority of a formal administrative hearing, to move him or her to segregation for a short time and then reclassify to another location. In both cases, the inmate must be evaluated by staff as to what the problem is and how best to correct it. The inmate must be counseled and advised that he/she must get along with others. Causes of incompatibility include the following:

- Hygiene: poor habits, not washing, etc.
- Controlling the television
- Harassing other inmates with threats of violence, horseplay
- Stealing food, property, etc. from other inmates
- Unusual behavior
- Sexual misconduct: masturbation, exposure, etc.
- Being overbearing and loud

Disciplinary Segregation

As a rule, disciplinary procedures against an inmate are usually handled by the classification section, but some institutions may assign staff solely for that purpose. Classification handles the assignment of inmates to *disciplinary segregation (D/S)* which is defined as an inmate being segregated, with loss of privileges as a result of rule breaking. After a finding of guilt in a hearing, the inmate is placed in segregation and loses privileges such as commissary, personal visiting, programs, television, and possibly accrued good time. The main goal behind a disciplinary code in a correctional facility is to both punish inmate troublemakers and isolate them (Cornelius, 1996, p. 68).

Disciplinary Codes

To have control in the facility, prisons and jails must have in place rules for inmates and consequences for breaking them. At the same time, correctional officers must understand that there are due process procedures including impartial hearings that must take place. These procedures are the result of litigation by inmates (see Chapter 13). Inmates must be given a copy of these rules and punishments.

An example of such procedures can be found at the Hampton Roads Regional Jail in Portsmouth, Virginia. It is written very clearly in the *Inmate Handbook of Jail Rules and Regulations*. It is very clear in the *Handbook:*

The Regional Jail has established rules of conduct to govern inmate behavior and to ensure that the facility operates safely and securely.... Disciplinary action will be taken against inmates who violate the rules of conduct. There are major and minor violations, depending on the type of offense and its severity. You may also face criminal prosecution if you violate the law.

The Rules of Conduct are divided into major and minor categories. Major Violations are serious and deal with actions against inmates or staff, either by physical means or violating the rules to disrupt security, such as possessing or introducing into the jail weapons, sharpened instruments, explosives or incendiary devices and engaging in sexual acts or forced sexual advances. Major Violations range from Killing a Person to Failing to Stand for Count or Interfering with the Taking of a Count. Other examples include:

- Escaping, attempting to escape or planning to escape.
- Creating a disturbance or acting in a way that disrupts or interferes with the security or orderly operation of the facility.
- Stealing.
- Misusing authorized medication
- Being in the cell of another inmate or in any unauthorized area.
- Creating a disturbance or acting in a way that disrupts or interferes with the security or orderly operation of the facility.
- Possession of contraband.
- Refusing to obey the direct order of a jail staff member.

Minor Violations are less serious, but are still important. Examples of Minor Violations include:

- Lying or giving false information to an employee.
- Smoking or possession of tobacco products.
- Obstruction of cell view.
- Not responding when called.
- Unauthorized contact with the public.
- Improperly passing or receiving notes or attempting to correspond with someone in this facility without approval.
- Throwing any item.
- Failure to follow posted rules and regulations.

There are punishments. For the finding of guilt of a Major Violation, punishment for one incident can be up to 60 days cell restriction or disciplinary segregation, and/or 60 days loss of good time or any combination of the two up to the maximum of each. When guilty of a Minor Violation, punishments include a maximum of 48 hours

cell restriction, or a maximum of 30 days cell restriction or disciplinary segregation. All or some the following privileges may be lost
during the term of the punishment: commissary, recreation, television,
telephone, visitation (except for attorney visits) and programs.
(Hampton Roads Regional Jail, *Inmate Handbook of Jail Rules and
Regulations*, 2003, pp. 14–18)

Due Process

In any case of the facility staff, namely classification conducting a hearing
on an inmate, there are due process procedures that must be followed. Inmates
cannot be "railroaded" into either disciplinary or administrative segregation
by correctional officers. To place an inmate in segregation is a major, life changing step for that inmate. To ensure fairness and prevent "kangaroo courts," the
courts, including the Supreme Court ruled that inmates must be afforded due
process in accordance with the Fourteenth Amendment to the U.S. Constitution (see Chapter 13).

To place an inmate on administrative segregation, a formal administrative
hearing has to be held. Generally, this is conducted by the Institutional Classification Committee (ICC). In some facilities this is called a "formal ICC."
The reasons must be clear, such as an ongoing disciplinary problem, incompatibility, protective custody, etc. Placement on administrative segregation can
be short term or for an extensive period of time, depending on the behavior
of the inmate and the security needs of the institution. This action can also
determine the conditions of confinement such as restrictions from programs
and recreation, staff escorts and restraints used when out of the cell. Criteria
for inmates being placed on administrative segregation can include inmates
under investigation for crimes or are pending a transfer.

To be placed on A/S inmates must be given a clear notice of the reasons for
placement in special housing such as A/S (Henderson, et al., 1997, p. 129). However, the notice to the inmate must be specific. To ensure fairness and due process,
a formal ICC hearing will be scheduled with a time frame to allow the inmate
to prepare for the hearing. The inmate will be notified of the time and date of
the hearing, can ask for staff or inmate assistance, and will be permitted to present his or her side of the case. Finally, the inmate will receive a written decision
including the reasons for it and will be given an opportunity to appeal to a higher
authority, such as the facility administrator (Cornelius, 2008, p. 195).

It is important that inmates facing disciplinary actions be afforded their due
process rights. By doing so, staff cannot be accused of being biased. These procedures include the following (Bales, ed., 1997, p. 18):

Direct supervision unit dayroom. Notice that there is no physical barrier between inmate dayroom and officer's station. The officer proactively controls the unit. Fairfax County (VA) Adult Detention Center. Photo by author.

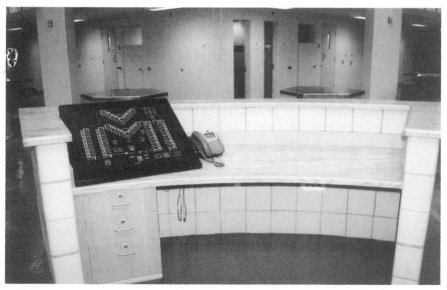

Officer's station in direct supervision housing unit. Fairfax County (VA) Adult Detention Center. Photo by author.

- The accused inmate receiving written notice of the charges. This can include a copy of the report or a document that specifies what rules are alleged to be broken.
- The inmate is afforded opportunities to present evidence on his or her behalf including the testimony of witnesses.
- The inmate is afforded the opportunity to ask for assistance either from another inmate or a staff person.
- The inmate is provided a written copy of the findings of the hearing officer or panel and the punishments to be imposed.

The inmate is also allowed to appeal the case to a higher authority, such as the jail administrator, prison warden, etc. The inmate should state the reasons for the appeal.

These rights have been expanded on, and many facilities give the inmate a more detailed explanation of his or her rights. For example, at the aforementioned facility, the Hampton Roads Regional Jail, inmates have a hearing notification period of 24 hours (which they can waive), and a time limit for the hearing being conducted—7 days from the date of the incident, excluding weekends and holidays. Inmates have the right to be present at the hearing unless they are unruly. Witnesses can testify by telephone or videoconferencing. Inmates can refuse to appear, but this will be understood to be an admission of guilt. There is an appeals process through a captain and the jail superintendent (the highest level). Inmates are advised that if they want to pursue litigation, they can do so without fear of harassment or reprisal (Hampton Roads Regional Jail, *Inmate Handbook of Jail Rules and Regulations*, 2003, p. 19).

Any type of administrative hearings must be impartial. COs and supervisors that have involvement either in the disciplinary charges or the reasons for administrative segregation should not be on the panel. They should testify as witnesses or be brought in to clarify the proceedings.

File Reviews

Inmates on special housing/segregation status must be reviewed periodically by the classification staff to ascertain if they are experiencing any problems or if they can go into the facility general population. Also, inmates on administrative segregation may be re-classified to the general population if circumstances change. A *file review* is defined as the ICC review of the case of an inmate's special housing status to determine if the inmate can be removed from administrative segregation or see how he or she is behaving on D/S. Inmates cannot be placed in segregation and "forgotten about." Staff must circulate in their housing status and ask each inmate at regular intervals if they are experiencing any problems or have any concerns. This information must be entered into the inmate's classification file for ICC review.

What is a reasonable schedule for file reviews? Should they be weekly, every other week or once per month? A supervisory body, such as the ICC or unit management team should review the inmate's status at least every seven days for the first two months and every thirty days thereafter. Mental health personnel should review the case every thirty days (Henderson, et al., 1997, p. 136). This can be modified into more frequent schedules. The inmate should also be able to request in writing a review, but not to the point of harassing the staff. Written decisions should be given to the inmate as much as possible. The key to accurate information about an inmate on special housing is information — information from all the facility staff that has contact with the inmate as well as accurate and factual incident reports from COs either referring an inmate to formal ICC hearings or supplying information that is useful in file reviews.

Each file review of an inmate on segregation status in the facility should look at the following information (Henderson, et al., 1997, p. 136):

- Reason for placement in segregation
- Disciplinary record
- Past criminal record
- Record of conduct in other correctional institutions
- Mental health status
- Involvement in criminal activity while in custody
- Attitude towards staff and authority, following rules
- Institutional work assignment history
- Adjustment and participation in facility programs
- Willingness and ability to get along with and/or live with other inmates
- Record of violent reactions to stressful situations
- Habitual conduct, language, actions that may provoke or instigate stressful or violent situations

To properly review the case of an inmate in special housing, supervisors and other key personnel should monitor operations by COs and other staff in segregation units. Their visits should be logged and conducted regularly, such as (Henderson, et al., 1997, p. 136):

- Shift supervisor or designee: once per shift
- Medical personnel: daily
- Caseworker, social worker or counselor: daily
- Religious representative (staff, not volunteers): weekly

Inmate in prison uniform, Maryland House of Correction.

- Chief of custody/security or designee: not less than weekly
- Deputy warden (custody) or designee: weekly
- Warden or head of facility (Chief Jailor, etc.): weekly
- Mental health staff: psychologist, psychiatrist, etc.: as requested by COs, staff or inmate, mental health staff should interview any inmate in segregation for over 30 days and prepare an evaluation or report with recommendations.

General Population: Three Styles of Management

While there are differences in the styles and architecture of correctional facilities in the United States today, there are three main designs that are still in widespread use in prisons and jails. These do not include dormitory style housing that may be used for inmate workers and trusties. One veteran jail officer remembered that when he started his correctional officer career in 1978, an open area that was used for storage was converted into a 30 bed dorm for work release inmates, with bunk beds and limited toilet and shower facilities. The jail was built in the late 1940s, and the sheriff had to use what space he had.

Linear

Long the standard design in jails, the *linear design* consists of cellblocks running off at right angles down a long central corridor. The linear design is considered the first generation of corrections architecture design (Cornelius, 2008, p. 46). Each cellblock has 4 or 5 cells opening into a *dayroom* or a central area where the inmates can congregate. Each day room has a television, a table or tables for eating, seats and toilet and shower facilities.

The linear design limits correctional officer interaction with the inmates. The CO can communicate with the inmates in the cellblocks through a Plexiglas window or by opening a slot in the cellblock door through which food, mail commissary items, etc. can be passed through. The CO can see into the dayroom, but not into the cells which are off of the dayroom. The only way for the CO to see what the inmates are doing is to physically go into the cellblock—and good safety procedure dictates that another CO watches his or her back (Cornelius, 2008, p. 46).

Podular

The second generation of correctional architecture is *podular remote surveillance* or *podular*. This system has the CO in a central control booth, observing the surrounding inmate living units or "pods" from a central vantage point. Intercoms from the control booth into the pods and visual sight are the main methods of communication (Cornelius, 2008, p. 47).

Both the linear and podular designs are *reactive*—when the CO sees an argument, a fight, a medical emergency, a fire, an assault, etc. he or she calls for assistance. He or she *reacts* to the situation. Both designs also have blind spots where inmates can engage in horseplay, manufacturing of contraband, fighting and assaults without being easily seen by the CO.

Direct Supervision

The third generation and the most novel of correctional architecture is *direct supervision*, where the correctional officer is stationed inside the inmate living area; there are no physical boundaries between him or her and the inmates. Communication is open, interpersonal and direct. This style of management is *proactive*. A CO can circulate among the inmates and go into any area that he or she is responsible for and see what is going on among the inmates. If the CO sees an argument, a fight brewing, inmates not obeying unit rules, or any misconduct, he or she can address it immediately. COs get to

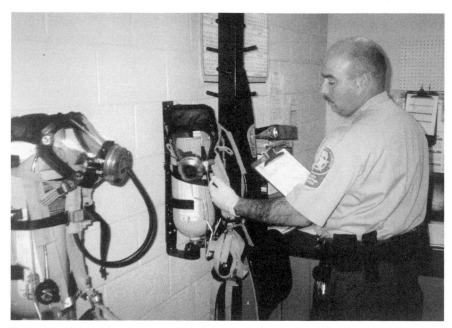

Inspection of fire safety equipment. Clarke-Frederick-Winchester (VA) Regional Adult Detention Center.

know the inmates who are carefully selected by classification or unit management to live in direct supervision, based on positive behavior and good institutional records. Also, COs who work in direct supervision have a sense of pride as the smooth operation of the unit reflects favorably on his or her ability to do the job and instill good behavior in the inmates (Cornelius, 2008, pp. 47–48).

Direct supervision has nine principles which aim for the fair, firm and humane management of direct supervision units. They are (Kemble, 1996, pp. 18–19):

- Effective control by being proactive with inmates and at the same time maintaining a sound security barrier.
- Effective management by assigning positive role models (COs) and the frequent supervision by facility management staff.
- Competent staff must be assigned; such as COs with good "people" skills, leadership skills and good decision making skills.
- Safety of staff and inmates: Both staff and inmates are cognizant of a safe environment, which makes both working and living in the unit easier.
- Manageable and cost effective results come from the fact that vandalism and negative behavior by inmates are reduced significantly, which re-

duces vandalism and the wear and tear on fixtures, furniture and security equipment.

- Effective communication is the basis and the critical element in the operational strategy and management of people. Direct supervision promotes open communication among staff and with inmates.
- Classification and orientation: A sound and effective classification system is necessary to operate direct supervision units. The CO is also familiar with each inmate in his or her unit.
- Justice and fairness is promoted in direct supervision. Problems with deviant inmates can be handled administratively or by a disciplinary system.
- Ownership of operations: A CO in a direct supervision unit develops a sense of pride and ownership in making the unit run effectively. Leadership and communication skills also develop which helps the CO learn job skills and may assist him or her in the promotion process.

Custody Levels

Classification or unit management will determine the custody level of each inmate and the corresponding housing that best suits it. There are three main levels of custody in corrections inmate management: minimum, medium and maximum (Henderson, et.al, 1997, p18):

- *minimum custody:* Inmates categorized at this level pose little or no management problems, and are considered to be at low risk for escaping or causing problems. Inmates at this level have freedom of movement throughout the facility (in approved areas), attend programs, and are under general supervision; they may be permitted to go outside the perimeter or into the community escorted by staff or may be participating in a community corrections program unescorted, such as work release. Examples of minimum custody housing include direct supervision units and dormitories.
- *medium custody:* Inmates at this level may be permitted to move about the facility during the day, but movement is more controlled at night. Inmates are under direct supervision when in programs or work details; they are also handcuffed and escorted when outside the perimeter. They are eligible for all activities and programs inside the facility. Medium security housing may or may not include dorms and direct supervision units, depending on agency policy.
- *maximum custody:* inmates are considered extreme and serious risks for violence, escape and threats to themselves, other inmates and staff, and

are under strict supervision. They are restrained and under escort whenever they are transported beyond the facility perimeter, and should remain in their units or cells when not attending programs, recreation, visiting or any authorized activities. In some correctional institutions inmates can be housed in secure cellblocks designated general population/ maximum security, or be housed alone in segregation; segregation being the most extreme maximum security housing. Examples of the most secure maximum security housing would be Death Row, any secure segregation unit, etc. Well known examples of maximum security are Pelican Bay, California (California Department of Corrections) and the federal correctional facility in Florence, Colorado.

Reclassification

Is it fair not to change an inmate's classification? In some cases, the crimes are so serious and the inmate's behavior is so negative, a maximum custody level is justified and will remain in place for as long as the inmate is confined in the facility. An inmate can request a custody level change from classification or the unit management team, but that does not necessarily mean that it will occur.

Some inmates demonstrate that they can behave in the facility, follow the rules and try to better themselves. The security needs of the facility and the needs of the inmates both need to be reevaluated as their sentences or incarceration progresses, court sentences are handed down, detainers are dropped, institutional conduct records are established and other factors such as program involvement are considered. To be fair, the inmate's classification custody levels must be reevaluated on a regular basis (Henderson, et al., 1997, p. 18).

The information coming into classification must be timely, accurate and factually based on observations of and encounters with inmates. Some inmates deserve a second look—if they earn it. The CO can relay to the classification staff or the unit management team pertinent information. All staff—COs, counselors, programs staff etc. can supply information. Reclassification to a lower custody level can result in a transfer to another facility, transfer to a work release program, or eligibility to a trusty or programs assignment. Basically, the staff conducting a reevaluation of an inmate's custody level will look at several factors, including (Henderson, et al., 1997, pp. 18–19):

- percentage of time served in the facility or in the case of jails, amount of time incarcerated.
- type, seriousness and frequency of disciplinary reports incurred.

- involvement with drugs and/or alcohol in the institution.
- mental and psychological stability.
- staff assessments and reports of the inmate's level of personal responsibility.
- family or community ties.
- participation in programs.
- conduct on jobs, work assignments and in living quarters.

The inmates must be informed that if their behavior warrants it, their custody level status can be also increased. Criminal charges filed while incarcerated, disciplinary problems or lack of progress in work and programs can increase their level from medium or minimum to maximum, with results that they will not like—such as removal from trusty status, being placed in more restrictive housing and being transferred to a more secure facility. The choice of behavior and the consequences it brings is up to them.

Summary

The correctional facility is more than a mere building to house inmates. It consists of several key areas: staff and inmate entry/exit points, perimeter, administration areas, control centers, visiting areas and service areas. Other key areas are reserved for inmate housing. The custody level or housing is determined by classification procedures: intake, housing decisions and handling of disciplinary cases.

Classification procedures are closely related to the security aspect of the physical plant. Classification processes include the gathering of information when an inmate enters the facility and making a team decision on the inmate's custody level and housing assignment. Two main decision making bodies in terms of housing and custody levels are the ICC or Institutional Classification Committee and the unit management team. Also of importance is the reclassification of inmates if circumstances dictate its necessity. The disciplinary system of a facility—its rules and punishments—is a main tool of control.

There are three custody levels—minimum, medium and maximum. Security measures and housing of inmates depends on what custody levels he or she is in. Segregation—either administrative or disciplinary—is the most secure housing available.

Review Questions

1. What are some security concerns concerning visiting?
2. What are the three important objectives of classification?
3. What should be asked of inmates in an in-depth classification interview?
4. Discuss what should be covered in an inmate orientation.
5. Define the ICC and unit management team.
6. What are administrative segregation and disciplinary segregation?
7. Why is due process important in administrative hearings and what basic rights do inmates have?
8. Explain each of the three custody levels in a correctional facility.

Terms/Concepts

administrative segregation
 (A/S)
AKAs
classification
classification file
contact visits
dayroom
direct supervision
disciplinary segregation
 (D/S) .
dispensary
file review
general population
incompatibility
initial interview
inmate request form

Institutional Classification
 Committee
 (ICC)
linear design
maximum custody
medium custody
minimum custody
perimeter
personal visiting
podular remote surveillance
 (podular)
pre sentence investigation (PSI)
professional visiting
protective custody
receiving area (booking)
unit management

References

Alexandria (VA) Office of the Sheriff. (2004). *Inmate Handbook*.

Bales, Don, (Ed.). (1997). *Correctional Officer Resource Guide, Third Edition*. Lanham: American Correctional Association.

Cornelius, Gary F. (2008). *The American Jail: Cornerstone of Modern Corrections*. Upper Saddle River: Pearson Prentice Hall.

Cornelius, Gary. (1996). *Jails in America: An Overview of Issues, 2nd Ed.* Lanham: American Correctional Association.

Duncan, Peria. (2008). *Correctional Officer Resource Guide: Fourth Edition.* Alexandria: American Correctional Association.

Hampton Roads Regional Jail. (2003). *Inmate Handbook of Jail Rules and Regulations.*

Henderson, James D., W. Harvey Rauch and Richard L. Phillips. (1997). *Guidelines for the Development of a Security Program, 2nd Ed.* Lanham: American Correctional Association.

Kemble, Tod. (1996, May–June). Jails in America. *Texas Journal of Corrections,* pp. 14–19.

Chapter 9

Key and Tool Control, Headcounts, Searches and Transportation

Security is a term that is used very frequently in a correctional facility. Officers might hear that the warden's new directive "improves security" or that an inmate was moved to segregation to "maintain the security of the institution."

Security is defined by Webster as "freedom from danger, fear or anxiety; a place of safety" and has two main principles: (1) the prevention of escapes by inmates; and (2) the maintenance of peace and order in the facility. It requires constant vigilance (Newcomb, 1989, p. 2). All people who live and work in the facility as well as the public must be protected from harm.

Basic Security Duties

This chapter will explore the basic security duties of the correctional officer: key and tool control, headcounts, searches for contraband and the transporting of inmates. These duties are an integral part of officers' daily responsibilities in the institution. If mistakes are made, the results could be deadly.

Key and Tool Control

Correctional facilities are locked facilities. Cellblock doors, security gates, staff area doors, exit doors, and food slots on cellblock doors all require keys. While some large doors may be opened electronically from a control center, the backup system in case of power failure is a key. Keys include the old fashioned metal kind *and* the newer computer lock "proximity cards" or "prox cards" that open a door by swiping it across a computer lock. Keys also include handcuff keys which could be a prized possession for an inmate if stolen or lost by a CO.

Key control is basically common sense and accountability. Basically, besides post or housing keys used by the officer inside the facility, there are emergency keys and restricted keys. *Emergency keys* are keys that allow the staff rapid access to every part of the facility in case of riot, fire, power outage or other emergencies. A master key that opens *all* security gates is an emergency key. *Restricted keys* are keys for certain areas such as commissary, staff offices, gyms, laundry, etc. They are issued only to staffs who work in those areas (Bales, ed., 1997, pp. 48–49).

In some large facilities, administrators have established *keyed zones* or areas that require only specific keys. If the inmates, for example, seize an officer as a hostage, they cannot gain access into another area. In no case, however, should officers working in inmate housing areas or with inmates be issued keys to external doors or doors that lead to the outside of the facility (Newcomb, 1989, p. 5).

The following key control procedures are recommended by the American Correctional Association (Bales, ed., 1997, p. 49):

- Keys must be cross-indexed and numbered. Records should show where the keys fit, what keys are on what ring, what staff members handle that ring, etc. Also keys must be checked out from a secure control area.
- Keys never should be tossed to another staff member or left in a lock. Keys should be physically *handed* from one staff member to another.
- Keys to such areas as the armory or tool storage areas should never come into contact with inmates, *ever.*
- Entrance keys, external door keys or grand master keys should not be in circulation in the institution.
- Employees should *never* take institution keys home.
- If appropriate, such as in minimum security institutions, inmates may possess keys for lockers, rooms or work assignments. Inmates should never see security keys or be allowed to handle them.

Homemade Keys

Hardware stores are not the only places where keys are made— inmates can make them, too! Take the case of a prisoner in the Florida Department of Corrections where officers conducting a strip search discovered in his possession a homemade key which could open doors throughout the institution. A subsequent investigation discovered more hiding places where several dozen weapons were found. When the officers conducted a body cavity search, they found in the inmate's rectum seven hacksaw blades, thirty-four razor blades, $2,000.00 in cash and six homemade handcuff keys (Sweet, 1994, p. 75–76).

Tool Control

Tools in the hands of inmates become weapons or instruments of escape. Correctional facilities, like other buildings that are heavily used, frequently are in need of repair: door locks, elevators, etc, all require maintenance. All maintenance workers should be escorted by COs and be responsible for safeguarding their tools when working in the facility. Upon leaving, the entire work area must be inspected to make sure no tools or discarded material was left behind that could be fashioned into weapons by inmates.

All tools used by facility staff must be accounted for, either by a tool control officer who signs tools in/out to staff and supervised inmate workers or by a check in/out system, where staff logs out tools for use and logs in returns. Inventories are a must, preferably in the form of a daily check. Some institutions use shadow boards where officers can see quickly at a glance if any tools are missing. Tool control can also cover kitchen utensils and janitorial equipment (Bales, ed., 1997, pp. 46–47).

Headcounts

One of the most important duties that the correctional officer performs is the headcount. Inmates must be accounted for *at all times* even when out of the facility on a transport, at a doctor's appointment, at a police lineup or while in court. Corrections facilities are required legally to know where inmates are. If an escape occurs, it is a criminal offense, but authorities—the police, sheriff, or corrections agency will want to know how it happened and what the CO did or did not do properly.

There are three types of counts that are performed. They are:

1. *Formal count:* a regular count required by staff at certain times such as at shift change, before lockdowns and at meal times. Formal counts may be counted five or six times per day or as often as two hours in maximum security institutions.
2. *Census count:* verification of inmate presence at a program, work detail or activity (i.e., recreation).
3. *Emergency count:* count taken because of an emergency such as a fire, riot, disturbance, power outage, escape, etc.
   (*Correctional Officer Correspondence Course,* Book III, 1997, p. 72)

If an inmate wishes to escape, he/she needs to successfully thwart the count. Such methods may include having another inmate be counted twice, using a dummy in a bed (for night counts) or convincing staff by forged pass or verbal manipulation that they are supposed to be in an area, program or activity, but in reality, they are not (*Correctional Officer Correspondence Course*, 1997, Book III, p. 72). In reality, officers can conduct counts anytime they feel it is necessary. In fact, the inmates should be well aware that they are subject to a count at any time. Good security means that inmates are always "looking over their shoulder" for the CO.

Guidelines for Effective Headcounts

Concerning headcounts in any type of correctional facility, officers should:
- be aware that they, not inmates, control the count. If necessary, inmate movement can be stopped. Inmates may be required to stand in front of their cells or stand in line. Two officers may be necessary to conduct counts of large numbers of inmates;
- counts only should be conducted by officers, and never by inmates. Inmates should never be permitted to assist in a count;
- if the count is interrupted, start over;
- all inmates should be checked by physical observation in their living/work/programs areas at least every thirty minutes;
- when conducting a headcount, the officer should see skin and breathing if the inmate appears asleep. Inmates have escaped using life-like heads and lumps made of clothing under bed clothes to fool officers;
- inmates should be observed for changes in morale or mood. Emotional changes in inmates can "tip" the officer off that something is wrong such as violence, escape attempts/plans, sexual assaults or suicides;
- all counts—formal, informal, census or emergency—must be documented in a log or on a form. In training, it must be stressed that when an officer signs for a count, he/she is signing an official record that he/she physically accounted for the inmates;
- if the officers' count cannot be verified by the official roster, the count must be retaken.
  (Newcomb, 1989, p. 5, *Correctional Officer Correspondence Course*, 1997, Book III, pp. 73–76)

Searches

Besides headcounts, another crucial duty of the correctional officer is searching: searching common areas, living areas, incoming mail, laundry carts, book carts, vehicles entering and leaving the facility, inmate property and belong-

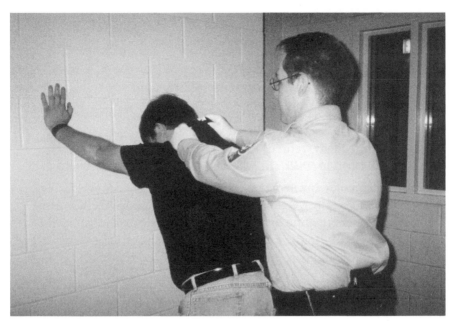

Jail officer searching an inmate. Note that the officer places the inmate at a safe distance, off balance. The officer proceeds to check the inmates body for contraband or weapons. Note the gloves. Clarke-Frederick-Winchester (VA) Regional Adult Detention Center.

ings, and the inmates themselves. Thorough searches are very instrumental in maintaining tight security in the institution.

Contraband

The goal of any good search is to ascertain if the inmate has contraband or items not authorized by the facility administration such as illegal drugs, weapons (including homemade weapons), etc. (see Chapter 3). Contraband can also include excess authorized items such as an inmate having two extra blankets when inmates are only issued one (Cornelius, 1996, p. 67). Contraband covers a broad range of items and its definition can include anything that correctional officers thinks is a threat to institutional security.

Generally, contraband is defined differently in each correctional facility; but other general guidelines and definitions parallel the aforementioned definition. Contraband can be any item not permitted to be received by inmates, sold inside the facility, received from the outside, or if approved, changed or modified (*Correctional Officer Correspondence Course, Book III*, 1997, pp. 22–24). Possession or trafficking in contraband is a disciplinary offense and in some jurisdictions, a criminal offense. For example, an inmate selling illegal drugs within the institution can be charged with an in-house disciplinary offense and a criminal or "street" charge.

Contraband in its many forms is a testament to *inmate ingenuity*. Inmate ingenuity is defined as the unlimited imagination and ideas that inmates exhibit in terms of contraband, manipulation of staff (see Chapter 11) and escape attempts.

Maintaining Safety and Security by Managing Contraband
by Edward W. Szostak
Superintendent (retired) Albany County Correctional Facility
Published in *American Jails*, July/August 1998, pp. 62–64

Contraband is any item that is prohibited in a correctional facility. Contraband in a correctional facility is a very serious matter. It requires diligent attention by correctional staff daily to combat the creativity of inmates in their efforts to create or acquire these forbidden items. Contraband may be a pen, a paper clip, currency, gum, pow-

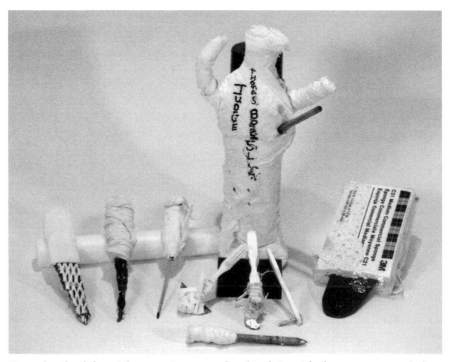

Contraband—left to right: two wire screens, handmade ice pick, three weapons made from toothbrushes and sharpened metal, sponge with sharpened metal from a radio speaker; bottom: sharpened bolt; top: "voodoo" doll made from toilet paper with a judge's name printed on the doll. Albany County (NY) Correctional Facility.

dered coffee creamers, cigarettes, matches, lighters, or even certain types of shoes or sneakers. Contraband varies at each facility depending on the level of security and classification of inmates. Some form of contraband exists in most correctional environments.

The Albany County Correctional Facility is currently a 1,005-bed facility (mega jail) that has experienced many phases of construction since 1982. The original facility was built in 1931 and had a 350-bed capacity.

The facility has an average daily population of 739 and currently employs a staff of 325. The 1998 budget has allocated the hiring of 32 new corrections positions and 7 registered nurses. We are in the process of filling these positions.

[Author's note: According to the Albany County Sheriff's Office website, the institution now has a maximum capacity of 1,029 beds, employs a sworn and civilian staff totaling 420, and has an average daily population of over 800 inmates. In the past year (2008) over 7,000 offenders were booked into the jail (Albany County Sheriff's Department, 2009).]

The Albany County Correctional Facility is proud to state that as of January 27, 1997, we became an accredited facility by the New York State Sheriffs' Association and the New York State Commission of Correction.

The Albany County Correctional Facility has experienced a variety of contraband items, i.e., homemade knives (shanks), homemade alcohol (home brew), and in order to create contraband hiding places inmates have hollowed out books and bars of soap. We have found bars of soap carved into various shapes including the shape of a small handgun. The gun appears quite genuine once colored with a black magic marker or pen. Broom and mop handles can be fashioned into spears, shanks or clubs; bed sheets braided like rope; broken Plexiglas mirrors and pens can be sharpened and made into shanks. Even harmless powdered coffee creamers can be dangerous. When the powdered creamer is blown through a hollow pen or straw-like device onto a flame, it becomes a crude flame thrower.

Construction Projects

Correctional staffs working in facilities that have experienced construction projects, whether major or minor, need to be attentive. We all recognize our business is somewhat unique; therefore, we must look at and handle things differently than businesses not concerned with the security issues we encounter. Common equipment or items used by contractors must not be left abandoned or improperly disposed of because inmates can acquire them and use them for entirely different purposes. Account for everything. All construction workers and managers will need to be informed of security requirements long before the job begins and reminded throughout the project. Pre bid conferences, preconstruction meetings, and all construction-related documents must clearly state the requirements that will be enforced. Security staff must constantly review deficiencies, address them, and notify supervisors immediately.

Contractors must be prohibited from bringing in glass soda bottles, pocket knives, money, and medications. The contractors should also be instructed not to have any contact with inmates. They need to be advised to properly inventory all materials such as screws, nails, and spent shell casings (unused ammunition for nail guns). Vehicle security procedures also need to be addressed, requiring that all vehicles and keys be secured at all times. Tools and heavy equipment must be secured and ladders are to be removed at the end of each day and properly secured.

Contraband Type and Methods of Obtaining

Some items once allowed, but now forbidden, introduce a whole new array of security problems. For example, the Albany County Correctional Facility is now a smoke free facility and has been for over three years. This has generated some interest by inmates who illegally obtain smokes of any kind and something to ignite them. Smuggling tobacco products by mail and/or packages, visitors, and even bribing staff are current methods used to introduce contraband. Other methods include inserting drugs or weapons into a rubber handball, sealing it, and then throwing it over perimeter fences or walls into recreation areas for the intended recipient. Obviously, correction officers need to be diligent in their efforts to search for and detect such methods. Contraband has also been introduced by the inmates' family members, even going so far as to placing contraband in an infant's diaper. Shoes, boots, and sneakers are also sources of contraband. Most foot apparel contains a metal arch support that reinforces the firmness of the footwear. This metal arch has been removed by inmates and then sharpened into homemade shanks or shivs.

Major Facility Searches/Shakedowns

To minimize the amount of contraband over the years the staff of the Albany County Correctional Facility has conducted three major shakedowns, all following the 1991, 1993, and 1996 construction projects. The entire facility was shut down and searched from top to bottom. It was estimated to cost approximately $10,000.00 per search, each search taking between 8 to 12 hours to complete. Teams needed to be established. Our teams consisted of a K-9 unit and their handlers from local law enforcement agencies, identification officers for photographic evidence, property officers to account for confiscated items, maintenance staff to provide access to plumbing and electrical areas, additional correction officers, supervisors, and administrators.

An announcement was made to all inmates the night prior to lockdown time (22:00) of the shakedown at 07:00. Reports of toilets flushing continuously throughout the night were noted by correction officers working the midnight shifts. Officers also found items thrown into common areas during their routine rounds.

Contraband Control

Once a method of making a weapon or obtaining prohibited items has been identified, measures are taken to minimize future access and opportunity. Such measures include inmates found in possession of contraband being prosecuted to the fullest extent of the law; daily searches of individual housing units; portable metal detectors; and K-9 patrols being used during inmate visitations.

Additionally, changes have been made to equipment and supplies to reduce availability of articles that can be used as weapons. Such measures include stainless steel toilets and sinks replacing porcelain fixtures, plastic replacing metal mop handles, and mop heads that had metal frames and screws now having plastic frames and clips. We purchase our cleaning supplies in plastic containers instead of containers that use metal lids. Factory-sealed bakery products with plastic clips replace items that were once sealed with metal twist ties. These metal twist ties can be used as a conductor of ignition in electrical outlets. Heavy duty non breakable plastic footlockers replace metal footlockers and all-plastic chairs replace metal and wood office furniture. Only clear trash liners are used because they permit visual inspection of contents.

The most recent step we have taken is seeking and obtaining the funding for the purchase of orange-colored canvas foot wear for all inmates upon admission. Sheriff James L. Campbell persuaded the Albany County Legislature to provide the $20,000.00 needed to purchase the canvas sneakers. Fortunately, the Albany County Sheriff's Office has experienced a good working relationship with the legislative branch of our county government.

Once the canvas sneakers are purchased and received, all inmates' personal shoes, boots, and sneakers are confiscated and placed with their property and held until their release. They will then be issued a pair of bright orange facility-issued canvas sneakers. Surprisingly, during the budget hearings, the media took great interest in this topic. This resulted in positive public relations for the facility with state and local media groups.

Sheriff James L. Campbell and I are proud to say that we have a very dedicated and professional staff. Training plays an important role in ensuring that officers and civilian staff *always practice safe techniques* during their everyday routines. These factors and our conscious efforts greatly reduce contraband in the Albany County Correctional Facility.

* * *

Edward W. Szostak retired from the Superintendent's position of the Albany County Correctional Facility, located in Albany, New York. He began his career as a corrections officer in January 1975. He rose through the ranks of sergeant, lieutenant, captain, chief, and assistant superintendent, moving to acting superintendent in 1990 and earning the full-fledged title the following year. During his tenure the facility expanded from a 350-bed institution to its now 1,005-bed capacity, went smoke free, and was awarded a Certificate of Accreditation in January 1997 by the New York State Commission of Correction and the New York State Sheriffs' Association. He formed Szostak and Associates, Criminal Justice Consulting, 89 Latham Ridge Road, Latham, NY 12110, phone 518-783-1641, e mail EWSzostak@aol.com.
Photos by Al Roland, Sr. Identification Officer.
Reprinted by permission of the American Jail Association.

Inmates have made shanks from the metal arches in shoes (Szostak, 1998, pp. 62–64) and have even sharpened toothbrushes. One jail officer reported that an inmate took a hollow plastic pen barrel and glued (by melting plastic) a sharpened coin on the end to make an arrow! Inmates have placed razor blades upright in deodorant sticks and made "bongs" out of light bulbs. One inmate had a jar of peanut butter mailed to him from the outside. When the COs inspected it, they discovered a two shot derringer pistol concealed inside the jar in a plastic bag. The jar had been resealed. There is no end to "inmate ingenuity." COs must remember the following throughout their careers: **Never underestimate the imagination and intelligence of inmates** (Cornelius, 1998, p. 34).

While contraband cannot be eliminated entirely, it should be controlled for these primary reasons (*Correctional Officer Correspondence Course*, Book III, 1997, p. 25):

• Possession and trafficking of contraband gives inmates power.

- Inmates can make weapons or poisons from contraband for use against staff, other inmates or on themselves.
- Inmates can escape or cause a disturbance with the use of contraband.
- Limiting and the aggressive control of contraband results in the better control of inmates and safety in the facility.

Basic Types of Searches

Searches in correctional systems fall into three categories: individual inmate searches, housing unit/work area searches, and vehicle searches. Searching inmates as well as all areas where they live, attend programs, and when transported to and from the facility is a fundamental part of the job of the CO. To be a good CO, one must put his or her hands on inmates and their belongings. There is no room for doubt and hesitation. Correctional facilities and inmates must be searched.

Individual inmate searches: There are three types (*Correctional Officer Correspondence Course*, Book III, 1997, p. 36):

1. *Frisk ("patdown"):* This is the most general type of search. It encompasses inspection of the inmate's clothing and body through the cloth-

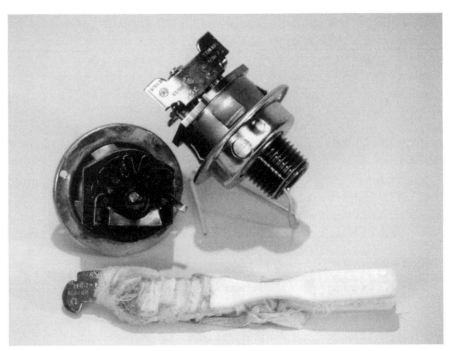

Contraband—standard sprinkler head modified into a weapon at the end of a toothbrush. Albany County (NY) Correctional Facility.

ing. Officers run hands over clothing to ascertain if anything is hidden in cuffs, under arms, etc. (see p. 213). Dentures, toupees and prostheses are removed and inspected.

2. *Body (strip search):* Strip searches examine the skin surface of the inmate, including hiding places in hair, behind the ears, under breasts (females), armpits, genitals (male), behind the knees, on the soles and between toes, and between the buttocks. Dentures, toupees and prostheses are removed and inspected.

3. *Body cavity search:* This type of search examines inside body openings such as the anus, vagina, etc. It should be done due to a reasonable suspicion that the inmate has concealed contraband inside a body opening. It should be performed *only* upon authorization of the warden, staff duty officer, etc. Also, it *must* be performed either manually or by instrument by trained medical personnel. Dentures, toupees and prostheses are removed and inspected.

Pat downs do not have to be in private, but strip and body cavity searches must be in private and performed in a way not to offend the dignity of the inmate. Officers should be located behind inmates for safety. All searches should be documented, such as pat searches entered in a log or shift report; strip and body searches written in an incident report.

Housing unit/work area searches: Inmates refer to these types of searches as "shakedowns." These searches of dayrooms, cells, kitchens, closets, classrooms, libraries, etc., should follow the principle of being "*systematically unsystematic.*" This means that the staff has a plan where to search, but makes it appear random to keep the inmates off guard. Correctional officer conducting searches of this type should ask themselves: **"Where would I hide contraband in here if I was an inmate?"**

Everything in the area should be searched, including bedding, furniture, wall cracks, holes, books, magazines, newspapers, large cans (for false bottoms), window bars, frames, ventilators, shelves, drawers, cabinets, etc. However, in this era of AIDS and diseases passed by blood borne pathogens, inmates do secretly hide needles for tattooing or drug usage and an officer searching "blindly" can get stuck (Bales, ed., 1997, p. 45).

Vehicle Searches: All commercial vehicles such as delivery trucks, trash trucks, etc., should be searched when entering and leaving the perimeter. Some institutions use mirrors, mechanics' "creepers" or inspection pits to check underneath the vehicle for contraband or inmates. Narcotics or pharmaceuticals should be unloaded in a secure area away from inmates. Also, the contents list of shipments and/or vehicles must be checked against the payload or cargos,

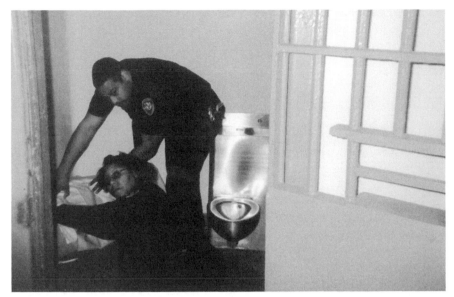

No matter what type of correctional institution, any areas where inmates have access should be searched frequently and thoroughly. Maryland Department of Corrections.

particularly paying close attention to boxes that are partially opened, damaged, marked in an unusual way or are extra (Bales, ed., 1997, p. 45).

Staff must remember that inmate workers (trusties) are the "movers and shakers" of contraband in the facility. Trusties also have access to materials that other inmates do not. When inmate labor, including trusties, is used, there is a strong possibility that security will be breached (Newcomb, 1989, pp. 5–6).

Transportation

Transporting inmates, even for short distances, is one of the most dangerous tasks for a correctional officer. Transporting an inmate, who must always be considered an escape risk, is dangerous when out of the secure environment of the institution. Inmates have escaped while on a transport and some of these escapes have been very daring. For example, an inmate charged with carjacking, kidnapping, making terrorist threats and false imprisonment escaped from jail officers at a local hospital where he was to have a broken wrist recast. As soon as the hospital elevator doors opened—out he ran. Unconfirmed reports said that two females were waiting in a vehicle to pick him up (Bay City News, 2004).

To have as safe a transport as possible, the American Correctional Association (ACA) recommends the followings steps:

Good security mandates that all visitors and vehicles entering the facility should be identified, logged, and searched if necessary. Maryland Department of Corrections.

1. *Planning*: Officer should plan the basic route of travel *and* an alternative route in case of emergencies. Transporting officers should check the inmate's file for security violations and behavioral problems. The inmate's identity also must be verified before transporting.
2. *Preparing*: Officers should never assume that an inmate and his/her belongings have been searched satisfactorily by another officer. The inmate may complain that a search has already been done; this could be a ploy to throw the officer off guard. Inmates should be strip searched before transporting and after the inmate returns to the facility. Inmates' belongings must be thoroughly searched. The transporting vehicle must be checked for contraband left by an inmate or worker and to see if the vehicle and equipment (such as a radio or emergency beacon) are operable.
    (*Correctional Officer Correspondence Course, Book III*, 1997, pp. 137–138)

Every inmate, though appearing to abide by the rules, may attempt to escape if an opportunity presents itself. Restraining devices must be used. The most common are:

- handcuffs: two connected metal rings, locked, placed around the wrists. They should be double locked with the holes facing the inmate's body or head. Inmate's hands should be facing in opposite directions. Handcuff keys are small as are paper clips which can be used to pick the locks if inmates have them hidden on their person.
- waist chain: effective because it lowers mobility of inmate's hands. It is placed through the inmate's belt loops and attached to handcuffs.
- ankle shackles: larger and sturdier, they act like handcuffs, but around the ankles.

Other guidelines are that transporting officers should follow procedures at all times and *always* be cognizant of the fact that *any* inmate may seize an opportunity to escape. Inmates should be visible to the CO at all times, seated away from officers' weapons and not be allowed to change seats or come into any contact whatsoever with the public.

Patrol Techniques

Correctional officers, like their counterparts on the street (police officers), must patrol their "beats." That beat could be the facility perimeter, a dormitory, a housing unit, a floor of cellblocks, etc. Each inmate housing area is a community just like each street or subdivision in an outside community. Each "community" has its security flaws, different inmate personalities, conflicts and problems.

Officers on patrol should be aware of all possible and existing security breaches, fire hazards, etc. in their areas and report these conditions to their supervisors and request corrective action. Also, the officer should know as much as he can about inmates in his/her area, activities that are going on and the whereabouts of all inmates in the designated area. He/she should know who comes, who goes, and who is authorized to be in an area.

Checks of areas and unusual occurrences must be logged. The elements of security discussed in this chapter—counting, key/tool control and searches—all interact during the officer's shift.

Officer checking perimeter fence, Maryland House of Correction.

Complacency

The officer's worst enemy besides the inmates is complacency. Complacency resulting in boredom can be an ally to the inmate. Officers working the same routine for a long period of time can become complacent, especially when a false sense of security sets in because serious incidents rarely occur. Examples of officer complacency include: failure to check identification of inmates, conducting poor searches, sleeping on post, exercising inadequate control of tools and keys, watching television on post, playing computer games on post, conducting poor inspections, exhibiting sloppy work habits, submitting poorly written reports, not entering critical information in observation logs and failing to exercise control and discipline when dealing with inmates. In one institution, the command staff, as a training exercise, planted a laminated card along the facility outside perimeter. The card read: "Bring this to the Chief of Security." At least seventeen officers walked by this card over a six-day period before it was discovered! (Czerniak and Upchurch, 1996, Cornelius, 1996, pp. 28–29). Rotation of personnel, training exercises and close supervision all can combat complacency.

Informants

The use of informants to aid law enforcement officers is as old as the law enforcement profession itself. Police officers get the information needed to solve crimes from those close to or are engaging in criminal activity.

The corrections officer, as part of his/her daily patrol duties, uses confidential informants. Simply defined, a *confidential informant* is an inmate who gives information to a correctional officer on the condition that his/her identity will remain anonymous. Inmates who act as informants usually want something and what they want may not be entirely clear to the officer. However, some motives of an inmate informant are as follows (*Correctional Officer Correspondence Course, Book III*, 1997, p. 102):

- *fear*: the inmate feels threatened by other inmates' activities *or* planned activities such as an escape plot, contraband manufacture/smuggling or taking of a hostage. The informant wants no part of them.
- *revenge*: the inmate believes that he/she has been treated unfairly or harshly by other inmates.
- *animosity*: to eliminate competition from other inmates, such as in trafficking contraband or making a "power play," the inmate may turn informant.
- *egotism*: the inmate wants the staff to think well of him/her.
- *reward or favor*: the inmate may relate information to an officer in hopes of receiving a reward or favor such as a trusty job, special visit, etc.
- *desire to reform*: an inmate may become an informant because they feel remorse for their crime and wish to do a "good deed" for society.
- *playing a game*: an inmate may give false information to confuse officers, especially new, inexperienced officers.

Officers must use common sense when dealing with confidential informants. In addition to ascertaining the motives of the informant, the CO should never promise any type of reward and all information should be relayed up the chain of command to the officer's supervisors for discussion and follow up. The officer should *never* reveal the identity of the inmate, either verbally or in writing. It does not matter if the CO needs or wants the information given (*Correctional Officer Correspondence Course, Book III*, 1997, p. 102). Many correctional officers use the terms "confidential source," "reliable source," or "anonymous source/inmate" all which mean confidential informant.

Correctional officers realize the value of inmates giving up information to the staff—being a "snitch." Many inmates are snitches in one way or another and are in prison because they were informed on, according to an officer at the Lebanon (Ohio) Correctional Institution. The trait is brought into the prison. One ten year veteran of Lebanon says that snitching "stops a lot of things … it prevents drug deals … escapes … and it prevents people from getting hurt" (Wojda, Wojda, Smith, Jones, 1991, p. 29).

Escapes

A fundamental goal of a good correctional security system is the prevention of escapes. Every inmate thinks of escape at one time or another. Some dismiss the thought while others try. To the correctional officer, *every* inmate is an escape risk, no matter what his/her charge, demeanor or time left to serve.

The term *escape* can be defined as "an inmate's criminal absence from the confines of the institution or extended confinement area" with the intent to remain at large" (Camp, 2003, p. 49). The absence is unauthorized and the inmate is subject to criminal prosecution as well as in-house disciplinary action. The extended confinement area could be the community, program, job or work detail outside the facility that the inmate is legally permitted access to. An inmate could be charged with escape if he/she was on work release and did not report to a job. An inmate can be charged with escape if absent without authorization from a work detail or transport. Also, this extended area also includes being in the legal custody of a correctional officer or a law enforcement officer, such as on a transport to a police station, court, another facility, etc.

The Desperation of Escapes

Correctional officer should remember at all times that the lives of inmates have been disrupted by incarceration. The things important to them on the outside can impact them inside, such as the family moving on, a significant other ending the relationship; the children are growing up without them, etc. Desperate people may do desperate things:

- A desperate escape occurred in 1983 in Alabama where eleven inmates ran through holes hacked in fences under a barrage of shotgun fire. Within forty-five minutes, nine were recaptured (*Washington Post*, 8/29/83).
- Women inmates desperately try for freedom, too. In 1984, five inmates, including two convicted killers, escaped from maximum security by squeezing through steel bars covering a window. The women, ranging

in size from 5'2", 110 lbs, to 5'6", 150 lbs., squeezed through bars fifteen inches high and less than eight inches apart (*Washington Post*, 12/17/84).

Staff mistakes can make an escape easy. For example, in 1982, two Pennsylvania county prison employees were suspended after one left his post to get coffee, leaving his keys on his desk and two doors unlocked. An inmate charged with rape and kidnapping escaped. A few months before, the same inmate escaped from a West Virginia jail by crawling through a ventilation system to the jail roof! (*Pittsburgh Press*, 12/31/82). Two inmates from a Southern jail used a piece of light fixture to open a jail door latch. It was easy because the door installer hung the door *upside down!* (*Detroit News*, 1996).

Inmate Ingenuity: Escapes

How far will inmates go in devising escape plans and carrying them out? Here is a sampling:

- Three Texas inmates purchased hundreds of yards of dental floss at the jail's canteen (commissary). Authorities discovered that they braided it into a rope and used cardboard salt and pepper containers for stirrups on a ladder.
- A convicted forger escaped from an Arizona jail by having a forged release order faxed to jailors.
- In one facility, booking received a telephone call from a probation officer (PO) requesting that a certain inmate be released. However, there was no PO; the phone call came from the inmate himself calling from one of the facility's pay telephones (Sweet, 1994, pp. 72–79, Stinchcomb, 2005, p. 220).

Courthouse Escapes

Jail correctional officers' duties extend frequently to the courthouse. Inmates must be escorted from the jail to court and defendants appearing in court are often remanded to custody. Correctional officers no matter what their assignments are must remember that whenever an inmate is out of his or her cell or living area, he or she may seize an opportunity to escape. Desperate people do desperate things. Consider these escapes from court:

- An inmate just sentenced to life in prison escaped from a Florida courthouse by slipping out of his handcuffs, hitting a deputy with a five foot ladder and prying open a metal garage door that led to the street. He managed to pry the door open through brute strength and squeeze out a one foot opening. He was recaptured after leading police on a high speed chase in a stolen vehicle. As he was being placed into a sheriff's vehicle he proclaimed "I am going to make them kill me" (*Pensacola News Journal, 2008*).

• An inmate suspected of serious crimes, including attempted murder escaped from a group of inmates returning to a prison minimum security honor farm. Not only did the CO fail to escort the inmates, the escapee changed prison uniforms with an inmate who had a Honor Farm classification and resembled the escapee. The change took place in a toilet space in a holding area. After switching uniforms, the two inmates lined up to go to their classified destinations. The escapee got into a van that was idling nearby reportedly driven by his girlfriend. As a result a security overhaul was planned including the implementation of a fingerprint scanning security system that scans the offenders' index finger and identifies them with offenders in the county law enforcement database (Thompson, 2007).

Escape Policies and Procedures

While escape policies and procedures vary from facility to facility, certain items are basic in nature. To prevent escapes, policies should include these measures (Henderson, Rauch and Phillips, 1997, p. 187):

1. Reporting unrest, tension, changes in inmate behavior or conduct;
2. Basic security accountability: tool and key control, counts, searches, inspections, etc.
3. Classification review of all inmates including designating high risk inmates;
4. Proper work and living assignments;
5. Prompt correction/repair of security breaches and plans to cover breaches until repairs are completed.

A functional escape plan provides procedures for maintaining security, notifying law enforcement agencies, and strategies for capturing the escapee. The American Correctional Association (ACA) recommends eighteen points.

Escape Plan

No matter how secure the institution, inmates will try to escape. During an escape attempt, officers must act quickly to stop the attempt and recapture the inmate(s). That is why a functional escape plan is vitally important for every institution. While the methods used by inmates in escape attempts vary, escape plans should contain the fundamental search and surveillance techniques that cover most situations. A functional plan includes the following elements:

Defining an escape. A clear definition is needed of what specifically constitutes an escape and the use of deadly force to stop escapees, in the particular jurisdiction involved, as opposed to an inmate being "off-limits," "out of bounds," or some other lesser infraction.

Reporting an escape. Staff in the institution must know whom they should notify in the event they believe an inmate is missing. In most cases, this is the control center.

Alerting the perimeter and gateposts. As soon as an inmate is believed to be missing, the perimeter and gatepost staff and any outlying patrol staff should be notified.

Securing the area. The entire institution should be secured; inmates must return to their quarters/cells.

Providing a count. The inmates in the institution should be counted immediately, to determine the identity of the missing inmates; in most cases, a picture card (identification) count will be needed to verify the identity of those missing.

Notifying top staff. The plan should specify the order in which top staff should be notified, usually starting with the warden.

Stating hostage information. The plan clearly should state that no inmate with a hostage is to be released, and that no hostage has any authority.

Identifying key posts to continue to staff. Some areas can be secured and their staff assigned to the escape hunt; others, such as the powerhouse and food service, must continue to operate; these positions should be identified in advance so no confusion results from removing staff from a critical post.

Establishing a command center. This area includes not only internal communications and command functions, but also communication with local and state law enforcement personnel assisting in the escape hunt.

Recalling staff. Using a current list of all employees and pre established call-up procedures, off-duty employees should be told to report.

Notifying local law enforcement. This section of the plan should state who is authorized to notify local law enforcement personnel of the escape, and by what means; it also may involve distribution of escape flyers.

Using internal searches to apprehend hideouts. The plan should specify internal search procedures to apprehend inmates who may be hiding inside the facility, awaiting darkness, fog, or some other time when it may be more favorable to try to escape the secure compound.

Planning external searches. Plans/procedures need to be in place that includes the use of force regarding "fresh pursuit," and coordination with allied agencies.

Establishing outside escape posts. The plan should establish fixed and roving escape posts, identify the equipment that should go on each post, and describe the other procedures necessary to staff these posts, including issuance of equipment.

Providing staff support on escape posts. The plan should provide for the regular relief, feeding, and checking of staff on remote posts.

Offering strategies for apprehending and restraining escapees. The plan should provide staff with clear guidance on actions they should and should not take when apprehending an escapee. At least two officers should be present to search any escapees after they are captured; if only one officer captures an inmate, the inmate should stay "spread-eagled" on the ground until backup assistance arrives.

Notifying of capture. When inmates have been captured, the procedures must specify who will notify all law enforcement agencies, communities, and the media.

Interviewing escapees. The plan must ensure that any interviews with escapees are done in a way that does not hamper the criminal prosecution of an escapee by compromising any constitutional rights.

[Reprinted with permission from the American Correctional Association, Alexandria, VA: "Chapter 7: Emergency Plans and Procedures," *Correctional Officer Resource Guide, 3rd Edition,* edited by Don Bales, ed., 1997, pp. 66–67.]

One thing that law enforcement agencies must have in order to successfully recapture an escapee is escape intelligence. *Escape intelligence* is defined as a comprehensive package of information that lets law enforcement agencies know as much information as possible about the escape, safety concerns and who should be contacted in case of apprehension. The following information should be in this summary: (Henderson, et al., 1997, p. 188):

- name of escapee, including all known aliases or nicknames;

- escapee's sex, race, nationality/ethnic origin, birth date, age, height, weight, hair/eye color, scars, marks, tattoos, state of residence and social security number or numbers, if the inmate uses more than one;
- recent photos of escapee;
- escapee's crime, sentence and any detainers (detainers are charges pending from another jurisdiction);
- Federal Bureau of Investigation numbers, state police numbers and/or local police case numbers;
- fingerprint classification;
- last known residence, past associates, likely places, residences, groups, etc., to which he/she could return;
- driver's license and vehicle information, if available;
- information as to whether the escapee is considered violent, dangerous or armed;
- name and title of the agency staff person who should be contacted if another agency captures the escapee.

Intelligence must be gathered when an escape occurs. Not only does staff have to file a detailed report, other information must be gathered from inmate informants, staff observations, the family of the escapee (if cooperative, etc.). The incident must be analyzed for causative factors, security breakdowns, etc., for use in training and revising procedures. One key part of an escape investigation is the gathering of information from the inmate's file, visiting lists, property and mail (Henderson, et al., 1997, p. 189).

Summary

Security in a correctional institution is an ongoing process involving observation of inmates through key and tool control, headcounts, proper searches, safe transportation of procedures and escape prevention and apprehension. The basic definition of security is "freedom from danger" for staff, inmates and the public. Lack of control can cause assaults, escapes and security breakdowns. Procedures must be in place and followed.

Keys and tools can become serious security problems if placed in the hands of inmates. Common sense methods of control, such as logs, etc., can help in their control.

Headcounts are crucial to security and must be conducted properly, either formally or informally. Searches of inmates and facility areas reduce the risk of contraband.

Transporting inmates safely takes careful planning and preparation. Inmates in desperate bids for freedom can escape during transports or by "inmate ingenuity"—schemes and daring plans, sometimes involving contraband. No less important is the fact that desperate inmates will attempt to escape from courthouses.

Inmate informants can pass along information to the officer, but an informant's motive may be self-serving.

Review Questions

1.   Why is the control of keys and tools important?
2.   Name four guidelines for successful headcounts.
3.   Define contraband and describe several examples.
4.   Describe the three types of inmate searches.
5.   How should a correctional officer prepare for a safe transport?
6.   What motives could a confidential informant have in supplying information to staff?
7.   Name four points of a good escape plan.

Terms/Concepts

body cavity search   *formal count*
body (strip) search   *frisk (patdown)*
census count   *inmate ingenuity*
confidential informant   *keyed zones*
emergency count   *restricted keys*
emergency keys   *security*
escape   *systematically unsystematic*
escape intelligence

References

Albany County Sheriff's Department: www.albanycountysheriff.com/correction facility.html (Accessed April 17, 2009).

American Correctional Association. (1997). *Correctional Officer Correspondence Course Book III: Security Issues.* Lanham: American Correctional Association.

Around the Nation: 11 Escape Top Security Prison in Alabama. *Washington Post*, 8/29/83.

Bales, Don, (Ed.). (1997). *Correctional Officer Resource Guide, 3rd Ed.* Lanham: American Correctional Association.

Bay City News. Dangerous Prisoner Escapes Custody in Calif. Corrections.com (January 9–11, 2004) www.corrections.com/ (Accessed January 9, 2004).

Camp, Camille Graham, (Ed.). (2003). *The Corrections Yearbook: Adult Corrections 2002.* Middletown: Criminal Justice Institute, Inc.

Cornelius, Gary. (1998, Summer). No. 36: Inmate Ingenuity Revisited. *The Journal of Correctional Training,* International Association of Correctional Training Personnel, pp. 33–34.

Cornelius, Gary. (1996, Winter). Complacency: Our Own Worse Enemy. *The Journal of Correctional Training,* International Association of Correctional Training Personnel, pp. 28–29.

Cornelius, Gary. (1996). *Jails in America: An Overview of Issues, 2nd Ed.* Lanham: American Correctional Association.

Czerniak, Stan W. and James R. Upchurch. (1996, July). If It Ain't Broke, Break It: Continuous Improvement in Prison Security. *Corrections Today,* pp. 62–64.

Detroit News. The Lighter Side. Home Page: 1/11/96. http://www.det news.com/menu/stories/31707.htm.

5 Inmates Escape. *Washington Post,* 12/17/84.

Henderson, James D., W. Hardy Rauch, and Richard L. Phillips. (1997). *Guidelines for the Development of a Security Program, 2nd Ed.* Lanham: American Correctional Association.

Newcomb, Walter. (1989). Basic Security Principles. *Jail Operations Bulletin. American Jail Association, Vol. 1, No. 7.*

Pensacola News Journal. (2008, October 24). Prisoner captured after courthouse escape. pnj.com. [Online]. Available: http://www.pnj.com (November 3, 2008).

Two Suspended After Jail Escape. *Pittsburgh Press,* p. A-5. 12/31/82.

Stinchcomb, Jeanne B., Ph.D. (2005). *Corrections: Past Present, and Future.* Lanham: American Correctional Association.

Sweet, Roland. (1994). *Law and Disorder—Weird News of Crime and Punishment,* N.Y., Signet.

Szostak, Edward. (1998, July–August). Maintaining Safety and Security by Managing Contraband. *American Jails,* pp. 62–64.

Thompson, Ellen. (2007, May 28). Safety concerns at Calif. Courthouse following prisoner's escape. Policeone.com news [Online]. Available: http://www.policeone.com/pc_print.asp?vid=1267316 (November 3, 2008).

Wojda, Grace, Raymond Wojda, Norman E. Smith and Richard Jones. (1991). *Behind Bars.* Waldorf: American Correctional Association and St. Mary's Press.

Chapter 10

Interacting with Inmates

Correctional officers are locked into a controlled environment just as the inmates are. However, correctional officers can leave after their shift and the inmates stay. During that shift, whether it is eight, ten or twelve hours, the correctional officer must be able to effectively: (1) communicate with inmates in a two-way or reciprocal fashion; and (2) give instructions in a way that the inmates willingly comply. In other words, inmates and staff must "get along."

Correctional officers do not carry weapons inside the institution. Their primary means of not allowing tensions to escalate are their brains, their behavior and the words that they speak. Good communication with inmates means much more than just talking with them; it means interaction and effective interpersonal communications. One rule to remember is:

Think about what you are going to say *before* you say it.

Another basic rule that officers should keep in mind is that inmates must be viewed as people. An officer who stereotypes inmates into "slang" categories such as "slugs," "scumbags" and a few more colorful terms will find his/her job very difficult. These prejudices will be felt by the inmate. Interacting with inmates is only part of the whole being of the correctional officer. This "being" or "makeup" is called *officer comportment.*

Officer comportment simply means the manner in which an officer presents himself/herself in doing the job or carrying out his/her duties (Halford, 1990, p. 2). While the duties, both formal and informal, of the correctional officer have been discussed in Chapter 2, how correctional officers carry themselves shape opinions by the public, other staff and inmates. Not only do these opinions shape views about the officer, but also about the agency. If the correctional officer presents a negative demeanor and appearance to inmates and staff, two-way communications and a positive work climate where inmates obey rules and get along with officers will not occur.

Realistically, how a correctional officer presents himself/herself depends on three key components: professionalism, ethics and mental outlook on the job. In turn, these three affect these forms of communication with inmates: non-verbal communications, verbal communications and correct assertiveness. Officer comportment means that the officer follows a code of ethics and good work standards. Good officer comportment permits the officer to deal with stress, enhances a sense of self-esteem, promotes job satisfaction and enables contributions to the corrections profession and his/her agency (Halford, 1990, p. 4).

Professionalism

Professionalism is a word that is used often in society today. Officers and staff are told to look and act "professional." The term means adhering to a professional occupation having both standards and requiring special skills. In 1978, Rudoni, Baker and Meyer examined the basic aspects upon which professionalism in any job or occupation is defined or structured (Gilbert, 1989, pp. 13–26):

- *public recognition:* citizens know that pre-trail detainees and convicted offenders are kept securely in our nation's correctional facilities by correctional staff;
- production of a valued or highly regarded social function: safe custody, rehabilitation of criminals and returning the criminal to society as a law abiding citizen. We, as a nation, pride ourselves on not having a cruel, barbaric and biased correctional system;
- special knowledge and job skills: to be professional correctional officers, COs must possess special knowledge about the inmates in their care. Special job skills include communication skills, interpersonal relations and correct assertiveness;
- special education or training: to obtain the above knowledge and skills, officers undergo specialized training: law, weapons, self-defense, security procedures, etc.;
- discretion and autonomy in performing duties: officers have discretion in many cases of whether to charge inmates (in-house or criminal) with infractions; they also have a wide leeway in dealing with inmates and their problems in ways that benefit the security of the facility and often the well being of the inmate;
- performance in accordance with minimum standards: duties and actions must be in compliance with federal/state statutes, court decisions, federal/state correctional standards, and standards from organizations such as the American Correctional Association and the National Commission on Correctional Health Care;

- peer review: to enforce performance standards for acceptable professional conduct and job performance: this is accomplished through review boards, promotional exams and promotional processes.

Other views of professionalism echo the view of officers having a high degree of competency. James A. Gondles, the Executive Director of the American Correctional Association (ACA), states that "professionalism is achieved through programs of recruitment and enhancement of the employees' skills, knowledge, insight and understanding of the correctional process" (Hutton, 1998, p. vi).

To break this down further, a professional employee possesses skills such as proficiency at security procedures; knowledge of the facility rules, polices and inmate population; insight and discretion in dealing with inmates; and understanding of the legal process including the civil rights of inmates. For the purposes of this chapter, dealing with inmates in a mature way through clear communications and being a positive role model are professional job skills.

The Honorable Helen G. Corrothers, former ACA president and a former commissioner of the U.S. Sentencing Commission, wrote in the ACA publication *The Effective Correctional Officer* that "… Corrections' rehabilitative objective can only be accomplished in the appropriate environment … in which inmates feel safe and where rehabilitation is encouraged and supported. The correctional officer's attitude and degree of professionalism contribute to this type of environment" (Corrothers, 1992, p. 6).

To be professional around inmates who have an underlying mistrust and disdain towards the staff, a correctional officer must have a professional appearance exhibiting self pride and confidence. Clean uniforms, shined shoes and a proper bearing tells inmates that this officer cares about his/her appearance and will pay attention to details on his/her posts.

Along with a professional appearance, another key factor is knowledge of policies and procedures. A professional officer knows the policies and procedures of the facility and how things are supposed to be done.

Policies and procedures are important to enhancement of the professionalism of the correctional officer. They perform these key functions (Hutton, 1998, pp. 68–69):

- policies and procedures enable the facility to meet standards: state, federal or by professional organizations such as ACA;
- state what the mission of the facility is and what is to be done. For example, policy might state that all inmates will be treated humanely and will not be harassed, etc.;
- procedures state how the policies will be carried out such as all inmates will be given a medical screening upon entry;

- policies and procedures supply employees with guidelines (general orders or standard operating procedures) on how to do the job and ensure uniformity among all shifts;
- policies and procedures protect both the employees and agency against (1) inmate lawsuits and (2) unfair actions and evaluations from supervisors;
- policies and procedures are tools that aid supervisors in managing and directing employees;
- policies and procedures are guides that inform employees what they can/cannot do and serve as references in case of a question.

To be effective, policies and procedures must change with the help of staff review and employee input (Hutton, 1998, p. 68). Professional officers should be thinkers and make suggestions to supervisors in writing. Not only is this good for the agency, but can be looked at when the CO is going for promotion or reassignment.

Ethics

Closely related to the professionalism of an officer is his/her adherence to ethical conduct. Like the word professionalism, ethics is a term used in describing the ideal correctional officer.

Ethics is defined by Vincent Barry and Lawrence Sherman as the "study and analysis of what constitutes good or bad conduct" (Pollock, 1994, p. 4). If an officer treats all inmates fairly and in a dignified manner, his conduct is ethical. If he subjects them to ridicule and brutality, he is behaving in an unethical manner.

While the above definition is rather simple and direct, a more detailed definition of the term is promulgated by the FBI National Academy. Ethics in policing and which could include corrections are the "standards of conduct that govern behavior." Also, the philosophy of ethics raises such questions as:

- What is a good person?
- What is it that an officer should and should *not* do?
- What actions are right and what actions are wrong?
- What principles guide good behavior?
- What are officers' obligations and rights?
  (Sirene, Kelly and Malone, 1994, p. 2)

An officer who practices good ethics has a good moral foundation. He/she applies the basic definition of ethics to the agency and institution's policies, rules and regulations and the laws/codes of the government (Sirene, Kelly and

Malone, 1994, p. 2). While this philosophy has been recognized as police ethics, it can be applied to the profession of corrections.

Lack of Ethics

Unethical behavior by correctional officers is embarrassing to the agency and has a definite impact on staff morale.

In 1993, one corrections agency experienced about forty employees being arrested and charged with bribery or drug violations inside a correctional facility. Eight were convicted and twelve pleaded guilty. One officer agreed to smuggle cocaine into the facility for only $300.00. The undercover police and FBI operations also resulted in employees being charged with introduction of contraband into an institution. An arraigning judge asked "If we can't trust the guards, who can we trust?" *(Castaneda, 1993, Washington Post, 04/08/94)*

The above true example illustrates an example of severe lack of ethics. To officers and staff doing their utmost to do a professional job, the public example of bad officers can discourage them, especially when citizens may think that all the officers in the agency are bad.

Surveys that have been conducted of good work performers reveal that they exhibit themes based on the following:

discipline and obedience
working
religion
doing the "right" thing in the face of unpopularity or difficulty
frugality: not being wasteful
making an individual effort in achieving success.
(Black, 1996, pp. 55–56)

Most supervisors would agree that these are desirable traits for correctional officers, especially doing the right thing even if other staff thinks that the action is unpopular. One veteran officer states that he was made fun of when he called inmates "Mister" or "Miss," even when the other COs in his squad thought that he was being "too nice."

How do these philosophic views apply to corrections? The best answer is by Harold W. Clarke, Director, Department of Correctional Services, Lincoln, Nebraska, and clear behavioral guidelines.

Ethics

Emanating from all debates on ethics and morality is a charge to all citizens directing us to reflect on our personal moral and ethical principles for the betterment of our society. We need to review both our professional and personal ethical postures. Leaders of public and private agencies, professional disciplines, associations and corporations have an additional responsibility to develop ethical and moral codes of conduct to guide the personal behaviors of the individuals affiliated with their organizations. Doing so will help the organization attain its goals.

Those of us in corrections, in view of the public scrutiny we endure, must move hastily to ensure that we have sound ethical codes in place. Those codes, consistent with the mission of the agency, should embody the intent of the applicable positions of the U.S. Constitution and state laws. Once we have implemented such codes, our concerns about scrutiny from the public and the media should diminish.

Every correctional employee should have a personal and professional sense of duty to forward the interest of corrections. That means our behavior on and off the work site should strive to be beyond reproach. We must strive to be honest, upright, virtuous, decent and credible. We should be lawful people, because law, not chaos, is the dominating principle in the universe.

Correctional leaders need to be ethical people. As Robert Noyce, the inventor of the silicon chip said, "I don't believe unethical people get ahead in business. If ethics are poor at the top, that behavior is copied down through the organization." The "do as I say but not as I do" approach to management can be disastrous to any organization.

For corrections to attain and sustain a posture beyond reproach, we must engage in self-regulation; regulation beyond that which is imposed on us by other authorized entities. To be successful in this endeavor, all correctional employees have a duty to report violations committed by co-workers. Why should we engage in such reporting? Because the image of all correctional employees and the overall health of our profession are at stake. We must become whistle blowers. For corrections to be successful and respected as a profession, we must demonstrate deference, respect, allegiance, loyalty and dedication to our missions and objectives.

We should report all behavior engaged in by co-workers on or off the work site that could potentially bring discredit on us. Examples of such behavior include alcohol and drug abuse, converting government property to one's own, trafficking, dereliction of duty (including abusing inmates), and inappropriate language in the workplace. We must police ourselves. If we ignore problems, we should not expect to see the violators change for the better. It was J.W. Sullivan who once said, "Some people are like dirty clothes—they only come clean when they are in hot water."

Reasonable people will adapt to change when they know the results will be good. Individuals who only seek marginal accomplishments need only to make small sacrifices, but those who are to achieve much must sacrifice much.

[Reprinted with permission from the American Correctional Association, Alexandria, VA: "Examining the Role of Ethics in Corrections" by Harold W. Clarke, Director of Correctional Services, Lincoln, Nebraska in *State of Corrections*, Proceedings, ACA Annual Conferences 1992, pp. 68–69.]

Informal Ethics: The Correctional Subculture

In a perfect world, correctional officers would adhere to policies and procedures to the letter. In reality, correctional officers have to survive and get along with their peers. Kauffmann in 1988 listed the rules of the correctional officer's subculture:

1. Always go to the aid of another officer.
2. Don't buy [smuggle] drugs. This action puts all correctional officers in danger.
3. Don't inform or "rat" on another correctional officer.
4. Never make another officer look bad in front of inmates no matter what the correctional officer did.
5. In an inmate/officer dispute, always side with the officer.
6. Always support officer sanctions against an inmate (including illegal use of force).
7. Don't be a "white hat" or good guy. This could be seen as being "buddies" with the inmates.
8. Maintain officer solidarity against outside groups, public, administration or the media.
9. Show positive concern for fellow correctional officers. Don't dump problems, help them out.
(Kauffman cited in Pollock, 1994, pp. 182–183)

Mental Outlook on the Job

The view that an officer has towards the job determines his/her ethics and the degree of professionalism he/she exhibits. In a perfect world, the ideal correctional officer knows all of the general orders, his/her uniform is "spit and polish" and mistakes are never made. But in reality the world of the correctional facility is far from perfect.

In reality, a serious threat to a correctional officer's sense of ethics and professionalism is making mistakes concerning relations with inmates. In dealing with them day after day, officers find that it is easier to overlook infractions, operate with some favoritism, and be "easy" in order to get inmates to comply with orders and the running of the post. This may contribute to officers crossing into a hazily defined gray area resulting in getting *too* friendly or personal with inmates (Crouch, 1980 cited in Pollock, 1994, p. 180).

How officers view their jobs and function as correctional officers have a direct bearing on how ethical and professional they appear around inmates. If the view is negative against supervisors and the agency, correctional officers may feel that they and the inmates have more in common with each other. If that occurs, infractions are overlooked and the maintenance of good security practices is compromised; unethical conduct and possibly corruption may take root. Bernard McCarthy calls this practice an incentive for corruption (McCarthy, 1991 in Pollock, 1994, p. 183).

In the simplest terms, correctional officers have a choice in how they feel about their jobs. According to Robert Johnson of American University, officers can be either "hacks" or "human services officers." In a positive to negative framework in terms of how inmates are treated, hacks represent the negative while the human service officers represent the positive (Johnson, 2002, pp. 201–202).

Smug Hacks

As Johnson explains this type of officer, the public image of the prison officer is often one of a "mindless and brutal custodian." Researchers Toch and Klofas in 1982 labeled these officers as *smug hacks* or "sub cultural custodians." A summary definition of hacks could be (Johnson, 2002, p. 201):

> An officer who is alienated from the positive aspects or goals of corrections; an officer who uses violence and negative communication to keep order.

Alienation is a key part of the definition. The hack may feel that he/she is a "uniformed prisoner" or one who has a lot in common with inmates. Both are locked in, both have to go by rules that are at times unrealistic and both get reprimanded by supervisors and the officers. The stress that these negative feelings cause is not dealt with in a positive way and is often taken out on the inmates (Johnson, 2002, p. 210).

This model of working can be described as a war-like "us versus them" philosophy where officers are the "good guys" and the inmates are the "bad guys." Naturally, the good guys are always right. Hacks do not want to hear the inmate's side of an issue. Non-compliant inmates are forcibly coerced into submission by threats, intimidation or *goon squad* tactics.

Lee Bowker in 1980 defined goon squads as "groups of physically powerful correctional officers who enjoy a good fight" and are used to restore the status quo by muscle power (Bowker, 1970 cited in Johnson, 2002, pp. 216–217). Hacks may respect the goon squad members as their kind of officers who do not waste time talking to inmates. They use force and the job gets done.

Other research in this area, especially by Kauffmann, illustrates the negative effects of being a smug hack and looking upon the job in a negative way. According to her research in the 1970s at the Walpole, Massachusetts State Prison, smug hacks can create a clique which promotes a subculture of violence. Inmates are not seen as human beings in distress or who have problems, but as "dehumanized creatures beyond the reach of care or compassion (Johnson, 2002, p. 218).

The following are examples of the behavior of "smug hacks." Often their actions were underhanded or indirect and at times served them as ways to "mentally get to them," aggravate them or punish them (Kauffmann, 1988, pp. 65–71):

- withholding toilet paper, matches or food;
- playing "head games" or as one officer said: "guy wants to make a phone call? You can make him wait ten, twenty minutes. Guy wants some writing paper? Tell him you don't have any;"
- adapting the "Hard Ass" role where the officer becomes coldly indifferent to inmates and the surrounding violence.

Crouch and Marquart in their research in Texas prisons found that some officers had similar beliefs: to cow or deceive convicts so as to gain their compliance. Commonly referred to "messing up their minds" and "keep them off balance," these methods involved making the inmates feel uncertain. One officer asked an inmate several times if he "slumbered" in bed. Confused, the inmate asked "do I sno?" [snore]. Everyone but the inmate knew what "slumber" meant. Other officers stared at selected inmates for long periods in order to make them uncomfortable and worried (Crouch and Marquart, 1980 cited in Johnson, 2002, pp. 221–222).

In an institution where everyday dealings with inmates are governed by the smug hack mentality, the inmates learn to resent the officers and distrust them, feeling that their welfare is not important. As a result, positive, two-way communication between correctional officer and inmates is not firmly established.

Human Services Officers

Correctional officers can look at their jobs in another way: the correctional system is an important function of the criminal justice system and some inmates can be changed if they encounter staff that not only act positively, but communicate to them in a mature, caring way. According to one prison officer, in order to be a professional, an officer's conscience should be his/her guide. The officers should care enough about inmates and themselves to do the job in a responsive way without violence and the use of force is a last resort (Johnson, 2002, p. 236).

Human service officers can achieve control in their areas without displaying a hostile or superior attitude. Influence over inmates and positive leadership can be attained with a minimum of friendliness and respect. Officers who are known to be friendly and fair are obeyed most readily as well as being liked (Glaser, 1969 cited in Johnson, 2002, p. 238).

The human service officer is the opposite of the smug hack. Instead of isolating themselves in their jobs, human service officers try to foster positive relationships with inmates and try to make a difference. The actions of these officers are based on these three themes:

1. *Providers of goods and services:* inmates' needs of food, clothing, medication, etc., are met. The officer uses positive communication skills to persuade dirty inmates to bathe, sloppy inmates to clean up, etc. Inmates will respect the officer as one who makes sure things run right. Officers report that if a promise is made to an inmate to take care of a problem that promise should be kept, even with routine problems like getting a towel. Promises that are ignored or not kept lower the inmates' respect for the officer and he/she is marked. As COs will say—the inmates see you all the time, and a negative reputation on your part will only make your job tougher.

2. *Referral agent or advocate:* cutting through the facility's "red tape" is important. For example, an inmate is desperately requesting placement in a drug program. He has written requests, but has not heard anything. An officer calls the counseling office, finds out information for the inmate and recommends that the counselor at least talk to the inmate. The inmate calms down and the officer has defused a tense situation.

Officers know, however, that they cannot do this all the time, but occasionally it is beneficial.

3. *Institutional adjustment:* this may be one of the most important aspects of the human service mentality. Many corrections workers report seeing themselves in different roles: psychiatrists, doctors, social workers, parental figures, etc. Also, many officers say that when they interact with an inmate experiencing a personal problem, they would listen and offer advice. Others say that they would approach such an inmate and offer help.
   (Lombardo, 1988, pp. 60–64)

In the daily world of the correctional institution, human service officers are given opportunities to assist inmates and inmates respect them as staff who will listen. Being able to empathize, not overly sympathize, with the inmates secures their cooperation (Lombardo, 1988, p. 63). As one corrections officer says:

> *Sure, we can sit at our posts all day, but these inmates are people with problems. Recently, an inmate was worried about his paycheck. He needed someone to get it, bring it to the jail so he could sign it over and get it cashed. His family needed the money. The work place would not take collect calls, so I gave him a call after verifying the number. He went back to the block relieved and a lot less tense.*

The attitude of the officer will translate into how he/she communicates with inmates either verbally or non-verbally. An officer practicing good, professional communication skills will maintain good, direct eye contact with the inmate, walk straight and erect, stand facing him/her and not slouch or appear disinterested. In making rounds or conducting business on the post, the officer should be dressed neatly, be well groomed and not distracted.

Verbal communication, to be effective, is dependent on the officer practicing good listening and speaking skills. An officer has to realize that in the correctional environment, they are the first persons that inmates will go to with requests, problems and questions. Secondly, the officer must realize that each inmate has his/her own unique way of speaking: some speak clearly; some are somewhat abrasive, some speak mostly in street slang, etc.

Good Interpersonal Communications

Many agencies instruct new personnel in the Interpersonal Communication (IPC) model of communications which has been a main staple of communications training in corrections for almost the past twenty years. It is a detailed model of communication, but for brevity, the National Institute of Corrections identifies these basic components (Stinchcomb and Fox, 1999, p. 298).

- positioning: the officer is close enough to the inmate, still maintains a safe distance, and is alert to the inmates' presence;
- posturing: the officer stands erect and maintains direct eye contact with the inmate. The officer may lean forward a little. Distinctive mannerisms such as pen clicking, foot tapping, etc., are avoided;
- observing: the officer is careful to see, hear and interpret what is happening, while watching verbal and non-verbal clues in the inmate such as voice tremors, agitation or nervousness. What is important here is that the officer makes inferences on what facts are observed: a calm inmate is nervous, the inmate is agitated, etc.
- listening: the officer hears out the inmate and suspends judgment. He/she concentrates on key words and determines the inmate's mood and/or intensity of the message. Listening is one of the most critical aspects of good inmate/staff communication.

While these aspects are the ideal forms of good interpersonal communication, the reality is that in a busy institution, staff must order inmates about quickly to ensure compliance with regulations, defuse arguments or take action in emergencies. For example, an officer trying to defuse a possible fight between two inmates tells them to quickly move apart—NOW! Later if the inmates have complied, the officer can practice positive communication skills to hear their problems.

Over time, correctional officers learn to balance personal concern for the inmate with professional caution. By doing so, objective judgments and rational decision making occur. This is called detached commitment (Stinchcomb and Fox, 1999, p. 298). As one veteran officer recalls:

One Sunday morning an inmate, who I knew quite well, told me that he had tried the night before to kill himself with a shoe lace noose, which had broken. I listened to the guy's problems: drinking, debts, unfaithful wife, etc. I felt sorry for him and thought that if I was in his shoes, I might be suicidal, too. But, I moved him to a high observation receiving cell on restricted issue until the psychologist could check him out. This was on Super Bowl Sunday. He swore that he was over his crisis and wanted to see the game. I stuck to my decision. After listening to him and offering advice, I just felt that I could not take the chance.

According to Daniel Stieneke, Director of the North Carolina Department of Corrections, Office of Staff Development and Training, practicing effective communication skills with inmates is one of a correctional employee's most important tools. Effective communication starts by the officer *listening* to the inmate, to their problems, fears, concerns, emotions, etc. They have them, like staff members do. While many inmates may not open up at first, if they see that the officer is trustworthy and concerned, that may change. Not only is listening crucial, so is speaking. Verbal messages to inmates should be in clear, respectful tones (Bayse, 1995, p. 50).

Correct Assertiveness

All of these positive ways of dealing with inmates and effectively communicating with them come together for the officer in work tool called positive assertiveness or *correct assertiveness.*

First researched by corrections stress pioneer Francis Cheek in 1984, this term means simply that the officer gets his/her point across without causing arguments, tension or stress. It incorporates common sense communication as well as calmness, seeing the other's point of view, looking at the whole situation with respect and consideration for other people's thoughts and feelings (Cornelius, 2005, p. 77).

At times, especially during emergencies, orders must be given and complied with immediately with no time for debate. However, most daily communication with inmates is non-emergency and routine, but may include disagreements, denials and resistance. Officers must remember in overcrowded institutions that even the routine can escalate into the dangerous. There are seven components to correct assertiveness (Cornelius, 2005, pp. 77–79).

Components of Correct Assertiveness

In using correct assertiveness in communicating with inmates, the correctional officer should strive to balance the communication with what he/she and the inmate both want to say and what they both want heard. In a situation when interacting with inmates, the officer should (Cornelius, 2005, pp. 77–79):

- *Consider the context:* What is the environment? Are other inmates present? Good communication should be away from noise, interruptions, distractions, etc. Also, how is your mindset? Are you tired, tense, and upset? Don't criticize in front of other inmates.
- *Maintain calm:* good communication is enhanced if all parties are not upset; understanding and cooperation increase.

- *Consider the other's point of view:* in good two-way communication, each party should try to see the other's viewpoint. Listening is important. Both officer and inmate should explain his/her side. The officer may disagree, but will be looked upon as a staff person who will listen and try to understand.
- *Explain your side:* it is important that inmates receive an answer to a request or question. They may not like it, but they will feel that at least they are being treated as people. They will respect officers for explaining the situation. If a reason can be given without violating security, it should be, instead of a curt "NO!"
- *Come to a solution:* both parties should work together to come to a solution. At times with resistant inmates, an officer may have to say that both sides have been heard and the inmate has several choices. Compromise is important.
- *Consider the consequences:* after hearing both sides and all factual information, officers make decisions. An officer must weigh the consequences or what may or may not happen.
- *Don't run hot and cold:* inmates respect an officer who is even tempered and not moody. Communication style can be affected by moods.

Staff Stress

One thing that can affect the way that staff members deal with inmates is how well stress is managed. Whereas twenty years ago, scant, if any, attention was paid to corrections officers' stress. Corrections officers were supposed to "hold it in," not showing any signs that the job is getting to them, etc.

The profession of corrections has come a long way in the past few decades, similar to the progress made in suicide prevention. However, if correctional officers allow themselves to be "burned out," positive interactions with inmates will suffer.

Stress and Stressors

Stress is the reaction of our bodies and minds to demands (called stressors) made upon us (Cornelius, 2005, p. 5). For correctional officers the list of stressors in their work may seem endless. Research by George Mason University and the American Correctional Association has shown that correctional workers, including jail officers, prison officers and probation and parole officers report the following as major stressors (Cornelius, 2005, p. 39):

- Short staffing
- Lazy coworkers
- Conflicting decisions from supervisors
- Poor communication
- No recognition for good work
- Lack of support from supervisors
- Conflicting operations among shifts
- Large caseloads
- Tight deadlines
- Lack of input into decision making
- Low salaries
- Bureaucratic red tape/paperwork

Effects of stress among corrections staff have included headaches, impatience, anxiety, difficulty sleeping, low energy and fatigue, inability to relax, anger, poor concentration, and pain in the back and neck (Cornelius, 2005, p. 38). A CO suffering any of these symptoms will find interacting with inmates in a crowded and busy correctional institution very taxing, along with maintaining security.

Burnout

Many COs look at irritable, angry and negative colleagues as "burnouts." While many definitions of burnout have been offered, the consensus is that it is a debilitating condition resulting from a long period of unrelieved work stress, characterized by emotional and mental exhaustion. Burned out COs exhibit a constantly angry and negative attitude towards their work, and say that "they don't give a damn." They forget that the discipline of corrections is a human service and a caring profession (Cornelius, 2005, p. 15).

Stress Management Techniques

The study of corrections stress has resulted in many books and publications on the subject. It is a vast subject, and COs suffering from unmanaged stress have many choices of coping techniques. Many agencies and criminal justice academies offer training in stress management as well as employee assistance programs. Stress can hurt correctional officers' professional and personal lives. Some COs develop health problems such as ulcers, heart conditions and high blood pressure. Some turn to alcohol and drugs as a way to self medicate their problems and escape the negativity.

To function properly in a correctional facility, COs must recognize that stress in corrections exists, how it affects the body and mind, and find ways to maintain both mental and physical health. Some techniques include:

- Getting enough sleep
- Practicing relaxation
- Talking to supervisors, family and friends about things that bother them
- Maintaining a proper diet and weight level
- Engaging in exercise and activity
- Quitting smoking
- Having hobbies
- Taking time off
- Avoiding excessive alcohol use
- Finding humor in life
- Doing things with friends and family
- Practicing time management
- Doing something nice for yourself—often

Correctional officers must manage stress if they are to have successful careers. One word of caution—if you are stressed out—get help. Talk to someone. Do not under any circumstances talk to inmates about your problems—the stress management they suggest will result in their manipulation of you.

Summary

Interacting with inmates has generally been regarded as staff having good communication skills. In reality, it combines professionalism, ethics, how staffs look at their jobs and good non verbalized and verbal communication.

Officers must view inmates as people as this shapes how positive communications can be. Professionalism in corrections means the job has special standards and skills; ethics means to know what must be done correctly and not incorrectly. A tool of the corrections professional is adherence to policies and procedures.

Officers can either be smug hacks, whereby they hate their jobs and act accordingly or can be human service officers trying to get the most positive results from their jobs. A tool for this officer is correct assertiveness, which provides for balanced communications.

Finally, unmanaged stress can take its toll on the CO and hinder both performance and job outlook. Stressed out COs must avoid burnout and seek help to manage their stress.

Review Questions

1. Discuss three key functions of policies and procedures.
2. What are ethics?
3. Discuss the rules of informal ethics in the correctional officer subculture.
4. Discuss the differences between smug hacks and the human services officer.
5. What is correct assertiveness?

Terms/Concepts

correct assertiveness   *officer comportment*
ethics   *professionalism*
goon squad   *smug hack*
human services officers

References

Bayse, Daniel. (1995). *Working in Jails and Prisons: Becoming Part of the Team.* Lanham: American Correctional Association.

Black, Lee Roy, Ph.D. (1997). Development of a Strong Work Ethic. In *The State of Corrections 1996 Proceedings ACA Annual Conferences* (pp. 55–60). Lanham: American Correctional Association.

Bowker, L. (1980). *Prison Victimization,* Elsevier: NY.

Castaneda, Ruben. (1993, November 5). Corrections Officers Held in Smuggling. *The Washington Post.*

Clarke, Harold W. (1993). Examining the Role of Ethics in Corrections. In *The State of Corrections 1992 Proceedings: ACA Annual Conferences.* Laurel: American Correctional Association.

Cornelius, Gary F. (2005). Stressed Out! Strategies for Living and Working with Stress in Corrections. Lanham: American Correctional Association. *See also:* Cheek, Frances, Ph.D. (1984). *Stress Management for Corrections Officers and Their Families.* Laurel: American Correctional Association.

Corrothers, Hon. Helen G. (1992). Career v. Job: Why Become a Correctional Officer? In M. Nunan (Ed.) *The Effective Correctional Officer* (pp. 1–10). Lanham: American Correctional Association.

Crouch, Ben, (Ed.). (1980). *Keepers: Prison Guards and Contemporary Corrections.* Springfield: Charles C. Thomas.

Crouch, B.M. and J.W. Marquart (1980). "On Becoming a Prison Guard." In B.M. Crouch, (Ed.). *The Keepers: Prison Guards and Contemporary Corrections.* Springfield: Charles C. Thomas, pp. 63–105.

Gilbert, Michael J. (1989, July). The Challenge of Professionalism in Correctional Training. *Journal of Correctional Training*, International Association of Correctional Training Personnel, pp. 13–26.

Glaser, D. (1969). *The Effectiveness of a Prison and Parole System.* Indianapolis: Bobbs-Merrill.

Halford, Sally Chandler. (1990). Officer Comportment. *Jail Operations Bulletin. American Jail Association, Volume II, No. 8.*

Hutton, Scott D., Ph.D. (1998). *Staff Supervision Made Easy.* Lanham: American Correctional Association.

Johnson, Robert. (2002). *Hard Time: Understanding and Reforming the Prison.* Third Edition. Belmont: Wadsworth.

Kauffmann, Kelsey. (1988). *Prison Officers and Their World.* Cambridge: Harvard Univ. Press.

Lombardo, Lucien X. (1989). *Guards Imprisoned: Correctional Officers at Work 2nd Ed.* Cincinnati: Anderson.

McCarthy, Bernard. (1991). Keeping an Eye on the Keeper: Prison Corruption and its Control. In M. Braswell, B. McCarthy and B. McCarthy (Eds.). *Justice, Crime, and Ethics* (pp. 239–253) Cincinnati: Anderson.

Pollock, Joycelyn M. (1994). *Ethics in Crime and Justice, Dilemmas and Decisions, 2nd Ed.* Belmont: Wadsworth. *See also:* Barry, Vincent. 1985. *Applying ethics: A text with readings.* Belmont, CA: Wadsworth and Sherman, Lawrence.1981. *The teaching of ethics in criminology and criminal justice.* Washington, DC: Joint Commission on Criminology and Criminal Justice Education and Standards, LEAA.

Sirene, Walt, James M. Kelly and Marita Malone. (1995). *Leadership in Developing the Organizational Ethic: Ethics in Policing, 3rd Ed.* Quantico: FBI Academy.

Stinchcomb, Jeanne B., Ph.D. and Vernon B. Fox, Ph.D. (1999). *Introduction to Corrections, Fifth Edition.* Upper Saddle River: Prentice Hall.

Toch, H. and J. Klofas. (1982). Alienation and desire for job enrichment among correctional officers. *Federal Probation, 46.* 35–44.

Washington Post, 04/08/94.

Chapter 11

Avoiding Manipulation

Staff in correctional facilities deal with many different types of inmates: varying in physical size, varying in degrees of criminal backgrounds, varying in the usage of alcohol and drugs, and varying in behavior and personality. The same is true for staff: some are hacks, some practice the human service approach, some are weak, some are strong willed and some are "by the book."

There is one common denominator running through the above—staff by their positions and authority—attempt to control the environment in the facility. The inmates would like to gain a significant amount of that control for themselves. The inmates attempt to gain this control by the practice of manipulation.

Importance of Resisting Manipulation

When a staff member falls victim to inmate manipulation, a small but *significant* crack appears in the facility's security network. The result can be the injury or death of staff/inmates/visitors, escape, introduction of contraband, etc. The list can go on. Ultimately, the inmate gains power and stature over the staff.

There is a line between inmates and staff. When correctional officers cross this line, they put many things at risk—namely their careers, the safety and security of the facility, their personal and professional reputations, the trust of the public and colleagues, and most importantly—their lives. Many inmates have no qualms whatsoever about using COs to get their way. Inmates have plenty to gain and little to use; the CO has plenty to lose and nothing to gain (Cornelius, 2001, p. 1).

James Bennett served as Director of the U.S. Bureau of Prisons from 1937 to 1964. He observed that the niche (see Chapter 6) is important to the inmate as the manipulation process. He wrote that "one of the first challenges for new prisoners ... is to try to make a place for themselves with the other men ... Sometimes the 'snow' job is crucial ... how to impress everybody with one's potential importance" (Bennett, 1970 in Leinwand, ed., 1972, p. 186).

Resisting inmate manipulation is a skill that should be learned and practiced by *all* staff members, civilian or sworn who interact with inmates on a daily basis. Also, volunteers and counselors who come into the institution to assist in programs should also have this training.

To successfully resist inmate manipulators, staff should have knowledge in three areas:

1. The personality of the inmate;
2. How inmates do time; and
3. The process of manipulation.

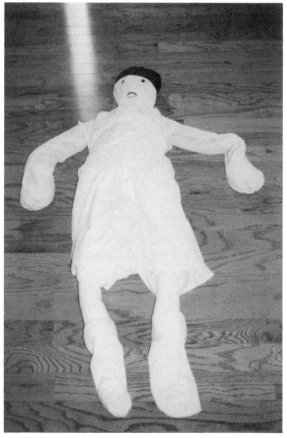

Never underestimate the intelligence of an inmate. This mannequin was made by a jail inmate "for fun." Mannequins have been used in escapes. Courtesy, Hampton Roads Regional Jail. Photo by author.

The Personality of the Inmate

Offenders are not born inmates; they *become* inmates through prisonization and the development of niches (see Chapter 6). While much research has been done concerning the personalities of inmates, this section will focus on observations from Dan Bayse, veteran correctional counselor and author for the American Correctional Association, Stanton E. Samenow, Ph.D., respected criminal psychologist and James Bennett, Director of the United States Bureau of Prisons from 1937–1964. Veteran staff members are aware of the distinct personalities and behaviors of street-wise criminals in terms of manipulation.

The Inmate Personality

According to Daniel Bayse, author of *Helping Hands: A Handbook for Volunteers in Prisons and Jails* (see References) and a former corrections counselor, inmates exhibit the following traits (Bayse, 1993, pp. 18–27):

- *Inmate masks*: inmates will wear different personalities like "masks" to suit the environment and their needs. For example, to a volunteer or counselor, inmates may seem attentive, contrite and remorseful, especially if it gains them sympathy. Back in the unit, they may brag about "fooling" people. Before a parole board hearing, an inmate may brag about his criminal record and how he will not get caught next time. In front of the board, he says that he is sorry and swears to stay out of trouble.
- *Narcissism*: many inmates feel that they are "number one" and the world has to suit them.
- *Need for power and control*: criminals like the excitement that comes with wielding power over victims: drug dealers having addicts beg, sex offenders forcing people to have sex with them, etc.
- *Lying*: lying is fundamental in the criminal lifestyle. Denials that they were involved in a crime are common.
- *Frustration*: the theme of "I want what I want when I want it" could be the inmates' theme song. Many are impatient and do not have the self-discipline to complete treatment programs. They may blame others: the police, correctional officers, counselors, etc., for their shortcomings and legal predicaments.
- *Distorted ideas about love:* Mature people in relationships care for their partners and the love and respect shown is sincere. Inmates "claim" to love others, put it may be just a tool in their manipulation toolbox to

use people. May inmates are narcissistic and only look out for themselves—"number one."

- *Violence and Anger:* Inmates may appear violent and/or angry in attempts to get others to be fearful of them and to do their bidding. Often, anger is an emotion just below the surface in inmates due to their frustrations.
- *Lack of remorse or guilt:* inmates often convince themselves of their innocence—they blame the victim. For example, an inmate serving life for the murder of a state police officer implied that it was the trooper's fault because he reached for his gun when the inmate went for his.
- *Lack of empathy:* inmates have little or no concern about the impact of their acts on victims. They may say: "He [she] wasn't *really* hurt when I stabbed him [her]. He [she] only spent an hour in the hospital and will be fine in no time."

Dr. Stanton Samenow is a respected, well known criminal psychologist in Alexandria, Virginia. In his book, *Inside the Criminal Mind* (see References), he observes that being incarcerated does not change the inmate's view that he is "top dog." Their motto is "If you serve time, let time serve you." Manipulation schemes continue and obeying rules is due to wanting the staff to look at him/her as being a "good" inmate, not due to rehabilitation. The life-long attitude of the criminal is to do as he pleases and this continues behind the walls (Samenow, 1984, p. 140).

The "Model Inmate"

Samenow also discusses a common term used to describe some inmates—the "model inmate." He says that some inmates may think that direct confrontations with staff are futile, so they will restrain themselves. They may "play up to the COs and any staff having authority over them, all the while holding the staff in contempt. Samenow describes the model inmate as "the consummate actor." The staff may think: "Wow—this inmate can be a trusty" or "this inmate should be awarded good time [time off their sentences for good behavior or program participation]." However, this "model inmate" may be scheming, wheeling and dealing all the while. Appearing to be a model inmate throws the staff off their guard (Samenow, 1984, p. 140).

Old Inmates v. New

The above views represent observations of inmates' behavior by professionals. Other traits have been observed, such as having less remorse and conscience than inmates in years past.

One of the best illustrations of this is reporter Miles Corwin's (Los Angeles Times) interviews with older inmates incarcerated in California's Tehachapi State Prison. The article appearing in 1993 revealed that newer inmates were more violent and exhibited little or no remorse for hurting their victims. A Los Angeles police psychiatrist, Dr. Michael Zona, said that this behavior can be attributed to sociopaths—people who have no feelings or concerns and have an anti-social personality (Cornelius, 1995, pp. 8–9).

How Inmates Do Time

The reader should review Chapter 6 to gain insight into how inmates do time. Underlying the aspect of having needs met and the development of a niche is the idea of comfort. Inmates want to do their time as comfortable and "hassle free" as possible and avoid the pains of imprisonment.

Correctional institutions are regimented places with schedules, the lack of comforts that offenders enjoy on the street, a lack of privacy, and people that an inmate may not want to have to deal with, including staff. Inmates want the environment to be more to their liking and to do time on their terms.

To meet the needs of activity, privacy, emotional feedback and safety, inmates may lie, scheme, cheat; steal or play "head games" with COs. Lies and concocted stories may get them a transfer to protective custody, for example. To obtain a sense of emotional feedback, inmates may "warm up" to staff, trying to portray themselves as "regular people" and not criminals.

The Process of Manipulation

According to Robert Johnson of American University, inmates have lived a lifestyle of lying and using people and manipulating others is a way of life. In fact, manipulation has been described as the "name of the game" in prison as well as on the street. In these environments, people are expected to be "cagey" and only naive persons tell the truth. The criminal victimizes weak people in and out of prison; they are "fair game." While the law-abiding citizen is honest, truthful and solves life's problems using legitimate means, the criminal/inmate will deceive and use lying and violence to cope. The result of living like this is that inmates who survive prison life become tougher and less able to feel for themselves and others (Johnson, 2002, pp. 90–92).

A complacent, sloppy officer will be a target for inmate manipulators.

Using people, finding niches, wanting things their way all exhibit a need for control. To understand inmate manipulation, staff must understand the definition of the word. *Manipulation* defined has three components:

1. to control or play upon
2. by artful or unfair means
3. especially to one's own advantage
   (Cornelius, 2001, pp. 4–5)

For correctional staff, manipulation follows these components, but with the attempts to control comes attempts to change staff by subtle means that can be very artistic. The result is to get something that is wanted, needed or achieved.

To properly guard against manipulation, correctional staff must ask themselves, "What do the inmates want to control? What might they really want? Are they telling the truth?"

Inmates' Views of Manipulation

Some inmates' views of the staff are that they are gullible; some are "do gooders" and are inferior. Some inmates think that they are more intelligent than the staff, and staff members and COs are there to do the inmates' bidding. Probably the best summary of this view is from writings in 1967 by H. Schwendinger and J. Schwendinger appearing in American University's Robert Johnson's work *Hard Time: Understanding and Reforming the Prison* (2002): "Whether on slum streets or in prison, the world is populated by victimizers who exploit others and a host of prospective victims variously known as 'punks, chumps, pigeons or fags'.... Even one's friends are presumed to be less than fully trustworthy and thus are potential candidates for exploitation" (Johnson, 2002, p. 91).

What does this mean to the CO? Simply it means that inmates (not all) view manipulation as a valuable tool in living life. Not only are staff and COs to be marked and manipulated, but also fellow inmates. Veteran COs will tell you that often they break up arguments and fights among inmates concerning stealing property such as canteen, magazines, radios, etc. and lying. Savvy street smart inmates will manipulate and take advantage of anyone if they can see some profit or gain by it.

Verbal Deception and Situational Deception

Inmates often practice **verbal deception** or simply lying or making statements that are not true. A competent officer can check things out and uncover the lie. If the inmate lies to cover up a lie, a good CO can confront him or her with questions and challenges to details (Knowles, 1992, p. 2). For example—an inmate tells his tier CO that his father is sick and he needs to make a long distance call to his family. The officer's questions should include: "What is the illness?" or "what hospital is he in?" Be careful—some inmate manipulators can add a lot of details, talk a lot and make the story appear very plausible.

Also, inmates engage in *situational deception*—misleading someone by actions without lying. For example, an inmate going by a cellblock wants to pass in contraband. Two inmate friends distract the officer by getting his attention by asking questions, etc. They did not actually lie—but the ruse worked—the CO was distracted and the contraband got passed (Knowles, 1992, p. 2).

Short Term v. Long Term Schemes

The manipulation schemes may be either small scale, one-time requests by inmates to staff or larger, more elaborate schemes. Short term or small schemes require very little planning and is one on one. Also, the inmate will see how "easy" the officer is (Knowles, 1992, p. 2).

Smaller versions may be pictured like an inmate asks an officer on post if he can go to a certain block to pay a friend back some cigarettes. The officer says yes, thinking "what's the harm?" A larger scale version could be several inmates each asking an officer for favors that involve bending or breaking the rules over a long period, such as a few months. At the appropriate moment, the officer is threatened with exposure to supervisors if he/she does not do a big favor for the inmates such as bringing in drugs. Over time, the manipulative demands on the COs get more serious (Knowles, 1992, p. 2).

Applying Basic Common Sense to the Definition

In addition to understanding what the term manipulation actually means, the best method of defense is to examine each component with a corrections "common sense" approach:

1. *To control or play upon:* the facility staff controls the environment: the housing assignments, mail, television, phone, food, etc. The inmate wants to control the environment and get contraband in, get into a housing unit that he/she likes, for example. They want what they want, and COs and other staff are not to get in the way.
2. *By subtle means:* Inmates will target a staff person. A staff target is not the ethical, professional officer, but the sloppy, lazy, inattentive officer.
    Studies of con games in jails indicate that inmates target officers who exhibit the following behaviors: (Knowles, 1992, pp. 2–3):
    • are naive or are too trusting of inmates;
    • are too friendly or familiar with inmates—they want to be "friends" with inmates;
    • are lacking professionalism and ethics;
    • exhibit low self esteem;
    • are apparently isolated or divided from colleagues, either by post locations or having personality clashes such as "he or she is hard to work with."
3. *Especially to one's own advantage:* The inmate may want sex, money, to escape, to have power over other, drugs and weapons smuggled in, etc. One negative aspect of inmate manipulation is sexual misconduct by officers (see Chapter 13). Now considered a sex offense and a serious crime, there are still COs that become romantically involved with inmates.

An officer or staff member who is a target may turn to inmates for conversation and company, forgetting that *the inmate is an inmate.* When staff becomes too familiar with inmates, a threat arises to the staff's professionalism. According to pioneer corrections researcher Gresham Sykes, staff is dependent on inmates to obey rules and complete tasks. Staff may overlook inmate rules, infractions, and this can be dangerous if staff members feel more comfortable around inmates than staff; they get too personal. Over long periods of time and due to close proximity with inmates, COs may become less objective, thinking that they have a common bond or friendship with the inmates. If COs are disgruntled they may identify with the inmates' feelings of victimization (Pollock, 1994, p. 183).

CO Supervisory Styles

Inmates may categorize staff into soft, hard and mellow categories of supervisory style. *Soft employees* are generally very trusting, overly familiar with inmates and naive. *Hard employees* are those who go by the book and pay strict attention to policies and procedures. *Mellow employees* are those who are soft and hard at the appropriate times; through experience they know when to be soft and they know when to be hard—they practice discretion. Manipulators tend to go after soft employees because they hesitate to say no and are reluctant to take charge; hard staff is targeted because inmates believe that the exterior hardness displayed by a CO hides a weakness. Inmates feel that the mellow employee would take too much time to work on by subtle means (Arizona DOC, 1984, p. 6). Also, if a CO is known to be overcautious and hard, the inmate manipulator can "butter up" him or her by saying how safe that the unit feels and it's a relief to see a CO that *really* pays attention to security, etc.

Testing

Inmates also may engage in "testing of limits" of a CO individually or as a group. This is called *fish testing*. The testing of limits is as it says; the manipulator asks or pushes the employee into bending or breaking the rules. In other words, the test is to see how far the manipulator can go before the employee says no, takes decisive action or makes a decision in accordance with policy (Arizona DOC, 1984, p. 6). The testing of limits or fish testing does not usually happen quickly. Inmates may work on the correctional officer for weeks or months, all the while doing favors for the officer such as getting coffee, running errands as a trusty, etc. and helping the CO do his or her job. The idea is to get the staff member to see inmates as nice, friendly, people, "buddies" and not inmates who are incarcerated for breaking the law.

Other methods include inmates over complimenting the staff member, saying things like "you care, not like the other officers," "we can talk to you," etc. The goal is to befriend the staff member, especially a soft one, who will find it hard to say no (Arizona DOC, 1984, p. 7).

Many of these processes overlap. For example, Officer Jones works a general housing unit in the prison. He is newly graduated from the academy and has been on the job for about eight months. Trusty Smith notices Jones does not move around his area too much and seems rather shy. Over the next few weeks, he offers to get Jones coffee, run messages to other officers, etc. He compliments Officer Jones repeatedly saying that he [Jones] really cares about the inmates, more than officers on the other shifts. Jones finds Smith welcome company and talks to him more frequently. One day, Smith asks Jones if he could go to the far end of the tier and say hello to an old friend, for "just a minute." Jones says sure, why not, not knowing that Smith is delivering some contraband. CO Jones has passed the test—with flying colors. Soon word will spread among the inmates that if you "butter up" CO Jones, he will be a "pushover."

Empathy v. Sympathy

When inmates manipulate, they are hoping the officer or staff member is sympathetic instead of empathetic. *Empathy* is a shared understanding or an experience of feelings, thoughts or attitudes. A staff member can empathize with an inmate's problems *without* feeling sorry for him/her. *Sympathy* is defined as sameness of feelings with pity and compassion (Arizona DOC, 1984, pp. 8–9). Sympathy is less objective than empathy. For example, an inmate manipulator approaches an officer supervising visiting and asks for more visiting time with his girlfriend. He tells the officer he misses her, has been locked up for a while, etc. An empathetic officer understands the pains of incarceration and tells the inmate that he understands his predicament, but the inmate will have to request it in writing through channels. A sympathetic officer will pity the inmate, feel sorry for him and give him extra time right away.

There appears to be no end to the mind games that the inmate manipulator will use on the staff; so the staff see them as other people, friends, etc., and not strictly inmates. These methods may range from the inmate saying "only you [staff person] can help me" to sexual references and touching (Arizona DOC, 1984, p. 12). If the staff person does not correct the inmate firmly when "brushed," lightly touched or flirted with, this may be a green light to the inmate to go ahead further and press the manipulation.

Staf
the "se
plays i
ing th
will th
son, v
sure tl
the ru
piece
perso
mates
ficult.
inmal
to col
14–1!
Nc
up. F
are ol
sides
ual, r

esult in what is called
targeted unknowingly
ng sympathy and test-
staff person. Inmates
inmate by a staff per-
may later use to pres-
?s. It could be bending
iced or letting a minor
is presenting the staff
r the COs from the in-
ıre. Refusal is now dif-
l and will do what the
the employee is forced
ırizona DOC, 1984, pp.

part of an elaborate set
o thinking that "inmates
ıe manipulator uses, be-
olve luring staff into sex-

Staff Sexual Misconduct

In 2003, President George W. Bush signed the Prison Rape Elimination Act or PREA (see Chapter 13). This federal law is designed to afford inmates protection against sexual misconduct from both correctional staff and inmates.

One disturbing aspect of inmate manipulation is that some correctional staff fall victim to inmate schemes and sexual seduction, despite the provisions of PREA and state codes making the carnal knowledge of inmates a crime. Inmates come from lifestyles of poor hygiene, drug usage, and poor health, including sexually transmitted diseases. One would think that COs should know better, but some get mired in this situation and risk their personal and professional lives and reputations. The inmate, whether it is male or female may take advantage of an officer's friendliness or grappling with stress, and "move right on in." Inmates will use the emotional feedback need on the CO, frequently by identifying with the problem the CO may be experiencing. For example, an inmate finds out that a CO is going through a divorce or a relationship is breaking up. The inmate may say that he or she is also going through the same problem, he or she knows how the CO feels, etc. Subsequently, the CO may come to see the inmate as not a criminal, but as a person having the same troubles in life. Sooner or later, the inmate may make his or her move, and a sexual encounter occurs. This is not to say the CO is blameless; he or she has to bear some responsibility.

There are "red flags" of staff sexual misconduct, and COs must report them to supervisors if they observe them. The National Institute of Corrections (NIC) has conducted training in this area. Some of these red flags include (Center for Innovative Public Policies, 2008):

- over-identifying with inmates such as saying "my inmate," or being blind to inmate actions/behavior
- sexual horseplay, joking and interaction between staff and inmates
- telephone calls to and from staff/inmates
- staff coming into the facility during off duty hours or during non business hours to see inmates
- staff sharing food with inmates; or giving or receiving gifts from them
- staff cannot account for time while on duty
- staff having excessive knowledge or inquiring a lot about an inmate and his or her family
- information received via the inmate "grapevine," rumors or from informants
- staff assisting inmate with inmate's legal or personal affairs
- inmates and staff members improving their appearance, makeup, hair, etc.
- inmate and staff member have notes, photos, letters and personal phone numbers from each other
- staff member showing favoritism and looking the other way to inmate infractions.

One excuse that a CO may use is that the sex was consensual or that the inmate "loves me." These are not valid reasons to engage in this behavior, and are not a defense according to PREA.

Examples of Inmate Manipulation

The boundaries of inmate manipulation are only limited by the boundaries of imagination and daring, sometimes involving others. Consider these examples of subtle means where inmates manipulated staff:

- An inmate in a maximum security prison ran a drug ring using drugs received from visitors and guards. He also attempted to entice a corrections employee to change his release date on his prison record to make it appear that he was close to release.

- In 1992, a criminal justice professor gave two prison inmates a cutting tool and helped them break out because "he was in love with one of them."
- Two officers lost their jobs because they were convinced to put $1,500.00 into an outside bank account to purchase a motorcycle from an inmate. The trouble was that the motorcycle never existed.
- An inmate persuaded three correctional employees to head an investment scheme to raise money for a treasure recovery from a sunken Spanish galleon. The inmates even printed stock certificates in the prison print shop and sold them to their friends. What was recovered from their $50,000.00 investment? Nothing.
- An inmate being transported back to a jail from a psychiatrist appointment persuaded his guards to stop at a hotel for dinner. He went unescorted into the restroom and escaped out the back door. Officials described the inmate as "… so glib and friendly that they [officers] said it was easy to forget he is a prisoner" (Bayse, 1995, pp. 65–66, Jordan, 1996, pp. C1, C5, Duggan, 1995).

Guidelines to Resist Inmate Manipulators

One of the most difficult things for staff in working in a correctional facility is knowing when an inmate is trying to manipulate them. Not all inmates are schemers and engage in deceit. Some inmates genuinely want to follow the rules, be left alone, be released, and rebuild their lives. However, many are so "slick" that the COs have difficulty reading their true intentions.

The safest practice is to keep a guard up all the time and assume that no matter how friendly the inmate appears or how apparently sincere they are, a manipulation scheme may be in the works. Staff members are always targets to get something that is wanted or needed by the inmate. Remember—you—the correctional officer—have access to the outside world—and the outside world contains things that inmates want.

Common Sense Rules

According to veteran CO Sgt. F.E. Knowles of the Hillsborough County (Florida) Sheriff's Office, the following are "common sense" rules that staff should follow to keep their guard up against manipulators (Knowles, 1992, pp. 1–6):

1. When informed of a situation by an inmate, a personal problem re-
    quiring action, a request, etc., check it out before taking action.
2. There is a line between staff and inmate. Never share personal infor-
    mation such as social life, significant others, children, etc., with an
    inmate.
3. Always look and act professional. Follow policies and procedures and
    keep supervisors informed, especially when an apparent manipula-
    tion is attempted. Use body language and posture to present an image
    of self confidence.
4. Be decisive. Never appear to be indecisive or at odds with colleagues
    in front of inmates. Inmates will use these as a wedge to separate a
    staff "target" from other staff. Say NO and mean it.
5. Be aware of where you are, what you are saying, and who may be lis-
    tening. As one jail officer said: "The inmate grapevine is better than
    AT&T." Control rumors; inmates love them and the staff dissension
    that results from them.
6. Documentation is important. Incident reports, memos, etc., being
    written informs staff of inmates' actions and makes it more difficult
    for the inmate to keep a secret.

The CHUMPS Approach

Many inmates think that those they want to manipulate, both inmates and
staff, are "chumps." Inmates think that that they are superior intellectually, and
it is permissible to use "CO chumps." The correctional officer can use the word
chumps as an acronym for sound, effective tools for keeping the guard up
against the inmate manipulator. The CHUMPS approach is (Cornelius, 2001,
pp. 112–116):

- *C = Control yourself and do not be complacent.* Say NO firmly and assertively. Do not bend the rules. Keep control of activities on and around
  your area of responsibility or post. Be nosy—ask an inmate for details
  concerning a request. Control inmate traffic and do not get overwhelmed
  by inmate conversation, etc.
- *H = Help inmates to help themselves.* Require that inmates follow the rules,
  including the institution chain of command. Encourage inmates to work
  through problems by legitimate means. Do not allow inmates to "shop
  for staff" where if they do not get the answer that they want from one staff
  member, they "shop around" until they find a staff member who will
  give them the answer that they want or will do what they want.

- *U = Understand the offender subculture and understand yourself:* Take advantage of all learning activities, seminars, articles (including on line material) and classes about the inmate sub culture. Observe inmate behavior, especially observing the niches that they have created for themselves. Take a self inventory—or better yet—ask a colleague to rate your job performance especially when dealing with inmates. Are you easily distracted? Are you assertive? Do you look and act like a professional?

- *M = Maintain a safe distance:* NEVER tell inmates about your personal life, family life, where you live, etc. Keep relations with inmates formal and require that they call you by your official title. Shut down sexual innuendoes and flirting quickly and firmly; document this behavior and inform your supervisor. Do not trust inmate overtures of friendship—*you are not there to be their friend.* NEVER accept a gift or a favor from an inmate, no matter how small or trivial.

- *P = Practice professionalism in policies and procedures:* Follow your agency's code of conduct. Have a working knowledge of the facility's policies and procedures; when there is a question; consult your supervisor for clarification. Be neat and well groomed, and carry yourself as a professional. Do not spread rumors and gossip about staff. Do not act like or speak like an inmate, act professional and proud of your profession at all times.

- *S = Stop yourself from being stressed out so that you are not vulnerable:* Strive to maintain your strengths and overcome your weaknesses. Learn how to manage your stress in positive ways such as talking about problems to family and friends and not to inmates. Avoid burnout and if you feel burned out, get help. Take charge of your life and do not let the job and inmates run you.

Summary

To be an effective part of the correctional facility's security network, staff must be trained in resisting inmate manipulation. To accomplish this, staff must be trained in the personality of the inmate, review how inmates do time, and the process of manipulation. The inmates' personality is often one of wearing masks and lying to hide their real intentions. Manipulation is basically an attempt to control someone by subtle means, which sometimes are well planned. Officers and staff must be empathetic and not sympathetic. There are common sense approaches for staff to guard against manipulation. One approach is the CHUMPS approach.

Review Questions

1. To successfully resist manipulation, staff should have knowledge in what three areas?
2. What does it mean when it is said that inmates wear masks?
3. What are the three components of the act of manipulation?
4. Inmate manipulators target staff members who exhibit what traits?
5. Explain the differences between empathy and sympathy.
6. Name four protectors against manipulation.
7. Discuss the CHUMPS approach.

Terms/Concepts

empathy   shopping list
fish testing   situational deception
hard employees   soft employees
lever   sting
manipulation   sympathy
mellow employees   verbal deception
set up

References

Arizona Department of Corrections (DOC). (1984, May). *Academy Core, Inmate Games and Set Ups.*

Bayse, Daniel J. (1993). *Helping Hands: A Handbook for Volunteers in Prisons and Jails,* Lanham: American Correctional Association.

Bayse, Daniel J. (1995). *Working in Jails and Prisons: Becoming Part of the Team,* Lanham: American Correctional Association.

Bennett, James V. (1970). *I Chose Prison.* New York: Alfred K. Knopf.

Center for Innovative Public Policy. *Red Flags—Are We Paying Attention to Staff?* http://www.cipp.org/pdf/redflags.pdf (Accessed November 13, 2008).

Cornelius, Gary F. (2001). *The Art of the Con: Avoiding Offender Manipulation.* Alexandria: American Correctional Association.

Cornelius, Gary F. (1995, Fall). The Changing Inmate. *The Twenty Minute Trainer, The Journal of Correctional Training,* International Association of Corrections Training Personnel, pp. 8–9. *See also:* Corwin, Miles. (1993, December 26). Recent Crimes Shock Old-Timers Doing Time. *The Washington Post,* p. A19.

Duggan, Paul. (1995, January 25). D.C. Jail Escape: A Clean Getaway. *The Washington Post.*

Johnson, Robert. (2002). *Hard Time: Understanding and Reforming the Prison, Third Edition.* Belmont: Wadsworth.

Jordan, Mary. (1996, April 25). Millionaire Convict Gives Guards the Slip. *The Washington Post,* C1, C5.

Knowles, Sgt. F.E. (1992). Con Games and Inmates: What the Line Officer Needs to Know. *Jail Operations Bulletin, American Jail Association, Vol. IV, No. 7.*

Leinwand, Gerald, (Ed.). (1972). *Prisons.* New York: Pocket Books.

Pollock, Joycelyn M. (1994). *Ethics in Crime and Justice, Dilemmas and Decisions, 2nd Ed.* Belmont: Wadsworth.

Samenow, Stanton, Ph.D. (1984). *Inside the Criminal Mind.* Times: New York.

Chapter 12

Inmate Violence

When anyone is locked up against their will, especially in overcrowded correctional institutions, it is logical to assume that violence—inmate on inmate and inmate on staff—will occur. Corrections staff must be concerned with the daily possibility that they will either be victims of violence or have to intervene in or defuse a violent situation. The concerns are many: fear of death, fear of being injured or contracting a disease (exposure to HIV, etc.). Every facility, no matter how well operated and secure, is prone to violence.

Violent acts in corrections facilities range from isolated incidents such as fights, assaults, etc., to larger, more serious incidents such as homicides, sexual assaults, disturbances and riots. This chapter will give the reader an overview into violence including riots, disturbances and other emergencies such as fires.

For correctional officers to understand inmate violence and work to prevent it (or at least reduce it), they have to know the definition of the two types of inmate violence. They are, according to researchers Braswell, Montgomery and Lombardo (Seiter, 2005, p. 347):

- *Interpersonal violence:* violence occurring between two or more individual inmates; the reason being a personal issue between them. Examples are small disturbances, assaults, attacks on individuals due to arguments, thefts of property, insults, etc.
- *Collective violence:* violence occurring between groups of inmates, including riots and disturbances, assaults on staff by groups of inmates, gang fights; the differences are issues of values and positions of the two groups. Examples are gang rivalry, racial bias, etc.

Reasons for Inmate Violence

The reason for inmate violence has been a subject of much research. Prisons and jails have an appearance and a reputation of being tough places with emphasis on security: walls, locks, cameras, razor wire, guard towers, etc.

Even with strict security procedures and state-of-the-art hardware, highly volatile inmates continue acts of stabbing, raping, gang warfare and rioting. New inmates must learn that to survive, he or she must look and act as tough as other inmates. The highest priority of an inmate is survival—they realize that it is every man [or woman] for himself (Samenow, 1984, p. 145).

Interpersonal Violence

Inmates who are locked up and hard core may expect to do as they please and to maintain status among their peers will choose disciplinary punishment rather than obey orders or give in to the staff. This quest for status may cause a physically aggressive inmate to use profanity or hit or punch an inmate or staff member when feeling threatened or infringed upon. An inmate switches TV channels and is punched. A staff member may be attacked unaware with a chair after denying an inmate's request. One inmate did not like the vegetable soup at lunch, demanding another portion to replace "the dregs of the pot" or "slop." The worker ignored him and the inmate threw soup in his face (Samenow, 1984, pp. 143–144).

The roots of inmate violence could possibly be traced back to deviant acts on the street. According to Katz, many young offenders are *bad asses* or become persons who overtly take on symptoms of deviance that other inmates regard as good. An offender who is "real bad" is described as tough and not easily influenced. He is not yielding. A "bad ass" axiom to live by is that others do not know who he is or where he is coming from and quickly he can cross the distance and destroy the others. They might say: "I'll jump you on the street good; I'll come upside your head; I'll fuck you up good" (Katz, 1988, pp. 80–81).

Correctional institutions, especially prisons, are places of unrest and frustration for inmates. Many inmates seethe inwardly, but keep a lid on their emotions. They may "mouth" words of disobedience or defiance, but know where to stop. Others have less self restraint; they verbally insult staff, defy orders and try to assert their individuality. Others act aggressively by physical attacks on property, staff and other inmates. Many staff members see inmate violence as routine or as a built-in component in corrections. The reasons are possibly overcrowding, under staffing, where the safety of inmates is jeopardized, and changes in good time and parole policies (Stinchcomb and Fox, 1999, p. 384).

Inmates do not cope with life and its problems in a mature fashion. Whereas the moral citizen addresses problems without deception or violence except for self defense, inmates use deception (see Chapter 11) and violence as coping mechanisms. Inmates live in a social jungle where "the weak versus the strong."

Inmate being escorted in restraints at Maryland House of Correction. A safe escort technique is to have two officers walk behind the inmate.

One factor in the development of a violent lifestyle in the inmate is the absence of a normal type of upbringing. Abusive parents, criminal behavior at an early age, foster homes, frequent clashes with authority and incarcerations as a juvenile offender all add up to a lack of maturity and a lack of positive life experience. This background serves to propel the person into a life of violent crime and anger (Johnson, 2002, pp. 143–145).

State Raised Convict

This culture of inmate violence can be symbolized by the type of inmate known as the ***state-raised convict***. This type of inmate is described by Johnson as "men [and women] reared on rejection and abuse in orphanages, detention centers, training schools and youth prisons." In other words, they were raised by the staff in tough state institutions and find themselves locked up for long periods in their lives in prison or other correctional facilities. One inmate called being in prison being in the "belly of the beast" (Johnson, 2002, pp. 141–143).

These hard core convicts have many interpersonal failures in life and view violence as their only way of being taken seriously as a person of importance. In predatory groups or cliques, singly or as gang members, they victimize weak and defenseless inmates while maintaining a cool, hard manliness over emotions that are impulsive and raw (Johnson, 2002, p. 143). Many inmates realize that engaging in violent acts such as assaulting staff or other inmates, or letting their tempers get the best of them will only worsen their position in the facility. Being a "hard case" may look good in front of other inmates at first, but reality sinks in when they are confined in disciplinary segregation, they lose their good time credits, their custody levels increase and they realize that they will have to adjust upon release from disciplinary segregation to a new housing unit and new inmates. But then again—some inmates don't care.

This is a frightening climate in which all staff has to be on their guard. COs cannot show fear or anxiety, but inwardly they must be on their guard. While inmates are always wary of violence, the CO has to be also.

Inmates may fight over a television program, food on a tray, a perceived insult about a girlfriend or boyfriend—the reasons may vary. Some inmates accuse others of tampering with their mail; stealing a book, insulting them; the list of possible reasons can go on endlessly. Whenever a correctional officer gives a hostile inmate a direct order or attempts to gain compliance with rules and regulations, underlying anger and resentment in the inmate can spill over and explode. Sometimes the violence is unleashed instantly; sometimes officers are later ambushed.

Inmates' Views on Violence

Inmates have their views on violence, and they can range from "survival of the fittest" to "kill or be killed" to "saving face." Consider:

> Polite guys [inmates] are never rude. They'll always say "excuse me" before burying a knife in another man's chest (Washington, 1991, p. 43). An inmate released from a maximum security prison dreams of knifing victims screaming in shock, of fights involving himself pounding relentlessly on a faceless prisoner. He used to wake up angry in prison and not talk to anyone until noon. In his sleep he still remembers where he kept his shank (Milloy, 1983).
>
> To a prisoner it is an insult to grapple hand to hand with anyone. If someone ever strikes him with his hand (another prisoner), he has to kill him with a knife ... All the violence in prison is geared for murder, nothing else. You can't have someone with ill feelings for you walking around. He could drop a knife in you any day. You learn to "smile" him into position. To disarm him into friendliness. So when you are raging inside at anyone, you learn to conceal it, to smile or feign cowardice (Abbott, 1981, pp. 88–89).

Attacks by inmates on inmates and on staff can be swift and savage. In 1995, in an eastern U.S. prison, a 45-year-old inmate was stabbed by a fellow inmate and was pronounced dead twenty minutes later (Metzler, 1995). A correctional officer, age 34, was fatally stabbed while securing inmates in their cells after dinner (International Association of Correctional Officers, 1995, pp. 36–37). Correctional officers have been assaulted by inmates hiding in showers, by inmates attacking from behind, by intoxicated inmates "bucking" on COs during processing and inmates' resisting being put in restraints—the danger is always there.

Collective Violence

Collective violence occurs when groups of inmates engage in riots, disturbances, and racial/gang violence—all involving large groups of inmates. Realistically, there is not a set number of inmates when discussing this type of

Superintendent Ed Szostak with Secretary Amy Comproski of the Albany County (NY) Correctional Facility examines a metal weapon fashioned from parts of a sprinkler head.

Chief Criscone (left) of the Albany County (NY) Correctional Facility inspects a metal knife (shank) fashioned from a sneaker's arch support; Superintendent Ed Szostak (right) examines a new type of contraband resistant sneaker which does not contain metal arches.

violence, but realistically this involves groups. These groups can consist of 10 inmates, 20 inmates, 8 inmates, etc.—there is no way to accurately predict how many.

Riots and disturbances are nightmares to the correctional staff—from the warden down to the line officer. Riots and disturbances can result in injury or death to staff members and inmates, property damage and a complete breakdown of authority.

Every correctional officer must keep alert to the fact that in a facility where people are being held against their will, riots and disturbances can occur. The key to their prevention is to not only understand what they are, but how they can be prevented.

Riots and disturbances are similar, but not exactly the same. The American Correctional Association (ACA) Dictionary of Criminal Justice Terms gives a practical, clear definition of each (American Correctional Association, 1998, pp. 35, 54, 101–102):

Riot: coming together of a group of persons [inmates] who engage in violent and tumultuous conduct. Their actions create a serious risk of causing injury, property damage and public alarm. In a correctional institution, rioting inmates control a significant part of the facility for a period of time.

Disturbance: an action by inmates not as large in scope or seriousness as a riot. Fewer inmates are involved, the duration is shorter in time, and there is no control or minimum control of a part of the institution.

A step down from a disturbance is an ***incident***, an event where only one or two inmates are involved and there is no inmate control over any part of the facility. Examples of incidents can be fights between two or three inmates, a cellblock refusing to obey an officer's order, or an act or acts against facility authority such as refusing to clean their cells, throwing waste, etc.

Examples of Collective Violence

In correctional history, large scale events at Attica and Santa Fe prisons were riots and became notorious for death and destruction. However, there are countless events of collective violence annually in correctional facilities throughout the United States. Here is a sampling:

- On February 8, 2006, nearly 500 inmates fought in racially charged melees in the Pitchess (California) Detention Center, part of the Los Angeles (LA) County jail system. Nineteen inmates were injured, including four cases of hospitalization, one having a serious head injury. The inmate violence spread to other nearby correctional facilities. In the Men's Central Facility in downtown Los Angeles 40 inmates battled each other and 10 were injured. The violence in the LA system had been going on for 5 days. Over 1,000 inmates had participated in the unrest by throwing bunk beds and using their fists and legs to combat each other. Conflicts were due to unrest and street conflicts between black and Latino criminal gangs. The toll was reported as one inmate dead, at least 28 sent to hospitals and nearly 90 injured. Methods used by jail deputies to stop the fighting included sting balls, tear gas, and pepper balls (Pierson and Garvey, 2006).
- In 2002, two Bristol County (Mass.) jails were locked down after inmates threw urine, feces and clogged toilets in order to flood cellblocks. They were protesting the sheriff's new $5.00 per day fee for facility services such as haircuts and visits to the jail doctor (Associated Press, 2002).
- A fight between a Mexican-American inmate and a black inmate over who owned a pair of trousers hanging in a washroom erupted into a riot involving over 300 inmates. Six barracks were smashed and the infir-

mary was burned down at a minimum security honor ranch in California (*Washington Post*, 1978).

- A thirty-minute disturbance involving fifty inmates fighting left a maintenance foreman dead from stab wounds when he rushed to help staff in a Virginia maximum security federal prison. The fight involved rival inmate groups (Gregg, 1982).

When one hears the word "Attica," he or she recognizes it as the site one of the worst prison riots in the United States. To understand collective violence, one has to examine what happened in Attica in 1971.

Attica: Synonym for Riot

The Attica Correctional Facility is a maximum security state prison located in upstate New York. In September, 1971, Attica held 2,243 inmates; many were recidivists convicted of violent crimes. Most of the inmate population was young, black or Puerto Rican inmates from urban areas. This background contrasted with the makeup of the 380 correctional officers, who were mostly white and were hired from the surrounding rural area. They had little or no training and because of post bidding per a union contract, the officers who had the most contact with the inmates were young and inexperienced. Due to budget constraints, employees' salaries were low and inmate programs or rehabilitation activities were almost non-existent.

Differences in the inmate population and the officer corps led to the officers' feeling that they were losing control. It was difficult to deal with inmates from New York City spewing revolutionary speeches and rhetoric. Some officers only communicated with inmates by banging clubs on the wall, signaling move, line up, etc.

A group of inmates formed the "Attica Liberation Faction," labeling Attica as a "classic institution of authoritative inhumanity upon men." Rumors of brutality were common.

The facility was a pressure cooker waiting to boil over and on September 9, 1971, it did. Speculation exists to this day if the riot was "sparked" or was planned. Some inmate calendars had the date September 9 circled. At 8:30 a.m., a group of inmates refused to line up for a work detail and an inmate fight with the officers resulted. Another incident involved a lieutenant being assaulted. Two inmates involved in the incident were assigned to disciplinary housing and rumors abounded that officers were retaliating violently on the inmates. One of the officers involved in the incident was attacked while returning a group of inmates to their cells after breakfast. The riot had started.

The riot spread quickly. A security gate was defective; the staff had too few officers and the communication system was outdated. There was no riot control plan, which caused confusion. Over 1,200 inmates took over four cellblocks and seized over forty hostages. Officers were outnumbered—there were under 100 to supervise 2,243 inmates over fifty-five acres. Homemade weapons surfaced among the inmates: knives, pipes, baseball bats and spears fashioned from scissor blades and broom handles.

With tear gas, part of the prison was regained by officers. However, some 1,200 inmates held cellblock D and the yard it faced. Ingenious inmates, using captured equipment, welded gates shut and shredded prison fire hoses.

The inmates released twelve hostages so they could receive medical attention. One hostage later died. The other hostages were stripped, dressed in inmate clothing and blindfolded.

State Corrections Commissioner Russell G. Oswald met with the inmate leaders in the yard and agreed to an inmate demand to let in the news media. He also agreed to let in outsiders including newspaper columnist Tom Wicker, Congressman Herman Badillo, and attorney William Kunstler to "oversee" negotiations. As a result, there were over thirty negotiators.

The negotiators and inmates compromised on a list of twenty-eight demands, many for improved procedures and conditions. However, the inmates refused to accept any plan which did not include unconditional amnesty and transportation for inmates wishing to go to a "non imperialist country" and the removal of the Attica superintendent.

Meanwhile, pressure from officials and the hostages' families was building to retake the prison. Following the inmates' refusal to release the hostages in exchange for the twenty-eight points, New York State Police and the National Guard moved into the prison to regain control. In the confusion, there were inadequate advance planning, uncoordinated leadership, the use of weapons (shotguns) not conducive to precision firing, and the lack of adequate medical personnel; thirty-nine people died (including ten hostages) and eighty were wounded.

Officials learned much from Attica. The Attica Commission investigated and recommended that:

• the possibility of negotiated settlement should be explored before using lethal force.

- authorities should retake a facility without lethal force, if possible.
- negotiations will not be productive if conducted in the presence of hundreds of inmates.
- negotiations must be private, on neutral ground, without the press, and if outsiders are admitted, limitations on their function must be set.
  (Leinwand, ed., 1972, pp. 125–147; Stinchcomb and Fox, 1999, pp. 389–392)

Riots: How They Start

How do riots start? Some researchers think that an event, such as a fight, a staff/inmate confrontation, an inmate transfer, etc., serves as a "riot spark" and ignites an already volatile atmosphere. Others think that inmate leaders plan a riot in advance.

Sometimes just staff enforcing rules can touch off a riot. A 1986 riot in a Florida detention center started when guards tried to stop inmates from taking other inmates' shoes and renting them back at $1.00 a day (Barber, 1986).

Pre-Disposing Factors

The vulnerability of a facility to the occurrence of a riot or disturbance is determined by the presence of pre-disposing factors or factors of corrections institutions that can reinforce the potential for trouble (Stinchcomb and Fox, 1999, pp. 386–387). These underlying causative factors are (Henderson, 1990, pp. 8–13):

- institutional environment regimentation, lack of privacy, sexual deprivation, separation from loved ones and friends, gang activity, brutality, poor food, etc.;
- substandard facilities: aging institutions that are old, in need of repair and overcrowded;
- inadequate funding: lack of funding and deficit financing leads to lack of repairs, lack of programs, etc.;
- overcrowding: results in tension, anger, predatory inmates, taxing services beyond reasonable limits. As one inmate said after a 1986 riot: "they made us sleep eight inches apart ... Lord, it is hot. That's why were did it [riot]." (Anderson and Lewis, 1986);
- inadequate staffing levels: increasing number of inmates being supervised by too few staff resulting in lack of proper supervision, lack of responses to requests and grievances, etc., and a climate of depersonalization where inmates are not treated like humans, but more like numbers or crowds;

CERT Team approaches scene of inmate disturbance. Manatee County (FLA) Sheriff's Office.

- idleness/lack of programs: idleness and tension can be reduced through positive programs such as education, vocation and recreation. Satisfying activities can maintain emotional stability and enhance self-esteem;
- public apathy: the public's lack of concern over prison conditions and rehabilitation can result in staff taking the same attitude;
- punitive attitude: society can demand retribution and harsh punishments, and these are dangerous attitudes to take in a tense, riot-prone facility. Supervisors must oversee staff who are positive towards their jobs and the treatment of inmates;
- inequities in the criminal justice system: tensions and frustrations increase when inmates see disparity in court sentences and what they perceive are unfair practices by the parole boards.

Causative Factors in the Inmate Population

In the environment of a correctional facility are a variety of inmate groups and types: the sociopathic inmate who is anti-social and who schemes against facility staff, racial and ethnic minorities, prison gangs, radical organizations and inmates who are mentally disordered whose behavior can be unpredictable and bizarre. A type of inmate, the ***political prisoner***, may emerge. Not to be confused with the noted political prisoners in other countries who are imprisoned for their political beliefs, the correctional "political prisoner" is an inmate, usually a member of a minority group, who blames society, the rich, prejudicial courts, etc., for his/her incarceration. In a riot situation, this type of inmate could act as a leader for a radical or racial group (Henderson, 1990, pp. 14–16).

Principles of Collective Behavior

In a flammable mix of the institution environment, overcrowding and different types of inmates living in a facility, one might ask what brings different inmates together to start a riot or disturbance *and* what keeps this cohesiveness going?

To understand inmate unity in a riot or disturbance, facility staff must understand the *Principles of Collective Behavior.* These factors serve to keep the riot or disturbance fueled by bringing inmates together as a group, and making the correctional staff's task of resolving the situation harder. These factors are (Henderson, 1990, pp. 16–17):

- Unity: inmates are likely to unite over *common* issues: issues that affect all or most of the inmate population. Common issues could be: visiting, food, medical care, etc. An example is the 1987 disturbances in the Federal prisons at Oakdale, Louisiana, and Atlanta, Georgia. Cuban inmates/detainees held 125 hostages without harm and negotiated a uniform agreement. The central issue binding them together was the possibility of repatriation to Cuba which affected them all.
- Frustration: agitators have an easier time recruiting inmates to their cause if inmates are angry, fearful, frustrated and feel that they have grievances. This was illustrated at Attica, where the inmates' list of demands showed frustration and anger about how the institution was run.
- Highly charged atmosphere: when a riot or disturbance is imminent or has started, the atmosphere is ripe for rumors which can turn a group of inmates into a mob. Police, sirens, fire equipment, news media, etc, can result in the inmates banding more tightly together.

Staff Countermeasures

Control of inmate violence and the prevention of riots, disturbances and incidents in a correctional facility are the job and the duty of everyone who works there. While the main responsibility of this task falls upon the line correctional officer, counselors, service staff, etc., all can help by reporting inmate behavior and keeping classification and custody staff informed of unusual occurrences or information about inmates. It is a never ending battle, especially in overcrowded correctional facilities.

Recognition of the Problem

Probably the best defense against inmate violence is for any COs and staffs who work around inmates is to remember at all times that they as well as inmates can be a target for an inmate assault. Also, staff in inmate housing, work and program areas must realize that fights between inmates or an assault on an inmate can happen quickly at any time.

Many officers fear the kind of violence which is unprovoked by them, and is unpredictable and spontaneous. As one Massachusetts prison officer said, this type of violence "... could happen any time, any day, [and] any minute. In this business, you just don't know" (Kauffman, 1988, p. 125).

While violence among inmates could be a result of personality conflicts, gang warfare, arguments over the television, etc., the reasons that inmates turn on officers can also vary. According to personal observations by the author, inmates may have just received bad news from home, their jobs are gone, an inmate in their cellblock is engaging in rowdy behavior, taunts and harassment, they may be under the influence of homemade alcohol or smuggled drugs or their anger levels are out of control. It is a negative atmosphere with a lot of unpredictable variables.

Unprofessional officers who lack maturity and ethics can provoke violence. Calling inmates names, using racial slurs, or embarrassing inmates in front of other inmates can, figuratively, turn up the heat on a boiling pot, causing the inmate to lose his temper. One Massachusetts prison officer said that other officers can get hurt because of an officer using insults on inmates such as "maggot." He said that "... I can get hurt because this [officer] is acting non-professional or stupid, out and out dumb" (Kauffman, 1988, p. 128). Correctional officers who provoke inmates or taunt them must be reported to a supervisor for counseling and/or disciplinary action.

Recognition of Warning Signs

The inmates will be the first to know if something is about to occur and may behave in certain ways that could be noticed by any staff member (Montgomery Jr., and Crews, 1998, p. 50). Observation of these behaviors should be documented by "information only" reports or by memorandum. These documents should be sent up the facility chain of command to upper level su-

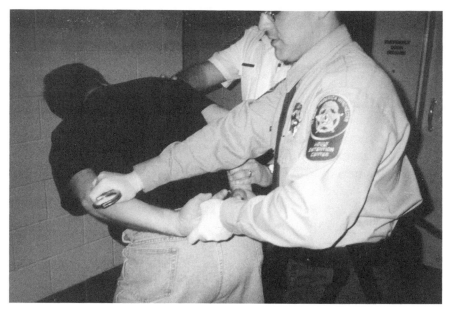

Some inmates object to being searched, and "break bad." The officer has to be ready for anything. Clarke-Frederick-Winchester (VA) Regional Adult Detention Center.

pervisors for distribution to the staff. All facilities should have an intelligence officer or committee whose function is to analyze the institutional climate. To simplify in "weather forecasting" terms, information received about inmate behaviors could act as a barometer on the atmosphere of the inmate population: Tense? Apprehensive? Prone to violence?

Different researchers have devised different lists of warning signs. However, the underlying theme is that inmates are acting abnormally in their interactions with staff and each other.

Riot/Disturbance Warning Signs

The following list is a compendium of warning signs that a riot or disturbance may be imminent, or that the atmosphere is tense (Stinchcomb and Fox, 1999, p. 387, Henderson, 1990, p. 74, Montgomery Jr. and Crews, 1998, p. 50):

Increases in:
- contraband and weapons found
- reports on misbehavior/incidents
- requests for cell change
- assaults on staff
- defiance of and confrontations with staff members

- purchases of food from canteen/hoarding
- smuggling of contraband by visitors
- manufacture/possession of weapons
- sick call attendance
- protective custody requests/admissions
- removal of food staples from dining hall
- requests for anti-anxiety or anti-depression medications
- requests to go to infirmary or outside hospital
- excessive or specific demands from inmates
- number of calls from family or friends about institution conditions
- number of grievances, especially about an unpopular policy change, called *grievance flooding*
- suicide attempts
- employee resignations
- appearances of anti authority and inflammatory material.

Warnings:
- to family and friends not to visit
- to well liked staff to take leave or a sick day
- anonymous warnings that something is going to happen
- mailing home personal belongings

Decreases in:
- attendance at movies, meals, recreation
- number of inmate workers

Avoidance:
- Inmates may also avoid staff with whom they had been friendly
- Inmates separate into groups along racial/ethnic lines, cluster in groups with "lookouts" posted or even change the seating arrangements in the dining hall by race, or make changes in the recreation yard by designating gang/race/ethnic "territory." The atmosphere may be tense and silent.

In summary, there usually are signs that something may happen. The correctional staff has to be alert for them or anything that frequently appears out of the ordinary, especially with a large number of inmates.

Controls of Inmate Violence

How do staff and correctional officers work to prevent or reduce violence in the facility? Sometimes the answers to this question are present in the everyday operations of the facility, and also may be inherent in the behavior of the

CERT Team members prepare to subdue an inmate. Manatee County (FLA) Sheriff's Office.

inmates. In other words, these controls to curtail violence are around the staff and inmates already—every day. Based on research by Lee H. Bowker, these controls are identified as (Bowker, in Braswell, Dillingham and Montgomery Jr., 1985, pp. 9–11):

- *Physical control:* This is simply hands on use of force by staff to protect inmates from each other, staff from assault or to enforce the rules of the institution. For example, an officer strikes an inmate who is assaulting another officer; a fight is physically broken up by officers restraining inmates. An inmate or inmates may be destroying property and legally can be restrained. An inmate refuses a direct order to go to his or her cell, and must be physically guided or led to a segregation area to await disciplinary charges.

Officers can use ***non-lethal use of force*** or physical force (holds, restraints, blocks, etc.) that overcome resistance, ensure compliance and does not cause death. ***Use of deadly force*** means that the officer can use force that is "likely to cause death or great bodily harm," generally as a last resort to protect someone's life or the officer's own life. The use of deadly force should be regulated by agency policy and state or local law (ACA, 1998, p. 30).

Firearms are usually thought of when discussing deadly force. For non-lethal force, items such as pepper spray, batons, and "stun guns" can be used.

Officers must document all uses of force, including the reasons for such actions. Also, the inmate upon whom the force is used must receive immediate medical attention. This includes inspecting restraint devices used on an inmate such as handcuffs, etc.

Physical control also includes the "hardware" of the facility: perimeter walls, gun towers, electrified fences, security gates, doors, locks, cameras, etc. These can serve to limit violence by controlling inmate movement and keeping them under observation. Also, the physical presence throughout the facility of officers in uniform—the *uniform presence*—can limit violence. Large numbers of staff in uniform (custody, classification, recreation, etc.) reminds the inmate constantly of staff physical presence and line of sight observation by officers.

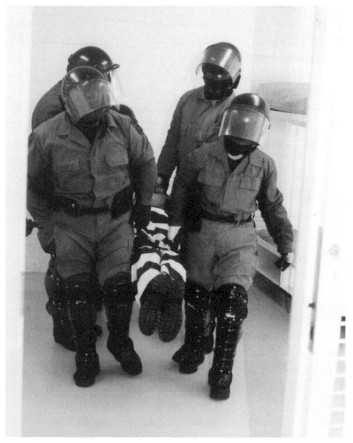

CERT Team transporting inmate to secure housing. Manatee County (FLA) Sheriff's Office.

- *Legal and administrative sanctions:* Inmates want out and to be released as quickly as possible. Violent inmates run the risk of having time added to their sentences by disciplinary committees removing good time [the time off an inmate's sentence for attending programs, good behavior, working in the institution, etc.]. Also, a classification committee can increase the custody level of an inmate because of violent behavior. Finally, the inmate population should realize that if they commit crimes such as homicide, sexual assaults, felony assaults, simple assaults, etc., they will be charged with a *street charge* or inmate jargon for getting charged with a crime defined by statute while incarcerated. A conviction could mean more time added on to the original sentence.
- *Supporting anti violence norms, values and beliefs:* Many inmates, like citizens in the general public, do not believe that violence is the answer to all of life's problems, especially those encountered with other inmates and staff. Most inmates want a calm atmosphere and violent inmates upset the "status quo." Inmates should be complimented by COs for solving a problem without resorting to violence. Inmates who are violent, threaten others, or delight in confronting staff may not be socially accepted by other inmates.
- *Housekeeping considerations:* Inmates should be frequently reminded that their cells, rooms or dorms are their homes for however long they are incarcerated. They are comfortable there with their property and surroundings. They have made friends with other inmates and may feel somewhat safe. If they engage in violence, they run the risk of being charged by statute, in house under the inmate disciplinary code, or both. If that happens, they will be moved to segregation. They will lose that "comfort zone."

Emergency Response Teams

An increasing trend in U.S. jails and prisons has been the development of *Emergency Response Teams (ERT)*, sometimes called Disturbance Control Teams or by similar names.

An ERT is a team of COs, on call, who are specially trained to respond to serious incidents, such as fights, riots, disturbances, forced cell moves, hostage situations, shakedowns, etc. Team members are trained in squad tactics, crowd control, use of force, non-lethal weapons, special weapons and emergency response strategies (Henderson, 1990, pp. 6–7).

The American Correctional Association recommends that ERT members be in good standing in their agency, including being in excellent physical shape and demonstrating proficiencies in weapons, riot control techniques, use of

Correctional Emergency Response Team, Manatee County (FLA) Sheriff's Office.

force procedures, repelling, tactical response, and facility emergency plans. They should be reliable, stable and of sound judgment in emergencies. Other specialized training, such as security hardware, is undertaken regularly (Henderson, 1990, pp. 6–7).

Correctional Emergency Response Team (CERT)
and
Tactical Apprehension and Control Team (TACT)

The Manatee County, Florida, Sheriff's Office has developed an effective response to inmate disturbances and other emergencies. This response is in the form of highly trained, well equipped law enforcement officers in the CERT and TACT teams.

Over fifty deputies are assigned to the CERT and TACT teams, drawing from a pool of correctional and law enforcement deputies. CERT can take care of problems inside the institution and TACT can handle outside problems.

CERT team members receive specialized training in:
cell extractions
riot control
high risk transports
shakedown (searches)
perimeters for hostage situations.
TACT team members are trained in these areas:
protests or marches

mass arrests
riots
parades
general crowd control

On September 16, 1996, illegal immigrant detainees trashed POD G-1 in a protest for better food, television and sneakers. Some ninety inmates were locked down. Warnings from staff went unheeded and the trashing was repeated on the following day. CERT and TACT were called in and the inmates got quiet due to a show of force. Order was maintained and each inmate was interviewed by immigration authorities. Without the show of force and discipline of CERT and TACT, the situation could have escalated into a riot.

"A professional approach by a professional agency—ready to respond, prepared for the worst, with a single mission of maintaining peace." That is the view of the teams.

[Source: Videotape: "Correctional Emergency Response Team and Tactical Apprehension Control Team, Manatee County Sheriff's Office, c. 1997. Special Thanks: Lt. Jim Conway.]

Prison riots can end or be terminated by a variety of means. Available data from U.S. prison riots and disturbances from 1990–1995 indicated the following ways the events ended, in descending order of frequency:

Use of force/assault	28.23%
Show of force	24.70%
Negotiation with inmates	21.56%
Use of chemical agents	11.37%
Voluntary surrender by inmates	9.41%
Threats by prison administration	4.70%

(Due to rounding, total may not equal 100%)
(Montgomery Jr. and Crews, 1998, p. 79)

While negotiation with inmates without the use of force or the show of force is always hoped for as a way to end the event peacefully, it is not always the case. Statistically, using and showing force have been the main factors in riot and disturbance resolution.

All staff should be aware of the workings of the facility's riot response plan. The American Correctional Association recommends that a riot/disturbance response plan incorporate these elements (Henderson, 1990, pp. 34–37):

- *prevention techniques and recognition of signs of tension:* good inmate/staff communications, staff recognition of the warning signs, proactive responses.

- *reporting incidents:* procedures for the immediate reporting of a riot or disturbance to a command center for immediate action, including isolating the area.
- *chain of command:* who is in charge until the regular command staff arrives is important, as is delegation of functions in the plan to personnel.
- *notification and call up procedures:* policies must be in place for shift supervisors, command staff and outside authorities (police, fire, etc.) and ERT members to be contacted. Also, other sections in the facility such as counselors, food service, programs, etc., must be contacted and given instructions for evacuation if necessary.
- *command center operations:* two command centers are needed—a primary one in a totally secure area in the facility and an auxiliary or backup out-

CERT members approach the inmate. Manatee County (FLA) Sheriff's Office.

side the facility in case the first is overrun. Communications to and from the command post must be established by radio, phone or intercom.

- *intelligence gathering:* information as to the event's location, who (inmate and staff) are involved, any injuries, etc., has to be gathered quickly *and* on an ongoing basis.
- *selection/assignment of emergency squads and options for action:* the plan should specify what response teams do what; what ERT members have been pre-selected to do what, and where teams are staged.
- *notification of outside parties and use of outside assistance:* Options for action must be thoroughly discussed: assault, utility cut off, negotiate, etc. If outside assistance such as police and National Guard are to be used, they must be trained personnel and know under whose authority they act and exactly what will they do.
- *developing options for actions:* each incident is different, but plans and options should be discussed as to personnel deployment, use of pepper spray, riot suppression activity, and the scope of the assault to take back an area or the entire facility.
- *equipment:* selection, use, accountability: the issue of batons, riot helmets, gas equipment, shotguns, etc., must be worked out in advance: who gets what. Weapons must be pre-prepared, loaded and ready. Also, since riots and disturbances are confusing and hectic, there must be a plan in place for the return and accountability of all equipment.
- *follow up:* after the event is resolved, the riot/disturbance should be thoroughly examined, noting good points of response and action and areas needing improvement. This information is helpful for recruit and in-service training.

As each facility is different, so are the nature of riots and disturbances. No two events are exactly alike. However, there are certain basic rules of dealing with the rioting inmates. They are (Henderson, 1990, pp. 38–39):

- Inmates who are rioting will not be granted illegal freedom;
- Authorities will not grant immunity or amnesty from prosecution. Prosecution will be pursued whenever possible;
- Persons under strain and duress, such as hostages, lose all authority and status. For example, if a prison shift supervisor is taken hostage, he is "no longer a shift supervisor."
- Keys and weapons are never to be surrendered to inmates. Authorities shall not provide drugs or alcoholic beverages to inmates.
- Authorities will not provide transportation to assist inmates in leaving the facility.

View from tower #2 at Maryland House of Correction.

Every facility, no matter how old, how constructed, or how big, should have a plan to deal with riots and disturbances. Even a county jail holding only fifty inmates could erupt in a disturbance.

In terms of prevention, the better the facility is operated, the less riot/disturbance prone the facility is. One of the best proactive strategies is staff simply being mobile and walking around. Staff presence meets the inmate need of safety. Also, inmates can ask the staff questions and a well-informed staff workforce can dispel rumors and look into inmates' concerns. By walking around, staff can also spot inmate troublemakers and the signs of possible unrest discussed previously in this chapter.

There are a variety of methods that staff can use to build a positive institutional climate and reduce inmate tension. They are (Montgomery Jr. and Crews, 1998, pp. 114–117):

- *Grievance process.* A method for resolving inmate complaints in a mature and reasonable manner, this mechanism gives inmates a forum for their complaints. Complaints are filed in writing and are either investigated by staff and a reply given to the inmate or a hearing with staff and inmate takes place.

- *Ombudsperson.* This is a staff person who will resolve problems and give satisfactory solutions to inmates' problems. In the military, a similar position is called inspector general.
- *Inmate councils:* The inmates elect representatives, who then discuss with the inmate population their problems, concerns, and anxieties. The representatives then bring this information to the council and subsequently the warden.
- *Inmate inventories.* Based on Likert's scale of measurement, the staff can measure how tense and riot prone the climate is. Questions are asked of the inmates and the responses contain the terms "easy" and "difficult" at each end of a scale having spaces from 1 to 5. Items could be:
  - opportunity to see the medical staff;
  - chance to speak to officer in housing unit;
  - opportunity to sign up for programs.
  - Inmates mark their feelings using the easy to difficult five point scale. Random surveys are taken periodically and the responses measured. If the staff, for example, see that a high percentage of inmates surveyed indicated that it is difficult to speak to an officer in their housing area, frustration may be building.
- *Staff training:* staff training on riot prevention must be on-going, emphasizing techniques to reduce tension and enhance security.
- *Emergency Response Teams:* ERT teams can serve to show inmates that violence will be responded to quickly and will also be contained.
- *Programs:* positive programs that promote self-help and self-esteem are healthy outlets for inmates instead of idleness. Recreation programs are always beneficial in reducing built-up tension.
- *Alternatives to incarceration:* any programs such as work release, electronic detention, community service, etc. are beneficial as they serve to reduce overcrowding and give inmates an incentive to be placed or court ordered into such programs as a result of good behavior.

Reexamining Corrections' Approach to Inmate Violence

With correctional facilities becoming more crowded, security threat groups becoming more problematic and corrections staff having to do more with less; correction's approach to inmate violence should be re evaluated frequently. This is an approach which encompasses the staff, the facility environment and policies.

According to Joseph D. Lehman, Commissioner of the Pennsylvania Department of Corrections, writing in 1992, these steps can be effective in dealing with inmate violence (Lehman, 1993 pp. 233–237):

Restrained inmate being placed in a cell. Clarke Frederick-Winchester (VA) Regional Adult Detention Center.

1. *Recognition of the stresses of prison environment:* Inmates feel little or no control over situations. Changes such as changes in goods, services and policies may provoke violence if perceived as harassment. The environment has an undercurrent of violence between inmates and inmates on staff, especially where primary contact with staff is over rules enforcement. Also, staff should recognize and correct negative aspects of the environment such as unsanitary conditions, sub standard heating, water, plumbing, toilets, etc. Encourage program, recreations and positive outlets for inmate energy.

2. *Separation of violence into categories based on victims' identification and the motivation of the aggressors:* Inmate protests, an officer's command, searches finding contraband, disciplinary actions, cellblock/institution transfer, etc. all have the capability of sparking inmate on officer violence. The aforementioned categories are generally reasons for inmate on staff assaults. Concerning inmate on inmate assaults, the reasons could be gang related, drug related or sexually motivated. COs should know what inmates are aggressors and what inmates are vulnerable targets.

Staff must track violent incidents relative to security, inmate classification level, the number of inmate assailants per incident and number of incidents per each inmate. Also, factors must be noted as to location of the incidents, time of occurrence, type of weapon(s), including fists, and the severity of the injuries.

3. *Identification of potential intervention points and development of a strategy:* Once data on violence is collected, staff must develop a strategy for the reduction of incident frequency and severity. Questions must be asked: Is more staff presence needed? What is going on with potentially violent inmates? COs should be aggressive in patrols throughout the facility; inmates should see many uniformed staff. Like searching for contraband in a "systematically unsystematic" method, COs should be unpredictable, such as backtracking through an area they just patrolled, walking assertively up to a group of inmates and asking "What's up?" and keeping inmates looking over their shoulders.

One strategy for the facility management is the recognition of the fact that hostage situations and fires can result from inmate violence. Fires may be contained without the evacuation of the inmate population. Fire emergency plans should follow the worst case scenario and have plans and training in place in case the entire facility has to be evacuated. A liaison with the local fire department and local law enforcement agencies is necessary. The worst thing that could happen besides an inmate or staff member dying in a fire is an escape by one or more inmates.

Hostage situations must be contained immediately and a security perimeter set up. The remainder of the inmate population must be locked down and all non essential security staff and civilians should be evacuated. Most facilities have some type of response plans for a hostage situation. The main goal is a peaceful, negotiated solution without injury or loss of life. One cardinal rule must be observed: If a sworn corrections officer, especially a supervisor such as a sergeant, captain or even sheriff is taken hostage, he or she loses all authority. By doing so, their rank cannot influence the negotiations.

4. *Evaluation of inmate activities and programs:* Based on information gained, classification procedures, contraband deterrence policies and inmate programs must be evaluated. Are classification decisions such as housing assignments objective and consider inmate behavior? Are strong predatory inmates placed with weak ones? Should certain inmates be segregated? Is the staff doing enough to counteract the flow and/or manufacture of drugs and weapons? Are inmates offered programs in skills training such as anger management, impulse control and cognitive skills?
5. *Strategies for staff:* Staff should be trained in interpersonal skills training, with emphasis on the best places and times to resolve inmate conflicts:

This may improve officers' skills in dealing with inmates and by defusing tense situations, assaults on staff may decrease in number. Training should include information gained from officers who keep things calm—the "level headed" ones. Also, the "hot heads" in the staff should be observed. Training should incorporate how each do their jobs and the positive and negative results of their actions. Mature inmates could be questioned as to what they think of staff/inmate interactions and if anything can be improved. But—a basic fundamental approach should be what COs were taught in the academy—back up your fellow workers, be cautious, be aware what is going on around you, use your security hardware and think *security*.

Lehman concludes by stating that changing the prison culture is not easy, but it can be done. He advocates the implementation of policies that advocate a *zero tolerance* of violent behavior. Simply, this means that the institution staff will not tolerate violence by inmates on other inmates or on staff for any reason; no exceptions will be made. Conflicts and disagreements will be resolved in a mature, adult manner. Related to this strategy will be the use of alternative strategies of conflict resolution: "trouble shooters," mediators and arbitrators. These methods can supplement the inmate grievance procedures.

Communications must be improved from the staff to the inmates and the inmates to the staff. Both groups should feel free to talk to one another without negative reactions or behaviors. Also, staff should conduct audits and assessments to monitor the communications and "institutional climate." The "climate" is the mood of the institution: tense, frustrated, non-communicative, etc. Since violence may be born of frustration, the frequent examination of the inmates' mood and then taking positive steps to improve the situation are beneficial (Lehman, 1992, pp. 236–237).

Correctional Officers: The Ten Deadly Errors

What can the individual correctional officer do to promote his or her safety? Plenty. While the potential for death or injury from the hands of inmates is always present, the following are some errors that must be avoided, according to veteran correctional officers Marty Boisvert, Michael Raunig, Michael H. Tolliver, Eric VanArsdale (Cornelius, 2009):

1. *Your Attitude:* Are you complacent? Are you bored? Just because all in the facility is calm, that does not mean that things won't change in a moment's notice? Your attitude can affect the safety of other staff and inmates in the facility.

2. *Tombstone Courage:* Don't be a hero. Be safe and strive to retire. No one doubts your courage, but remember inmates can hurt you—get backup—it is common sense.

Recreation facilities can reduce inmate tensions by engaging in exercise and "burning off steam." Fairfax County (VA) Adult Detention Center. Photos by author.

3. *Not Enough Rest:* Alertness is a critical factor. Get rest and sufficient sleep.
4. *Putting Yourself in a Bad Position:* Always think "defensive mode." Do you walk in front of inmates? Are you aware of where they are? If cut off or confronted, do you know an escape route or how to quickly call for help?
5. *Failure to Recognize Danger Signs:* What concerning inmates is out of place? Is there unusual activity or inactivity? Know your post area, watch the inmates in your area and report and discuss with your supervisor your concerns. Trust your "gut."
6. *Failure to Watch the Hands of Inmates:* A potential assault from an inmate starts with the hands. Watch them.
7. *Relaxing Too Soon:* Never think that an inmate call for assistance is a routine one or a false alarm—be alert! Be ready for anything!
8. *Non Usage or Improper Usage of Handcuffs:* Know and follow the procedures concerning the proper handcuffing of inmates. Keep the inmate's hands restrained. Remember your training.
9. *Poor Search Techniques or Not Searching:* Other correctional staff members trust you with their lives to perform one of the most critical and basic duties of corrections: searching inmates, their living/work areas and their property. Be nosy. Be thorough. Search properly.
10. *Dirty or Inoperative Equipment:* Does your pepper spray work? Is your radio operable? How clean is your firearm when you carry it on transports? How old is your ammunition? Do you have trouble qualifying at the range? Do the cameras and intercom work? Does your flashlight work?

Think about these errors; please do not make them.

Summary

Violence is inherent to the field of corrections. Often, among inmates, it is a result of deviant backgrounds and life on the street, where conflicts are settled with violence. Many inmates are frustrated and have not learned mature coping skills.

There are two types of correctional violence: individual violence and collective violence. COs must recognize and deal with each. Also, COs must recognize, document and report to supervisors the signs of tension in the facility

State raised inmates use violence as a symbol of importance and being taken seriously. Staff must remember that they are targets at all times. Staff members who are immature and unprofessional open themselves up as targets.

Countermeasures include the use of physical control, legal/administrative sanctions, and strategies to manage behaviorally disordered inmates. A proactive strategy is needed, such as recognition of prison stress, examining violent occurrences, adapting zero tolerance policies, and improved staff training. A riot and disturbance plan must be detailed and carefully thought out.

Correctional officers are not perfect. COs must strive to not make mistakes, and should be familiar with the ten deadly errors of COs.

Review Questions

1. What is meant by an inmate being a "state-raised convict?"
2. Define "bad asses."
3. Explain three methods (Bowker) of staff control of inmate violence.
4. How can staff re-examine correction's approach to violence?
5. Identify and explain five of the Ten Deadly Errors of correctional officers.
6. Explain the Principles of Collective Behavior.

Terms/Concepts

bad asses
collective violence
disturbance
Emergency Response Teams (ERT)
incident
interpersonal violence
non-lethal use of force
political prisoner

Principles of Collective Behavior
riot
state-raised convict
street charge
uniform presence
use of deadly force
zero tolerance

References

Abbott, Jack. (1981). *In the Belly of the Beast: Letters From Prison.* Vintage: New York.

American Correctional Association. (1998). *Dictionary of Criminal Justice Terms.* Lanham: American Correctional Association.

Anderson, John and Nancy Lewis. (1986, July 11). D.C. Trying to Move Hundreds of Inmates. *The Washington Post.*

Inmates protest $5 daily fee by tossing human waste, flooding cellblock. Associated Press, corrections.com 7/02 on line.

Barber, Ben. (1986, May 30). Inmates shipped out after riot. *USA Today.*

Bowker, Lee H. (1985). An Essay on Prison Violence. In Michael Braswell, Steven Dillingham and Reid Montgomery, Jr. (Eds.), *Prison Violence In America* (pp. 7–17). Cincinnati: Anderson.

California Prison Riot. (1978, February 22). *The Washington Post.*

Cornelius, Gary F. (2009, Spring). The Ten Deadly Errors of Correctional Officers. *The Correctional Trainer* [Online]. Available: www.iactp.org Publication of the International Association of Correctional Training Personnel. *See also: Managing a Direct Supervision Housing Unit: Back to the Future,* Seminar at the American Jail Association 27th Annual Conference and Jail Expo, May 6, 2008. Speakers: Marty Boisvert, Michael Raunig, Michael H. Tolliver, Eric VanArsdale, CO.

Correctional Emergency Response Team and Tactical Apprehension Control Team, Manatee County Sheriff's Office, c. 1997. [video]. Special Thanks: Lt. Jim Conway.

Gregg, Sandra. (1982, December 26). Va. Jail Aide Killed, 1 Hurt in Disturbance. *The Washington Post.*

Henderson, James D. (1990). *Riots and Disturbances in Correctional Institutions.* Laurel: American Correctional Association.

In Memoriam Officer Philip K. Curry 1960–1994 He Served. (1995, Winter). *The Keeper's Voice.* International Association of Correctional Officers, pp. 36–37.

Johnson, Robert. (2002). *Hard Time: Understanding and Reforming the Prison: Third Edition.* Belmont: Wadsworth.

Katz, Jack. (1988). *Seduction of Crime: A Chilling Exploration of the Criminal Mind—From Juvenile Delinquency to Cold Blooded Murder.* Basic Books.

Kauffman, Kelsey. (1988). *Prison Officers and Their World.* Cambridge: Harvard University Press.

Lehman, Joseph. (1993). A Vision for Dealing with Violence in the '90s. In *The State of Corrections Proceedings: ACA Annual Conferences 1992* (pp. 233–237). Lanham: American Correctional Association.

Leinwand, Gerald, (Ed.). (1972). *Prisons.* New York: Pocket Books.

Metzler, Kristin. (1995, February 7). Lorton Inmate Stabs Prisoner, 45 to Death. *The Washington Times.*

Milloy, Courtland. (1983, February 17). Readjusting to Life on the Bricks. *The Washington Post.*

Montgomery Jr., Reid, Jr., Ph.D., and Gordon Crews, Ph.D. (1998). *A History of Correctional Violence: An Examination of Reported Causes of Riots and Disturbances.* Lanham: American Correctional Association.

Pierson, David and Megan Garvey. (2006, February 9). More Rioting Erupts at Jails. *Los Angeles Times* [Online]. A1. Available: http://articles.latimes.com/2006/feb/09/local/me-jails9 [2008, November 14].

Samenow, Stanton E., Ph.D. (1984). *Inside the Criminal Mind.* Alexandria: Time.

Seiter, Richard P., Ph.D. (2005). *Corrections: An Introduction.* Upper Saddle River: Pearson Prentice Hall. *See also:* Braswell, Michael C., Reid H. Montgomery and Lucien X. Lombardo (1994): *Prison Violence in America, 2nd Edition,* Cincinnati: Anderson.

Stinchcomb, Jeanne B., Ph.D. and Vernon B. Fox, Ph.D. (1999). *Introduction to Corrections, Fifth Edition.* Upper Saddle River: Prentice Hall.

Washington, Jerome. (1991). *Iron House: Stories From the Yard.* Vintage: New York.

Chapter 13

The Rights of Inmates

This chapter will discuss the issue of inmate rights. This is a complicated issue—dealing with a wide range of subjects ranging from the development of inmate rights, frivolous lawsuits and to recent court decisions that dictate to correctional staff that inmates are afforded certain civil rights. This chapter is meant to be a concise, basic guide. Correctional officers should also keep in mind that due to court decisions and legislative acts, this is an area that is constantly subject to change. Correctional officers responsible for staff training should keep up with cases and laws and pass the information onto the staff. The references used in this chapter can serve as a good foundation to cover inmate rights.

Although the subject of inmates' rights can also be technical, this chapter will present a practical, line staff approach to inmate rights. These areas will be discussed:

- history of the courts concerning the rights of inmates and inmate litigation
- liability of staff: negligence and deliberate indifference
- *basic inmate rights* under the First, Fourth, Eighth and Fourteenth Amendments to the U.S. Constitution
- how staff can protect themselves from inmate lawsuits.

The whole subject of inmate suits and litigation is a changing one, involving state courts, the federal courts, the Supreme Court and the U.S. Congress. Due to this changing nature, the discussions in this chapter will serve as a general guide. All corrections facilities should have access to a legal resource including retained attorneys—who can keep the staff advised and assist with training.

Another reason for department legal resources is that the issue of inmates' civil rights is a complex one involving procedures, standards, court rules and documentation. These areas involve procedures for staff to follow. Qualified legal help can advise facility correctional officers as to what rights are to be afforded to inmates.

For correctional staff, the first step in learning the civil rights of inmates is acceptance of these facts (Hemmens in Duncan, 2008, p. 21):

Law library. Notice the resources: law books and computers for research and writing legal work. Fairfax County (VA) Adult Detention Center. Photo by author.

1. Inmates do not lose all civil rights when they become incarcerated;
2. The courts have granted certain civil rights to inmates and they can exercise them whether correctional staff agree or not;
3. Under certain circumstances or conditions if staff causes these rights to be violated, they can be held liable and consequences may include loss of job and/or paying monetary damages to inmates and/or their families.

Acceptance of all of these points is crucial to understanding inmates' rights. Concerning number 2, common phrases among corrections officers are that "inmates have too many rights," and "inmates have more rights than officers." These phrases are the result of frustration and lack of understanding. The CO may incur liability if he conducts himself in accordance with this attitude.

The granting of inmate rights by the courts have resulted in better treatment for inmates resulting in higher professional standards for facilities and better training, as will be made clear in this chapter. For the sake of simplicity, this chapter will not be a detailed education of the American judicial system pertaining to inmate rights, or a listing of landmark cases. What are important are the decisions that are made and their impact on the work of correctional officers in our correctional facilities.

Correctional officers receive formal training in criminal justice academies and on site seminars concerning the organization and responsibilities of the federal and state court systems. Judges in these courts look to each other for advice and to see how other courts have resolved similar situations.

To get a framework so that civil rights can be discussed, the correctional officer should have a basic understanding of the court system and what avenues are available to inmates so that they can file civil rights litigation.

History of the Courts and Inmate Rights

The United States has a dual court system. Federal and state courts co exist; defendants are tried in either federal or state courts depending on the nature of the charge—whether a federal or state law was violated. A statute giving the court the authority to act or the effect of a law being broken in its geographical area is called the court's jurisdiction (Schmalleger and Smykla, 2008, p. 429). In some cases, inmates can be charged with both federal and state crimes, and will be tried in both courts, one charge at a time. For example, an inmate is charged with burglary of an office building (state crime) but an investigation leads to his being charged with assault in a national park (federal crime).

Federal Court System

The federal court system is nationwide; each state has one or more federal courts within its borders. A concise guide to the federal court system is as follows, from the top down (Schmalleger and Smykla, 2008, p. 429):

> *United States Supreme Court:* Highest court in the United States, rulings are binding in all state and federal courts. It has ruled that constitutional requirements for criminal procedure in federal courts can apply to the states. Inmates can file state appeals and federal lawsuits to the Supreme Court alleging violations of these constitutional requirements.
>
> *United States Court of Appeals:* These courts total 11 courts of appeal that are arranged by circuits containing specific district courts in a region. There is a federal circuit for United States District Courts as a whole, one District of Columbia Circuit for district courts in the District of Columbia, and nine other circuits having jurisdiction for specific states. For example, the First Circuit contains the district courts of Maine, Massachusetts, New Hampshire, Rhode Island and Puerto Rico. The Fourth Circuit consists of Maryland, Virginia, West Virginia, North Carolina and South Carolina.

United States District Courts: These are the trial courts of the federal judiciary system, trying offenders charged with violating federal law. Each state has at least one federal district court; some states such as New York and California have as many as four. U.S. District Courts are also located in the District of Columbia, federal territories and Puerto Rico.

State Court Systems

State court systems are structured in a similar fashion to the federal systems. State trial courts are at the lowest level, hearing trials of offenders charged with violating state laws. State trial courts are generally organized by county. At the level above them are the state intermediate appellate courts which can hear appeals from the trial courts. The highest state court is the state supreme court, highest court of appeals in the state. The state supreme court can refer cases to the United States Supreme Court (Schmalleger and Smykla, 2008, p. 429).

Three Eras of Inmate Civil Rights

To put inmate rights in perspective, the evolution of inmate rights can be divided into three periods or eras: the hands off, the hands on and the one hand on/one hand off (Collins, 2004, pp. 7–8).

The *hands off era* lasted for most of the history of corrections in the United States, ending by 1970. During this time, the courts did not get involved with inmate litigation. The reasoning by jurists was that they knew nothing about correctional administration and the guiding concept of federalism which means that federal courts should avoid interfering with the activities of state and local government wherever possible (Collins, 2004, pp. 7–9). During this era, correctional authorities wielded much power and enjoyed freedom from court inquiry. Public opinion was basically apathetic with little concern for the welfare of those incarcerated. Training was minimal, if conducted at all. Inmate complaints went unheeded in this era. The following cases are examples of conditions in U.S. prisons and jails at that time as well as the courts' response (Collins, 2004, pp. 8–9):

- In 1951, a case involving a federal jail in Alaska was examined by an Alaskan court. The jail was old, built of wood frame. Up to forty inmates were housed in a room so small that less than nineteen square feet per inmate was allowed. Only twenty bunk beds were in the room, there was only one shower, one toilet and heat was provided by an unsafe wood stove. There was only one exit. Young inmates (age sixteen) were housed there. The judge agreed that the conditions were bad, calling the facility a "fabulous obscenity," and stated that it was not fit for human habitation. However, no Eighth Amendment (cruel and unusual punishment) finding was concluded; the judge, while noting the poor conditions, said that the inmates' living conditions were better than U.S. soldiers fighting in Korea. The only possible relief in his view was to release prisoners.

- An Alabama case dealt with inadequate medical care. Inmates handled both treatment and records. Examples included a maggot infested wound that went untreated for twenty days; an incontinent inmate patient was forced to sit on a bench as not to stain his bedding and as a result, he frequently fell and his leg was eventually amputated. The case revealed poor sanitation and a shortage of qualified doctors in the prison.
- As recently as 1965, inmates in the Alabama prison system were tortured by a device called the "Tucker Telephone" which delivered electric shocks to inmates. Inmates were also whipped (Cornelius, 2008, p. 332).
- An 1871 Virginia case described inmates "slaves of the state" saying that inmates forfeit their liberty and all personal rights (Cornelius, 2008, p. 331).

With the attention to substandard prison conditions that these cases generated and the advent of the civil rights cases of the 1960s, the hands off period started to end. More attention was being given to the rights of minorities and the underprivileged. Lawsuits by inmates started finding their way into the courts, sometimes with or without attorneys.

With the courts beginning to pay attention to inmate litigation, the **hands on era** began and lasted through the 1970s. The courts began to respond to corrections conditions cases, disciplinary due process issues, religious freedoms and many issues under the Bill of Rights. Due to these cases, inmates gained new rights, the opinion of which are still being debated today (Collins, 2004, pp. 12–13).

A serious problem with the hands off era was that for many years, the courts did not interfere in corrections and now the trend was reversed. In the confusion that followed, the courts became very detailed in their decisions on how correctional facilities should be operated—including food, prison uniforms, double celling, etc. However, courts began to notice and rely on professional standards from organizations such as the American Correctional Association (Collins, 2004, pp. 12–15).

During this period, the media became a method to which the public could see conditions in prisons and the cases which were addressing them. For example, the case of *Ruiz v. Estelle*, [1980 F. 2d 115] was profiled in *Newsweek* in 1979. This case concerned the lack of medical care in the Texas Department of

Corrections. The suit combined eight inmates' complaints, alleging that an inmate whose arms were amputated in a farm machinery accident went without prompt medical care and was raped by another patient at the prison hospital. Other complaints included brutal conditions in solitary confinement; suturing without anesthesia an inmate who had mutilated himself; and an inmate, a former truck driver, performing surgery (Bonventre and Marbach, 1979, p. 74).

The last era, the "one hand on/one hand off era" represents a compromise between the first two eras. Sometimes called the *restrained-hands approach*, the courts sought to balance the rights of the inmates against the security needs of the correctional facility. Courts are not as quick to impose their own solutions to problems; they give correctional staff and administrators an opportunity to correct the problem (Stinchcomb and Fox, 1999, pp. 596–597).

The restrained hands approach era is where the corrections profession has been since the early 1980s (Collins, 2004, p. 8). It is a realistic approach: the courts are not getting too involved so as to hamper the legitimate efforts of correctional staff. Courts look to see if restrictions on an inmate's perceived constitutional rights meet a *legitimate penological interest* such as a function or need that promotes the safety and security of the facility (Stinchcomb and Fox, 1999, p. 596).

In general, the courts have recognized four legitimate penological needs that justify correctional authorities restricting at times the constitutional rights of inmates (Schmalleger and Smykla, 2008, p. 429):

- The maintenance of order in the correctional facility: having both a calm climate and discipline.
- The maintenance of security in the correctional facility: control of individuals and objects entering and leaving the facility.
- The safety of inmates and the staff: avoidance of physical harm, including sexual assault.
- The rehabilitation of inmates: practices that are necessary for the health, well being and treatment of inmates.

This is accomplished by use of the *balancing test*. The court looking at an inmate complaint will apply four common sense questions to decide if the restrictions that the inmate is complaining about meet a legitimate penological interest of the correctional facility. They are, based on *Turner v. Safley*, 482 U.S. 78 (1987) (Cornelius, 2008, pp. 336–337):

- Does a valid or reasonable connection exist between the rule/restriction/policy and a legitimate penological interest?
- Are inmates allowed to exercise their civil rights in other ways?

- If the inmates are allowed to exercise their rights, will this practice affect other inmates?
- Are there alternatives to accommodate both the inmate rights and the legitimate penological interests of the facility?

The balancing test is applied hundreds of times daily in correctional facilities, every time an inmate challenges a regulation or a policy. A simple example would be an inmate challenging the facility visiting policy. He may complain that the 20 minute length of visiting time with family should be extended to thirty minutes. The warden informs him that the 20 minute time is ample, other inmates wait in line and visit, and if the inmate wants to have more contact with his family he has access to the phone and the mail. The test is that the First Amendment, which covers visiting, is extended to inmates, but to keep an orderly facility and not to create any trouble, the facility imposes this policy.

Realistically, for correctional staff, the restrained hands approach is common sense. Inmates have limited rights; limitations are imposed by correctional staff pursuant to an important goal—security of the facility and the safety of all who live and work there. Inmates, through court actions, have tried to get some of these limitations lifted by alleging that their rights are being infringed on.

Mechanisms of Litigation

Correctional officers should never underestimate the resolve of inmates who initiate litigation. Inmates do not have to file lawsuits through an attorney, even though the inmate or his or her family may file litigation for them. Corrections officers should be very wary of the inmate known as the *jailhouse lawyer*, an inmate very well versed or self taught in the law who files litigation or assists other inmates in filing litigation. He/she usually has no formal training in the law. The actions of a jailhouse lawyer include filing lawsuits alleging violation of inmates' rights, representation of inmates in disciplinary cases, appeals of disciplinary cases and other legal matters such as assisting in their own defense in court (ACA, 1998, p. 60). Inmates can file appeals or other court actions themselves or through attorneys. However, the main mechanisms to file lawsuits against correctional officers are (Cornelius, 2008, p. 329):

- *Habeas Corpus Actions:* In these actions, inmates claim that they are being held illegally, and attack a correctional facility, court, etc. responsible for keeping the inmate in custody.
- *Torts:* Torts are court actions generally filed in state courts in which the inmate seeks damages; alleging that he or she is owed some duty by cor-

rectional staff. Tort actions accuse correctional facilities of causing harm to the inmate, through such things as failure to protect the inmate, medical malpractice, the staff lacking training, etc.

- *Civil Rights Actions:* This is probably the most preferred method of inmates: filing litigation alleging that their civil rights under the Constitution were violated by correctional staff, which is liable to pay monetary damages. Civil rights actions are based on a key piece of federal legislation, the *Civil Rights Act* or *42 United States Code 1983*. Commonly referred to as "Section 1983," it states that government officials, such as correctional officers, can be held for monetary damages if found liable in withholding an inmate's civil rights under the Constitution. This is important—because many civil rights that we enjoy are based on amendments to the Constitution.

Relief Sought in Inmate Litigation

To understand the reason that inmates can seek relief in the courts—by filing both civil rights litigation, appealing their cases and assisting their attorneys, COs must be familiar with the Sixth Amendment in the Bill of Rights. This amendment states that the accused has certain rights, such as speedy trials, to be informed of the crime or charge, be confronted with witnesses, and have the assistance of counsel for his or her defense. Through court cases as will be discussed, this has been modified to affirming that inmates have a right of access to the courts, namely through attorneys and the use of legal resources (Cripe, 2003, pp. 83, 98).

Correctional staffs encounter many inmates who state that they will file suit. Some inmates are quiet and sincere; otherwise are more threatening and try to intimidate staff, especially new officers. Inmates can sue if they desire, like any other citizen, but filing lawsuits and winning are two different things. However, inmates will sue and the COs will find themselves named as defendants in a lawsuit.

With the emergence of inmates' civil rights and their demands to be heard, there came into prominence the jailhouse lawyer or, as some staff say, the "writ writer." Jailhouse lawyers often assist inmates in legal matters and the courts have allowed such assistance to take place. Jailhouse lawyers are not to be underestimated. Many know what legal forms to file, what cases to research and what procedures to follow in getting their case—civil rights lawsuit or criminal—into court. Correctional officers have found themselves in federal courts facing inmates' lawsuits accusing them of using excessive force, denying them religious freedoms, using too many restrictions on mail, denying them medical care and so on. Just because an officer is sued does not make the inmate's case valid, but care and caution should be taken towards inmates who know their way around a law library.

A law library is a crucial part of inmates having access to the courts per the Sixth Amendment. The Supreme Court ruled as far back as 1941 in *Ex Part Hull 312 U.S. 546 (1941)* that inmates must have access to the courts to file habeas corpus petitions. Subsequently, there have been several landmark cases in this area. The case of *Johnson v. Avery* 393 U.S. 483 (1969) took on the question of jailhouse lawyers assisting other inmates. In *Johnson,* the Supreme Court ruled that prison authorities may impose reasonable limits and regulations on inmates assisting each other, but cannot prohibit such activity at least until some form of reasonable alternative of assistance is afforded to the inmates. With this case, the jailhouse lawyer became a mainstay of inmate populations (Collins, 2004, pp. 44–45, 55). Inmates can ask for the assistance of a jailhouse lawyer, but it is the decision of the correctional staff to allow such access based on security concerns, the classification custody level and the records of the inmates.

In 1974, the Supreme Court decided the landmark case involving due process for inmates, *Wolff v. McDonnell* 418 U.S. 539 (1974). Besides discussing due process, the Court also ruled that inmates' right of access to the courts was expanded to include civil rights actions. In 1977, in *Bounds v. Smith* 430 U.S. 817 the Supreme Court ruled that correctional facilities could not impose barriers between inmates and the courts and had an affirmative duty to assist inmates by having adequate law libraries or adequate assistance by persons trained in the law, such as law students, paralegals or attorneys (Collins, 2004, pp. 45, 55).

In 1996, the Supreme Court redefined the rights of inmates and access to the courts in *Lewis v. Casey* 116 S.Ct. 2174 (1996). Most correctional facilities tried, through purchases of legal books and materials to meet the requirements of the *Bounds* decision, rather than bringing into the facility persons trained in the law. Now questions arose as to what is an adequate amount of time in the law library, what space is adequate to store law books and how should segregated inmates be afforded access. The *Lewis* decision required that inmates must show substantive, actual harm or prejudice caused by a law library being obsolete, or the legal access system for inmates in the facility was causing the inmate problems with his or her litigation (Collins, 2004, pp. 47–49, 55).

For example, an inmate requests to go to the law library because he is working on his appeal. The CO in his housing unit purposefully and repeatedly loses the request forms; the inmate misses the appeal date. An inmate on administrative segregation asks over a month long period for copies of legal forms and a court case that he needs to file a lawsuit against the jail. The request is never answered nor is he given an explanation, only that "troublemakers do not need the law library." Or—an inmate alleges that the legal books in the law library are 10 years out of date. These can be seen by courts as actual harm.

One aspect of the *Lewis* decision must be noted. In that case, the Supreme Court ruled that the right of access to the courts protects the ability of the inmate to file civil rights litigation concerning facility practices and conditions; it also protects the inmate when he or she files challenges to convictions such as appeals. It does not protect the inmate's ability to litigate other matters such as divorce, child custody, etc. The cases do not require that the correctional facility turn inmates into "litigating engines capable of filing everything from shareholder derivative actions to skip and fall claims" (Collins, 2004, p. 49). In other words, correctional facilities are busy places and security must be maintained. Inmates, in order to use the law library must confine their activities to meaningful litigation, not as a "witch hunt" to sue people or file a lot of cases as a hobby. Also, law libraries are not social gathering places and COs should make frequent checks in them to make sure that inmates are engaged in legal work and not using word processors and computers to write to their sweethearts.

Forms of Relief

Correctional officers should keep in mind that just because an inmate files a lawsuit naming the officer, that does not mean that the lawsuit will be lost by the officer. Remember—anyone can sue, but not everyone wins. The usual motivation is money; inmates are convinced that correctional agencies and staff have "deep pockets." Inmate litigators are hoping to get their cases into court with a sympathetic judge and jury. Inmate lawsuits look for two things from corrections officials: liability and damages. If the court finds the correctional officer liable, the money will follow.

Two main forms of relief are available to be awarded to the inmate if he or she is successful. An *injunction* is simply a court order telling the agency to do or not to do something. For example, a prison's law library has out of date law books. An inmate sues, and the case goes to federal court. The court orders the prison, using an injunction—to completely revise the law library and bring it up to date. While injunctions are the most commonly used forms of relief under the Civil Rights Act, they have had a profound impact on reshaping corrections (Collins, 2004, p. 32).

The second category of relief is monetary damages. These take three forms (Collins, 2004, pp. 33–34):

- *Nominal damages:* Nominal damages are what they appear—in name only. The court agrees that the inmate had incurred violations of his or her civil rights, but the violations were very minor and showed no harm. The inmate may receive a small amount, such as $100.00.

- *Compensatory damages:* These damages compensate the inmate for medical expenses, lost wages, plus pain and suffering and mental anguish if the court deems necessary. For example, an unsafe fire condition exists at the facility; the inmate is burned in a unit fire and sues. Compensatory damages can pay for his burn treatments.
- *Punitive damages:* This is the nightmare of any correctional officer. While compensatory damages can be paid from an insurance company retained by the agency, punitive damages come right out of the correctional officer's pocket. Punitive damages are meant to punish, and are levied if the CO is found liable and intentionally or recklessly caused the inmate's civil rights to be violated.

State of Inmate Litigation

During the late 1970s and early 1980s, there were many inmate lawsuits filed against correctional facilities. With the passage of the Prison Litigation Reform Act (PRLA) containing specific guidelines on the filing of inmate lawsuits, it is clear to veteran staff that the number of these lawsuits has declined.

According to the Bureau of Justice Statistics, the number of inmate lawsuits filed in federal courts increased from 2,267 in 1970 to a peak of over 39,000 in 1995. In 2000, federal court inmate lawsuits numbered 1,041 and lawsuits by inmates filed in state courts totaled 24,463, for a combined total of 25,504. The total has declined, but the potential of inmates filing still exists (Collins, 2004, p. 19).

Recent research has given corrections professionals insight on the nature of complaints of Section 1983 litigation. The National Center for State Courts, in conjunction with the United States Bureau of Justice Statistics (BJS), studied Section 1983 cases disposed of in 1992 by U.S. District Courts located in Alabama, California, Florida, Indiana, Louisiana, Missouri, New York, Pennsylvania and Texas. These states have nearly 50% of U.S. Section 1983 litigation and are representative of the entire range of Section 1983 cases nationwide (Cornelius, 2008, p. 330).

In an examination of the subjects of corrections activities being challenged, the study found the following issues and corresponding rates of frequency (Cornelius, 2008, p. 330):

- Medical treatment (17%): failure to provide back braces, corrective shoes, dentures, necessary surgeries, etc.
- Physical security (21%): excessive force by officers, failure to protect from assaults and rapes by other inmates, harassments and threats by staff, no prevention of inmate property theft, unreasonable body cavity searches.

- Due process issues (13%): improper procedures in administrative segregation placement, intra-prison transfers, disciplinary actions, and classification.
- Living conditions (4%): diets that are not nutritionally adequate, inadequate clothing, denial/limitations of exercise.
- Physical conditions (9%): overcrowding, inadequate toilets/showers and sanitation, excessive noise, failure to protect against AIDS exposure and tobacco smoke.
- Denial of religious expression, assembly, visitation and racial discrimination (4%)
- Denial of access to courts, law libraries, lawyers, plus interferences with telephone calls and mail (7%)
- Harassment and assault by arresting officer (3%)
- Invalid conviction or sentence (12%)
- Other: denial of trial, denial of parole, etc. (11%)

Prison Litigation Reform Act

One of the best developments in recent years has been the reduction in what are termed frivolous lawsuits, or simply lawsuits without merit. According to an article in the June 23, 1995 *Corrections Digest*, examples of frivolous lawsuits are (Stinchcomb, 2005, p. 540):

- One inmate serving a life sentence for rape and murder of five teenage girls sued the California Department of Corrections for serving him a soggy sandwich and broken cookies for lunch.
- An inmate in Oregon sued over 100 times, including one allegation stating that prison officials refused to silence a nearby early morning train, which disturbed his sleep. He also alleged that he was denied a dry place to lie down because of the prison staff watering the grounds.
- An inmate filed approximately 600 lawsuits against the District of Columbia prison system that challenged prison conditions, including restrictions on his "church" he founded—and he is the sole minister.

The Prison Litigation Reform Act or PLRA of 1996 is a federal law that revolutionized the problem of corrections dealing with inmate litigation. It requires all inmates filing lawsuits in federal court to pay a filing fee; in some cases the fee may be waived. Besides restriction on attorney's fees in successful cases, PLRA requires federal judges or magistrates to screen inmate lawsuits and dismiss or "weed out" lawsuits that are frivolous and contain little merit (Cornelius, 2008, p. 356).

Another stipulation of PRLA is that it expands the grievance requirements first established by another federal law, the Civil Rights of Institutionalized Persons Act or CRIPA. CRIPA is a law enacted by Congress that allows the Justice Department to sue on behalf of all persons inside institutions, including prisons and jails. It also postpones all actions on an inmate lawsuit until the inmate has exhausted all administrative remedies that meet criteria established by the Justice Department or the federal judiciary. PRLA makes the inmate responsible for exhausting all grievances and appeal procedures that are available, not just those established under CRIPA mandates (Cornelius, 2008, p. 356).

Grievances

Some correctional officers are of the opinion that grievances are a waste of time, and allow the inmate to vent and gripe. The effectiveness of grievances depends on how they are implemented and the weight given to them by the facility staff. A *grievance* is a complaint, filed through channels to the appropriate institution staff in whose area of responsibility the complaint is concerned (Cornelius, 2008, p. 472). For example, an inmate has severe headaches and he thinks that the prison medical staff has misdiagnosed the problem, or is not giving him the proper medication. He has attempted to resolve the problem by speaking to the medical staff, but feels that the matter is unresolved. He requests and receives a grievance form. The grievance will be logged in, given a number (in most facilities) and assigned to the medical staff for resolution within a certain time frame. The inmate will receive a written answer and may appeal to a higher supervisory level in the facility administration.

The key to an effective grievance system, as illustrated in the example, is to get the inmate to try to resolve the problem with the facility staff by use of inmate request forms or other approved means. In other words staff should encourage inmates to voice their complaints and problems in a mature way, instead of yelling, demanding action or becoming angry.

An effective grievance procedure can be found at the Alexandria (VA) Detention Center. The inmates are informed through their Inmate Handbooks that certain issues are not grievable, such as disciplinary actions, housing assignments and classification status. The inmate must first try to resolve the problem with staff or COs involved, and if they do not like the way that the matter is resolved, they can file a grievance form. Staff has four on duty days to respond, and inmates may appeal to supervisors. Grievances are not to be a tool to "write up staff," they must have merit. Grievances containing profanity and insults will not be accepted (*Inmate Handbook,* Office of Sheriff, Alexandria, 2004, p. 23).

Inmates may try to "buffalo" COs by saying that the grievance system is "B.S" or a waste of time. If COs do not give credence to the grievance system or ignore inmate grievances, the level of anger and tension in the facility will increase. Inmates may also threaten COs and staff by saying "screw the grievances — give me a Section 1983 form." Staff and COs should try to inform the inmate that a grievance is required by the court; however, some inmates do not listen.

Liability of Staff

The goal of every correctional officer, besides doing the utmost to safely confine inmates and protect the public, is to not have to pay punitive damages in a finding of liability. In order to understand this concept, a CO must have a working understanding of liability.

Liability Defined

In the simplest terms, *liability* means "the responsibility for one's own behavior," based on the term liable which means "obligated or responsible according to law" (ACA, 1998, p. 67). To be liable in a civil rights case, a defendant (correctional staff) must have caused the constitutional violation on the inmates or have caused the injury. Under Section 1983, liability is imposed when someone such as a corrections officer "establishes a violation of a constitutional right" [such as denial of religious freedom]. Courts will focus on this aspect of the suit (Collins, 2004, p. 29).

While corrections officers and staff can be subject to *criminal liability* if litigation proves that an employee on the job broke a specific law or criminal statute, most inmate litigation involves *civil liability* — the violation of civil rights resulting in the payment of monetary damages or compensation (Stinchcomb and Fox, 1999, pp. 598–599).

Inmates know that the average line staff member has limited ability to pay damages so they file suits that challenge policies and procedures set forth by agency heads and supervisors. In other words, the agency that hires and supervises the employee can also be held liable. This concept is known as indirect liability or *vicarious liability* which goes beyond the actions of the line staff (Stinchcomb and Fox, 1999, p. 599).

Vicarious liability is defined as the responsibility for another's actions or failures to act [omissions]. Correctional supervisors are held responsible for the actions of employees under their supervision (ACA, 1998, p. 212).

Vicarious liability is a result of a situation where someone other than an employee, such as a supervisor, knew or should have known what was happening or about to happen, but did nothing to prevent the situation. As a result, the lack of action was the proximate cause of harm, injury or death to the inmate (Stinchcomb and Fox, 1999, p. 599).

For example, a shift supervisor knows that a certain housing unit holds hard core inmates that frequently fight. Security must be maintained at all times. A new correctional officer, a rookie, reports for duty and tells the supervisor that he has not gone through training. The supervisor assigns him to the housing unit, saying that he needs a "warm body" on that post. No instructions or pass on information are given to the officer. The rookie officer, thinking that all is quiet, leaves his post for an hour to take a break. One inmate then attacks another, who suffers a broken jaw and concussion. Is the shift supervisor subject to vicarious liability? *Yes.* He knew of a potentially harmful situation and by putting an untrained officer in that unit, the situation was a proximate cause of the assault. Perhaps the inmate would not have assaulted the other if a seasoned veteran officer (or maybe two) had been assigned to the unit.

Three key elements of vicarious liability are basically three critical jobs performed by corrections supervisors:

1. Failure to train: the employing agency could be held liable if the employee being sued could prove that he/she was not properly trained in their job.
2. Negligent supervision: a supervisor would be liable if he/she knew of a situation where an employee was doing something wrong and this was not corrected.
3. Negligent employment or retention: closely linked to negligent supervision, a problem employee is hired and/or retained on the job. For example, an employee with a poor performance record for sleeping on the job is hired. One night, he falls asleep on post and an inmate suffers a fall and is not immediately treated, resulting in complications. Another employee has a record of ignoring inmates' complaints. He ignores an inmate's request to move and as a result, the inmate is assaulted. In both cases, the supervisors, as well as the employees could be held liable, especially if it can be proven that these problems were known and supervisors did nothing.
(Stinchcomb and Fox, 1999, pp. 599–600)

Correctional officers pride themselves as working on a team—a squad, a section, a shift, etc. They must assist their supervisors in identifying and "weed-ing" out staff that can cause the agency liability. They must also remember that they may also be supervisors in the future.

Negligence

The term *negligence* is widely used in inmate legal actions. Basically, it is the inmate telling the court that the corrections staff owed a duty to protect, the treatment of a medical problem, etc., and it was not performed. Perhaps the best definition is by Dean Champion (Champion, 2005, p. 692):

> Tort [action] involving a duty from one person [staff] to another [inmate], to act as a reasonable person might be expected to act, or the failure to act when the action is appropriate; failure to exercise reasonable care toward another. Gross negligence includes willful, wanton and reckless acts, without regard for consequences and are totally unreasonable.

Negligence can take two forms—negligence itself is failure to act as a reasonable person would. For example, an officer pulling inmates for programs forgets to check the "keep separate list." Two inmate enemies come into contact and one assaults the other. *Gross negligence* involves the willful, wanton and reckless actions which are both unreasonable and have no regard for the consequences (Champion, 2005, pp. 425–426). For example, two inmates are known enemies and officers knowingly fail to keep them apart, a fight ensues and one inmate suffers a fractured skull. One of the officers is heard later to say: "I always did want to know who the best street fighter was." In this example, a staff member intentionally did something to cause harm. Another example could be that an officer is angry at an inmate who cursed at him the day before. The next day, the inmate slips on a wet floor and breaks his arm. The officer waits two hours before calling for a medical officer.

All correctional staff should receive training in negligence and how failing to do a proper job may lead to an inmate lawsuit.

Deliberate Indifference

Deliberate indifference is a form of negligence. It is what it appears: it occurs when staff knows of a condition or need of the inmate, and purposefully does nothing about it. The formal definition is that deliberate indifference occurs when correctional staffs [supervisors and line staff] know or should have known, because of obvious conditions, that what they are doing or not doing is a risk to the health, safety and well being of the inmate, but they take no action (ACA, 1998, p. 31). For example, the staff member knows that an inmate needs medical attention and ignores the problem. Examples of this would be chest pain, bleeding, etc. A reasonable person would call for medical attention, but the deliberately indifferent person does nothing.

Another aspect of deliberate indifference is sexual assault. For example, a young inmate approaches a correctional officer and says that other, bigger and more aggressive inmates are threatening to rape him that night after lights out. The officer advises the inmate to "be a man" and "stand up to those guys." That night the inmate is raped, injured, and later tests reveal that he contracted HIV. His attorney sues the agency and the correctional officer seeking punitive damages; the officer is found to be liable and deliberately indifferent to the safety needs of that inmate.

Basic Inmate Rights

The core of inmate rights—the foundation—is based on several amendments to the U.S. Constitution. An alert CO recognizes this, and keeps up with developments and changes dictated from the courts. This section will give each amendment an overview and explanation of the inmate rights affected by the courts.

First Amendment

This amendment—the first of the Bill of Rights, includes several freedoms that we hold very dear—namely the freedom of religion, the freedom of speech and the freedom of the press. The Supreme Court has determined that inmates are afforded those rights under this amendment which are consistent with the legitimate penoligocal interests of the correctional facility (Hemmens 1997, in Bales, ed., p. 19).

Freedom of Religion

While many COs, especially long time veterans, think that inmates "get religion" when they enter into jail or prison, the fact is that religion can be a good thing and a positive force in rehabilitation. That does not mean that inmates can practice their religion in any way that they choose. While courts have supported inmates being able to choose their faiths, they have not given inmates the total freedom to worship in a manner not conducive to facility security.

On the other hand, this does not mean that the facility can restrict an inmate's desire to practice religion because the staff may think that the inmate is running a game or is not totally honest or sincere. Courts will balance the inmate's request against the security needs of the facility.

Some inmates have tried to fabricate religions in order to make their incarceration more comfortable. In the 1970s, an inmate formed the "Church of the New Song" or CONS in which he stated that a sacrament of his "church" was steak and wine to be served occasionally. The courts eventually decided that CONS was a scam and did not afford it protection under the First Amendment. In another case, a court ruled that the Universal Life Church which grants such religious titles as "Doctor of Divinity" through paid mail orders was not a religion (Collins, 2004, p. 70).

The benchmark case concerning inmate religious rights was *O'Lone vs. Shabazz* (482 U.S. 342, 343 or 107 S.Ct. 2400, 96 L.Ed. 2d 282 (1987). A group of Muslim inmates sued prison authorities because they wanted to attend the Islam service Jumu'ah, which conflicted with a minimum security prison work detail. The prison argued that they did not have the staff to escort the inmates to the services and keep up the prison routine. They also said that the Muslims would appear to receive special treatment, a group could develop that could challenge prison authority and there were alternative ways for the Muslims to practice their faith, such as having access to a Muslim religious leader, special diets and other services. The Supreme Court, although ruling for the prison, adopted the balancing test, with Chief Justice Rehnquist saying that "when a prison regulation impinges on inmates' constitutional rights, the regulation is valid if it is reasonably related to legitimate penological interests" (Mushlin, Volume 1, 2002, p. 683).

What does this mean to the CO on the line? First, all religious requests should be directed to the chaplain and/or programs director. Second, if a facility policy is restricting an inmate from practicing a religious faith, it must show a good reason why, such as security, order, etc. Just saying "security" will not satisfy a court in a lawsuit. The reason has to be clear and backed up by documentation.

The courts now use several tools to deal with inmate religious requests and the First Amendment. The Religious Land Use and Institutionalized Persons Act (RLUIPA) passed by Congress and signed into law in September 2000 protects the religious rights of institutionalized persons. No government entity [such as a correctional facility] may impose a substantial burden on a person in an institution [such as a correctional facility] unless it can be shown the burden furthers a compelling governmental interest [such as order, security, etc.]; and the burden is of the least restrictive means of furthering that interest. Once an inmate claims that a facility policy places the burden, the burden shifts to the facility agency to demonstrate that there is a compelling need behind it (Mushlin, Volume 1, 2002, p. 690, 695). As mentioned before, line COs should not engage in debates over inmates in these matters, but refer them to the chaplain. The chaplain can then consult with agency supervisors.

There are several controversial areas within the framework of inmates and religion. The first is sincerity of belief. The inmate must be sincere in his or her religious beliefs, if they are not; the correctional facility is not under any legal duty to accommodate the inmate's request. Sincerity of belief is easy to prove or disprove, depending on the record keeping of the staff. In one case, a court ruled that an inmate was insincere. The inmate had failed to respond to a request for information about the religion in question from the staff, failed to request religious services for twelve years, failed to file an administrative appeal concerning being denied religious services, and was ambiguous and unclear about alleged religious beliefs (Collins, 2004, p. 71). To establish sincerity, inmates should be referred to the chaplain and be required to put their requests in writing. If the inmate fails to request religious information, does not request to see the chaplain, clergy or a religious volunteer, and does not participate in religious activities or services, he or she will have a very difficult time proving to a court that he or she is sincere about religion and that his or her constitutional rights under the First Amendment were violated. All of this can be documented and retained on file.

The second controversial area is the matter of religious diets, which has been the subject of much litigation. The faiths most involved have been the Jewish and Muslim faiths. A kosher diet is required of Orthodox Jews, including that food must prepared in a certain way, animals must be slaughtered conforming to Jewish rituals, and meat and dairy products cannot be eaten together, pork is not to be eaten, etc. Muslims must follow religious dictates of their faith and not eat pork. The courts have been willing to accommodate religious diet requests when the costs of doing so are not overwhelming and also when facility officials cannot show any rational reason for denying it (Mushlin, Volume 1, 2002, pages 734,737). All religious diet requests should be channeled to the chaplain. Many facilities have solved the no pork religious diet situation by simply eliminating all pork from the menu and making sure that food products served contain no pork or pork by products. Another alternative is to have all religious diet requests approved by the chaplain in agreement with facility food service, or instruct inmates who are vegetarian not to eat any meat from the meal line or trays.

The final controversial area is the attendance by inmates at religious services. While religious services can serve to aid rehabilitation and give the inmate a positive outlet for his or her religious faith, it must be noted that all inmates are not religious, the correctional facility must maintain order, safety and security, and inmates have been known to engage in gang activities and communications that have nothing to do with religion. Add to the mix inmates on disciplinary segregation, administrative segregation, and protective custody and the problem becomes more complex.

Courts have taken the position that the reasons for some inmates to be excluded—such as those on segregation—must be examined. A good alternative is cell visitation by a chaplain, a religious official such as a priest, pastor or imam that has approval to enter the facility or a volunteer. By doing so, segregated inmates can have their religious needs met to some degree. Also, holding many religious services among different faiths may prove infeasible. While some facilities may allow inmates to lead their own services, courts generally agree that if officiating clergy and personnel can lead a service, inmates have no right to officiate in religious services. Space, staffing and the number of inmates attending all impact security and operations (Mushlin, Volume 1, 2002, pp. 741, 744, 746).

First Amendment: Ties to the Community

The freedoms of speech and association can be met in correctional facilities through the mail and visiting. The courts have recognized that through these inmates can maintain meaningful connections to the outside world. This does not mean that inmates can visit and correspond with whoever they want.

Mail

Part of the concept of freedom of speech and expression is the sending and receiving of mail by inmates. For security reasons, most if not all institutions stamp outgoing mail with the name of the facility, so the recipient can see at a glance from where it originated.

Restrictions and regulations by correctional facilities concerning mail are due to the four penological needs recognized by the courts and have already been discussed in this chapter: order, security, safety of all in the facility and rehabilitation. For those reasons, incoming mail has to be inspected and packages have to be searched. For example, in one local facility an inmate had signed up for a college correspondence course in geometry. That was very good concerning rehabilitation and furthering the positive lifestyle of the inmate-education. However, when the package was opened it contained a ruler and a compass—both which could be used as weapons. The inmate could have the printed material, but not these items. Items such as these are not illegal, but are contraband. They can be placed in the inmate's property and given to him or her upon release or released by the inmate to his or her family.

Correctional administrators have serious concerns about inmate mail, including (Cripe, 2003, pp. 102–103):

- Correspondence that discussed direct breaches of security, such as riots, escapes, plans for illegal ventures (such as drug smuggling), homicides, assaults, gang activities and introduction of contraband.
- Planning for crimes such as robberies upon release or retrieval of drugs, stolen goods, or other fruits of a crime.
- Intimidation of and threats to witnesses.
- Contents of letters that criticize the facility administration—while inmates can criticize; such views inside a facility can be inflammatory.
- Inflammatory material that could incite inmates such as from hate groups, racial supremacist groups, etc. This may include groups masquerading as religious groups.
- Pornographic material—such as printed pages from pornographic internet web sites, books or magazines.

Complete censorship of inmate mail is not practical. What *is* practical is keeping an eye on mail on two levels. First—closely inspect incoming mail for contraband and second—keep a close watch and observation on the mail of inmates or groups of inmates identified as security threats. Incoming mail is of the utmost importance, as its contents may be of legitimate penological interest. Outgoing mail is of less concern as the threat diminishes because it has left the facility. In some facilities, where high profile inmates are housed and security is extremely tight, the contents of incoming and outgoing mail may be scanned very closely (Cripe, 2003, p. 103).

Still, correctional facilities must be careful about printed material in books, newspapers, periodicals, magazines and clippings from them. Generally, inmates may receive such materials by subscription or in separate mailings from family or friends. In *Thornburgh v. Abbott*, 490 U.S. 401 (1989), inmates and several publishers challenged a U.S. Bureau of Prisons regulation by which prison wardens could reject incoming publications if found to be "detrimental to the security, good order or discipline of the institution or if [they] might facilitate criminal activity." Examples included articles on how to make homemade alcohol, manufacture drugs, and making homemade weapons. Sexual content such as homosexuality or bestiality could be rejected if found to pose a threat to security—the main overriding standard. The Supreme Court decided that the standard to be applied was the balancing test discussed previously in this chapter from *Turner v. Safley*, stating that the prison mail regulations were central to security (Cripe, 2003, pp. 111–112).

Concerning jails, the case of *Bell v. Wolfish* 441 U.S. 520 (1979) ruled on "publisher only regulations," even though part of the case was a challenge to a Bureau of Prisons rule. During the litigation of this case, the Bureau of Prisons relaxed its guidelines to allow paperback books and magazines to be sent in by friends and family. However, the Supreme Court ruled that such a regulation such as publisher only for books and magazines dealt not with content, but with the cornerstone of all correctional facilities—security. The regulation was upheld for both convicted and pre trail inmates (Cripe, 2003, pp. 111–112).

The safest course for most correctional facilities has been the "publisher only rule." Inmates have the alternative of selecting books and magazines from a leisure type library, either by going to it, or in the cases of overcrowded institutions, having a book cart making rounds of population areas, including administrative segregation. Donations can be accepted from local citizens and the local library, but the material is screened for content and contraband. For example, a library or a citizen drops off several hundred magazines and books for the inmates. Staff looks for hidden contraband and any article or book that can be questionable, such as articles on how to pick a lock, or as one article stated in a magazine, "the best concealable handguns."

In one jail, the librarian brought to the attention of the programs director a book that graphically depicted the sexual abuse of females by a gynecologist. The book was summarily rejected and disposed of. Books may be restricted to paperback, as inmates have been known to use heavier hardback books for not reading, but weightlifting or as weapons with which to hit other inmates. In another facility, the staff librarian discovered that the reason that so many inmates wanted a certain book was because gang members were very secretively marking letters and passages of certain pages and text in order to pass gang messages to each other. In summary, not all inmates are interested in the First Amendment and good reading material.

Visiting and Phone Calls

The last aspects of maintaining ties to the outside are visiting and phone calls. While personal visiting with friends and family is recognized as being important, the Supreme Court has refused to say that inmates are guaranteed an absolute or unfettered right to visits. Nor do inmates have the right to visits without any physical barriers (called contact visits) or conjugal visits (where inmates may visit with members of the opposite sex in private, a significant other, or a spouse). Some correctional agencies do allow contact and conjugal visitation per policy (Collins, 2004, p. 79).

The bottom line is that the courts have left it up to the correctional facilities as to how to securely operate inmate visiting. Some institutions have visiting lists where staff approves a listing of family members and friends who are permitted to visit while others may have a system that instructs visitors to call the facility for an appointment. A new trend in visitation is *video visitation,* where visitors visit and talk to the inmate via a video hookup. By doing so, inmate movement is curtailed, as a "kiosk" set up is used—the inmate may speak into the video camera from his or her unit to a kiosk in the lobby where the visitors sit speaking into another camera. However it is operated, visiting procedures and scheduling are set by the correctional facility staff. In times of emergency, such as a fire condition, power outage, hostage, riots, escapes, etc. visiting can be canceled.

Probably the best illustration of courts deferring to correctional personnel concerning visiting is the case of *Block v. Rutherford* 468 U.S. 576 (1984), in which inmates in the Michigan prison system challenged restrictions on contact (no barriers) personal visiting. Prison officials had attempted to accommodate the wishes of prisoners in the lower classification grades concerning contact visiting, but prohibited inmates in the higher more risk classification grades from receiving contact visits. Faced with the security problems which always seem to accompany contact visitation, such as the introduction of contraband, including drugs and weapons and staff expenses for the screening of visitors, the prison system prohibited contact visits. A Michigan District Court sided with the officials, and this decision was affirmed by the Sixth Circuit. The Sixth Circuit also supported the Michigan visitation policies of allowing visitors under age 18 to visit only if they were the children of inmates, and/or a stepchild or grandchild; they also had to be accompanied by a legal guardian or immediate family member. Inmates could not visit with natural children if their parental rights were terminated; also inmates could have only ten non family members on an approved visitors list. Ex inmates could only visit if he or she was a family member or had unique qualifications such as being a lawyer, a member of the clergy or a government official or representative (Palmer and Palmer, 2004, pp. 38–39).

In this case, the Sixth Circuit made several profound announcements about correctional visiting. It mentioned that the Supreme Court has left the problems of prison administration to prison administrators. Also, when prison regulations [such as visiting] are reasonably related to and are supportive of legitimate penological interests [such as security] there should be no federal intervention, such as from the federal judiciary (Palmer and Palmer, 2004, p. 39).

Personal phone calls are another important avenue of inmate contact with the outside world. If inmates had their way, most would be on the phone all day and all evening. However, the courts have ruled that inmates retain rights under the First Amendment to communicate with family and friends. Also, the courts have said that there is no legitimate governmental purpose that corrections officials can achieve by preventing inmates from having reasonable access to a telephone. Inmates do not have the right to unlimited phone access and use, and legitimate penological interests can be the basis of rational restrictions on the phone, subject to scrutiny by the courts if necessary (Palmer and Palmer, 2004, pp. 72–73).

Examples of such restrictions are the hours that the phones in the housing units are available. Another restriction is the use of collect call phones, where calls placed by the inmate to people on the outside are collect and the charges must be accepted after the call is identified as coming from inside the correctional facility. If an inmate damages a telephone or breaks a rule and is found guilty his or her phone access may face further restrictions through the facility disciplinary process.

Another area of concern is inmates who use the phone to threaten witnesses, threaten people on the outside that they have become displeased with, or to plan criminal acts, such as gang activity or the smuggling of weapons or drugs into the facility. Corrections officials have a duty to prevent these acts when based on credible information through thorough investigation.

For example, an inmate obtains the phone number of a witness who is subpoenaed to testify against him in open court. The witness makes a formal complaint to the jail, and an investigation is commenced. Investigators listen to recordings of the inmate's phone calls and corroborate the complaint. The inmate can be segregated and all personal phone calls are made through the CO at his or her post. This takes place only after a due process hearing; COs cannot arbitrarily "shut down" an inmate's phone use. The correctional agency has a duty to protect the public, including citizens who are cooperating with law enforcement. However, in an emergency, such as inmate who has just been booked in and is abusing the phone, restrictions can be placed on an emergency basis pending a hearing.

Fourth Amendment

Searches are the main security tool of any correctional institutions. While some inmates can attempt to intimidate inexperienced COs and state that they have a right of privacy, in reality they do not. The Fourth Amendment guards against unreasonable searches and seizures. On the street, police must have a search warrant based on probable cause or search a person based on reasonable suspicion. In a correctional facility, COs search cells and work areas, pat search (frisk), strip search and conduct body cavity searches without getting warrants (Collins, 2004, pp. 85, 94).

The key term for correctional officers concerning searches is *reasonable*. COs do have the power and authority to search. That does not mean that a CO should awake an entire cellblock at 3:00 AM every night for a week because he or she thinks that the inmates are hiding something. Nor does it mean that a strip search be conducted in an open area observable by other staff and inmates. Actions such as these can cause the inmates to claim harassment and embarrassment. If sued, the agency would have to justify the actions of the CO in searching inmates in this manner.

Cell Searches

A landmark case that referenced the rights of inmates and staff searches of their cells was *Bell v. Wolfish*, cited earlier in this chapter. Inmates filed suit at the Metropolitan Correctional Center (MCC), a federal detention center in New York City that held both convicted and pre trial detainees. The inmates complained about MCC's search policy, alleging that their quarters were needlessly left in disarray with items damaged or destroyed. They wanted to be present when their cells were searched so that there would be "reasonable" searches. MCC officials said that inmates being present during searches would result in security problems, such as moving contraband ahead of the search team, or arguing with staff which distracted COs. Both the district court and the Second Circuit Court of Appeals ruled the MCC room search policy unconstitutional, but the U.S. Supreme Court reversed their rulings, saying that both pre trial and convicted inmates have no right of privacy with respect to his or her room or cell (Cripe, 2003, p. 150).

Strip and Body Cavity Searches

Correctional officers should be familiar with conditions that would dictate performing a strip search or a body cavity search. While pat searches are the least invasive, violating the inmate's privacy and dignity, strip searches and body cavity searches are uncomfortable for the inmate. No one likes to strip in front of a CO in a correctional facility; having someone checking a body orifice is more uncomfortable.

The more intrusive the search, the greater the burden placed on the correctional facility to show the need for it especially concerning strip and body cavity searches. Per *Bell v. Wolfish,* considering that the inmate has some expectation of privacy [such as not being harassed or embarrassed], courts hearing litigation has considered these four interrelating factors (Collins, AJA, 2004, p. 223):

- The correctional facility's need for the particular type of search—weighed against
  - How intrusive the search is on the inmate
  - The manner in which the search is performed
  - The place in which the search is conducted

One could argue that the word "security" is justification enough for any type of search. The courts have differed on this opinion. Security is not a magic word that justifies any type of search of inmates at any time. Courts want correctional officials to show them the need for the search. An example is "blanket strip searches" of all arrestees entering a facility. While jails argued that these searches were necessary to keep out contraband, the courts held that there has to be reasonable suspicion that an offender is concealing a weapon or contraband to justify a strip search in booking (Collins, AJA, 2004, p. 224). For example, a 70-year-old woman arrested for passing a bad check and having no criminal or drug history would not be strip searched as opposed to a 25-year-old chronic substance abuser arrested for possession. The arresting officer thinks that there may be more drugs on him than was found during the arrest pat search. Thus the jail staff would be wise to strip search him.

Reasonable Suspicion

To justify a strip or body cavity search, correctional officers should document the reason, based on reasonable suspicion, and consult with their supervisors. This can apply to other incidents or concerns in the general population, not just in booking. If there is a contraband problem in the institution and homemade weapons and illegal substances are frequently found, supervisors can justify cellblock searches and strip searching inmates. If an inmate who is a known high profile gang leader and escape risk is being transferred to another facility or going to court, a strip search may be justified. In all cases, the reasons for the strip search must be clearly written.

What exactly is *reasonable suspicion*? To frame it simply, it falls between a "hunch" and probable cause. Reasonable suspicion has been defined in several court cases. In *U.S. v. Payne,* 181 F.3d 781, 786 (6th Circuit, 1999) it was defined as the authority (corrections agency) conducting the search to be able to point to "specific and articulable facts that, when taken together with rational inferences from those facts, reasonably warrant a belief that the arrestee is hiding contraband or a weapon." A more clear definition is in *Spear v. Sowders* 71 F.3d 626, 631 (7th Circuit, 1995) in which the court ruled that "... reasonable suspicion requires only specific objective facts upon which a prudent official, in light of his experience, would conclude that illicit activity might be in progress." Simply translated, facts, when combined with prudence and experience, result in a CO having reasonable suspicion (Collins, AJA, 2004, pp. 225–226).

This is critical for body cavity searches as well as strip searches. The reasons must be documented with the image of the CO possibly testifying in open court as to why he or she thought it was necessary to conduct a body cavity search; the incident report justifying in writing the reasons had better be well written and clear.

Common sense must prevail. Searches of inmates must be same gender— male COs searching male inmates; female COs searching female inmates. While pat searches of inmates by a member of the opposite sex may occur in emergencies for safety, care must be taken to conduct the search in private and in a dignified manner. Correctional officers in many academies and in-service classes are being taught the method of using the flat or edge of the hand. However, *every effort* must be made to have inmates pat searched by a CO of the same gender. In no instance should a strip search or body cavity search be conducted by medical personnel or a CO of the opposite gender.

Eighth Amendment: Cruel and Unusual Punishment

Many inmates think that they are being subjected to "cruel and unusual" punishment, especially if they have had a physical encounter with correctional staff. Others think that when they did not receive the medical treatment that they felt that they deserved, the medical staff subjected them to cruel and unusual punishment. Correctional staff including correctional officers are not machines—mistakes have been made—but the correctional system in the United States is arguably the best in the world concerning medical care, treatment of inmates, safety of inmates, conditions of confinement and the training of correctional officers.

Although short in text, the Eighth Amendment has had the most significant impact on corrections and inmate litigation. It says that "excessive bail shall not be required, nor excessive fines imposed, nor cruel and unusual punishment inflicted." The phrase "cruel and unusual punishment" has been used by inmates to challenge medical care, food, overcrowding, protection and safety, being placed in segregation and the use of force by COs. Litigation by inmates under this amendment can challenge numerous conditions and practices in a correctional facility or throughout a correctional system with several facilities (Collins, 2004, p. 105).

Basic Human Needs of Inmates

In *Wilson v. Seiter*, 111 S. Ct. 2321 (1991), the Supreme Court clarified conditions of confinement as they apply to the Eighth Amendment. The Court said that for conditions to be considered cruel and unusual punishment, they have to be very bad where inmates *are not* provided with one or more basic human needs. Secondly, the staff members (defendants) knew of serious problems and deficiencies and failed to take corrective actions or were deliberately indifferent (Collins, 2004, p. 109).

The CO Self Test

When looking at whether conditions meet the basic human needs test, correctional staff should objectively ask themselves—"would I, if incarcerated, wish to live in this facility?" The basic human needs, according to the Supreme Court in *Wilson v. Seiter* are listed below, and must be considered separately, except when they combine to deprive an inmate of a single identifiable human need such as food, warmth or exercise (Collins, 2004, pp. 110–111):

1. *Food*: that is nutritious, adequate, and is served in a sanitary manner.
2. *Clothing*: that is protective from the climate and provides privacy and is in good repair.
3. *Shelter*: concerns the overall environment—noise, heating, cooling, ventilation, maintenance, cell sizes, etc. Shelter cases concern mainly the physical plant.
4. *Sanitation*: deals with cleanliness, leaking plumbing, vermin, etc.
5. *Medical care*: lawsuits are popular, focusing on how medical services are delivered, both medical and dental care.
6. *Personal safety*: asks "are the inmates reasonably safe?" Do procedures such as classification, CO supervision, etc., promote safety or cause deficiencies? Cases challenging overcrowding generally cite personal safety, but the Court said in *Bell v. Wolfish* and *Rhodes v. Chapman*, 101 S.Ct. 2392 (1981) said that crowding of inmates (i.e., double celling) is permitted if inmates' basic human needs are met. Inmates must be protected from harm by other inmates. Staffs are liable if they know of a situation of possible harm to an inmate and do nothing. Also, does staff use excessive force to control inmates?
7. *Exercise*: can be an issue if the lack of it amounts to cruel and unusual punishment, such as not being provided for long periods of time. Inmates in lockdown such as in maximum security units without exercise could result in a lawsuit.

Three areas of concern when combating litigation under the Eighth Amendment are medical, excessive force and personal safety.

Medical

Correctional officers are on the front line when recognizing medical problems and referring inmates to the medical staff. If inmates do not receive basic, decent medical care, or if staff is deliberately indifferent to their medical needs, the facility is open to liability.

The landmark case concerning inmate medical care is *Estelle v. Gamble* 97 S. Ct. 285 (1976). In this case, a Texas prison inmate complained of inadequate treatment for a back injury. The Supreme Court stated that deliberate indifference to serious medical needs of inmates constituted the "unnecessary and wanton infliction of pain," and while not specifically defining deliberate indifference and serious medical needs, suggested three examples of behavior that clarified this standard (Mushlin, Volume 1, 2002, pp. 365–367).

First, medical staff (doctors, nurses, facility medical personnel) must show indifference to the medical needs of the inmate. This could include not receiving treatment, treatment is inadequate, and post operative or treatment instructions were not followed. This also could include not receiving prescribed medications. Second, correctional staff intentionally delays or prevents access to health care. Third, staff interferes with the medical treatment once prescribed to the inmate. Concerning pre trial detainees, correctional law researchers are of the opinion that there is no foundation for distinguishing the medical needs of pre trial detainees and convicted inmates—in reality—they are treated the same. There is little "wiggle room" for correctional officials as the deliberate indifference standard of *Estelle* is similar to the deliberate indifference standard as it applies to other violation areas of the Eighth Amendment (Mushlin, Volume 1, 2002, pp. 367–373).

The issue now becomes the CO and medical care. Since the CO has more contact with the inmate than any other staff member, how he or she deals with inmates having serious medical needs is important. The courts have devised five factors that indicate if the inmate has a serious medical need (Mushlin, Volume 1, 2002, pp. 376–377):

- The medical need is serious if it is a condition that has been diagnosed by a doctor and treatment is mandated.
- The medical need is serious if a lay (non medical) person easily recognizes the need for a doctor's [or medical staff's] attention.
- The medical need is serious if it causes pain.
- The medical need is serious if it significantly affects the individual's daily acts.

- The condition can be serious if there is a possibility of a life long handicap or permanent loss.

One case illustrates this. In *Noland v. Wheatley*, 835 F. Supp. 476 (N.D. Ind. 1993), a court found unconstitutional the conditions under which a semiquadriplegic inmate without a colon or bladder was confined. He was housed in a safety cell because his wheelchair would not fit in a regular cell doorway; the cell had no bed, no toilet and no running water; and the inmate had to empty body waste from his urostomy and colostomy bags into a floor drain. Due to no running water, he had to wait until "bath day" to wash his soiled hands (Collins and Hagar, 1995, p. 23).

The CO has to "trust the gut" and be safe rather than sorry. While many inmate ailments may be minor or if the inmate wants to gain some sympathy through manipulation, some conditions may be very serious. The presence of pain and the apparent need for medical treatment are critical factors. If the inmate is complaining of serious pain, COs must call for medical attention and document the notification. Let the medical staff determine the condition of the inmate.

This is true especially in booking, where an adequate medical system in which staff performs a detailed screening of inmates to determine if there is a condition that needs medical attention or the existence of a contagious disease (Mushlin, Volume 1, 2002, pp. 378–379). Closely related to this is suicidal behavior, which is part of a good screening process that combines three staff areas: booking, medical and mental health. Inmates in correctional facilities commit suicides and exhibit medical and mental health factors such as depression, mental illness and substance abuse that make them high risk for suicide. The courts have ruled that even though an inmate decides to take his or her own life, that choice is irrelevant—there is a clear duty by correctional staff to take action to protect inmates from self destruction and self harm (Mushlin, Volume 1, 2002, p. 442).

Inmates have a right to care that is necessary to treat serious disabilities, including physical handicaps. Some courts have ruled that there is a duty by staff to provide prosthetic devices, such as artificial limbs. In addition, if a correctional facility does not provide a wheelchair or handicapped accessible facilities, they will be found liable. The Americans with Disabilities Act (ADA) is a federal law that prohibits discrimination against people with disabilities, and in some appropriate cases to inmates. Since 1998, courts have expanded ADA to include inmates who have AIDS or are HIV positive, reasoning that inmates have the same interest in accessing programs, services and activities available to other inmates who are not handicapped (Mushlin, Volume 1, 2002, pp. 462–467). Disabled inmates must be treated the same as non disabled inmates whenever possible. For example, inmates with prosthetic limbs should have access to showers, programs and some form of recreation, just like other inmates.

Excessive Force

Emotions run high in correctional facilities. Some inmates complain that correctional officers hurt them intentionally by using too much or excessive force, thus violating the courts' position of inflicting unnecessary pain.

The basic rule for correctional officers and the use of force is that correctional officers can use force to protect themselves, other staff and inmates (including from themselves, such as in an overt suicidal act) from serious bodily harm or death. Force can also be used to enforce compliance with rules and regulations. The courts, in inmate rights cases, look at whether the force was reasonable, justified and/or excessive.

The amount of force being used may escalate to the point that the inmate's resistance is overcome, but beyond that it may be excessive. For example, an unruly inmate refuses to leave his cell for a disciplinary hearing. He backs up to a far wall screaming at officers to come in and get him. Attempts to talk him down are fruitless. Obviously, this cannot continue. Discipline and order in the institution must be restored. Officers go in and grab the inmate who punches and kicks. The officers defend themselves, striking the inmate. The inmate is placed on the floor and handcuffs are applied. As he is led to a segregation unit, he goes limp and the officers have to drag him. At the segregation unit, before the restraints are removed, several officers punch and kick the inmate severely, causing internal injuries.

Are those last punches excessive force? Yes. After reasonable attempts to calm the inmate fail, officers were justified in physically moving the inmate, defending themselves against his blows, restraining him and even dragging him. The inmate's resistance was overcome and the situation was resolved. The "extra blows" at the end were not justified and the officers may be liable.

Courts in recent years have supported legitimate security-related polices and procedures that are deemed necessary to control violent and disruptive inmates or inmates who are "out of control." The courts may use a *malicious and sadistic test* to see if restrictions placed on disruptive inmates are excessive. This test can also be used to determine if the force used on an inmate was excessive and unnecessary. Five factors are considered:

1. The need for the use of force: the situation, events leading to it, etc.
2. The amount of force used: too much?
3. Extent of any injuries sustained by the inmate.
4. The threat perceived by a reasonable correctional officer.

5. The efforts by officers to temper the use of force.
    (Collins and Hagar, 1995, p. 25)

Point five is critical. In a use of force situation, the ideal way to resolve it is to "talk the inmate down" or use persuasion or a show of force in order to *avoid* the usage of force, whenever possible. Sadly, sometimes force has to be used, whether it is non deadly force, where the force used does not cause serious bodily injury or death, or deadly force, where the force used will most likely cause serious bodily harm or death (Palmer and Palmer, 2004, p. 22).

The courts are also looking at several areas concerning the use of force. In one case, *Jenkins v. Wilson* 432 F. Supp. 2d 808 (W.D. Wis. 2006), an inmate was refusing to obey an order to be handcuffed after the CO found contraband in his cell. The inmate verbally abused the officer and took a fighting stance. The CO called for backup; one CO responded and a physical struggle ensued due to the inmate's continued resistance. The two COs struck the inmate several times, including the head. Several more officers arrived; the inmate was restrained and treated for a small cut. No other serious injuries were reported. The court considered the malicious and sadistic test, but did not grant the defendants' (COs) motion for summary judgment. The question that a court may ask in a case similar to this one is why didn't the COs lock the inmate in his cell? An emergency team could have responded and/or the inmate may have calmed down. Cooler heads may have prevailed, and when they do, it is more difficult for the inmate to allege excessive force. It is not being suggested that all incidents be handled like this, it is just an option for COs and supervisors to consider (Collins, AJA, 2004, Chapter 3 Update, pp. 16–17).

Another area concerns the usage of such means as pepper spray, restraints, stun devices, mace, etc. Loud disruptive inmates, the ones who yell, scream and pound the cell door can make working in a correctional facility difficult. They can incite other inmates and be a major annoyance. The courts feel that the use of force on them is permissible in certain cases, such as in restoring order. In *Williams v. Scott* 1997 WL 321173 (7th Circuit, 1997) the court approved the actions of a CO who, after giving the inmate a direct order to stop his disruptive behavior (kicking the door), fired a two second burst of mace to restore order and discipline (Collins, AJA, 2004, p. 56).

Some courts have found for the inmate and their families when dealing with improper use of restraints, or the agency has had to settle in court with the plaintiffs. While the reason for putting the inmate in a device such as a restraint chair may be valid, courts will look not only at the reason, but whether the restraints (from a restraint chair to "hog tying" or tying the hands behind the back and linking them to the ankles tied together) causes the inmate actual harm, whether the restraints were left on too long, whether the inmate was checked by a medical staff person, and what was done for the inmate (receiving food, water, going to the bathroom, etc). Examples of settlements include an Arizona case where an inmate died after being placed in a restraint chair, gagged and shot with a stun gun; or a Utah case settled for $200,000 in which blood clots were determined to have caused the death of an inmate confined to a restraint chair (Collins, AJA, 2004, pp. 56–57). Inmates have been hog tied and have died due to their breathing being restricted, or what is known as positional asphyxia. This practice is now generally frowned upon by correctional authorities.

The courts are not supportive of COs using excessive force to have a little fun with inmates. One of the best cases to illustrate this is *U.S. v. Walsh*, 194 F.3d 37 (Second Circuit 1999). In this case, a jail officer, weighing over 300 pounds, stepped on an inmate's penis—on three different occasions. The inmate, who had a history of mental problems, wanted a cigarette and the jail officer—a lieutenant—told him that in order to get one, he had to put his penis across the bars. The jail officer, who proclaimed himself "Big Jack" or "Hammer Jack" promptly stood on the penis, causing the inmate to scream in pain. The inmate got his cigarette. "Big Jack" was convicted and received two years in prison concurrent on each count and two years of supervised release (*Correctional Law Reporter*, 2000, pp. 89–90).

Personal Safety

Inmates are to be kept safe from other inmates. They are not to be harmed or assaulted by other inmates. COs know that fights in jails and prisons can result in serious injury or death. If the staff knew of a condition or set of circumstances in which an inmate could be hurt by another inmate and did nothing, the courts have held that this is a violation of the Eighth Amendment. COs must circulate, talk to the inmates and see what is going on.

In *Farmer v. Brennan* 114 S. Ct. 1970 (1994), the Supreme Court set the standard on inmate attacks and violations of the Eighth Amendment. An inmate who was a transsexual undergoing a sex change treatment (he was biologically a male) including silicone breast implants and unsuccessful testicle removal surgery was sentenced to 20 years in the federal system. He continued to receive hormonal treatments and dressed and acted feminine. He was placed in a male facility, where within two weeks of his arrival he was beaten and raped by another inmate. He filed suit, claiming that prison officials were deliberately indifferent and violated the Eighth Amendment by transferring him to a prison that had a history of inmate assaults and violence. The Supreme Court noted that while the Constitution does not mandate comfortable prisons; it does not permit "inhumane ones." The Court said that prisons are dangerous places and inmates are stripped of "virtually every means of self protection" and access to outside aid. That does not mean that the prison officials are not free to let the "state of nature [or inmate violence] take its course" (Mushlin, Volume 1, 2002, pp. 63–64).

Sexual predatory attacks and misconduct by staff is another concern. To address this problem, one of the most profound legislative acts in recent years has been the Prison Rape Elimination Act (PREA) of 2003. Inmates, no matter how neither negative their behavior or serious their crime should not be the targets and victims of sexual assault by staff or inmates; nor should they be the victims of staff sexual misconduct. In hearings before Congress in 2003, testimony by corrections professionals revealed that the total number of inmates that have been sexually assaulted in the past 20 years most likely exceeds one million. Inmates who are mentally ill are at an increased risk of being victims of sexual assault while incarcerated; juveniles are five times more likely than adults to be sexually assaulted while incarcerated (*Corrections Professional*, 2003, p. 8).

This legislation is designed to do the following (*Corrections Professional*, 2003, p. 8):

- Establish in all types of correctional facilities a zero tolerance policy for incidents of rape, sexual assault and other forms of sexual misconduct.
- Make the prevention of such acts a top priority.
- Implement strategies for the detection, prevention, reduction and punishment for prison rape and sexual misconduct; accomplished through training.
- Increase the information and data on sexual assault and misconduct.
- Increase the accountability of corrections officials who fail to detect, prevent, reduce and punish prison rape and sexual assault.

For the CO, an inmate being sexually assaulted is a ripe formula for a lawsuit. A sexual assault by another inmate can result in the contraction of a sexually transmitted disease, continued harassment from other inmates, physical trauma, depression and despair that could lead to suicidal behavior. An inmate victim of a sexual assault can sue, alleging that the correctional facility placed him in housing with predators and he attempted to inform the staff and nothing was done.

Statistically, sexual victimization in U.S. prisons is mostly inmate on inmate, but staff assaults are not that few. According to a survey by the Bureau of Justice Statistics, inmate on inmate attacks number 62.5 percent and staff on inmate attacks total 37.5 percent. In approximately half of the staff sexual contacts, inmates indicated that they were willing participants (*Corrections Professional*, January 2008, pp. 1, 5). Consent does not matter; sexual misconduct and violence are just what the terms imply.

All correctional officers should be familiar with the wide ranging definitions of sexual violence as stated in the Bureau of Justice Statistics (BJS) report *Sexual Violence Reported by Correctional Authorities, 2006*, published in August, 2007. This annual report gives data on the problem of sexual violence in our nation's correctional facilities. In 2004, BJS developed uniform definitions of sexual violence and sexual misconduct. They are detailed and leave no room for doubt. All incidents of sexual inmate on inmate sexual violence involve sexual contact with any person without his or her consent, or with a person who is unable to give consent or refuse. Staff sexual misconduct includes any behavior or acts of a sexual nature directed by an employee, volunteer, official visitor or agency representative (all considered staff) whether consensual or non consensual. The definitions are (Beck, Harrison and Adams, 2006, p. 9):

Non consensual sex acts: Inmate on Inmate
- Contact between the penis and the vagina or the penis and anus; this includes penetration.
- Contact between the mouth and the vagina, anus or penis.
- Penetration of the genital or anal opening of another person by a hand, finger or other object.

Abusive sexual contacts: Inmate on Inmate
- Intentional touching of the genitalia, anus, groin, breast, inner thigh, or buttocks of any person; this includes directly or through the clothing.
- Incidents in which the intention is to sexually exploit—rather than to only debilitate or harm.

Staff Sexual Misconduct: Staff with Inmates
- Intentional touching of the following: anus, breast, buttocks, genitalia, groin, or inner thigh with the intent to abuse, arouse or gratify sexual desire.
- Completed, attempted threatened or requested sexual acts.
- Occurrences and incidents of indecent exposure, invasion of privacy, or staff voyeurism for sexual gratification.

Staff sexual harassment: staff with inmates
- Repeated verbal statements, comments, demeaning references, derogatory comments about body and clothing, obscene, profane language and gestures by staff to an inmate.

The liability factor is this: the correctional officer is the first line in preventing inmates from being victimized in any way—by other inmates or staff. It is unfortunate enough that some COs are charged with carnal knowledge of inmates—but the agency can be sued by inmates and their families alleging that agency personnel engaged in cruel and unusual punishment of a sexual violence or misconduct nature. No correctional agency wants media reports circulating throughout the community alleging that correctional officers in their facilities were engaging in rape, sexual assaults and intimate affairs with inmates.

Fourteenth Amendment

The *Fourteenth Amendment* is quite lengthy. For the study of inmate rights, a part of it reads: "... nor shall any State deprive any person of life, liberty, or property, without due process of law; nor deny to any person within its jurisdiction the equal protection of the laws" (Collins, 2004, p. 155). This clause has come to mean having due process or procedures in administrative proceedings including disciplinary hearings where the inmate may be subjected to a loss, such as being placed in disciplinary segregation, losing good time, being removed from programs and recreation, losing privileges such as commissary or having restrictions placed on visiting.

Closely related to this amendment is the *Fifth Amendment,* which reads that "No person shall be ... deprived of life, liberty, or property without due process of law." In layman's terms, a correctional agency cannot take away anything of importance to an inmate without some type of due process. Not every claim by an inmate that he or she was denied due process is valid—a significant deprivation or an adverse impact has to be shown. For example, an inmate cannot complain that the hours that the cellblock telephones are on is a due process violation, but if he or she is denied the use of the phone at all without a hearing—that could be a due process violation (Cripe, 2003, p. 164).

The Two Key Questions

When one puts the two amendments together, two key questions arise. The first is if there has occurred any deprivation of life, liberty or property. In a correctional facility, inmates are all ready deprived of liberty and property—they are not free citizens. If it is decided that an inmate has suffered a significant deprivation, the second question arises—what processes or procedures is due to the inmate who has been thus affected? The courts have termed this matter as "fundamental fairness." Fairness also means that the government (correctional agency) has the legal authority to act and that steps are taken to determine (procedures) that the facts are true and are as the agency says that they are (Cripe, 2003, p. 164). This is common sense to the CO. If anything of importance is to be taken away or modified and this impacts the inmate in a big way, then there must be fair due process hearing based on accurate documentation of facts and observations—not something that is falsified or vague. COs must also recognize the importance of accurate reports.

In the case of *Sandin v. Connor* 115 S. Ct. 2293 (1995) the Supreme Court revised the ways that courts have looked at due process issues such as the placing of inmates in administrative segregation. Instead of looking at the precise language of the regulations governing these decisions, courts now look at the seriousness of the loss of the inmate, such as being segregated, etc. If the rules were strict, it would increase the liability exposure of the agency, hampering its flexibility. Inmates could challenge decisions based on what was written or not written in the language of the rules. The *Sandin* case said that a liberty interest—something of value to the inmate, such as being in general population—will be created only if a deprivation is showed that is atypical and significant in relation to the normal incidents of prison life. This may appear unclear as to what an "atypical" deprivation is (Collins, 2004, pp. 158–160). An example may be an inmate spending a long period of time in disciplinary segregation for a minor rule violation even though a placement of inmates in disciplinary segregation is normal for a corrections facility.

Hearings

Reports form the basis of administrative hearings—the first being a formal classification committee hearing (ICC) to place an inmate on administrative segregation, remove or restrict a privilege, or place constrictions on the inmate such as two CO escort, being placed in hand and leg restraints when out of the cell, etc. This type of hearing is non disciplinary—the inmate has not broken a rule, but some action must be taken.

The other type of administrative hearing is a disciplinary hearing charging that an inmate has broken the rules of the facility; the inmate is facing sanctions such as disciplinary segregation, removal of a privilege or a reprimand—either verbal or written.

Disciplinary Hearings

A good rule for officers to follow is that inmates are due a hearing (or a form of a "trial") if they are accused of a disciplinary charge. The landmark case of *Wolff v. McDonnell*, 418 U.S. 539 (1974), put forth the procedural requirements that are required in inmate disciplinary cases. They are (Collins, 2004, pp. 160–163):

1. *A hearing*: the inmate has the right to be present, but he/she can waive this by words or behavior. The hearing personnel must be impartial. Hearings can be conducted by a panel of supervisors or a hearing officer. Many facilities have a designated hearing officer.
2. *Advanced written notice of the charges*: staff must give this to the inmate at least twenty-four hours prior to the hearing so that the inmate can prepare a defense.
3. *An opportunity to call witnesses and present evidence in a defense*: there is an exception, where the witnesses could be hazardous to safety—such as if a witness is an enemy, informant, etc. The facility must justify the denial if the accused inmate litigates. There is no right to cross-examine or confront witnesses. The hearing board or officer controls witness proceedings.
4. *Assistance*: legal references say sometimes. Inmates have no right to an attorney in disciplinary cases even if criminal charges are being considered. Some institutions allow them only to observe that due process is being followed. Usually inmates may have the assistance of another inmate or staff member, at the discretion of the facility. If an inmate is illiterate or it is apparent that he/she has difficulty understanding the proceedings, the role of an assistant is critical.
5. *Written decision*: a written decision must be given to the inmate as to the decision and the evidence used for the reasoning of the decision. This serves two purposes—the inmate can better understand what has transpired and the entire proceedings are better understood when reviewed by a higher authority, such as the facility command staff—or even in court. This document should be detailed, not just stating something like "guilty based on officer's report" or "guilty due to evidence."

Inmates can be placed in administrative segregation pending disciplinary actions without a hearing for the safety and security of the facility. For example, if an inmate refuses to obey an officer's order or commits a serious rule violation, he/she can be placed in segregation pending further action, such as a disciplinary hearing. Such moves are often immediate and necessary. Some inmates cannot, for the security and smooth operation of the institution, remain in population.

Classification Hearings

Another procedural due process hearing is the classification hearing. These hearings are held when inmates need placement in administrative segregation

(A/S). The inmate may not have broken a rule, but he/she may be unsuitable for living with other inmates due to mental instability, poor hygiene, argumentative personality, his or her charge, having a need for protective custody, etc. The inmate may also be disruptive in a program or recreation and his or her participation in those areas need review. In these cases, as in consideration of administrative segregation, some sort of due process is required. Even if an inmate requests protective custody, a hearing should be conducted to give the inmate the fairest consideration in examining all of the facts of the case.

The hearing should be less formal than a disciplinary hearing. Generally, the Institutional Classification Committee (ICC) holds the hearing. It is basically a review of the facts recommending administrative segregation or other actions. Its nature is non-adversarial, including an informal evidentiary review; the inmate must receive prior notice and be offered an opportunity to respond in a written or oral statement. Some courts have ruled that the inmate can present witnesses and documentary evidence; appeal the decision to a higher authority and mandate a required periodic institutional review of the classification decision. Also, the inmate should be advised as to what affirmative, positive actions he or she can do justify reclassification or another review of the case (Mushlin, 2002, Volume 2, p. 319).

Post Hearing Actions

Although not required by the Constitution, it is best to have a practice of *administrative review*, a practice whereby the classification proceedings and related evidence (and *only* these) are reviewed by a higher authority over the hearing panel/officer. Courts have suggested that inmates be able to appeal hearing decisions. The Fourteenth Amendment concerns equal protection, so if the facility regulations provides for an appeal procedure, all inmates *must* be notified of their right to appeal. All notifications of the right to appeal and answers must be in writing (Palmer and Palmer, 2004, p. 175). However, the inmate should appeal in writing within a certain time frame and state the reasons for his/her appeal. The written answer to the appeal is then delivered to the inmate.

Protectors from Inmate Lawsuits

Correctional officers *can* protect themselves from inmate lawsuits. They must not panic; they should keep in mind that anyone (inmates) can sue—but winning is another matter. Correctional officers should also be cognizant of the fact that their actions and decisions can directly impact the rights of inmates in their custody. They must be careful. That does not mean that COs must be fearful of the inmate litigator. What it means is that the CO must be confident that they are doing the right thing and performing their duties in good faith—within the framework of court decisions, agency policies, procedures and common sense.

Correctional officers should not feel that they must be lawyers, and know the latest court decisions and judicial philosophies concerning inmates. No CO can know everything at a glance. What COs must do is realize the importance of inmate rights, the seriousness of liability and strive to keep up with the most up to date information on the subject (Hemmens in Duncan, 2008, p. 21): COs should view legal updates taught by agency attorneys or guest speakers from the legal field not as boring training that they must sit through, but as important. They should try to connect the court decisions to their duties in the facility. For example, when the Supreme Court ruled that inmates must not be prohibited (within reason) from practicing religions that may not seem "mainstream," COs should see the connection—if an inmate wants to see the chaplain about obtaining Buddhist materials, the CO is handed the responsibility of seeing that the inmate's religious inquiry is not ignored or restricted.

Levels of Liability

The state of Michigan looked at the problem of law enforcement liability—especially corrections—and paid out claims. The Michigan Municipal Risk Management Authority (MMRMA) is a self insurance provider to police and local corrections agencies. Examining claims in the 1990s, it was discovered that almost two thirds of all claims and losses on behalf of MMRMA jurisdictions originated from local sheriff department operations—many of who run the local jails. It was costly—over a 15 year period, MMRMA paid out $35 million to defend personnel in these agencies (Ross and Page, 2003, p. 10).

According to this research and writings by Darrell L. Ross, Ph.D. and Bill Page, the potential of inmates to sue correctional staff is likely on two levels—the line staff and the supervisors and managers of the line staff. A common strategy is for the inmate to file a suit against the individual CO and also name his or her supervisors and agency administrators, alleging that they failed in their duty to properly train, supervise, direct and discipline the correctional officers in the proper performance of their duties and responsibilities. The inmate litigator feels that they could have done something to correct the situation or prevent the errant CO from making a bad decision. That is why numerous personnel are named in inmate suits (Ross and Page, 2003, p. 10).

Level One: Line Correctional Officers

Correctional officers make decisions every day in our nation's correctional facilities. These decisions merge with the limited rights afforded to inmates by the courts. These decisions are (Ross and Page, 2003, p. 10):

- Making decisions to search or seize inmate property
- Making decisions to use force on an inmate, including the level of force
- Making decisions that affect inmate safety, such as protective custody, enforcing discipline, etc.
- Providing for adequate security for the inmate population
- Providing for proper medical care.

Level Two: Supervisors and Administrators

The two critical areas concerning the liability of correctional supervisors are training and directing (supervising). A correctional supervisor might claim that the policies and procedures are good and protect staff from liability, but realistically—how well are COs trained and supervised? Are they given general orders in roll call and told to read them? Or—are they discussed at length with a realistic question and answer session to ensure that they are understood? For example, an area of liability for correctional officers is suicide prevention. Inmates must be protected from self harm. The warden and senior supervisory staff distribute a new, revised suicide prevention plan. Is training conducted in it? Do the COs *understand it?*

Supervisors have liability in several areas, namely hiring, retention, discipline and training. According to Melanie C. Pereira, director for the Howard County Department of Corrections in Jessup, Maryland, the test for supervisor liability under Section 1983 is whether (Pereira, 2007, p. 6–17):

- Control or direction is exercised by a supervisor: Is the supervisor giving orders or direction that violates constitutional rights? For example, an inmate is complaining of an excruciating migraine headache at 3 AM; the CO calls her supervisor for permission to take the inmate to the dispensary. The supervisor admonishes her saying his standing policy is for inmates to wait for sick call at 6 AM. The inmate is not seen and later suffers a stroke.
- Some form of personal participation by the supervisor: Did he or she set a policy, practice or custom that resulted in a violation? For example, a prison warden states that his officers will take no "crap" from inmates who do not obey the rules. Several inmates are roughed up being restrained and a subsequent lawsuit is lost by the agency; the COs used ex-

cessive force, believing that the tone of the directive was "hands on first, we'll talk later." There is a failure to supervise the CO: This could be if a supervisor does nothing while a CO improperly beats an inmate, a CO is a "loose cannon on the deck" and mistreats inmates and nothing is done, or other staff informs the supervisor of the misconduct of a CO and no disciplinary action is taken. The CO retains his position.

While these areas involve supervision and lack of action, training liability must be discussed. A big loophole for inmate litigators or their attorneys is the discovery that the agency supervisors conducted little or no training in critical areas pertaining to the confinement of the inmates. For supervisors to protect staff from both the "jailhouse lawyer" and inmate lawsuits, proper training and supervision must be conducted and exercised in the following areas (Ross and Page, 2003, p. 11):

Inmate Property:
- Officers losing, delaying access to or destroying inmate property and inmate clothing, especially legal and religious works/items
- Denial of inmate property during incarceration, especially in segregation

Medical:
- Inadequate medical diagnosis, treatment, monitoring, follow up or care
- Failure to provide medical care and medication, including the dispensing of improper medication
- Prompt alerting/summoning of medical and mental health staff
- Failure to recognize signs of distress, including depression, suicidal behavior, etc.
- Failure to adhere to sick call policy, ADA, etc. and to keep inmates under close observation

Use of Force:
- Tactics, restraints, self defense, proper use of force escalation in response to non compliance by inmates
- Cell extractions, multiple officer response
- Emergency plans: hostage, escape, riot, disturbance
- Medical response to use of force, emergency incidents and any event where an inmate is injured

Searches and supervision:
- Cross gender supervision
- Sexual harassment, general harassment ("revenge") and misconduct
- Unethical conduct/failure to follow security procedures

- Listening to inmate safety/hygiene/incompatibility issues
- Failure to be proactive
- Ignorance of rights in segregation/medical care/religion/privacy

Documentation:
- Booking and classification paperwork
- Pass-on
- Post and Observation Logs
- Request forms
- Report writing
- Investigations
- Grievances

PROTECTORS AGAINST INMATE LAWSUITS

1. *RECOGNITION:* Staff should be aware of conditions and or situations that could lead to an inmate lawsuit. Anticipate areas of liability. Be proactive. Take an interest in inmate welfare and put attitudes aside.
2. *EDUCATION AND TRAINING:* Ongoing education and training in constitutional issues and inmate rights is a must. Classes should be mandatory at the entry and in-service levels.
3. *SELECTION AND HIRING:* Staff who may be problem employees and may treat inmates unfairly should not be hired or retained. Use performance evaluations to bolster good behavior or to correct bad behavior.
4. *CORRECT POLICIES AND PROCEDURES:* Keep them up to date and in compliance with case law, state law, federal law, and standards of accreditation from the state or professional organizations such as the American Correctional Association if applicable.
5. *SUPERVISION:* Supervisors must know what is going on inside the facility and take corrective actions. Courts do not want to hear "I didn't know," especially from supervisors.
6. *DISCIPLINE:* Problem staff must be dealt with. Supervisors must take action against staff that are negligent and violate inmates' rights.
7. *COMMUNICATIONS:* The more communication that exists between inmates and staff, the easier problems can be solved. If you are not sure about a question of liability, ask your supervisor. Support a grievance procedure and encourage inmates to use it.
8. *DOCUMENT: Write it down*—clearly and legibly, whether it is a log, memo, report, etc. It could prove valuable in court. Keep a notebook.

Summary

Correctional staff must accept the fact that inmates do not lose all civil rights and constitutional protections when incarcerated. While most officers tend to say that inmates have more rights than staff, the state and federal courts see differently. Inmates are allowed to file litigation in habeas corpus actions, torts and civil rights actions under 42 USC Section 1983. Historically, inmates had been viewed as little better than slaves. After periods of non-involvement and detailed involvement (hands on and hands off eras), corrections is now in a period where the courts will intervene in a restrained way, balancing inmate rights versus security. Inmates seek money damages and liability from staff, and these each take several forms. The courts frown upon frivolous inmate lawsuits or legal actions without merit, and states are taking steps to combat them.

The law library is a crucial tool of inmates filing litigation, especially with the help of a jailhouse lawyer. Inmates have basic rights under the First, Fourth, Eighth and Fourteenth Amendments, with the biggest issues being religion, visiting, mail, searches, medical care, excessive force, personal safety, sexual assault and due process. Many legislative acts have impacted corrections, namely the Prison Litigation Reform Act, the Religious Land Use and Institutionalized Persons Act, the Americans with Disabilities Act, the Civil Rights of Institutionalized Persons Act, and the Prison Rape Elimination Act.

Line staff and supervisors are both the targets of inmate litigators, even though there are many protective tools that can be used to prevent inmate lawsuits or successfully defend against them.

Review Questions

1. Explain the three eras in the history of inmates' rights.
2. Describe conditions in jails and prisons before intervention from the courts.
3. Why are law libraries important?
4. Describe the four parts of the balancing test.
5. Concerning Section 1983 suits, what are the reasons that inmates file the most suits?
6. Why is sexual assault considered cruel and unusual punishment?
7. What is the malicious and sadistic test?
8. Discuss the rights of inmates pertaining to mail, visiting, religion, medical care and searches.
9. Discuss how staff can protect themselves from liability.

Terms/Concepts

administrative review
balancing test
Civil Rights Act
  (42 United States Code 1983)
civil rights actions
compensatory damages
deliberate indifference
grievance
gross negligence
habeas corpus actions
hands off era

hands on era
injunction
jailhouse lawyer
malicious and sadistic test
negligence
nominal damages
punitive damages
reasonable suspicion
restrained hands approach
torts
vicarious liability

References

Alexandria (VA) Office of the Sheriff. (2004). *Inmate Handbook.*

American Correctional Association. (1998). *Dictionary of Criminal Justice Terms.* Lanham: American Correctional Association.

Beck, Allen J., Ph.D., Paige M. Harrison and Devon B. Adams. (August 2007). *Sexual Violence Reported by Correctional Authorities, 2006.* U.S. Department of Justice: Bureau of Justice Statistics. Washington, DC: U.S. Government Printing Office, [available on line at www.ojp.usdoj.gov/bjs/].

Bonventre, Peter and William D. Marbach. (1979, January 15). Hell in Texas. *Newsweek,* 74.

Champion, Dean J. (2005). *Corrections in the United States: A Contemporary Perspective, 4th Edition.* Upper Saddle River: Pearson Prentice Hall.

Collins, William C., J.D. (2004). *Correctional Law for the Correctional Officer: 4th Edition.* Lanham: American Correctional Association.

Collins, William, Esq. (2004) *Jail and Prison Issues: An Administrator's Guide.* Hagerstown: American Jail Association.

Collins, William C. and John Hagar. (1995, May–June). Jails and the Courts: Issues For Today, Issues for Tomorrow. *American Jails,* 18–26.

Cornelius, Gary F. (2008). *The American Jail: Cornerstone of Modern Corrections.* Upper Saddle River: Pearson Prentice Hall.

Congress passes bill to deter prison rape, mandate reforms. (August 22, 2003). *Corrections Professional, Volume 9, Issue 1,* 1, 8.

Cripe, Clair A., A.B., J.D. (2003). *Legal Aspects of Correctional Management.* Sudbury: Jones and Bartlett.

Duncan, Peria. (2008). *Correctional Officer Resource Guide: Fourth Edition.* Alexandria: American Correctional Association.

4.5 percent of U.S. inmates report sexual victimization in prison. (January, 2008). *Corrections Professional, Volume 13, Issue 8,* 1, 5.

Hemmens, Craig, J.D., Ph.D. (1997). Corrections and the Law. In Don Bales (Ed.) *Correctional Officer Resource Guide, 3rd Edition* (pp. 15–21). Lanham: American Correctional Association.

Hemmens, Craig, J.D., Ph.D. (2008). Corrections and the Law. In Peria Duncan (Ed.) *Correctional Officer Resource Guide 4th Edition* (pp. 21–27). Alexandria: American Correctional Association.

Mushlin, Michael B. (2002). *Rights of Prisoners: Third Edition (Volumes 1–2).* Thomson West.

Palmer, John W., J.D., and Stephen E. Palmer, J.D. (2004). *Constitutional Rights of Prisoners: 7th Edition.* Cincinnati: Anderson.

Pereira, Melanie C. (2007). Vicarious Liability in 42 USC Section 1983 Cases. In *A View from the Trenches: A Manual for Wardens by Wardens* (pp. 6–17 to 6–19). Alexandria: American Correctional Association.

Ross, Darrell L., Ph.D. and Bill Page. (2003, January–February). Jail Liability: Reducing the Risk by Studying the Numbers. *American Jails,* 9–15.

Schmalleger, Frank, Ph.D., and John Ortiz Smykla, Ph.D. (2009). *Corrections in the 21st Century Fourth Edition.* New York: McGraw Hill.

Stepping on Inmate's Privates Violates Eighth Amendment. (April–May, 2000). *Correctional Law Reporter, Volume XI, No. 6,* 89–90.

Stinchcomb, Jeanne B., Ph.D. and Vernon B. Fox, Ph.D. (1999). *Introduction to Corrections, Fifth Edition.* Upper Saddle River: Prentice Hall.

Glossary

administrative review: classification proceedings and related evidence (and *only* these) are reviewed by a higher authority over the hearing panel/officer.

administrative segregation (A/S): housing where the inmate is housed separately from inmates in general population for other than disciplinary reasons; as much as is possible, the inmate receives the same privileges as inmates in general population.

AKAs: aliases or other names the inmate uses.

average daily population (ADP): measurement of daily average facility population by the adding the sum of the number of inmates confined in a correctional facility for one year and dividing it by the total number of days in that year.

bad asses: persons who overtly take on symptoms of deviance that other inmates regard as good.

balancing test: court looking at an inmate complaint will apply four common sense questions to decide if the restrictions that the inmate is complaining about meet a legitimate penological interest of the correctional facility.

basic training: training conducted in a training academy that is measured in a set number of hours, that newly hired correctional officers must successfully complete within their first year of employment, subjects covered include the agency mission, rules and regulations, and the skills that must be developed for job performance.

benefit of clergy: practice that protected any wrongdoer who could read at all from the death penalty; they then received a lesser penalty such as branding.

blood feud: acts of revenge and retaliation where the victims' people, families or tribes seeking revenge on the offenders' people, families or tribes.

body cavity search: examines inside body openings such as the anus, vagina, etc. *must* be performed either manually or by instrument by trained medical personnel.

body or "strip" search: examines the skin surface of the inmate, including hiding places in hair, behind the ears, under breasts (females), armpits, genitals (male), behind the knees, on the soles and between toes, and between the buttocks; dentures and prostheses are removed and inspected.

boot camp: a short term institutional type of confinement, modeled after military training, that includes strict discipline and regulations, and is designed to promote self discipline, respect for authority, responsibility, and a sense of achievement and accomplishment.

Bridewell: in 1757, a workhouse named after London's Bridewell Palace; dealt with wrongdoers by using them as cheap labor.

capital punishment: punishing an offender by taking his or her life.

census count: verification of inmate presence at a program, work detail or activity (i.e., recreation).

civil commitment: the action of a judicial officer, court or administrative body ordering a person to be confined in an institution or facility for custody, treatment, protection or deportation, including those administered by a mental health service.

civil death: early practice where the wrongdoer had many aspects of his life stripped away: his property was confiscated in the name of the state, his wife was declared a widow and could remarry, and had all status as a citizen and liberties taken away until death.

Civil Rights Act (42 United States Code 1983): commonly referred to as "Section 1983," it states that government officials, such as correctional officers, can be held for monetary damages if found liable in withholding an inmate's civil rights under the Constitution.

civil rights actions: litigation alleging that their civil rights under the Constitution were violated by correctional staff, which is liable to pay monetary damages; civil rights actions are based on a key piece of federal legislation, the Civil Rights Act or Title 42 United States Code Section 1983.

classification: an ongoing process and an inmate management tool, based on staff analysis and diagnosis of inmate information, resulting in informed inmate housing and custody level decisions.

classification file: the file generated by the classification section that serves as the central repository for information obtained from and about an inmate.

cold turkey: slang term for inmates withdrawing from a drug without maintenance doses of the drug.

collective violence: violence occurring between groups of inmates, including riots and disturbances, assaults on staff by groups of inmates, gang fights; the differences are issues of values and positions of the two groups.

community corrections facilities: corrections facilities, generally minimum security, that house low risk offenders who are participants in rehabilitative programs using community resources.

compensatory damages: damages compensate the inmate for medical expenses, lost wages, plus pain, suffering and mental anguish if the court deems necessary.

confidential informant: an inmate who gives information to a correctional officer on the condition that his/her identity will remain anonymous.

contact visits: visits where the personal visitor and inmate are allowed to visit without any type of physical barrier.

contraband: any item (illegal drugs, weapons, etc.) that is not authorized by the facility administration; can also be any authorized item in excess such as extra blankets, hoarded food, etc.

control: inmates are safely confined, through policies and procedure enforcement certain acts are prevented: escapes, criminal acts inside the facility, conspiracy to commit criminal acts outside the community, rule violations, assaults on staff and other inmates, gang activity, and contraband smuggling.

convicts: those adjudicated and sentenced to terms of incarceration.

corporal punishment: infliction of pain on the body by any device or method.

correct assertiveness: the officer getting his/her point across without causing arguments, tension or stress, incorporating common sense communication as well as calmness, seeing the other's point of view, looking at the whole situation with respect and consideration for other people's thoughts and feelings.

correctional ideology: a body of ideas and practices that pertain to the processing of offenders as determined by the law, either by punishing offenders, treating their problems or preventing future criminal behavior.

correctional officer (CO): a trained law enforcement officer in a correctional facility whose function is to supervise and manage inmates, enforce the laws of the jurisdiction, enforce the rules of the facility, maintain the inmates in a safe and secure environment and prevent escapes.

correctional staff: all of the workers in a correctional facility including the correctional officers, medical officers, counselors, programs staff and service workers.

corrections: a set of agencies, both public and private that attempt to control the behavior of persons either accused of or convicted of a criminal offense.

criminal street gang: an organization, association or group of three or more persons, whether formal or informal which has a continuity of purpose, seeks a group identity and its members engage [or have engaged] in criminal activities either individually or collectively.

cultural empathy: a mind set of COs putting themselves in other people's [foreign/ethnic inmate] "cultural shoes."

dayroom: central area where the inmates can congregate; contains a television, a table or tables for eating, seats, toilet and shower facilities.

deliberate indifference: occurs when correctional staffs [supervisors and line staff] know or should have known, because of obvious conditions, that what they are doing or not doing is a risk to the health, safety and well being of the inmate, but they take no action.

delinquent: category of juvenile offender involving criminal acts; has three components: minors who have committed acts which would be considered crimes if they were adults; status offenders who have violated juvenile regulations such as a curfew, attending school, etc.; and incorrigible or unruly juveniles who their parents, guardians or the juvenile court have deemed unmanageable.

delusions: symptom of mental illness, the mentally ill person believes that other people are controlling their brains, their thoughts, can read their minds or are spying on them.

detainers: charges that are on file from other jurisdictions, holding the offender pending transfer to that jurisdiction.

determinate sentence: sentence that fixes a flat maximum term (i.e., ten years) that the inmate must serve minus any time off for good behavior.

deterrence: to "send a message" to others that if they commit crimes, they too will suffer the fate of wrongdoers who are incarcerated or under some type of correctional supervision.

developmentally disabled offender: formerly known as "mentally retarded; these inmates are characterized by low intellectual ability (IQ) and show an inability in social or life skills.

direct supervision: inmate housing where the correctional officer is stationed inside the inmate living area; there are no physical boundaries between him or her and the inmates.

disciplinary segregation (D/S): an inmate being segregated, with loss of privileges such as commissary, personal visiting, programs, television, and possibly accrued good time, as a result of rule breaking.

dispensary: a form of "mini hospital" in the facility where inmates needing medical attention are housed under the supervision of the medical staff.

disturbance: an action by inmates not as large in scope or seriousness as a riot. Fewer inmates are involved, the duration is shorter in time, and there is no control or minimum control of a part of the institution.

doing time: inmate's concern for doing his/her own time, getting out with minimum pain in the shortest time.

dually diagnosed: offenders suffering from mental illness in combination with substance abuse.

Educational Doctrine: doctrine that believes if inmates are given opportunities for education in several areas, such as learning a trade, an occupation, reading/writing skills, and discipline, internal controls would result and lead to non criminal behavior.

emergency count: count taken because of an emergency such as a fire, riot, disturbance, power outage, escape, etc.

emergency keys: keys that allow the staff rapid access to every part of the facility in case of riot, fire, power outage or other emergencies.

Emergency Response Teams (ERT): a team of COs specially trained to respond to serious incidents, such as fights, riots, disturbances, forced cell moves, hostage situations, shakedowns, etc.; team members are also trained in squad tactics, crowd control, use of force, non-lethal weapons, special weapons and emergency response strategies.

empathy: a shared understanding or an experience of feelings, thoughts or attitudes.

escape: an inmate's criminal absence from the confines of the institution or extended confinement area with the intent to remain at large.

escape intelligence: a comprehensive package of information that lets law enforcement agencies know as much information as possible about the escape, safety concerns and who should be contacted in case of apprehension.

ethics: study of what constitutes good or bad conduct or standards of conduct that govern behavior.

ethnocentrism: a belief that one's own culture is "inherently superior."

fantasy: inmate having fantasies, daydreaming, etc., is conducted in private to shut out the drabness and despair of imprisonment.

farmed out: informal jail term meaning that an inmate has been transferred from one jail to another for overcrowding or security reasons; practice of transferring inmates to other facilities for management reasons including the reduction of overcrowding.

fee system: in early jails, fees were charged for every item (such as a bed, mattress) and process (being housed in squalid quarters or a private room).

field training officer (FTO): a veteran staff member who serves as the training supervisor of the new CO, requiring him or her to perform job tasks, such as searches, headcounts, writing reports, etc.

file review: the ICC review of the case of an inmate's special housing status to determine if the inmate can be removed from administrative segregation or see how he or she is behaving on D/S.

fish testing: testing of limits of a CO by inmates individually or as a group.

folkways: society rules such as customs and acceptable ways of doing things that controlled both prescribed and proscribed behavior.

formal count: a regular count required by staff at certain times such as at shift change, before lockdowns and at meal times.

free will: concept whose basic premises are that a person chooses good or bad actions and as a result of these choices, he/she must be held accountable for the consequences of them.

frisk (patdown): the most general type of search by inspection of the inmate's clothing and body through the clothing; running hands over clothing to ascertain if anything is hidden in cuffs, under arms, etc.

gang intelligence units: specialized units that investigate suspected gang members who are incarcerated, investigate crimes committed by gang members in the facility, assist in disciplining gang members, provide staff training, and work with local and federal anti gang law enforcement agencies.

gang member: an individual who participates in a criminal street gang and has knowledge of members engaging in criminal gang activities.

general deterrence: concept of overall punishing criminals and showing the general public that crime does not pay and the consequences are harsh.

general population: housing where inmates live together and are afforded all privileges, such as commissary or canteen, television, programs and recreation; inmates are considered to have the social skills necessary and the behavior to live with other inmates.

geriatric correctional facilities: separate correctional facilities or units that are specifically designed to supervise and provide services for inmates aged 55 and older.

gleaning: inmate taking advantage of any available resource, programs, counseling, etc., to better themselves and prepare for life after prison.

good time: time earned by an inmate through participation in rehabilitative, vocational and educational programs and activities, granted at the discretion of the correctional facility administrator.

goon squad: a group of physically powerful correctional officers who 'enjoy a good fight' and are used to restore the status quo by muscle power.

grievance: a complaint, filed through channels to the appropriate institution staff in whose area of responsibility the complaint is concerned.

gross negligence: willful, wanton and reckless actions which are both unreasonable and have no regard for the consequences.

habeas corpus actions: court actions in which inmates claim that they are being held illegally and attack a correctional facility, court, etc. responsible for keeping the inmate in custody.

habitual offenders: criminals who continue to engage in repeated criminal behavior despite repeated arrests, convictions and sentences.

hallucinations: symptom of mental illness where offender believes that he or she is seeing things and/or hearing voices that other people state that they do not hear or see.

hands off era: period where the courts did not get involved with inmate litigation; the reasoning by jurists was that they knew nothing about correctional administration.

hands on era: period where the courts began to respond to corrections conditions cases, disciplinary due process issues, religious freedoms and many issues under the Bill of Rights.

hard employees: employees who go by the book and pay strict attention to policies and procedures.

home detention/electronic monitoring: court ordered or screened inmates with approval by the sentencing judge may reside in their homes and go into the community to work, attend treatment programs, attend school and take care of emergencies with prior staff approval, usually monitored by an electronic transmitting device.

hulks: early method of housing of prisoners in old, abandoned transport ships anchored in harbors and rivers.

human services officers: opposite of the smug hack; instead of isolating themselves in their jobs, human service officers try to foster positive relationships with inmates and try to make a difference.

immigration detention facility: facility houses offenders who have violated immigration laws and are awaiting deportation, court action or other dispositions of their cases.

improvisation: inmate gathering whatever items or materials that are available and substituting them for "luxuries" on the outside, i.e., making homemade alcohol, making weapons, etc.

incapacitation: strict and controlled punishment that prevents criminal offenders from committing future crimes by making it physically impossible for them to do so; they are isolated.

incident: an event where only one or two inmates are involved and there is no inmate control over any part of the facility. Examples of incidents can be fights between two or three inmates, a cellblock refusing to obey a CO's order, or an act or acts against facility authority.

incompatibility: occurs when an inmate demonstrates by actions, behavior or request, that he or she cannot live with other inmates in the general population.

indeterminate sentencing: sentencing that sets a minimum and maximum range to serve, such as five to ten years, also known as presumptive sentencing.

initial interview: an in depth interview conducted by the classification staff where crucial information is first gathered about the inmate.

injunction: a court order telling the agency to do or not to do something.

inmate code: the social rules in prisons and jails that inmates live by; this code permits inmates to live by *their* own rules, not so much the institution's.

inmate ingenuity: the unlimited imagination and ideas inmates exhibit in terms of contraband, manipulation of staff and escape attempts.

inmate request form: a form used by inmates to communicate in writing to the staff; inmate indicates the appropriate facility staff where request is to be sent and writes a message.

in-service training: training designed to maintain certification and job skills; the CO is required to attend a specific number of hours of training in subjects applicable to his or her job during a particular time period.

Institutional Classification Committee (ICC): a committee consisting of various sections (custody, mental health, medical and classification staffs) of facility staff that has to consider and make decisions based on the behavior, criminal background, custody level and housing location of the inmate.

integrity interview: employment interview where applicants are asked questions about financial difficulties, drug and/or alcohol abuse, or any situation that could put the CO into a compromising position with inmates.

interior cellblock: construction of cells back to back in tiers stacked inside a large, hollow building; the cell doors opened out on a gallery or "catwalk" which was eight to ten feet from the exterior wall of the building.

interpersonal violence: violence occurring between two or more individual inmates; the reason being a personal issue between them.

Irish System: correctional system developed by Sir Walter Crofton in 1850, in which the indeterminate sentence was used as an incentive for inmates to move through stages toward release providing a model for parole supporters in the United States.

jail: a correctional facility administered by a local law enforcement agency, such as a sheriff's office or local corrections department; confines adult offenders and juveniles under certain circumstances who are awaiting trial or sentenced to one year (12 months) or less.

jail fever: a form of typhus in early jails and prisons; developed due to squalid and unsanitary conditions.

jailhouse lawyer: an inmate very well versed or self taught in the law who files litigation or assists other inmates in filing litigation; he/she has no formal training in the law.

jailing: inmate learning the inmate culture, similar to carving out a niche, getting very familiar with inmate life, looking on other inmates like family.

juvenile detention centers: facilities designed to provide specialized programming such as counseling and education to prepare the juvenile for an eventual return to the community; are responsible for the custody and/or care and treatment of juveniles determined by juvenile court authorities to be in need of care, services or to have allegedly committed criminal acts and offenses (delinquent).

juvenile offender: any individual who is subjected to the juvenile court jurisdiction for the purposes of adjudication and treatment based on his or her age (under age 18) and the limitation of offenses as defined by state law.

keyed zones: areas in the facility that require only specific keys.

large jails: jails having 250–999 bed capacity.

laws: mores and their sanctions (or punishments) that were written down and became rules for all to follow.

lever: acts toward an inmate by a staff person, viewed as kind and thoughtful, that the inmates may later use to pressure that staff person to perform favors.

lex talionis: concept of an eye for an eye and a tooth for a tooth.

linear design: cellblocks running off at right angles down a long central corridor, considered the first generation of corrections architecture design.

lockstep: inmates marching in close order, single file, each prisoner looking over the shoulder of the man in front, facing towards the right, feet stepping in unison.

lockup: a temporary holding facility, usually operated by a police department that holds offenders pending bail or transport to the local jail for processing, inebriates (those offenders arrested for public drunkenness) until they are ready or sober enough to be released, and juvenile offenders pending release to parental custody or placement in a juvenile detention center at the order of the juvenile court.

malicious and sadistic test: five factor test used by courts to determine if the force used on an inmate was excessive and unnecessary.

Mamertime Prison: prison underneath the sewers of ancient Rome described as squalid and inhumane.

mandatory sentences: the punishment is fixed by law through legislative acts at both the state and federal level for specific crimes.

manipulation: to control or play upon, by artful or unfair means, especially to one's own advantage.

mark of the slave: in ancient societies, the practice of identifying criminals by shaving their heads.

Mark System: earning marks by behaving and working hard for early release; better preparing inmates for a return to society, developed by Captain Alexander MacConochie in 1840.

maximum custody: inmates are considered extreme and serious risks for violence, escape and threats to themselves, other inmates and staff, and are under strict supervision.

maximum security: inmate housing designed to exercise maximum control and constant supervision over the inmate population through careful security measures such as escorts, restraints, locked doors, frequent searches, etc.

Medical Model: believes that the answers to crime were inside the individual; crime was to be treated after the problem was diagnosed much as in the way a physician diagnoses a disease; a treatment program attempts to "cure" the problem, and the inmate is released into the community on supervised release (parole) who would continue therapy and casework.

medical parole: parole under which an inmate can be released for medical reasons after serving a portion of his or her sentence.

medium custody: inmates may be permitted to move about the facility during the day, but movement is more controlled at night; inmates are under direct supervision when in programs or work details and are handcuffed and escorted when outside the perimeter.

medium jails: jails having 50–249 bed capacity.

medium security: inmate supervision where security measures are less strict. Fewer cameras and the allowance of inmates to move more freely and unrestrained typify some trust in the inmates.

mega jails: jails having 1000+ bed capacity.

mellow employees: employees who are soft and hard at the appropriate times; through experience they know when to be soft and they know when to be hard—they practice discretion.

military corrections facilities: correctional facilities that incarcerate offenders who commit crimes while active members of the United States Armed Forces; also known as "the stockade" or "the brig."

minimum custody: inmates at this level pose little or no management problems, and are considered to be at low risk for escaping or causing problems.

minimum security: supervision where inmates are allowed greater degrees of movement and responsibilities such as attending programs or in cases of community corrections facilities, attending programs or working in the community. Inmates are generally not a security risk and may be short term (close to release date).

mores: stricter rules that encouraged prescribed behavior or discouraged proscribed behavior.

negligence: tort [action] involving a duty from one person [staff] to another [inmate], to act as a reasonable person might be expected to act, or the failure to act when the action is appropriate; failure to exercise reasonable care toward another.

niche: a functional sub setting containing objects, space, resources, people and relationships between people; inmates will try to cope with incarceration as best they can using the people and resources around them.

nominal damages: court agrees that the inmate had incurred violations of his or her civil rights, but the violations were very minor and showed no harm; the inmate may receive a small amount, such as $100.00.

non-lethal use of force: physical force (holds, restraints, blocks, etc.) that overcome resistance, ensure compliance and does not cause death.

offender: a person convicted or adjudicated of a criminal offense, i.e. a violation of criminal law.

officer comportment: the manner in which an officer presents himself/herself in doing the job or carrying out his/her duties.

on the job training (OJT): training that is conducted on the job for a specific number of hours per agency policy, and usually after the new correctional officer graduates from basic training, but before he or she is permitted to work independently on a post or job assignment.

operational capacity: the level or population at which the correctional facility can operate safely and is usually decided by the agency head or person supervising the facility operations.

outlaw: wrongdoer staying away from society by choice; also offenders who eluded the law.

panopticon: a circular design for prisons that allowed guards to observe and monitor many prisoner housing areas from a central location.

parole: the conditional release of an offender into the community before the expiration of sentence based on good behavior and rehabilitative activities, such as work and attending programs.

penal servitude: ancient Roman society practice of using criminals sentenced to long terms as manpower to row galleys, building public works or working in mines.

penitentiary: from Latin; a place that a man is sent to do penance for sins against society.

perimeter: the secure boundary of the correctional facility.

personal visiting: defined as friends and family members of inmates coming to visit per facility policies and procedures.

podular remote surveillance (podular): the CO is in a central control booth, observing the surrounding inmate living units or "pods" from a central vantage point.

political prisoner: an inmate, usually a member of a minority group, who blames society, the rich, prejudicial courts, etc., for his/her incarceration.

pre sentence investigation (PSI): a comprehensive report about an inmate, written either by a probation officer or a social worker and is submitted to the sentencing judge in felony cases.

prescribed behavior: acts which were deemed acceptable by early society, such as marriage, bearing and rearing children, growing food, hunting, protecting the family, helping others, etc.

presumptive sentence: a minimum and maximum term is fixed, such as one to five years, six months to one year, etc.

pre-trial detainees: persons incarcerated but not yet convicted of a crime.

Principles of Collective Behavior: factors such as unity, frustration, and highly charged atmosphere that serve to keep the riot or disturbance fueled by bringing inmates together as a group, and making the correctional staff's task of resolving the situation harder.

prison: a correctional facility that houses convicted offenders under long sentences, usually over one year and are administered by state governments, the federal government or a private corrections company.

prison psychosis: a form of mental disorder where the inmate cannot cope with prison life any longer be due to prison routine, assault, fear of rape/assault, depression, falling apart of social life (family, marriage, etc.) and the deterioration of their lives on the outside such as their losing their jobs, their homes, etc.

prison wagons: "mobile cages" used in the post Civil War South to transport and house convicts, used when convicts were leased out to businesses; each could hold up to thirty convicts and provided sleeping quarters.

prisonization: the process by which the inmate learns, through socialization, the rules and regulations of the penal institution, as well as the informal values, rules and customs of the penitentiary culture.

probation: offender being released into the community by the court and being required to obey conditions (maintaining employment, participating in substance abuse treatment, going to school, etc.) enforced by a probation officer.

probationary year: first year of employment where new correctional officers must demonstrate that they or she can complete basic training and OJT.

professional visiting: visits from attorneys, social workers, police officers, psychologists, probation and parole officers, clergy, etc.

professionalism: adhering to a professional occupation requiring both standards and special skills.

proscribed behavior: wrong behavior such as murder, rape, thievery, kidnapping, destruction of another's property, etc.

protective custody: the housing of an inmate on administrative segregation in order to protect him or her from being harmed by other inmates.

punitive damages: damages come right out of the correctional officer's pocket; punitive damages are meant to punish the CO if found liable in recklessly or intentionally causing a violations of an inmate's civil rights.

Quaker Doctrine: the view that if a criminal was to free himself or herself from wrongdoing, he or she would have to repent sins and get in touch with God. Through religious instruction, prayer and Bible study, crime would decrease.

rabble management: practice of early American jails of housing people such as drunkards, vagrants, public nuisances, and the mentally ill.

rated capacity: the number of inmates or beds assigned to a correctional facility by an official body such as a jail board, a local corrections department, a sheriff's office, or a state or federal department of corrections.

reasonable suspicion: specific, objective facts upon which a prudent official, in light of his experience, would conclude that illicit activity might be in progress.

receiving area (booking): area where incoming prisoners must be legally committed, searched, submit their property to a search and be photographed.

recidivism: offenders being rearrested for new crimes or inmates being released and re incarcerated for committing new crimes.

regional jails: jails that are operated by several jurisdictions jointly by mutual agreement with each jurisdiction contributing funds for operations and staffing.

rehabilitation: an approach to offender management through the use of programs, counseling, etc., which attempts to change the offender's criminal behavior through appropriate treatment and return the offender to the community as a law abiding citizen.

reintegration: treatment model concept that states that offenders need to be released into the community as productive citizens, using community resources to teach them tools to handle problems.

restrained hands approach: era in which the courts sought to balance the rights of the inmates against the security needs of the correctional facility.

restricted issue (RI): taking from the inmate all items including clothing with which the inmate can make a noose, cutting instruments, any sharp objects including pencils, etc.

restricted keys: keys for certain areas such as commissary, staff offices, gyms, laundry, etc.; they are issued only to staffs who work in those areas.

retribution: revenge, or society giving the lawbreaker his or her "just deserts."

riot: coming together of a group of persons [inmates] who engage in violent and tumultuous conduct; their actions create a serious risk of causing injury, property damage and public alarm.

scenario based training: training that puts trainees in certain situations through the involvement of role players or by electronic means.

security: freedom from danger, fear or anxiety; a place of safety and has two main principles: (1) the prevention of escapes by inmates; and (2) the maintenance of peace and order in the facility.

security threat groups (STGs): groups, because of their organization, views, ability to recruit new members and carry out actions and illicit activities in support of their views, disrupt the security and orderly operation of the correctional facility.

set up: a process where the staff member who is targeted unknowingly plays into the inmates' hands.

shopping list: a list of demands for the COs from the inmates, to be performed under threat or fear of exposure.

sick call: a scheduled procedure where inmates that complain of medical problems can see the nurse or facility physician.

situational deception: misleading someone by actions without lying.

small jails: jails having 1–49 bed capacity.

smug hack: an officer who is alienated from the positive aspects or goals of corrections; an officer who uses violence and negative communication to keep order.

social control: the set of methods that are designed to encourage or force people to obey the norms of society.

soft employees: employees who are generally very trusting, overly familiar with inmates and naive.

special deterrence: concept that believes that those already convicted of crimes are made to say through severe sentences that "The results and consequences of my crimes are too painful; it was not worth it; it was not worth the risk. I do not want to be punished like this again."

specialized training: training in a specific task or job skill, often requiring certification or a showing of proficiency.

state-raised convict: inmates reared on rejection and abuse in orphanages, detention centers, training schools and youth prisons.

sting: final wrap up of the set up where the employee is forced to comply with inmate demands.

street charge: inmate jargon for getting charged with a crime defined by statute while incarcerated; a conviction could mean more time added on to the original sentence.

stupefaction: inmates learn to "blunt their feelings," fantasize and turn inward due to incarceration numbing them.

sympathy: as sameness of feelings with pity and compassion.

systematically unsystematic: the staff has a plan where to search, but makes it appear random to keep the inmates off guard.

therapeutic communities: corrections facility units where inmates live as a group, follow unit and program rules and guidelines and undergo treatment and therapy.

thought disorders: mental illness in which the offender's thought processes are severely affected, such as schizophrenia, delusional disorders and paranoia.

three strikes laws: laws that stipulate that any three felony convictions could lead to a life sentence.

ticket of leave: conditional release in the Irish System; convicts released under tickets of leave were supervised by the Inspector of Released Prisoners who secured employment for the released convicts, required them to report regularly to him, inspected their homes, and verified their employment.

torts: court actions generally filed in state courts in which the inmate seeks damages; alleging that he or she is owed some duty by correctional staff.

treatment: correctional rehabilitative approach that begins with qualified staff diagnosing the needs of offenders, designing a program or programs to address these needs and the application of the program.

trusties: carefully selected and screened inmates who perform work for the correctional facility.

truth in sentencing laws: laws that mandate that offenders serve a substantial time in prison, approximately 85 percent, before being released on some type of supervision or parole.

uniform presence: large numbers of staff in uniform (custody, classification, recreation, etc.) that reminds the inmates constantly of staff physical presence and line of sight observation by officers.

unit management: each housing unit has a management team, similar to the ICC that makes program, housing and classification decisions for inmates in the unit.

use of deadly force: force used that is likely to cause death or great bodily harm, generally as a last resort to protect someone's life or the officer's own life.

verbal deception: lying or making statements that are false.

vicarious liability: a situation where someone other than an employee, such as a supervisor, knew or should have known what was happening or about to happen, but did nothing to prevent the situation; as a result, the lack of action was the proximate cause of harm, injury or death to the inmate.

weekend confinement: offenders at the local level are sentenced to serve their sentences on weekends, from Friday to Monday and can be used to work around the local jail or in the community under staff direction.

work/study release: Through court order or screening and approval by the sentencing judge, inmates are permitted to reside in a community corrections center, pre-release center, or halfway house, and work and/or attend school in the community.

zero tolerance: the institution staff will not tolerate violence by inmates on other inmates or staff for any reason; no exceptions will be made.

Index

Note: *f* indicates illustration; CO indicates correctional officer